What does transnationalism mean fr- him?
Why pompeoz?

much more about individual [illegible]

Specific people drive the Processes/study

PLAYING AMERICA'S GAME

AMERICAN CROSSROADS

Edited by Earl Lewis, George Lipsitz, Peggy Pascoe, George Sánchez, and Dana Takagi

Playing America's Game

Baseball, Latinos, and the Color Line

Adrian Burgos Jr.

UNIVERSITY OF CALIFORNIA PRESS Berkeley Los Angeles London

University of California Press, one of the most
distinguished university presses in the United States,
enriches lives around the world by advancing
scholarship in the humanities, social sciences, and
natural sciences. Its activities are supported by the UC
Press Foundation and by philanthropic contributions
from individuals and institutions. For more information, visit www.ucpress.edu.

University of California Press
Berkeley and Los Angeles, California

University of California Press, Ltd.
London, England

Library of Congress Cataloging-in-Publication Data

Burgos, Adrian, 1969–.
    Playing America's game : baseball, Latinos, and
the color line / Adrian Burgos Jr.
        p.   cm. — (American crossroads ; 23)
    Includes bibliographical references and index.
    ISBN 978-0-520-23646-2 (cloth : alk. paper)
    ISBN 978-0-520-25143-4 (pbk. : alk. paper)
    1. Hispanic American baseball players—History.
    2. Baseball—United States—History.   3. Racism
    in sports—United States—History.   4. United
    States—Race relations.   I. Title.

GV863.A1B844   2007
796.357—dc22   2007002883

Manufactured in the United States of America

16   15   14   13   12   11   10   09   08   07
10   9   8   7   6   5   4   3   2   1

This book is printed on New Leaf EcoBook 60,
containing 60% post-consumer waste, processed
chlorine free; 30% de-inked recycled fiber, elemental
chlorine free; and 10% FSC-certified virgin fiber, totally
chlorine free. EcoBook 60 is acid-free and meets the
minimum requirements of ANSI/ASTM D5634–01
(*Permanence of Paper*).

In memory of those who entered the U.S. playing field and were not recognized, and for Dolly, Miranda, and my parents, Aida Burgos and Adrian Burgos Sr.

Contents

Illustrations

Preface

Baseball was never far away as I was growing up in northern New Jersey and southern Florida. My earliest baseball memory is of a game I attended at Yankee Stadium in 1976, the year the stadium was reopened. There were also Sunday afternoon games where church members would congregate after morning service. The sounds of people conversing in Spanish and English, bats striking balls, and gloves popping have been forever etched in my childhood memories. After we moved to Florida, I could be found on about any afternoon playing baseball, whether in a league, on a school team, or dueling with my neighbor in our own version of the game. He turned out to be quite a ballplayer, winning Broward County's high school player-of-the-year award and starring in Division I college ball while I played at the Division III level.

Baseball provided a forum among my relatives to discuss broader issues about sports, history, and community. My grandmother Petra Maldonado's dinner invitations to watch Yankee games were opportunities to talk baseball and family history as she shared stories of old-time players and of her experience living in Puerto Rico during the first half of the twentieth century. My grandmother Mercedes Rivera imparted similar historical lessons during the year I lived with her while I taught high school in Spanish Harlem. Listening to her recollections as a Puerto Rican woman who participated in the migration to New York City during the 1950s was truly a seminar in Latino history. Together, my grandmothers exposed me to the lived experience of cultural continuities and change, Latinidad, and transnational practices before these terms were part of my academic vocabulary.

My passion for baseball and history ultimately led me to a more easily attainable goal than a big-league career—writing a history of Latinos in America's game. My interest in this history started in my youth when I followed the game in local and national publications, caught whatever games came on radio or television, and collected baseball cards. Baseball cards taught me the geography of baseball. The cards of Ed Figueroa, Luis Tiant, Dennis Martínez, John Candelaria, Mike Torrez, and Rennie Stennett taught me that baseball was popular throughout much of the Spanish-speaking Americas: Cuba, Dominican Republic, Puerto Rico, Mexico, and Panama. These players provided a connection with generations of Latino players, and their professional achievements sparked a sense of pride. The extent to which Latinos participated in the Negro leagues, however, remained hidden to me until much later.

The oral history of the feats performed in black baseball has made it hard to separate lore from actual events. These stories have captured the imagination of baseball fans everywhere—recall how Negro leaguer Buck O'Neill's appearance in Ken Burns's PBS series *Baseball* transformed the retired player into a national spokesman. The hundreds of Latinos who performed in the Negro leagues have not been so fortunate. Predominantly foreign-born and overwhelmingly Spanish speaking, Latinos have been rendered mute in the retelling of baseball's racial saga despite the efforts of baseball historians and exhibit curators. Barred from the major leagues and overlooked by chroniclers of black baseball, Latino players like José Méndez, Cristobal Torriente, Martin Dihigo, Francisco "Pancho" Coimbre, and Horacio Martínez have remained on the sidelines of history.

Researching and writing this book have involved an intellectual journey that took me from the archives of the National Baseball Library in Cooperstown, New York, to the sugarcane fields of Cienfuegos, Cuba, and from classrooms at the University of Illinois to the homes of dozens of retired Latino players in the United States, Puerto Rico, and Cuba. At those various stops I gained important insights into the experience of Latino players. Listening to the stories of Latino Negro leaguers and their families underscored the importance of re-inserting this vital chapter into the story of baseball. Black Latino players Rodolfo Fernández, Rafael Noble, Charlie Rivera, and Armando Vásquez shared stories that illuminated how they dealt with the dual impact of their race and ethnicity on and off the playing field. Their memories affirmed the importance of placing their particular experiences, along with those of other Latinos, in a broader analysis about race, Latinos, and the color line.

The history of Latinos and baseball is rife with misconceptions. I first grappled with one of them while writing my senior's thesis at Vassar College. This early work revealed a flawed working hypothesis, that baseball's popularity among Caribbean Latinos was primarily an outgrowth of U.S. imperialism. Baseball's infusion into Latino cultures involved a much more complicated process of transnational exchange among those who moved within the professional baseball circuit, from players and executives to fans, émigrés, and others who followed the sport. In different contexts, Latinos adopted "America's game" and gave the sport meaning that went beyond athletic competition. For them, baseball also became a site for building community, making citizens out of colonial subjects, teaching appropriate class behavior, and displaying masculinity. And as the game became professionalized and opportunities to play in the United States increased, baseball also developed into a possible avenue of escape for impoverished Latinos.

This initial investigation revealed another significant misconception: during the Jim Crow era (late 1880s to 1947) nearly all Latinos played in the Negro leagues, not in the major leagues. This stunned me as a lifelong baseball fan. Unsatisfied with the explanation that Latinos who gained entry to the majors were simply viewed as fellow whites and that all those who performed in the Negro leagues were black, in my doctoral studies I explored the historical context of Latino participation and the policing of the color line during Jim Crow. This story, I was convinced, revealed the racialization of individuals from the Spanish-speaking Americas in U.S. society and demonstrated how race structured opportunity in America's game.

The timing of my doctoral research was somewhat serendipitous. In 1994 Burns's documentary *Baseball* sparked a revival of popular interest in the history of the Negro leagues. After the series, a plethora of Negro league books was published, oral histories were collected, and additional documentaries composed. Burns was not the first to acknowledge the centrality of the Negro league story to the history of baseball. Ted Williams, in his Hall of Fame induction speech in 1966, called for the

Hall to honor black baseball's greats. Four years later Robert Peterson published *Only the Ball Was White,* the book that inspired many to pursue research on the Negro leagues. A decade later, Donn Rogosin in his book *Invisible Men* labeled Latinos and the Latin American story the missing link in the story of the Negro leagues. This notion inspired me when I read Rogosin's book while in graduate school; I noted in the margin of a page, "This is where I enter."

Historicizing the experience of Latinos in the Jim Crow baseball world and beyond proved challenging on multiple levels. The premise that studying the inclusion of Latinos in organized baseball would unveil the workings of baseball's color line drew vocal dissenters. My aim, they speculated, was to prove a Latino player had surreptitiously "broken" the color line, and thus to diminish the historical role of Jackie Robinson. Much to the contrary, this focus ultimately reinforces Robinson's role in baseball's racial saga, revealing how organized baseball officials opened access to a limited number of Latinos during segregation on the basis of racial ambiguity and plausible deniability. Indeed, I argue that it took Robinson as a clearly identified African American to shatter this ambiguity and begin dismantling the racial barrier.

Popular ignorance about Latino participation on either side of baseball's racial divide has posed a significant hurdle. Rediscovered in the mid-1990s, typical accounts of the Negro leagues continue to minimize the Latino dimension. Attending Negro league conferences, I discovered much myopia to be overcome in broadening understandings about Latino participation. While browsing the vendor exhibits at a conference in 1996, I noticed a T-shirt bearing the insignia of Negro-league teams. The vendor proudly took credit for its design. When I asked, "Why exclude the New York Cubans?" he said the Cubans' franchise was not significant enough in the history of the Negro leagues. This response underscored the public education still needed to recapture the era when African Americans and Latinos joined forces to create a transnational circuit that operated outside of organized baseball. Understanding this circuit, the actors who created and participated in it, the institutions of which it was made, and the communities that sustained it required an approach that stressed the connections, not the differences, between the English- and Spanish-speaking baseball worlds.

The quest to understand the everyday lives of migrants who cross national borders as part of labor streams or in response to economic dislocation or political conflict compelled scholars to think beyond nation-states. An international framework would not work. Rather, an approach was needed that recognized processes whereby institutions, commerce, information, laborers, and communities transcended the geography of nation-states. Fruitful collaborations with colleagues at the University of Illinois, Urbana-Champaign, and with Frank Guridy and Gina Pérez convinced me that to fully grasp the world inhabited by historical actors like Alex Pompez necessitated transnational approaches. This did not mean the nation or nation-state lost all meaning, but that these units of analysis did not contain or dictate the ways the actors under examination here formed meaning, built community, forged new forms of group identification, and challenged or transformed racial understandings. This book traces the travels of such actors within professional baseball and tells how what transpired in Havana, Santo Domingo, and San Juan reverberated in Harlem, Chicago, and Cincinnati.

Little did I know that a decade after I began this line of research, the National Baseball Hall of Fame would call on my expertise for a special election on the Negro leagues. The inclusion of a Latino baseball expert on the Screening and Voting committees represented an important step in ensuring that Latinos were not considered merely as an afterthought. The February 2006 election moved us closer to a fuller rendering of black baseball history as it included five Latino candidates: José Méndez, Orestes Miñoso, Alejandro Oms, Alejandro Pompez, and Cristobal Torriente. The election of Méndez, Pompez, and Torriente meant Martin Dihigo would no longer be the sole Latino Negro leaguer in the Hall. Yet the first black Latino in the major leagues, Miñoso, fell between the lines; his role as an integration pioneer was diluted in the minds of some due to his Latino cultural heritage, as if growing up in a Spanish-speaking society diminished the significance of his black skin and African ancestry as the game was being integrated. The story described in these pages is largely about understanding the historical context of Latinos who entered the U.S. playing field before and after Miñoso by explaining how the color line worked when it came to Latinos and how Latinos' cultures affected their place in America's game.

Acknowledgments

Countless hours of working with others have left an imprint on this book. Special thanks go to those who shared parts of their life stories and to those who hosted my research stays. Worthy of special mention for sharing so much of their experience and connecting me with others who lived the history documented on these pages are Albertus "Cleffie" Fennar, Charlie Rivera, Claritha "Peaches" Osborne, Rodolfo Fernández, Emilio "Millito" Navarro, Vic Power, Julio and Ana Navarro, and Martín Dihigo Jr.

This book benefited from the mentorship and intellectual guidance of Earl Lewis and Fred Hoxie. They have provided sage advice and intellectual support through their work and interaction as scholars committed to social justice and diversity in the academy. George Sánchez's enthusiastic support and insights have continued to profoundly affect my thinking. Richard Cándida Smith, Donald Deskins, David Scobey, Rebecca Scott, and Tom Trautman, scholars at the University of Michigan, invested their time and intellectual insights, which have challenged and influenced my intellectual formation. A diverse group of intellectual collaborators at Michigan also shaped this project: Maria Elena Cepeda, Matt Gladue, Tom Guglielmo, Larry Hashima, Riyadh Koya, Kate Masur, Aims McGuinness, John McKiernan González, Pablo Mitchell, Natalia Molina, Tom Romero, Merída Rúa, Nicole Stanton, Wilson Valentín, and the members of the African People in the Industrial Age Reading Group. Frank Guridy is worthy of special mention for having hosted several research stays, read drafts, and engaged in hours of conversations that forced us to rethink critical concepts and approaches to our work.

A number of grants and fellowships facilitated this project. The University of Michigan's Rackham Graduate School provided me (and other underrepresented students) a Rackham Merit Fellowship. Additional support from other units at Michigan included: A Spring/Summer Research Partnership Grant from the Office of the Vice President of Research; a History Department summer research block grant; a Cuban Regional Archives Project Research Grant for an initial research trip to Cuba; a Latin American and Caribbean Studies Exploratory Research Grant to travel to Puerto Rico and collect interviews with retired players from the Puerto Rican Winter League and Negro Leagues. The Center for Afro-American and African Studies, especially associate director Evans Young, supported me through research grants, teaching assistantships, and a place to hold meetings of the African Peoples in the Industrial Age Reading Group. External support in the form of a Huggins-Quarles Dissertation Grant from the Organization of American Historians (OAH) funded a research trip to the National Baseball Library and Archive (NBLA) in Cooperstown, New York; and a Ford Foundation Doctoral Dissertation Fellowship enabled me to complete the dissertation. A Ford Postdoctoral Fellowship later enabled extensive book revisions.

Research support from the University of Illinois at Urbana-Champaign (UIUC) immensely aided this project's completion. The UIUC Research Board awarded a Humanities Release Time Grant and a research grant to conduct follow-up research and to hire a research assistant. The Scholars Travel Fund and the Latina/o Studies Program provided conference travel grants. The Center on Democracy in a Multiracial Society underwrote the Capitalizing on Sport conference I co-organized with CL Cole. Other support from UIUC allowed me to hire additional research assistants. Will Cooley, Jennifer Guiliano, David Hageman, and Matt Wiemer all worked diligently to locate materials and keep me on schedule. Guiliano in particular has contributed invaluable assistance to this and other, ongoing projects at UIUC.

Intellectual collaboration with colleagues has both challenged me and furthered this project's development. James Barrett, Vernon Burton, Pedro Cában, Sundiata Cha Jua, Jason Chambers, CL Cole, Fred Hoxie,

Fred Jaher, Mark Leff, Cynthia Radding, Leslie Reagan, David Roediger, and Damion Thomas all engaged in critical conversations with me or provided feedback on versions of different chapters. Another collection of scholars also served as my teachers, critics, and collaborators. Among those who read drafts, commented on conference papers, or engaged in developmental conversations are: Frances Aparicio, Elsa Barkley Brown, Mia Bay, Fred Cooper, Jorge Duany, Juan Flores, Kevin Gaines, Michael Lomax, Alejandro Lugo, Robin Kelley, Nancy Mirabal, Michelle Mitchell, Tiffany Patterson, Gina Pérez, Lou Pérez, Samuel Regalado, Dorothee Schneider, Arlene Torres, Jules Tygiel, Penny Von Eschen, Carmen Whalen, and Francille Wilson. C. Keith Harrison started as a professor who mentored up-and-coming scholars and became an intellectual collaborator and friend.

Refinement of this work also benefited from audience participants at invited talks, workshops, and conference presentations. Challenging and insightful questions by engaged students and faculty at Oberlin, Vassar, and Wheaton College; workshop participants at the University of Chicago's Social History Workshop and Caribbean Studies Workshop; fellow attendees at University of California at San Diego's Symposium on Sport and Globalization; and audience participants at the 2003 OAH Conference and the Latino Studies Symposium in the Midwest at Ohio State University all pushed me to rethink critical points. Special thanks to the organizers of these symposiums and workshops for envisioning this project as contributing to a broader conversation about race, Latinos, sport, and U.S. history.

Archivists and librarians at a number of institutions provided invaluable assistance in locating materials. Jim Gates, Tim Wiles, Scot Mondore, Pat Kelley, Bill Burdick, and Greg Harris, as well as the NBLA research staff, proved an all-star cast. Orlando García Martínez and the staff at the Archivo Provincial de Cienfuegos made research trips to Cuba very productive. The entire staff at the Center for Puerto Rican Studies at Hunter College capably assisted me during my many visits. Research on nineteenth-century Latino pioneers benefited from the assistance of Patricia Kane, head archivist of Fordham University's Special Collections, and Rick Stattler, curator of manuscripts at the Rhode Island Historical Society.

A network of baseball historians, journalists, and media relations officials that stretches across the Americas also aided me in this endeavor. This network included Luis Alvelo, Greg Bond, Joel Franks, Mario Longoria, Bob Timmerman, Eduardo Valero, and Juan Vene. Media relations officials for the Chicago Cubs, New York Mets, and New York Yankees, along with Jeff Idelson at the National Baseball Hall of Fame, issued me press credentials to interview current and retired players. Todd Bolton, Dick Clark, Leslie Heaphy, Larry Hogan, Larry Lester, Jerry Malloy, and James Overmyer, all members of the Negro League Committee of the Society of American Baseball Researchers, have kept the history of black baseball alive. Notably, Jerry Malloy shared research materials and read early chapter drafts before his all-too-early death left a void among those working on black baseball history.

This work has benefited immensely from the guidance of two wonderful editors, Monica McCormick and Niels Hooper; George Lipsitz and the other American Crossroads Series editors; and Jules Tygiel and the other outside readers. Stacey Krejci served as my "book coach," reading drafts and challenging me to write more concisely. Collectively, they have truly helped make this book more than just a history of Latinos in baseball. Finally, this project would not have been completed without my most significant intellectual collaborator, Dolly Túa-Burgos. She has been my number-one fan, best friend, unwavering supporter, sharp-witted editor, and provider of balance.

Introduction
Latinos Play America's Game

LIVING WITH THE COLOR LINE

The indelible mark segregation left on the American collective memory goes beyond posted signs and the official enforcement of Jim Crow laws in the South. Segregation was more than Eugene "Bull" Connor and his police officers letting loose their dogs and turning water hoses on civil rights marchers in Birmingham, Alabama. Segregation involved both official and social acts that restricted access to public and private facilities and institutions along lines of race. More than a southern phenomenon, segregation's impact also came from everyday acts of citizens emboldened by their own racial beliefs and, at times, by law enforcement or social custom. Its legacy is in the actions of neighbors who informed black families attempting to integrate neighborhoods that they were not welcome in the Midwest, and of residents who barred "colored" children from entering local schools in the Northeast or Southwest.[1]

Tension along the color line was heightened in the late nineteenth century by three major changes in U.S. society: the rise of the new industrial order, urban migration, and African American migrations north. During this period of demographic shift and economic change, whites, blacks, and other racialized groups contested the location of the exclu-

1

sionary point along the color line. Their continuous efforts to open or limit access to public and private facilities and institutions inspired African American intellectual W. E. B. Du Bois's contention that the color line would figure as the problem of the twentieth century.

Hailed as the national pastime, no sport confronted the problems of race and the color line more publicly than professional baseball. The problem of the color line emerged in part from a number of contradictory principles that guided professional baseball's operation. Viewing baseball as a commercial enterprise, league organizers and team executives desired new markets for league expansion, strove to attract new consumers, and attempted to locate ever more affordable sources of talent while exerting labor discipline over the "work" produced by their players. These pursuits combined to create a league whose elite status resulted from its control of critical markets and exclusive claim to the sport's top talent, which, hypothetically, attracted consumers. As an operational policy, racial segregation limited management's ability to introduce labor competition (from among racialized minorities) to counter demands from its players. Segregation thus forced team owners and league officials to balance their commercial goals of expanding markets and dominating labor with the goal of maintaining a racially restrictive system that restrained their domination of labor.

These contrary impulses reigned within organized baseball from the late 1870s through the middle of the twentieth century. Efforts to open or limit participation pitted league management against players, players against one another, and whites against racialized minorities. Throughout the Jim Crow era each group fought for its place within organized baseball. Indeed, establishing exclusivity was critical to each group's position. Management's control of key markets and talented players elevated a league's status within the hierarchy of professional baseball. By supporting segregation, white players boosted their own claim as the only men who possessed the skill and individual attributes to perform as professionals. Such claims sought to neutralize management's effort to discipline them as a class so that professional baseball would thrive as a commercial venture. Those who suffered racial exclusion endeavored to challenge claims that they lacked playing skill and "gentlemanly" comportment. Through their performance on the professional ball fields and their conduct before the sporting public, these men attempted to change perceptions of who could be viewed as a professional ballplayer and as a man. In the end, management held the ultimate authority over access to organized baseball. These men always had the capacity, but not necessarily the will, to break the unwritten agreement against signing colored players. Brooklyn Dodgers general manager Branch Rickey demonstrated this ability in 1945 when he broke stride with the other organizations in signing Jackie Robinson as organized baseball's first African American player in the twentieth century.

My analysis of the dynamics of the color line in professional baseball focuses on individual agency—how specific actors sought to alter, negotiate, and transform terms of inclusion—and on professional baseball as a social institution in which difference became manifest in its economic, cultural, and social policies. The book's argument centers on four points. First, the workings of baseball's color line may best be examined in the most notable case of inclusion, Latinos. Second, the terms of inclusion within this segregated institution depended on a racial system that featured five major "colored" racial groupings—white, brown, red, yellow, and black. Third, until the Dodgers signed Robinson, transnational actors who exploited racial understandings to open up organized baseball to Latinos were typically driven by management's desire to secure new sources of labor without disrupting the color line. And fourth, racialization persisted in the midst of inclusion, most prominently in the denigration of Latino cultural practices within the major leagues after integration.

PLAYING IN A BLACK AND WHITE FIELD OF DREAMS

Throughout the Jim Crow era, individuals undertook everyday acts that either challenged or affirmed segregation. Those who struggled daily against segregation's dehumanizing effects included riders moving the colored sign on the public bus, domestic workers doing their own laundry at their employer's home, and shoppers refusing to enter businesses that discriminated. Historian Robin Kelley's apt description of Birmingham public buses as moving theaters where riders negotiated the color line within the marketplace also illuminates a dilemma entrepreneurs faced when it came to segregation and the marketplace: their desire to expand their consumer base to include blacks was counterbalanced by concerns that white consumers preferred racial exclusivity. Such considerations were even more difficult for management when it came to the workplace repercussions of including blacks or other racialized minorities in the labor force. Would an integrated workplace prompt organized protest on the part of whites? All of these concerns arose in debates over the integration of organized baseball and in the policing of the color line from the late nineteenth century into the mid-twentieth century.[2]

The terms of inclusion in the segregated major leagues were not so clearly delineated as the chalked lines that separate fair and foul territory on the baseball diamond. From the late 1890s through the early 1940s big-league organizations ever so slowly widened access to "colored" players by openly signing Native American and Latino players. The changing terms for including Latinos throughout this period reveal that policing baseball's color line was a complicated process.

As racialized individuals from the Spanish-speaking Americas, Latino participants in U.S. professional baseball blurred any line between inclusion and exclusion, racial eligibility and ineligibility. The existence of brown in a perceived black and white playing field disrupts the generally accepted story that only whites performed in the major leagues and only African Americans played in the Negro leagues. Nearly all players from the Spanish-speaking Americas performed in the black baseball circuits during the Jim Crow era, outnumbering those who appeared in the majors (fifty-four) by more than a five-to-one margin.[3] Thirteen of the sixteen major league teams that existed prior to 1947 had at least one Latino player perform in uniform before Jackie Robinson's 1947 debut. That these players, most of whom were racialized as nonwhite Others or of "Spanish" ancestry, secured access illuminates how team and league officials manipulated their league's racial policy to sign players who occupied locations along the color line other than that of blacks.

Latinos did not enter the U.S. playing field as simply black or white. Rather, most occupied a position between the poles of white (inclusion) and black (exclusion). First manifested in the racialization of Vincent Nava as a Spaniard and as a Spanish catcher in the early 1880s, this in-between racial position not only sustained the elevation of European whiteness but also revealed Latinos' own differentiation from the white mainstream within organized baseball. Just as significant, the process of incorporating Latinos illustrates the participation of league and team officials in the production of racial categories to accommodate the limited inclusion of nonwhite Others.

Rather than stories of individuals passing for white, the history of Latino participation in organized baseball reveals a tradition of collaboration among league management, members of the sporting press, and individual players by which the terms of inclusion were gradually altered. Together, baseball executives, sportswriters and editors, and players manipulated racial understandings and recast group identification to facilitate the increasing participation of nonwhites in organized baseball.

My focus on Latinos as central actors in the negotiation of the color line breaks with the convention of writing baseball's history in terms of black and white. I do not, however, invent a history that did not exist. To the contrary, this approach presents a nuanced understanding of the individual actors who influenced baseball's color line as well as the socio-economic forces that contributed to the construction and, later, dismantling of baseball's racial barrier. I find inspiration for this pursuit in anthropologist Michel Rolph Trouillot's argument that history at its roots is a relationship between those who live in the present and the events of the past. History cannot alter the facts of the past: what occurred did occur.[4] Our *understanding* of the past, however, evolves through new perspectives and analytical frameworks that produce new insights.

Players from the Spanish-speaking Americas did perform before, during, and after organized baseball's adoption of a Jim Crow policy. The story of which Latinos gained access, when, and under what circumstances sheds light on the principal actors who altered the terms of inclusion within organized baseball. Their actions changed what a racially eligible player looked like in terms of skin color and other physical features. That these actors brokered access to organized baseball's segregated leagues affirms historian Alexander Saxton's position that "by looking at racial categories and their fluidity over time, we glimpse the competing theories of history which inform the society and define its internal struggles."[5] The story of who was included in or excluded from America's game therefore adds an important chapter to the broader history of how individuals from the Spanish-speaking Americas have been racialized in U.S. society.

The evolution of racial understandings within U.S. professional baseball reveals *racial knowledge* in operation. Whether it was a major-league team official manipulating racial understandings to reconfigure racial eligibility, or a Latino Negro leaguer attempting to get service at a segregated restaurant by emphasizing his Spanish accent, individuals employ racial knowledge to negotiate power and the meaning of difference in local and institutional contexts. Athletes and team managers are not alone in this regard. The press, fans, and other people also used racial knowledge.

Racial knowledge, as historian Frank Guridy theorizes, operates in a number of ways. At its simplest level, it functions as "a system of thought that assigns meanings to human biological characteristics" and that enables us to place individuals in racial categories. As a form of knowledge, it is "constructed in relation to, and altered by, interconnected social, economic, cultural, and political processes" that give it the quality of "trans-historical 'truth.'" The appearance of a Mexican category in the 1930 census and its removal from the following census offer a prime example of the interconnected political, social, and cultural processes: the category's removal coincided with the end of a massive repatriation campaign against people of Mexican origin. Finally, racial knowledge functions as a "mode of interpreting the human social world" by means of which members of various social classes and gendered and racialized groups analyze their peers, community, and environment.[6] Organized baseball's adoption of categories such as Spanish, Castilian, and Latin to determine who was racially eligible encapsulates all three modes of racial knowledge in action.

The machinations involved in positioning individuals along the color line constitute a social version of America's racial game, one played with dire consequences and life-altering stakes. In professional baseball this version of America's game included not just those wearing uniforms but also those who hacked away on typewriters to make deadline, fans who cheered or heckled, and team personnel who decided racial eligibility. These actors used racial knowledge to negotiate local racial understandings, forge new group identifications, or reformulate racial categories to accommodate different participants in Jim Crow baseball and in different locations within baseball's transnational circuit. Their actions resonate with what scholars Michael Omi and Howard Winant term racialization, a concept that seeks to unveil "the sociohistorical process by which racial categories are created, inhabited, transformed, and destroyed."[7]

Racialization occurred in professional baseball on both the structural and individual level. At the structural level the formation of racially segregated institutions had concrete consequences. The institutions' existence elevated the value of whiteness since one's position along the color line influenced earning potential and since positive attributes required to play in organized baseball, such as respectability and masculinity, were ascribed to whites. At the individual level, the institutions affected participants as they fashioned identities for themselves and recast racial understandings. Individuals from throughout the Spanish-speaking Americas began to see themselves as fellow Latinos based on their experience of racialization and of participating in baseball's transnational circuit.[8] The use of transnational labels for players from the Spanish-speaking Americas first emerged during segregation and became increasingly articulated as greater numbers of Latinos participated in U.S. professional baseball.[9]

THE DIAMOND AS CONTESTED TERRAIN

From the late 1860s through the late 1880s, lively debates raged about the professionalization of baseball and the role of sport in U.S. society. Should individuals make playing baseball their livelihood? Did baseball really constitute work? The rise of the industrial age influenced responses to these and other questions about who should play professional baseball and under what terms. By the 1880s the nation's population had begun to shift from rural to urban areas, Reconstruction had come to an end, and African Americans had begun to migrate to the urban North. These changes in the national landscape altered the course of professional baseball's commercial development. The changing demographics transformed the characteristics of consumer markets, local talent pools, and the ethnic and racial composition of the fan base. The successes of organized labor in advocating for the increasing numbers of industrial workers, moreover, created the conditions for the development of commercial entertainment in urban centers throughout the Northeast and Midwest.[10]

Within professional baseball circles, league management, players, and the sporting press debated the best means to create stability in a volatile business environment where turnover was constant and several leagues vied for attention. Baseball entrepreneurs argued that league success required contractual terms that guaranteed a stable talent pool and controlled salaries. Management resolved to insert a reserve clause into player contracts that would force players to remain with one team. First instituted by National League founder William Hulbert in 1879, the reserve clause exchanged the security of guaranteed employment for labor peace.

The reserve clause profoundly affected professional baseball's labor relations, in effect transforming professional ballplayers into organizational property. Conflicts over its impact started in the mid-1880s and remained unresolved until the advent of free agency in 1976. The reserve clause also contributed to the significance of racial boundaries. The agreement between management and white players to institute the reserve clause and a reservation system effectively limited management's ability to introduce labor competition from talented nonwhite players. This in conjunction with the implementation of the color line made a career in organized baseball a profession designed for white men.

AMERICA'S TRANSNATIONAL GAME

Starting in the late nineteenth century, a transnational circuit began to take shape that linked New York, San Francisco, and Chicago with Havana, San Juan, and Santo Domingo through exchange of players, management expertise, and information. With the new opportunities this circuit offered, talented players, whether from the United States or the Caribbean, enjoyed a financial boon. North American professionals' first documented travel in this circuit took place in 1879 when future major-league manager Frank Bancroft led the Rochester-based Hop Bitters baseball team on a tour of Cuba. Other professional teams followed over the next two decades, touring the Spanish colony when political conditions permitted. The end of Spanish colonial rule in 1898 turned Cuba into a regular winter stop for teams and players from the elite minor leagues, the major leagues, and the Negro leagues.

For the first half of the twentieth century, racial and economic realities affected which teams and players participated at Latin American points within baseball's transnational network. First, the most talented African American players, ironically, enjoyed greater liberty to perform in Latin American leagues than their white counterparts from organized baseball. Because black baseball teams lacked the power and the financial standing to enforce a reserve clause as the better-financed major leagues did, more Negro leaguers left the United States to play in Latin America. Second, white major leaguers had to weigh the opportunities offered by the Latin American leagues against the power of organized baseball to blacklist players who violated league management's stated policies.

Professional opportunities within the transnational circuit fueled a migration of talented Latinos who moved from their native countries to play elsewhere in the Americas. In the segregated era, Santos Amaro, Pelayo Chacón, and Luis "Lefty" Tiant participated in this movement. Santos Amaro, the senior member of the Amaro ball-playing clan, played extensively in Mexico after learning the game in his native Cuba. A native of Mexico, Ruben Amaro Sr. enjoyed a major-league career spanning the 1960s and 1970s. Born in the United States, the youngest Amaro ballplayer, Ruben Jr., played in the majors in the 1990s.[11] After one generation toiled in the Negro leagues, the Chacón and Tiant families witnessed their sons perform in the major leagues when the U.S. playing field was transformed after integration. Modern examples reveal the continued impact of migration on America's game. Modern ballplayers such as Nomar Garciaparra and Alex Rodríguez are children of immigrant, first-generation U.S. Latinos. Edgar Martínez, José Rosado, and dozens of others were born stateside but were reared in Puerto Rico or in the Dominican Republic. Another group of notable Latinos, including Manny Ramírez, José Canseco, and Rafael Palmeiro, came to the United States as children accompanying their parents. They came in different waves of migration prompted by political instability, war, and economic restructuring brought about by such events as the Cuban Revolution (1959), the assassination of Dominican dictator Rafael Trujillo (1961), and the signing of the North American Free Trade Agreement (NAFTA).

These migrations and such transnational practices as sending remittances disrupt static geographical definitions of *Latino*. Traditional nation-bound identities predicated on one's birthplace fail to adequately account for the ways that the Amaros as individuals, as a family, and as members of different communities maintained and built ties of affinity in new locations. This traditional usage of national identity divides generations of migratory Latinos, positioning some as ethnic Americans and others, even their own siblings, as immigrants. These seemingly arbitrary distinctions raise the issue of what identity labels mean in the everyday lived experience of Latinos, whether U.S. or foreign born, as they participate in labor markets and communities that grow increasingly fluid and transnational.[12]

The common experiences in baseball's transnational circuit of those from the Spanish-speaking Americas contributed to a coalescence of identity around a shared experience of racialization. These individuals rallied around one another's play as fellow sojourners in the U.S. ball fields, whether in the major leagues or Negro leagues, and inscribed their presence with multiple meanings. In this fashion playing America's game consolidated some forms of group identification while also reiterating racialized understandings of difference. European immigrants, for example, felt eminently more American watching fellow first- and second-generation ethnic Americans such as Joe DiMaggio or Hank Greenberg excel in the big leagues. On the other hand, it mattered little to most North American fans, big-league officials, and newspaper reporters whether a player came from Cuba, Mexico, or the Dominican Republic or was even U.S.-born. At different moments, league policies formulated to deal with "Latin" player issues treated all those from the Spanish-speaking Americas as sharing a common identity, whether it was Negro-league officials responding to the Dominican League's 1937 player raids or the major-league baseball commissioner's pronouncement about Latinos who performed in the Caribbean winter leagues in the mid-1950s. Within this context it is clear that *Latino* as an ethnoracial category represents a process of racialization that affected many groups from the Spanish-speaking Americas.[13]

MORE THAN A GAME

The experience of Latino ballplayers draws on a history of interconnections between the United States and the Spanish-speaking Americas that has long perplexed baseball historians. Part of this puzzlement arises from players identifying and acting in transnational ways that reveal a circuit not fully controlled by organized baseball or North American league officials. The shaping of U.S. professional baseball by such transnational actors as black baseball entrepreneur and later major-league scout Alejandro "Alex" Pompez often goes unrecognized, leading baseball historians and sportswriters to describe Latino participation as a recent phenomenon, a boom.

The *lack* of history imposed on Latino baseball received little attention until Marcos Bretón, David Fidler, Alan Klein, Arturo Marcano, Samuel Regalado, and Rob Ruck began to address this void. Their works assessed the individual and collective impact of Latinos playing in organized baseball in the post-integration era, calling attention to the profits major-league organizations realized from developing players in Latin America.[14] Collectively, they shed light on the "boatload mentality" major-league officials have long held toward Latin American talent from impoverished countries and exposed its effects in baseball, on individual Latino players, and on local communities in the Dominican Republic, Venezuela, and elsewhere in the Spanish-speaking Americas.

The participation of individuals from the Spanish-speaking Americas during baseball's Jim Crow era prompts my consideration of a question historians of race and baseball have not fully explored: given baseball's color line, what were the exact terms on which Latinos gained entry into the segregated major leagues? A simplistic response is that those admitted were all *white*. Examination of contemporaneous sources, however, reveals that the vast majority of Latinos who participated in the major leagues were not received as fellow whites. Given the popular perceptions of "Latin" Americans as mixed-race people, a related question is why the one-drop rule was not so stringently applied to Latinos as it was to African Americans. These concerns can be adequately addressed only by examining those players who actively participated in baseball's transnational circuit and its incorporation of Latinos.

The approach I employ here eschews previous models of analysis that divorce Latino populations in the United States from those in the Caribbean and Latin America. Instead I use the concept of the Spanish-speaking Americas. This geographic concept encompasses these ballplayers' national origins and accounts for the impact of over three centuries of Spanish colonialism, two centuries of U.S. territorial expansionism and imperial activity in Latin America, and waves of overlapping migrations within the Americas. This remapping of the Americas temporarily discards current nation-state boundaries, which can obscure how these individuals perceived commonalities within the circuit in which they participated. "Spanish-speaking Americas" thus focuses on the positions Latinos occupied as participants in U.S. economies of politics, labor, and race.[15] The approach also responds to calls for the broadening of American Studies by incorporating a "critical internationalism" that engages the powerful forces that have shaped the history of Latinos in what Cuban patriot José Martí calls *nuestra America* and addresses the manner in which geographical and cultural borders come to affect the daily interactions of all Americans.[16]

To some, this book's focus on the experience of Latino ballplayers requires justification; the athletes' experience is certainly atypical compared with other Latinos in the United States. As highly skilled labor, professional ballplayers enjoyed a distinct advantage in securing legal entry into the United States. These men, however, did not spend their entire lives on the baseball field. At the end of the day, they returned to their roles as brothers, fathers, sons, workers, immigrants, and citizens or noncitizens. They lived lives as individuals embedded in multiple relationships and affiliations, occupying what scholars refer to as subject positions, wherein persons exercise varying levels of agency while also remaining subject to the authority of others, whether institutions or individuals.[17] The multiple subject positions these men held—as professional workers, citizens of different countries, men, and so on—did not make them unique. The public manner in which their careers were lived and discussed did, for in American life few social areas are more closely observed than the sporting world. As a result, sport offers a critical location for theorizing about the everyday, and thus learning about race, place, and identity.[18]

COVERING THE BASES

Playing America's Game explores historical and social questions about the working of baseball's color line. I argue that Latinos were not at all tangential to the working of baseball's color line. To the contrary, in the face of African Americans' outright exclusion, Latinos were the main group used to test the limits of racial tolerance and to locate the exclusionary point along the color line. This book interrogates the operation of power within the social institution hailed as "America's game" and reveals the agency of different actors as they worked to maintain or challenge the status quo in terms of race and access.

An inclusive history that details Jim Crow's impact on individuals from the Spanish-speaking Americas entails certain potential pitfalls. Two of these concern sources: the accessibility of oral and archival sources, and the privileged position given to North American voices. The media's role as transmitters of racial knowledge through their descriptions of particular events and actors must be counterbalanced by amassing an eclectic group of sources that avoid silencing or minimizing the role of certain participants and that illuminate the multiple influences on baseball's racial system both on and off the playing field, inside and outside the United States.

The project of documenting the experience of Latinos in America's game on either side of the racial divide initially seemed daunting. It required gleaning materials from sources from throughout the Americas to retrace the players' travels within baseball's transnational circuit. This meant utilizing untapped personal collections in Puerto Rico and archives in Cuba and interviewing former and current players. In contrast to the relative dearth of records on the actions of Latino community leaders in the United States, the careers of Latino players are much more readily documented in newspapers and sports periodicals. These sources enabled me to follow how the Spanish-speaking Americas were incorporated into U.S. professional baseball, and understand the working of its color line by following the travels of different individuals in and out of organized baseball.

Divided into three parts, the book's chapters detail the labor, race, and gender politics of baseball's color line. Part I examines the formation of professional baseball's color line in the late nineteenth century. Chapter I analyzes the influence of class, labor, gender, and race discourses on the positions taken by league management and players as members of different social classes and as racialized subjects. A central event in the period was the development of the reserve clause. The second chapter interrogates the formation of Latino racialized positions within professional baseball by examining the entry of Vincent Nava into the National League in the early 1880s, and the emergence of the Cuban Giants in the mid- to late 1880s as a response to the color line. Chapter 3 focuses on the elite minor leagues' limited experiments with racial inclusion in the mid- to late 1880s, and the formation of black professional baseball as response to the hardening racial climate that ensued.

The expansion of U.S. professional baseball's reach into the Spanish-speaking Americas in the aftermath of the War of 1898 is the focus of Part 2.[19] To highlight the social and economic forces that prompted the manipulation of organized baseball's racial barrier, I examine how Latinos helped form baseball's transnational circuit and participated in U.S. professional baseball during the Jim Crow era. Chapter 4 describes baseball as a cultural industry seeking to tap into new consumer markets and sources of talent in the Caribbean. Yet once the U.S. national game became firmly racially divided, baseball faced the dilemma of how to justify incorporating Latino talent. The fifth chapter illustrates the manipulation of racial understandings that produced limited Latino inclusion in the major leagues from the early 1910s into the 1930s. The following chapter, "Making Cuban Stars," discusses Latinos in the Negro leagues to reveal ways that they along with African Americans developed new understandings of race and community. Chapter 7 looks at the acquisition of Latin American talent by the Washington Senators, which became organized baseball's most active team in Latin America in the 1930s and 1940s.

The book's final part, "Beyond Integration," examines the impact of Latinos and baseball's transnational circuit on the integration of U.S. professional baseball. Chapter 8 engages the increased participation of Latinos on either side of the racial divide in the decade preceding the Brooklyn Dodgers' 1945 signing of Jackie Robinson. The following chapter, "Latinos and Baseball Integration," discusses the participation of Latinos within the pioneering group of ballplayers who integrated minor-league and big-league teams throughout organized baseball. Chapter 10 analyzes the racial antagonisms and the cultural shock that Latino players encountered in the integrated major leagues. In particular, I discuss the racialization of Latinos as a continuation of previous racial understandings wherein Latinos occupied a category (brown) as neither black nor white. The chapter "Latinos and Baseball's Global Turn" scrutinizes major-league baseball's globalization strategies that continue to position foreign-born Latinos as a highly exploitable labor source; the chapter also details some of the local responses formed to counter or seize the exploitative system already established. The final chapter, "Saying It Is So-sa," analyzes the cultural production of a Latino identity as the perpetual foreigner who has only a recent history in America's game.

PART ONE

THE RISE OF AMERICA'S GAME
AND THE COLOR LINE

1

A National Game Emerges
The Search for Markets
and the Dilemmas of Inclusion

Baseball . . . requires the possession of muscular strength,
great agility, quickness of eye, readiness of hand, and many
other faculties of mind and body that mark a man of nerve. . . .
Suffice it to say that it is a recreation that anyone may be
proud to excel in, as in order to do so, he must possess the
characteristics of true manhood to a considerable degree.
Henry Chadwick, *Beadle's Dime Base-Ball Player* (1860)

A CUBAN IN AMERICA'S GAME

Little fanfare surrounded eighteen-year-old Esteban Bellán's decision to
leave Rose Hill College in 1868 after completing just three years of grammar preparation classes (the equivalent of high school). A member of the
Rose Hill varsity baseball club for those three years, the Cuban native aspired to turn his talent on the diamond into a career in professional baseball. This ambition, however, meant joining a profession that was still experiencing growing pains and had yet to establish a stable economic footing.

The professionalization of baseball had undergone uneven development
by the time Bellán embarked on his professional journey. Although newspaper coverage attested to the improving levels of skill and performance
on its diamonds, professional baseball remained loosely organized. A strong
national league had yet to emerge, and professional teams had yet to begin
conducting national tours. Players took advantage of the weak organizational structure by "revolving"—jumping from one team to another in spite
of established contractual agreements. This and other practices sullied the

1. Esteban Bellán *(standing, far right)* with the 1869 Troy Haymakers. The first Latino in the major leagues, the Cuban native appeared with the Haymakers in the National Association from 1869 to 1871, after attending Fordham University (then Rose Hill College) from 1864 to 1868. The Cuban teenager was part of a wave of Cuban children sent to the United States to receive their education as anti-Spanish sentiment grew among the Cuban elite in the mid- to late 1860s. (National Baseball Hall of Fame Library, Cooperstown, New York.)

game's reputation and prompted calls for the formation of a stronger league that would ensure the respectability of the professional game.

Into this profession ventured Esteban Bellán, whose Cuban elite parents sent him to New York initially to study at the Rose Hill campus of St. John's College (present-day Fordham University). The Cuban established a reputation as a solid player within two years of his 1868 professional debut. The *New York Clipper,* in its 1870 season preview, praised him as "an efficient and faithful guardian" of third base and "one of the pluckiest of base players."[1] His most productive season came as a member of the Troy Haymakers in 1872, when he compiled a .278 batting average. The following year Bellán returned to Cuba, where he participated in the formation of the island's first baseball club, the Habana Base Ball Club, and helped lay the foundation for baseball's emergence as Cuba's national game.

Baseball had arrived in Cuba a decade before Bellán's return, at about the time the sport started to flourish in the United States. During the Civil War the military had served as a catalyst for baseball's spread to different regions of the United States. Away from the battlefront, soldiers from both sides played the game at recreation and prison camps.[2] After the war, soldiers returning home transported the game throughout the land. In the case of baseball's spread to Cuba, political strife and economic instability on the Spanish-controlled island produced waves of emigration during the last half of the nineteenth century that set the conditions for the game's introduction there.

Geographical proximity enabled Cuban émigrés to move easily between the States and Cuba to escape labor strife or political conflict, find better economic opportunities, or reunite their families.[3] Nearby cities in Florida such as Key West, Tampa, and Jacksonville developed into popular destinations. New York City, Philadelphia, and New Orleans also became destinations as port cities connected to Cuba by steamer lines.

Wherever they settled, Cuban émigrés formed a variety of organizations. Mutual aid societies helped them adjust to their new surroundings. In New York, Tampa, and Philadelphia, they established political organizations such as Partido Revolucionario de Cuba y Puerto Rico that pushed for Cuban independence or for the creation of an Antillean nation.[4] Many Cubans also embraced baseball, forming their own clubs and local leagues.

Migration during Cuba's Ten Years War (1868–78) worked to facilitate baseball's assimilation into Cuban national culture as part of a broader shift in the cultural orientation and attitudes of the Cuban elite. During the Ten Years War, Spanish colonial authorities grew increasingly intolerant of anti-Spanish protests among university students, imprisoning the many whom they viewed as the most egregious offenders.[5] Frustrated with Spanish colonial domination and worried about their children's future, disenchanted members of the Cuban elite either emigrated or sent their children to be educated in the United States.

The elite's decision to send their children to the United States was an extension of the battle to claim independence from Spain. Cubans chose to enroll their students in religious schools, among them Springhill College, St. John's College, and Georgetown University. This enabled Cubans to adhere to their religious beliefs, but on their own terms, thus maintaining cultural continuity. Other members of the Cuban elite sent their offspring to U.S. military academies—a decision that further revealed a desire to place the next generation beyond the purview of Spanish colonial authority, and to possibly prepare future leaders of the anti-colonial struggle.

Scores of Cubans who figured prominently in the game's development on the island received their baseball indoctrination as émigrés or students in the United States. Nemesio Guilló, credited by some chroniclers as the "father" of Cuban baseball, attended Springhill College in Mobile, Alabama, for six years, returning to Cuba at the age of seventeen in 1864. Reportedly included among his possessions were a bat and a baseball, "the first to be seen in Cuba," according to a 1924 account in *Diario de la Marina*.[6] Throughout the late nineteenth century countless Cubans returned from their North American sojourns with similar cultural artifacts. In transporting the game to different parts of the island, this generation acted as the vanguard of Cuban baseball, teaching others how to play the game and forming baseball clubs that laid the foundation for the game's development.[7]

When Cuban teenager Esteban Bellán arrived to attend Rose Hill in 1864, a Spanish-speaking enclave was already forming in New York City. Starting in the 1820s, Cuban émigrés fleeing political persecution and seeking improved economic opportunities chose to relocate in New York City.[8] By the 1860s, Cuban émigrés, from common laborers in the cigar-making sector to nationalist leaders such as José Martí and Rafael Serra, joined Puerto Ricans and others to form a Spanish-speaking enclave centered on barbershops, restaurants, cigar stores, and other storefront businesses.[9]

New York City had also developed into a baseball hotbed, and the Rose Hill campus was no exception with students and faculty regularly playing on campus.[10] Organized in September 1859, the Rose Hill Base Ball club was the school's first club. Two years later, the first Spanish-surnamed student appeared with the Rose Hills: Uladislaus Vallejo, a native of Sonoma, California. Among Spanish-surnamed students, who ranged between 15 and 25 percent of the student body from the 1860s through the 1880s, several partook in the baseball scene.[11] A number of Cubans who helped form baseball clubs and served as league officials in Cuba studied at the Bronx-based school. This group included the Zaldo brothers, Carlos and Teodoro, who studied at Fordham from 1875 to 1877 and later formed the Almendares Baseball Club, one of Cuba's most storied teams.[12] But it was Esteban Bellán who left the biggest mark. The first Cuban to play in U.S. professional baseball, his entry into the profession created little stir as baseball management and the sporting press focused their attention on building up the professional game and creating a stronger organization.

PROFESSIONALIZATION AND MAKING THE LINE

Like many of his professional peers, Esteban Bellán took advantage of professional baseball's weak organizational structure.[13] After he left Fordham, the young Cuban performed for different teams in each of his first three seasons. Players exercised this mobility because most professional teams and leagues lacked the power to enforce their contracts. Turbulent conditions abounded: Players jumped contracts. Clubs raided one another's rosters. Unable to maintain a stable pool of talent, teams and leagues regularly folded.

Commentators and journalists noted that the unenforceability of contracts threatened professional baseball's economic stability. Baseball management operated at a disadvantage since its capital investment in grounds, infrastructure, and local communities was immobilizing. By contrast, players enjoyed the ability to ply their skills wherever they could find a good contract. This created a peculiar dilemma for management. "On the one hand," baseball historian Warren Goldstein has written, "as relatively immobile sources of capital, clubs wanted players to be free to move to them. On the other hand, these same clubs wanted to have some way of keeping players from revolving away from them as easily as they had come."[14] Baseball management attempted to solve this problem by creating a contractual system that bound players to an organization and by continuously expanding its search for new talent.

Earnest attempts to build national associations to counteract the practice of revolving started in the late 1860s. The first association to develop a national membership, the National Association of Base Ball Players (NABBP), was formed in 1857 "to promote the standardization of playing rules, to regulate interclub competition and to encourage the growth of baseball." Initially composed of amateur clubs from New York, the NABBP's membership grew and extended as far west as Oregon and south as Virginia.[15] This expansion forced the association's membership to consider two significant issues: the color line and the professionalization of baseball.

Baseball lacked a uniform policy regarding race-based segregation. The question of the color line was viewed as a local matter for individual associations and professional teams to consider for themselves. Importantly, the issue was not limited to teams and associations in the South, but was debated primarily in the Northeast and Midwest, where the majority of amateur and professional teams and associations were based.

At the second annual convention of the NABBP following the Civil

War, the association's nominating committee summarily rejected the application of the Philadelphia Pythians, a team of African American players. The committee's report described its stance regarding applications for new membership: "It is not presumed by your committee that any club who have applied are composed of persons of color, or any portion of them; and the recommendation of your committee in this report are based upon this view, and they unanimously report against any club which may be composed of one or more colored persons."[16] Baseball's first national association thus adopted a color line. The nominating committee's decision not to consider these applications was widely trumpeted. Sportswriter Henry Chadwick, for one, agreed with the spirit of keeping any subject that had a "political bearing" out of the convention.[17]

Three years after NABBP's decision, delegates at the annual meeting of the New York State Base Ball Association took up the same question. Delegates unanimously adopted a resolution that called for the rejection of all applications by clubs that included "colored men." The Troy Haymakers' delegate voted for the exclusionary measure even though that team employed Cuban native Esteban Bellán. The association's decision drew a few vocal critics. Chadwick, for one, objected to the exclusionary resolution on the grounds that it introduced "a political question . . . as a bone of contention in the council of the fraternity.[18] Chadwick's position did not emanate from empathy for African American players; the baseball "fraternity" was not interracial.

Formal consideration of the racial question bothered Chadwick and others, for it brought into the open what others had accomplished covertly. Passage of these formal bans along with gentlemen's agreements to exclude "colored" players in other associations asserted lines of racial separation and created race-based privilege for white men.[19] These efforts at the start of Reconstruction illustrate local responses to the demographic shifts and legal changes whereby African American males had begun to attain full citizenship status protected by constitutional amendments.

MAKING PROFESSIONAL BASEBALL RESPECTABLE WORK

Professional clubs and associations encountered a series of challenges in transforming the amateur game into a professional business. In addition to gaining control of finances and personnel, organizers had to convince baseball aficionados that the professional game was both compelling entertainment and respectable work. Altering public perceptions posed a major hurdle. Since the late 1850s many had viewed baseball, sporting-goods mogul Albert Spalding noted, as little more than a pastime "to be played in times of leisure, and by gentlemen, for exercise, and only incidentally for the entertainment of the public." Spalding, a former professional player who starred in this early era, explained that this view represented the majority, who feared that baseball "would suffer by professionalism." Specifically, they worried that professionalization would open the sport to any man "who could play the game skillfully, without regard to his race, color, or previous condition of servitude." They also feared "the introduction of rowdies, drunkards, and dead-beats" into the stands during games. The potential change in the composition of on-field participants and spectators contributed to the concern that "the game would lose in character if it departed from its original program."[20]

Baseball management thus had to convince a skeptical audience that professional baseball was an appropriate evolution of the popular pastime and that amateur and professional baseball differed qualitatively. Advocates offered that professionals demonstrated greater mastery in their athletic performance due to their regular practice in preparation for league exhibitions. Amateurs performed a weaker brand of baseball since they played the game only as a leisure pursuit.

Distinguishing between the rough-and-tumble play of boys and the work of professional men required the regulation of behavior. The sporting press and baseball management cooperated formally and informally to ensure social control by disciplining labor for actions that could impugn the game's standing. Sportswriters openly discussed the ideal qualities in a model player. In the first edition of *Beadle's Dime Base-Ball Player* (1860) author Henry Chadwick listed a series of offenses for which clubs should levy fines, among them players using profane language either in club meetings or on the field, disputing the umpire's decision, not obeying the team captain, and being absent without excuse from the club's business meetings. Clubs soon amended their constitutions and bylaws to include player codes of conduct. Historian Warren Goldstein found that disciplinary action taken by clubs typically focused on the four transgressions outlined by Chadwick. Common to these offenses was the player's loss of self-control as evident in behavior unbecoming a gentleman.[21]

Class- and gender-based discourses used to cast the sport as respectable work best performed by gentlemen reflected nineteenth-century tensions "between the culture of respectability and the culture of the street." As professional men, players on the field were expected to demonstrate self-control, mastery over their emotions. This ability separated the men

from the boys, the professionals from the amateurs. The boundary between the construction of boys and men within baseball was less chrono-
logical than conceptual, one "more concerned with the 'manly' or 'boy-
ish' behavior of adults than with the activities of boys."[22]

The task of turning potential consumers into paying spectators hinged
partly on whether professional baseball was respectable work. Rather
than a game any boy or rowdy man could learn to play with proficiency,
organizers redefined the athletic performance involved in professional
baseball as highly skilled work of respectable men. Numerous com-
mentaries from this era, Goldstein notes, "employed almost exclusively
the language of work: discipline, training, skill, and specialization." The
sporting press regularly participated in this discourse. "When they praised
or criticized particular players or clubs," Goldstein explains, "they ap-
pealed not to a concept or realm of leisure and play but rather to the
standards of the workplace—a workplace in which craftsmen still exercised considerable collective autonomy over the pace and organization
of their labor."[23]

Efforts to affirm the game's respectability focused on attracting the
right type of spectators and celebrated a game that both men and women
could attend. In this era of Victorian class and gender sensibilities, women
spectatorship bolstered the claim that professional baseball was respectable work, not mere "boys' play." Women provided a form of social policing, since they "personified standards of behavior that could,
theoretically, keep men's behavior within certain boundaries."[24] Their
spectatorship did not necessarily challenge gender norms nor dissuade
those who profited from their attendance from believing that the limits
on women's involvement within the national pastime should remain.
"Neither our wives, our sisters, our daughters, our sweethearts, may play
Base Ball on the field," Spalding wrote in his 1912 history of baseball;
"they may play Basket Ball, and achieve laurels; they may play Golf, and
receive trophies; but Base Ball is too strenuous for womankind, except
as she may take part in grandstands, with applause for the brilliant play,
with waving kerchief to the hero of the three-bagger."[25]

Dissociation from gambling and alcohol was also considered necessary to establishing the professional game's respectability. In *America's
National Game* Spalding identified the influence of the "gambling element" as a significant barrier to the advancement of professional baseball. A former player who had joined forces with management, Spalding worried that the presence of "gamblers, rowdies, and their natural
associates" would deter "honest men or decent women" from attending

professional games. The sale of liquor at the ballpark particularly concerned him, for it increased the likelihood of drunkenness and the presence of "rowdies." Henry Chadwick lambasted those who attended games to indulge in gambling: "the class of fellows who patronize the game simply to pick up dollars by it, indulge in the vilest abuse and profanity in their comments on those errors of the play which damage the chance of winning their bets or pools."[26]

Public scrutiny of player behavior contributed to the broadening of management's disciplinary power. Chadwick called for the suspension and even expulsion of players who repeatedly broke team rules and codes of professional behavior. The call for discipline reflected tensions between the middle and working classes within professional baseball circles. Middle-class members of baseball clubs, Goldstein notes, "brought to their baseball playing and socializing the characteristic Victorian fear of unregulated passion and concern for self-control."[27] The opening up of the playing field to athletes from working-class backgrounds exacerbated this concern as middle-class sports writers and editors, players, managers, and executives wrestled for control over the game's future.

AN ASSOCIATION FOR PROFESSIONALS

The NABBP's amateur members watched uneasily as the balance of power within the association shifted toward its professional members. The association's rule against professional players was, Henry Chadwick admitted in the 1867 *DeWitt Base Ball Guide,* ineffectual. "Though ostensibly all were amateurs," Chadwick observed, "it is well known nearly all the leading clubs . . . employed professional players." Even many of the amateur clubs engaged in practices—such as charging gate fees—that further commercialized the game. This shift prompted a reconsideration of membership rules. In its annual meeting following the 1868 season, NABBP membership approved a new classification of players, amateur and professional. The altered balance of power within NABBP was demonstrated the following year when the professional clubs repealed the dual player classification system, "effectively banishing the amateurs" from the association.[28]

By the late 1860s, gambling scandals had wrecked the reputation of the National Association of Base Ball Players and brought its collapse. Players guilty of throwing games to the benefit of gamblers were expelled, but the damage had been done. Public confidence in game results as free from the influence of gamblers and dishonest players had been lost. Even players "lost faith" and "began to lose hope in the future of the pastime itself."[29]

The gambling scandals pitted advocates of amateurism against supporters of professionalization. Amateur clubs in the NABBP viewed professionalization as the corruptive influence. Professional clubs held that the lack of a strong central organization capable of controlling labor and protecting the game's reputation was the greatest obstacle to baseball's development. The two factions split the NABBP, and in March 1871 the professional clubs formed the National Association of *Professional* Base Ball Players. Known simply as the National Association, the new organization aspired to become the nation's premier professional league. To bring stability to the professional game, organizers agreed to charge clubs a ten-dollar entry fee to join the league, enacted governing rules that penalized players who attempted to jump their contracts, and barred league clubs from raiding each other's rosters.

The National Association lasted for five seasons of haphazard operations. Its ten-dollar entry fee allowed teams from smaller markets to join the circuit and resulted in fluctuating numbers of teams participating each season. Industrial boomtowns such as Troy, New York, and Fort Wayne, Indiana, ultimately proved less capable of sustaining a professional franchise than Boston, Chicago, New York City, and Philadelphia.

Unstable operating conditions convinced baseball entrepreneurs that additional reforms were needed to better capitalize on the game's commercial possibilities. Albert Spalding contended that "the system in vogue for the business management of the sport was defective." For him, the National Association's economic instability demonstrated the need for professional baseball to operate "like every other form of business enterprise."[30] He called for a new system that "separated the control of the executive management from the players and the playing of the game."

The crisis in professional baseball was a familiar one to entrepreneurs, Spalding claimed. "It was, in fact, the irrepressible conflict between Labor and Capital asserting itself under a new guise."[31] To his mind, in professional baseball's evolution, players had retained too much power. When baseball clubs had first started to venture beyond their local circles in search of competition in the 1860s, team captains had been both laborer and manager at once. While performing as one of the starting nine players, captains also scheduled games, signed new talent, commanded players on the field, and made in-game management decisions. With a strong captain at the helm, a team of players offered a package whose operational responsibilities were squarely in their own hands. This was an unhealthy mixture for Spalding. The former professional player argued that "no ball player, in my recollection, ever made a success of any other business while he was building up his reputation as an artist on the diamond. The two branches are entirely unlike in their demands. One calls for the exercise of functions differing altogether from those which are required in the other."[32]

The solution to professional baseball's operational problems and lack of institutional control, Spalding believed, was the formation of a new national league. The new league would embrace a management system that diminished the team captain's role. A team would operate with a manager, a general/business manager, and executive officers responsible for the oversight of everyday operations to a group of investors. The new management system placed all players squarely in the realm of labor; all a player now offered the market was his individual skill (a commodity), effectively weakening the players' collective bargaining position.

A TRULY NATIONAL LEAGUE

Planned covertly by Spalding and William Hulbert, the National League was formed by disenchanted owners who pulled out of the National Association. Spalding explained the founders' motivation: "The National League was organized in 1876 . . . to rescue the game from its slough of corruption and disgrace, and take it from the hands of the ball players who controlled and dominated the National Association of Professional Base Ball Players."[33] The new league transformed the role of baseball clubs. Their new function "would be to manage Base Ball *Teams*. Clubs would form leagues, secure grounds, erect grandstands, lease and own property, make schedules, fix dates, pay salaries, assess fines, discipline players, make contracts, control the sport in all relations to the public." In so doing, baseball clubs would relieve players "of all care and responsibility for the legitimate function of management, [and] require of them the very best performance of which they were capable, in the entertainment of the public, for which service they receive commensurate pay."[34]

The National League founders created an exclusive organization and enacted a multipronged approach to maximize profits through domination of labor and cultivation of new markets. The league now dealt with players as "club subordinates" and adopted a new contract that "provided a penalty of expulsion for any player violating his contract, and anyone thus expelled was to be forever ineligible to reinstatement in any League club."[35] The reserve system and the National Agreement would prove management's most enduring tools in limiting labor costs. These two innovations represented the cornerstone of William Hulbert's plan to give baseball a coherent structure and institute a level of cooperation that solidified its foundation.[36]

Over the first five years of the National League's operation, William Hulbert, part owner of the Chicago White Stockings, urged team officials from other professional leagues who desired protection from player raids to join the National Agreement.[37] A cooperative effort among several leagues, the Agreement established a process to sign and transfer players that directly confronted the problem of player raids and contract jumping. The hierarchy created through the National Agreement ensured that talent flowed upward within what was later known as organized baseball. A revised agreement signed by the National League, American Association, and Northwestern League in 1883, the Tri-Partite Agreement set the financial parameters for the transfer of contracts between major and minor leagues, established a formal ranking system for the minor leagues, and set a salary scale for players according to the league in which they performed.[38]

National League teams relied heavily on the minor leagues in acquiring new talent. Until the advent of the National Agreement, big-league teams were not required to compensate minor-league teams for signing away their players. The Agreement thus extended an important protection to minor leagues that joined—a structured process that required a team interested in signing a minor-league player to purchase his contract at a scheduled transfer or option fee. Teams operating outside the Agreement, however, were still susceptible to raids.

Heeding a further lesson learned from the missteps of their predecessors, National League organizers created a strong central authority to supervise league operations. Unlike the National Association, the National League established strict requirements whereby franchises desiring to join the circuit could be screened and the number of member clubs limited. For example, clubs had to be based in cities with population greater than 75,000, ensuring a market large enough to sustain a league franchise. The upstart circuit also empowered league officials to actively supervise operations to ensure, among other goals, that teams fulfilled their required allotment of league games. League officials were thus commissioned to protect the game's reputation, assuring consumers that the circuit was not under the influence of gamblers and that the league itself would deliver a competitive and complete schedule.

PROFESSIONAL MEN OR CHATTEL PROPERTY?

Introduced in 1879, the reserve system proved management's most effective weapon in controlling escalation of player salaries and limiting player mobility. Assured by owners that the reserve clause enhanced the league's viability, National League players agreed to its insertion into the standard player contract. Initially set for National League teams to reserve four players each, the reserve system was unilaterally extended over the next eight seasons to cover the entire team roster. This decision by baseball management produced labor strife.

The reserve system drastically reduced labor's ability to engage the market as free agents. In the pre–National League era, ballplayers enjoyed mobility within a weak league structure, changing teams with relative ease. They lacked the collective power, however, to control the operations and structure of the professional game.[39]

Early on under the reserve system, players exercised inordinate influence in determining who was hired as their teammates. In other words, they controlled access to the game's "shop floor." A combination of factors positioned players to contest management's attempts to introduce nonwhite labor competition without their consent. First, National Leaguers initially cooperated with management in the creation of the reserve system. This provided players in organized baseball economic security, though less salary escalation than what they might have garnered in a free-agent system. Second, labor also collaborated with management in shaping popular perceptions by engaging in class- and gender-based discourses that presented the professional game as respectable work performed by gentlemen.

Discourses about masculinity and respectability also contributed to justifying the exclusion of colored players. By collaborating with management in the formation of a color line, players wielded influence in determining who could participate in organized baseball. The color line boosted the status of white players as professionals while also creating an artificial scarcity of available talent. Indeed, the reserve system and the color line were interdependent factors in empowering white professional players in their struggles with baseball management. Players knew that management risked a major upheaval among the rank and file should it unilaterally introduce nonwhite labor competition. Moreover, there was materially little for white players to gain collectively from racially integrated leagues. To the contrary, these players risked losing gains in salary or even jobs if the artificial scarcity of talent, and whatever collective bargaining advantage they held, were eliminated.

The reserve system radically altered labor relations by binding a player to an organization for his entire professional career. The system's enduring impact compels us to ponder the status of professional players. Were they labor or organizational property? Outspoken players complained of being treated like chattel, mere property to be bought and sold by team owners. Treatment as property at a time not far removed from the era of slavery imposed on ballplayers a condition associated with blackness. Concerned players sought to avoid the subordinated status of "colored" Americans, who had been excluded from organized baseball.

Management's collaboration with players in implementing a color line created a dilemma. The color line limited management's quest to find markets for new talent that could serve as labor competition and help them control labor costs. Whatever new talent management attempted to introduce needed to pass a series of litmus tests, among them acceptance by their professional peers as either fellow whites or acceptable nonblacks. Thus management often weighed the possible reactions of current players in determining the racial eligibility of new talent from different ethnic or national backgrounds.

BARNSTORMING THE AMERICAS

Word-of-mouth recommendations from established professional players, team officials, or sportswriters provided big-league teams with valuable information about players who performed in semiprofessional and sandlot leagues. Typically scheduled for the off-season, barnstorming tours involved traveling through a region (such as the West or the Caribbean) to play local semipro and professional teams, exposing players to new talent. Barnstorming teams were composed of either intact teams from the regular season or squads formed specifically for the tour. Big-league players participated in these tours to supplement their regular-season income as attendance revenues were split between the traveling and local teams based on a predetermined percentage, usually 60–40 for the winner.

Although not always profitable, barnstorming trips into new territory permitted teams to capitalize on the direct exposure to local talent or on the scouting reports provided by barnstormers. In the 1870s California was the new territory in which to barnstorm and locate promising talent. At the end of the decade, Cuba emerged as another option as barnstorming teams sought out new markets to tour and as players searched for additional employment opportunities in the island's newly formed professional circuit.

The Hop Bitters team from Rochester, New York, arrived in Havana in December 1879 to help launch the Cuban professional league's inaugural season.[40] Formation of Cuba's professional league a year after the end of the island's Ten Years War signaled a new beginning. Given the fragile peace after the war, Spanish rulers closely monitored the economic and cultural exchange between the United States and the island colony.[41] Baseball's popularity among Cubans, particularly among nationalist sympathizers, worried Spanish rulers, who maneuvered to minimize public engagement with the sport.

Trouble surfaced as soon as the Hop Bitters contingent docked in Havana. The Cuban promoter-businessman who arranged the tour greeted them with bad news: their previous arrangement, which guaranteed the Hop Bitters $2,000 plus half of gross receipts, was null and void. According to Hop Bitters manager Frank Bancroft, Cuba's governor-general had "issued special orders that the Spanish government would levy a tax of 50 per cent on the gross receipts during the club's sojourn there, or else they would not be permitted to charge any admission."[42] The first North American barnstorming tour of Cuba almost ended before a single pitch had been thrown.

The new tax made charging admission unfeasible, effectively preventing the Hop Bitters from playing their scheduled slate of games. Undeterred, Bancroft located a North American entrepreneur in Havana to bankroll the Hop Bitters' stay on the island. Under a new arrangement, the team would play Sunday games through the rest of December, and no admission would be charged, thereby circumventing the tax.

Colonial authorities closely monitored the activities of Bancroft and his club. When Bancroft's publicity campaign, which involved distributing U.S. flags with "hop bitters" printed on them throughout Havana to spark attendance, caught the attention of the Spanish government, police officers took the manager into custody and interrogated him. Authorities released him on condition that he not distribute any more American flags, because "it would encourage the Cubans to rebellion."[43]

The Spanish were rightly concerned about the impact of more liberalized exchanges between Cuba and the United States. Politicians and capitalists in the United States had long taken an interest in the political and economic climate in the Spanish possession. As historian Felix Masud-Piloto notes, on at least four occasions the United States approached Spain about purchasing Cuba, in 1869 (while the Ten Years War raged) offering $100 million for the island. Moreover, enclaves of Cuban nationalists and entrepreneurs in the United States served as vital links with the network of nationalists in Cuba, raising funds, stockpiling arms, and recruiting soldiers to fight for a free Cuba.[44]

The first professional venture in Cuba was not a financial success for the North American tourists. Despite the lack of competition—the Hop Bitters handily defeated the Cubans in the two games they played—and though unprofitable, the tour "paved the way and made other visits there of American teams profitable."[45]

The Hop Bitters' visit helped Cubans celebrate the launch of their new league and marked the beginning of a continuous North-South exchange of talent, information, and technical expertise. The inaugural Cuban season saw not only the participation of Cubans who had learned the game while studying in the United States but also the signing of North American professionals to perform in the Cuban league. Cubans enlisted the support of U.S. sporting papers in this effort. A September 1879 *New York Clipper* column announced the Havana team's interest in "importing a first-class pitcher" for the 1879–80 campaign.[46] Although Havana failed to sign a North American player, their starting line-up featured Esteban Bellán, Nemesio Guilló, and Emilio Sabourin, all of whom had attended U.S. schools. Colón, another Cuban league team, did sign two future major leaguers, Warren "Hick" Carpenter and Jimmy Macullar. The two later told the *Chicago Tribune* they had been "highly pleased with Havana and its players."[47] Other big leaguers who followed, such as Billy Taylor, Billy Earle, and John Cullen, agreed that the circuit made North American professionals feel welcome.[48]

A contentious debate arose over the inclusion of North Americans. Some Cubans worried that the North American influence would corrupt the Cuban game, privileging playing for pay over virtuous competition. Others such as player Wenceslao Galvez decried the unfair advantage that hiring North American players gave clubs since Cuban professional baseball was still in its infancy. Despite this debate, Cubans continued to organize barnstorming tours and use their contacts to solicit applications and hire North American players. The Cuban league thus initiated the recruitment of U.S.-born players decades before organized baseball would begin to scout Cuba for talent.

The increased number of exchanges with Cuba would prompt organized baseball's management to formulate policies about the incorporation of Latino talent. Among other issues, team officials would consider how to protect their property in the reserved players who participated in Cuba and elsewhere, preserve the reputation of their leagues and member clubs, and incorporate Latino talent without drawing charges that they were circumventing the color line. The end of Spanish colonial rule in 1898 would make these concerns even more immediate as barnstorming became an annual occurrence and Cuban talent only improved.

Organized baseball's expanded search for new markets and talent underscored the need to establish a firm strong organization in the face of contract jumping, gambling scandals, and league failures. Management's goal of controlling salaries and labor mobility prompted the creation of the reserve system. The quest for greater economic stability also resulted in the National Agreement, which established a hierarchy for organized baseball. Professional baseball's economic reorganization pitted the players' desire for economic security against their concerns about being treated like chattel. The reserve clause created in players a sense of lost independence and threatened racial status, apprehensions heightened by the rhetoric about respectability and masculinity used to defend racial exclusivity in organized baseball.

The geographic expansion of baseball and the development of links with Cuba in the 1870s exposed those in organized baseball to the different racial regimes that existed in the South, the frontier West, and the Spanish-speaking Americas. Expansion forced professional teams and leagues to consider signing individuals from these regions and to ponder the meaning of racial and ethnic difference. The issue of whether to incorporate African American players was simplified by the constancy of the color line that barred blacks. More difficult for management was figuring out how to categorize individuals of "Spanish extraction" and whether some or all were racially eligible to enter organized baseball. Management also had to gauge the reaction of the league's players and fans and the press: would they accept a "Spanish" player into their midst?

2

Early Maneuvers

Vincent Nava, the Cuban Giants, and the Color Line

"The Spanish Catcher of the Providence Club": that was the tag Providence (Rhode Island) Grays team officials and the local press attached to Vincent Nava when he first appeared in the National League. Nava's arrival in professional baseball's most elite circuit was news in 1882. Over the next three seasons, Providence boosted attendance at the league's games and local exhibitions by strategically using team photographs and advertising postcards featuring their catcher Nava to pique the curiosity of baseball fans.

Vincent Nava's entry into the National League drew more notice than had Esteban Bellán, his Latino predecessor in the National Association. Bellán and Nava share a historical bond due to their similar experience of racialization as individuals from the Spanish-speaking Americas. In the eyes of North Americans, the two were Spanish, whether they came from Cuba or Mexico. Just as significant, they occupied the position of exotic Others within baseball's racial system and were situated in between the white and black poles of baseball's color line.

Speculation that either possessed African ancestry arose long after the two departed the U.S. playing field. In both cases contemporaneous materials do not support assertions that either was widely perceived as black and therefore had successfully circumvented the gentleman's agreement. To the contrary, coverage from the sporting press and mainstream newspapers reveals that the two Latinos embodied a different masculine and racial position than those held by white European American and African American players.

The United States had undergone significant change in the nine years between Esteban Bellán's 1873 departure from and Vincent Nava's 1882 arrival in the big leagues. Reconstruction had ended in 1877 as federal troops were withdrawn from the South as part of the resolution of a disputed presidential election. After the withdrawal southern states began to dismantle the work of Reconstruction legislation by passing Jim Crow laws restricting access to public facilities and accommodations. The end of Reconstruction and rise of Jim Crow prompted African American migrations west to Kansas (the "Exodusters") and the Midwest. As the nation expanded westward, settlers encountered Native Americans, Mexicans, and other earlier settlers, producing great excitement and anxiety. Reporting on the success of traders, explorers, and homesteaders in the plains and Southwest and on the Pacific Coast, the press also described with great alarm violent clashes with Indians whose way of life and homelands were threatened by the new arrivals. Indeed, settlers, prospectors, and federal troops continued to make incursions into territory assigned to the "Plains" Indians by the Treaty of Fort Laramie (1868). Continued white encroachment led to the battle at Little Bighorn in 1876, where Sioux and Cheyenne Indians annihilated George Custer's troops. The massacre led to a reformulated federal policy, exemplified by the Dawes Act (1887), which focused on relocating and remaking Native Americans into individual landowners and members of mainstream society.

Professional baseball underwent its own reorganization in the 1870s while expanding its operational sphere. Expansion beyond its original geographic contact zone into California and the Southwest introduced into organized baseball individuals whose ethnoracial identities accounted for the regions' different mixtures of indigenous and Spanish-speaking groups. The process of clearing such individuals for participation in organized baseball would involve differentiating them from blacks by emphasizing Spanish or some other European ancestry.

Contributing to confusion about Vincent Nava's identity and place in baseball history are his family history, the timing of his entry into the National League, and inconsistent information in primary sources. Sources created after Nava retired from the professional diamond are equally muddled, referring to him as a Cuban, an Italian, and a Spaniard.[1]

The conflicting information has allowed different individuals and groups to claim Vincent Nava in telling their story of America's game.[2]

The maternal roots of Vincent Nava's family tree reach to Mexico. Records uncovered by Nava biographer Mario Longoria document that Nava's mother, Josefa Simental, was a native of Durango, Mexico. When Nava was a young boy, his mother married William Irwin. A druggist, Irwin is identified in the 1870 U.S. Census as white and a native of England. In marrying Simental, Irwin also adopted Nava as his stepson, adding ten-year-old "Vincente" to a household that already included two Irwin boys.

Questions persist about Nava's paternal ancestry, in particular the origins of the Nava surname. Based on Latin American custom, one may surmise that his biological father's surname was Nava. The future big leaguer would have been born Vincente Nava Simental, or simply Vincente Nava according to U.S. customs.[3] The 1870 census suggests that both sides of his family were from Mexico. Living next door to the Irwins was a sixty-year-old woman listed as Eregoria Naba. A woman of some means with a personal estate valued at $3,000, the Mexican native's exact relationship to Vincent Nava cannot be ascertained.[4] Historian Joel Franks suggests she was Vincent's maternal grandmother. A case could also be made that she was from Nava's paternal side of the family, since she did not share a surname with Josefa Simental.

Growing up the adopted son of William Irwin allowed Vincent Nava to break into professional baseball in California under the Irwin surname. The name not only recognized the relationship between the two men but also counterbalanced the young ballplayer's olive complexion and other physical features that could indicate his Mexican ancestry or possible indigenous or *afromestizo* roots. Players with Spanish surnames had appeared in California's amateur and professional circuits prior to Vincent Irwin embarking on his professional career, indicating that having a Spanish surname did not by itself preclude one from participation.[5] Rather, given the intricacies of race and place in California, a combination of the appropriate class status, ethnic stock, and physical features had enabled these players to perform alongside Anglos.

As California in the 1870s was little more than a generation removed from its former status as a Mexican possession, Californians inside and outside the Mexican community were eager to clarify, and even dissociate themselves from, "Mexican" as a racially mixed identifier. Anthropologist Martha Menchaca's recovery and interrogation of the "black" roots of Mexican Americans, in addition to their European and indigenous roots, is instructive here. Menchaca traces the historical role of the African diaspora in Mexico from the time of Spanish arrival through the migrations of *afromestizos* (individuals of Spanish, African, and indigenous ancestry) within Mexico and into its northern territories (what is today the U.S. Southwest). She demonstrates how the legal system in Mexico and in the United States inscribed racial difference in a way that denigrated indigenous, black, and mixed roots. Within both contexts, access to first-class citizenship and to land ownership was a battleground in which people jockeyed for racial position. These individual and collective struggles were part of the backdrop whenever an individual of Mexican ancestry entered the public arena; they were no different for Nava.[6]

AN UNPRECEDENTED JOURNEY

Vincent Irwin made his professional debut in 1876 and developed a reputation for handling fast pitching that enabled him to progress up the state's professional ranks. He apparently was reconsidering his choice of occupation in 1879; the San Francisco city directory listed him as a blacksmith. His mother's death that year no doubt gave him pause; the teenaged catcher missed over a week of play due to what a local San Francisco paper labeled "domestic affliction." The following year, his baseball aspirations seemed back in line as he was once again listed in the directory as a "baseball player."[7] The 1881 winter campaign would change his career trajectory entirely.

Observed by National League standouts John Montgomery "Monte" Ward and Jerry Denny, who were also performing in the California scene, the young catcher's play inspired Providence teammates to convince their management to sign him.[8] Ward and Denny witnessed firsthand what those who followed the California baseball scene already knew: Nava possessed that rare ability to catch fast pitches that gave teams a competitive advantage since it permitted pitchers to throw with greater velocity.[9]

Impressed by the catcher, Ward wrote exuberant letters to Providence's manager, Harry Wright, to secure permission to sign him for the upcoming National League campaign. A February letter claimed Irwin had "the reputation of being the best catcher on the Pacific Slope."[10] Jerry Denny, a product of the California circuit, conveyed another glowing report. Henry Chadwick shared Denny's report that he had found a catcher in San Francisco "who handles Ward's delivery in fine form" and, just as significant, "*is a Spaniard*." In late March, Harry Wright sent along his own enthusiastic report to Chadwick, describing "Vincent Irwin the Spaniard" as a "splendid thrower and untiring catcher" who would "prove a great favorite."[11]

The newly signed catcher knew little of the discussions that preceded his arrival in Providence. In late January, the Providence Grays' Board of Directors meeting to discuss preparations for the 1882 campaign included a debate about the merits of signing the "Spaniard." Initially, the board's chair, Henry Winship, viewed the signing as an "objectionable" proposal. Winship worried how others in the National League would react to Providence's open inclusion of a Spaniard. He was rightfully concerned. Almost ten years had passed since Cuban Esteban Bellán had departed from the National Association, and no other Spanish-surnamed player had appeared in the big leagues since. Fellow Providence board member Horace Bloodgood countered Winship's concern by suggesting that a Spaniard could serve as "a strong advertising card" for the club, drawing fans who would consider him a curiosity.[12]

In their deliberations Providence's team management recognized both the economic reality of professional baseball and the ambiguity of the in-between space on the color line. Economic survival had pressed management to locate new means of attracting more spectators. Some professional leagues flouted social prohibitions by having Sunday games or selling beer and liquor at the ballpark. The American Association (1882–91) openly sold alcohol at its league games, earning the derisive label the "Beer and Whiskey League."[13] Other teams highlighted the ethnicity of their players. Boston's National League club proudly tied its team's on- and off-the-field fortunes to player-manager Mike "King" Kelly's ability to draw fellow Irishmen, starting in 1887. A few minor-league teams signed ambiguously white ethnics or, in rare instances, African Americans. Still other teams hired mascots or featured other curiosities to draw fans. It was in this vein that the Providence board agreed to sign Nava, not as a challenge to the gentleman's agreement or the color line, but rather as an exotic drawing card.

Fully aware that their new catcher came from Spanish stock, the Providence board agreed to sign the catcher sight unseen. Providence's success in employing him as an "advertising card" would hinge in large part on its success in winning approval from several parties.[14] Team officials, league management, and National League players—all white men—had the power to veto the inclusion of a racially ambiguous player in the circuit. Typically, the issue did not come to an actual vote. In the Providence case, however, careful deliberations and tactical planning occurred over how to introduce the league's first Spaniard.

BECOMING VINCENT NAVA

A neglected figure in the story of race in America's game, Vincent Nava's participation as a "Spanish" player in the majors from 1882 to 1886 illuminates the fuller spectrum of experience along baseball's color line. In baseball's racial scheme, he was its first *brown* player. His presence prompted the adoption of ethnoracial categories to explain to the baseball public the difference he embodied.

Vincent Nava's travels inside and outside professional baseball illustrate how individuals used their racial knowledge, collaborated to create new racial understandings, and altered local, regional, and even international understandings of race.[15] The transformation of Vincent Irwin into Vincent Nava showcases his collaboration with Providence team management to capitalize on the way racial perceptions and the categories used to identify individuals vary according to location. The racial positioning of Nava within organized baseball, moreover, underscores the role of geographic mobility in allowing individuals to accumulate knowledge about how race worked in different locations. Some of those who relocated to a region with a different racial regime could transform (or have altered) their racial positioning. This did not occur without fear of exposure or resistance.

Battles over the fluidity of racial positioning did occur and were at times accompanied by violence. This dynamic was central to the story, as told by historian Linda Gordon, of forty "white" orphans who in 1904 became embroiled in a racial controversy when they were transported from a New York City orphanage to a small Arizona mining community to be adopted by Mexican parents. The prospect of these children potentially "becoming" Mexican and thereby losing their "whiteness" led to their abduction by members of the community's European settlers.[16]

The chameleon-like transformation of Irwin into Nava long puzzled baseball historians, prompting them to consider the question, What brought about the name change? What was it a response to? A popularly cited interpretation by baseball historians contends that the olive-complexioned California native was part black and had successfully passed for white in getting into the majors.[17] Within the context of professional baseball's expansion in the 1880s into California and the Southwest, this interpretation does not withstand scrutiny. It ignores the racial-

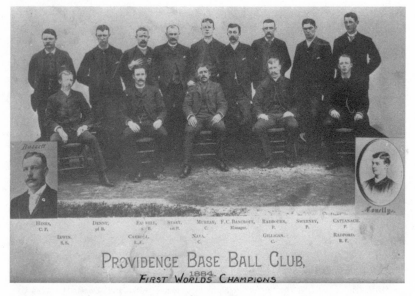

2. Vincent Nava *(seated front row center)* in an 1884 Providence Grays team photo. Frank Bancroft is in the second row, fourth from the right. Raised in San Francisco, Nava was the first U.S. Latino to perform in the National League; while with the Providence Grays (1882–1884), he was publicized as the "Spanish catcher" in the hope of drawing fans wherever the team performed. (National Baseball Hall of Fame Library, Cooperstown, New York.)

ization of Nava as "Spanish" while he played in organized baseball. Moreover, it fails to explain why the ballplayer would hazard a move from a surname that clearly indicated an Anglo background, *Irwin,* to *Nava,* which marked him as a curiosity, a foreigner, a "Spaniard."

Providence's new catcher accommodated to the team's strategy of promoting him as a drawing card, even though it meant becoming a curiosity. For him, accommodation was the price of entry into the nation's most elite professional league, along with the financial compensation and respect that came with being a big leaguer. The decision not to bear his mother's name (Simental) on entering the National League and less than three years after her death makes sense if his biological father's surname was *Nava.*

Local newspapers that followed developments in the National League reported the name change with little speculation. Before the 1882 campaign started, the *New York Clipper* referred to him as *Don* Irwin, Sandy Irwin, the little Spaniard, and *Señor* Irwin. After the season opened, the paper listed him as "Nava" in its box scores and game summaries. Other periodicals followed suit. *Chicago Tribune* writers called him "Nava the little Spaniard"; the *National Police Gazette* identified him as "Nara [*sic*] the plucky little Spanish catcher." Describing him as having a "dark olive complexion and distinctive features of his race," the *Providence Journal* explained the name change in its April 3 edition: "His name is Vincent Nava, the name Irwin adopted by him being that of a step-father."[18] Unstated in this article was Providence's plan to take advantage of its new catcher's ethnic stock. A name that marked him as a foreigner, a Spaniard, was critical to these plans.

Providence immediately put its Spanish catcher to work to bring in the crowds, literally and figuratively. On opening day of the 1882 campaign, the team sent Nava and its other reserve players to the ballpark's entrance to collect tickets from fans. A local paper commented that, put in "charge of the grandstand," Nava was the "observed of all observers."[19] Although he did not develop into the star player Ward and Wright predicted, Nava nonetheless attracted fans. The April 22, 1882, issue of the *New York Clipper* noted that among the crowd gathered for Providence's game against the New York Metropolitans, "much curiosity [was] evinced to see the play of the Spaniard." New Yorkers were not alone in wanting to see Nava, who proved an enduring attraction. When the Grays visited Portland, Maine, for an August exhibition game in his third season with Providence, the *Portland Advertiser* noted that the "tight built little Spaniard . . . was a favorite with the spectators from the first."[20] The use made of his ethnicity gained Nava a status that surpassed what his on-field performance would normally have garnered.

PLAYING IN THE BIG LEAGUES

Fans who never personally interacted with Nava learned about the "Spanish" presence in America's game through press coverage. The racial knowledge they gained from direct and indirect encounters influenced their perception of him. In this way, baseball aficionados learned about the racial significance attached to gradations of skin color when it came to individuals from the Spanish-speaking Americas.

Neither a star player nor a full-time starter, Nava did fulfill a crucial team role as Providence's reserve catcher. The physical demands of the position made it difficult for a catcher to start every game of a season. Rule changes in the early 1880s that for the first time permitted pitchers to throw overhand made catching even more hazardous. Standing less than twenty feet behind home plate, catchers wore only a facemask and unpadded leather hand mitts that provided virtually no protection. Broken fingers, sprained hand ligaments, and broken hands were facts of life. A catcher's high susceptibility to injury in conjunction with the fourteen-player roster made it doubly important for a club to have a capable reserve catcher at the ready. According to baseball historian Rick Stattler, Nava caught some of the nineteenth century's greatest strikeout pitchers, and this "sums up what seems to have been Nava's main talent, and what kept him in the major leagues for parts of five seasons despite a lifetime .177 batting average. He could stop the fastest fastballs of his day with his bare hands."[21]

The era's baseball scribes paid special attention to the masculinity that players demonstrated on the diamond. In Nava's case observers focused on his resiliency as a "plucky" player who did not let pain rule him. In April 1882 a Providence paper related an account of Nava's pluck from his San Francisco playing days: "Denny tells a story that in his [Nava's] first game with Ward he dislocated an ankle but refused to retire and caught several innings by jumping on one foot." Nava thus fulfilled the gendered expectations of a professional ballplayer: performing despite injury and contributing to the team's victory signified courage, professionalism, and manly ability. Because of these expectations, starting players were ashamed to leave a game since it was a sign of an inability to endure pain.[22]

Nava's pluck drew notice throughout the 1882 season. "Although suffering from a dislocated finger," a May 31 *New York Clipper* column noted, "Nava, the Spaniard, caught splendidly." The *Providence Journal* elaborated on this performance. "The plucky Spaniard faced Ward's delivery with true heroism, and flinched but once when the sphere struck fairly in the injured member." Nava's ability to play through the pain even inspired a poem in a local Providence paper.[23] Ten days later, Providence faced off against Chicago's National League club led by Adrian "Cap" Anson. In neither instance did Anson protest about the olive-complexioned Nava participating in the series. The *New York Clipper* did note that Ward's wild pitching re-injured Nava's badly bruised fingers, knocking him out of action for ten days. Nava's uninspired performance when he returned on June 21 contributed to a Providence loss and drew criticism from the *Providence Evening Telegram*. "Come on, Don Irwin, you must Nava do that again, let in two runs by a couple of passed balls."[24] In criticizing his performance, the midseason article reminded readers of Nava's name change and of his ethnic status.

The most apt example of media participating in the construction of

Nava's difference came in the form of a Gilbert and Sullivan parody. Initially published in the *Detroit Free Press,* "Nava Pinafored" (see below) appeared in several newspapers throughout the National League circuit.[25] Through its reprinting, the parody circulated ideas about Nava's ethnoracial difference that shaped countless individuals' racial understanding. Followers of the National League circuit may never have met the "Spanish catcher of the Providence club" personally, but the parody's lyrics helped them understand that he was different from them—he was Spanish.

NAVA PINAFORED

Solo—
I am the catcher of the Providence club.

Chorus—
And a very good catcher, too.

Solo—
You're very very good,
And be it understood,
There's one thing he don't do.

Chorus—
He's very very good,
And be it understood,
There's one thing he don't do.

Solo—
Tho' at wielding the ash
I seldom make a dash,
And sometimes pop an easy fly,
When I don my little mask
I'm all you can ask,
For I Nava let a ball go by.

Chorus—
What, Nav

Solo—
No, Nava

Chorus—
What, Nav

Solo—
Well, hardly Ava.

Chorus—
Hardly Ava lets a ball go by;
Then give three cheers, and a rub, dub, dub,
For the Spanish catcher on the Providence club.

Sportswriters made puns and occasionally presented Nava's words phonetically to mark his difference. Such practices persisted after his rookie campaign. A late March 1883 *New York Clipper* column reprinted several items from Chicago newspapers about Nava. Of Providence's catcher, one Chicago sportswriter wrote that he "Nava saw better catching," and another observed that "He'll Nava do so any more" after an indiscretion for which Nava had been fined. An item that mocked Monte Ward's attempt to coach his "Spanish protégé" represented the most flagrant example of using language to depict ethnoracial difference: "Hi, Senor! quito offi il firsto basilo et makadagio towardso secundo basilo liki hellio!" [Hi, Senor! Quit off first base and make a dash toward second base like hell!].[26] The mocking portrayal of the Providence teammates' communication contradicts Nava's status in the U.S. Census as an English speaker.

Heralded as the best catcher on the Pacific Coast, Nava failed to meet expectations after he entered the National League. The catcher's inconsistent play, repeated injuries, and off-field capers upset the team's management.[27] Although 1883 was his best big-league campaign, Providence's new manager Frank Bancroft lost confidence in the catcher that year and reduced his playing time. Nava would not be in Providence uniform to enjoy the team's ultimate triumph in 1884, when the Grays claimed the National League pennant and won the first "world series" over the American Association winners, the New York Mutuals.[28] Rather, late in the season, Bancroft loaned Nava and pitcher Joseph "Cyclone" Miller to a military team at Fortress Monroe, Virginia. The loan proved a harbinger. Bancroft released Nava after the 1884 season.[29] The catcher latched on with Baltimore's American Association club, but his skills had atrophied. He bounced around the minor leagues during the next three seasons and occasionally took employment outside of baseball. His appearance in two games with Baltimore in 1886 would be his last big-league action. In 1887 he retired from the diamond and settled in Baltimore.[30]

EVIDENCE OF THINGS NOT SEEN

The years Vincent Nava lived in Baltimore exposed the limited choices available to those who resided in a Jim Crow city: one was either white or "colored." Nava's death in 1906 presented local officials with a quandary: where to bury an individual who had a dark-olive complexion but was not African American. The former big leaguer's final resting place, according to biographer Mario Longoria, was a Baltimore cemetery created for those born without Anglo ancestry and perceived as nonwhite.[31] Burial in a "Negro" cemetery contradicts official designations of Nava's racial status. The 1900 U.S. Census entry for the Baltimore resident listed him as white, as did his 1906 death certificate. In both cases, one is tempted to ask who identified Nava as white. In the former, was it the census taker or Nava himself? In the latter case, did the medical officer who filled out the death certificate or the informant, Nava's housemate Thomas Healy, identify the deceased as white?

The intriguing question of Nava's family background and identity has led historians to speculate that Nava was a black man who passed for white. Baseball historian David Voigt places Nava in the middle of racial tensions percolating within 1880s baseball. "In Anson's era facts about blacks were damning," Voigt observes. "At best, baseball fans regarded black players as curiosities; at worst, they badgered them with insults. . . . Such was the case of Vincent Nava. . . . Racist taunts made Nava's baseball life a nightmare." Writing almost a full century after the catcher's 1882 National League debut, Voigt asserted that Nava's "dark skin repeatedly branded him a Negro."[32] In so doing, Voigt intimates that Nava's contemporaries suspected that he was not really a "Spaniard," but a "Negro" player passing.

Sporting papers that covered the National League circuit or that focused on the Providence club offer little evidence to sustain Voigt's assertion. These papers do reveal two important dynamics involved in Nava's inclusion in the National League. First, they pointed to the complicity of Providence team officials in brokering Nava's entry into the league. Second, these print sources illuminate the consistent racialization of Nava as an individual who occupied a position distinct from that of players perceived as unambiguously white or black.

Racialization of Nava as a Spaniard was a tactical choice that emphasized European ancestry. This tactic reveals the hierarchy that individuals from the Spanish-speaking Americas faced within professional baseball circles. As a Spaniard, the young catcher was more palatable to the discriminating baseball public than he would have been as a Mexican, due to the denigration of Mexicans in U.S. racial understanding. This tactical labeling also avoided the possibility that a Mexican might have *afromestizo* heritage.[33] The point here is not to preclude that possibility in Nava's case, but rather to acknowledge that, at a time when African American players confronted increasing discrimination as individual teams and leagues erected a racial barrier, Nava's contemporaries did not racialize him as black.

Nava's racialization as a Spaniard occurred before the first recognized African American (Moses Fleetwood "Fleet" Walker) participated in the big leagues. While Nava was an active player, the leading sporting sheets— the *New York Clipper,* the *National Police Gazette,* the *Sporting Life,* and the *Sporting News*—consistently stated that Providence's catcher was of Spanish stock, occasionally speculating about his national origins. The *Chicago Tribune* occasionally referred to him as "Nava the Cuban."[34] And not until after Nava retired did claims emerge that he was not of Spanish descent (such as the suggestion in a May 1899 column in the *Sporting News* that he was the big league's first Italian) or that the San Francisco native was passing.

Importantly, Nava's time with Providence was more than a one-game occurrence. This was in stark contrast to William E. White, a first baseman whose sole big-league appearance with Providence in 1879 received little attention until 2004, when baseball historian Peter Morris uncovered the Georgia native's racial background. White attended Brown University, where he played on the varsity team before serving as an emergency replacement for Providence's injured first baseman in 1879. Identified as a white man in the 1880 U.S. Census, White was listed in the 1870 Census as a nine-year old mulatto living in Georgia.[35]

Morris's discovery raised immediate questions among baseball scholars about race and the color line. Should White be considered a racial pioneer as the first black player in the majors? How do we account for the ballplayer having enrolled at Brown University as a white student before he appeared in his one game for the Providence Grays? Did his contemporaries view him as a white man, or had someone uncovered White's family background after his sole appearance for the Grays? The answers to these questions affected the timing of the imposition of organized baseball's color line. In the end, for whatever reason, White pursued a different career path than Nava or Fleetwood Walker, and would not bear the full brunt of racism in the professional baseball scene that African American players such as Walker, Bud Fowler, and those involved in the formation of the Cuban Giants would encounter in the 1880s.

BECOMING CUBAN GIANTS

Neither Vincent Nava's 1882 arrival nor his 1886 departure from the big leagues was marred by public calls for his exclusion. That would be the burden borne by African American contemporaries Walker, Fowler, and George Stovey, among others, who attempted with varying degrees of success to participate in organized baseball during the turbulent 1880s. African Americans faced more limited choices than Nava had, due to a growing commitment to maintain black exclusion within organized baseball. Attempting to pass for white to break into organized baseball remained a dangerous pursuit. The passing individual lived precariously, ever fearful of exposure and subsequent reprisals. In 1885 one group of enterprising men devised a less dangerous alternative—masquerading as "Cuban" Giants.

The genesis of the Cuban Giants team is tied directly to the formation of alternative institutions founded to serve African Americans who suffered the exclusions of segregation. From as early as 1870 black hotels featured baseball games played by their wait staff as entertainment for patrons. A hotel circuit emerged that boosted baseball's popularity within the African American community. The Chicago Blue Stockings club evolved from this circuit and in 1870 toured the Midwest as a professional club.[36] In the East the "baseball craze" among black hotels started in the early 1880s but quickly subsided, giving way to a more formal organization of black professional teams.[37]

The Cuban Giants made the transition from the hotel circuit to the professional baseball world. The team's founders had worked at black hotels along the Eastern Seaboard and participated in their baseball circuit. This work experience had placed the founders in position to acquire racial knowledge about Cubans and other groups of "colored folks," as well as to assess the playing abilities of those participating in the circuit. Employed as headwaiter at Long Island's Argyle Hotel in 1885, Frank Thompson assembled the hotel's wait staff as much for their ball-playing talent as for their wait skills.[38] Realizing black baseball's potential as a source of commercial entertainment, Thompson along with the managers of two other teams, S. K. Govern and C. S. Massey, secured financial backing and pooled the talents of their respective clubs—the Manhattans of Washington and the Philadelphia-based Keystone Athletics and Orions— to form a new team, the Cuban Giants.

Whether any of the team's organizers or players had traveled to Cuba prior to forming the Cuban Giants remains an open question. Such a trip would have allowed them to witness firsthand the game's popularity among Havana's Cuban elite and perhaps to observe Cubans of various skin colors playing baseball. Afro-Cubans quickly formed their own baseball clubs on the heels of slave emancipation (1886), and by 1887 several Afro-Cuban teams competed in a championship tournament in Havana among *clubs de color*.[39]

The extent to which the Cuban Giants team manipulated racial types to masquerade as Cuban has been widely debated. Black baseball historian and former player Sol White's account of the genesis of the Cuban Giants stands at the center of this debate. "Most old-timers today are vague as to the origin of this name," journalist Alvin Harlow wrote in a 1938 *Esquire* article, "but Sol White . . . says the version which came to him is that when that first team began playing away from home, they passed as foreigners—Cubans as they finally decided." White informed Harlow that the team's players concealed their identity and "talked gibberish to each other on the field which, they hoped, sounded like Spanish."[40]

Most baseball historians initially accepted White's narrative. Several issues, however, call its veracity into question. More than fifty years had elapsed between the formation of the Cuban Giants and White's admittedly secondhand account in 1938 (he had not joined the team until five years after its formation). The timing of White's account was doubly significant. He shared his account in the late 1930s, in the midst of the largest influx of Latino players into the major leagues during segregation. Nineteenth-century sources, moreover, suggest an alternative narrative and do not affirm White's version. Published just two years after the team's formation, an October 1887 *New York Age* column made no mention of the Cuban Giants speaking gibberish, nor did it intimate any other racial performance except selection of the team's name.[41]

The decision to name themselves the Cuban Giants drew on the ambiguous racial position Cubans occupied in U.S. professional baseball and within U.S. racial understanding. In the Northeast, the label *Cuban* made sense to the region's baseball fans, especially those who followed the development of baseball's transnational circuit. The choice Frank Thompson and fellow team organizers made reveals an acute awareness of the place of Cubans within the baseball world.

By the mid-1880s, any close observer of the Cuban baseball scene could see that the U.S. national pastime had sunk deep roots into Cuban soil. North Americans could follow the game's development in Cuba in U.S. sporting papers such as the *New York Clipper,* the *Sporting News,* and *Sporting Life.* Cuban publications such as *El Score* and *El Baseball* likewise covered compatriots who participated in North American baseball. North Americans and Cubans also interacted directly on the diamond. Cuban squads bearing names such as *Yara, El Progreso,* and *America* played against black and white teams in Key West and Tampa, as evident in published box scores in locally and nationally distributed papers in the United States and Cuba.[42]

Cuban migration to the United States produced additional points of contact. Fearing government reprisals for their political activities, nationalist sympathizers migrated to the United States, where they continued their agitation for independence. Wherever they settled, Cuban émigrés established mutual aid societies, social clubs, and labor unions that linked them in building local, national, and transnational communities and helped them adjust to life in the United States. The organizations also disseminated news about the independence movement and conditions on the island and enabled émigrés to contribute funds to the Partido Revolucionario Cubano, the Cuban insurgent army. They also hosted dinners, dances, lectures, and other social events; some also sponsored baseball teams that carried the names of their hometowns or symbolized support of the nationalist cause.

By the time the Cuban Giants were formed, Cuban émigrés had established *colonias* in New York City, New Orleans, and Philadelphia and in smaller cities like Key West and Tampa, where they were vital contributors to the economic infrastructure through the cigar-making industry. *Colonias* served as critical contact points, exposing North Americans to the diversity of the Cuban people and also to the ideology articulated by the Cuban independence movement. Cuban and Puerto Rican nationalist leaders such as José Martí, Sotero Figueroa, and Francisco Gonzalo "Pachín" Marín published tracts and newspapers and gave lectures that made clear the nationalists' belief in a nonracial national identity. In such a politically charged environment, Cuban émigrés with nationalist leanings undoubtedly reminded their North American neighbors to avoid confusing Cubans with Spaniards, those fighting for national independence with those seeking to maintain colonial rule. The diversity of Cubans involved in this movement, ranging from Afro-Cuban cigar makers to lighter-skinned professionals and cigar factory owners, surely affected, if not surprised, North American observers, who were also witnessing the retreat from Reconstruction in the States.

Coverage of New York City's Cuban community within the black press shed further light on the struggles of the Cuban people. In the early 1880s several black newspapers published tracts calling for the abolition of slavery in Cuba and editorials supporting Cuban national independence. On August 11, 1883, the *New York Globe* published "Slavery in Cuba," a column by the American Foreign Anti-Slavery Society that called the attention "of colored people of America" to the lingering question of slavery in Cuba, unresolved by wars fought on the island.[43] Coverage of political events in the black press associated the freedom struggle of Cuban people with the plight of African Americans. Coverage of Cuba attempted to prick the awareness of African Americans to the broader dimensions of black politics in the Americas, and also worked to ensure that some Americans would see Cubans as fellow people of the darker races.

Frank Thompson and fellow team organizers premised their baseball venture on the idea of a baseball team composed of darker-skinned individuals who identified as Cuban. The Cuban Giants' manipulation of racial perceptions departs from what scholars refer to as passing—whereby individuals assume a totally new racial identity and assimilate themselves into that racialized community. Arthur Thomas never changed his name to Arturo Tomás, nor did William Whyte rename himself Guillermo Blanco. Rather the charter members of the Cuban Giants opted to place themselves in the same sort of ambiguous position that accommodated Latinos such as Vincent Nava within U.S. professional baseball; they did so to secure temporary sanctuary from the full brunt of Jim Crow segregation.

The success of this ploy hinged in part on the Cuban Giants' geographic mobility. As a team that barnstormed extensively, the Giants visited towns throughout the Northeast and, later, in the midwestern and mid-Atlantic states, where they could manipulate fans unfamiliar with Cubans. Reaction to the Cuban Giants varied, from respect to amusement, passive acceptance, and defiant retaliation. Tensions that erupted before a scheduled game in New York City's Williamsburgh section represented the worst-case scenario for the Cuban Giants. "Who are the Cuban Giants?" the *National Police Gazette* began a June 1886 article. "That is what the mob were trying to find out last Sunday, when they chased them for their lives." Local police and the Cuban Giants' manager had to intervene to quell the disturbance; otherwise, "there would not have been a single giant left to carry news back to Cuba."[44] The predominately Irish fans who gathered for the game, described by the *Gazette* as "flannel mouthed Micks," were not at all amused by the ruse. Certain that they could distinguish between Cubans and African Americans, they decided the Cuban Giants were clearly *not* Cuban. Their response illustrates how ordinary people who differentiated between black and Cuban attempted to minimize the racial ambiguity that the Cuban Giants hoped to capitalize on through their ploy.

Sporting papers used racial images and language to remind readers that, despite the team's name, these were not really Cuban Giants.[45] Journalists described the team as "snow flakes" and "swarthy manipulators of the Spaulding [*sic*] sphere" and used more racially incendiary descriptors such as *nigger* and *coon.*[46] A *Binghamton Daily Leader* sportswriter avoided all subtlety in a June 1887 column, suggesting that the "Cuban Giants might develop some phenomenal ball playing if the manager would place watermelons on the home plate."[47] Print coverage thus conveyed the ambivalence and at times outright hostility toward the racial position the Cuban Giants sought to occupy within professional baseball.

LEAVING A MARK

Through their on-field prowess and their manipulation of racial understandings, the Cuban Giants set an important precedent. The team projected an understanding of Cubans as not always colored white, a position informed by coverage within the black press and direct interactions with Cubans in cities such as New York, Philadelphia, and Tampa. In so doing, the Cuban Giants ensured that within certain sectors of the U.S. professional baseball world, Cubans would be perceived as racially ambiguous.

Journalists from the mainstream and sporting press effectively ensured that terms used to refer to individuals from the Spanish-speaking Americas would not automatically connote whiteness. In the mid-1880s sportswriters began applying labels such as *Cuban, Spanish, Portuguese,* and *Mexican,* and even *Italian, Arabian, Indian,* and *Irish,* to African American players such as International League members Moses Fleetwood Walker, George Stovey, Frank Grant, and Bud Fowler.[48] On April 23, 1887, the *Sporting News* reprinted an item from a Newark newspaper that referred to Walker and Stovey as the "Spanish Battery." That same month, the *Toronto Daily Mail* reported that Newark's two African American players were hailed as "Spanish beauties" in the International League circuit and that Buffalo's manager described his African American second baseman, Grant, as an "Indian." Along the same lines, the column added that Binghamton's manager said Fowler "was from Portugal."[49] That these practices developed as an oft-injured Vincent Nava was departing from the big leagues has produced confusion on two points. First, it led some well-intentioned historians to speculate that contemporaries suspected the Mexican American catcher was a Negro who passed for white and therefore was ultimately bounced from organized baseball. Second, it prompted others to argue mistakenly that *Spanish* and *Spaniard* developed within baseball circles as referent terms for black.[50]

Newspaper coverage of Vincent Nava's big-league career validates the argument that Nava occupied a different location along baseball's color line from his black contemporaries. Reaction to Nava's participation in the big leagues differed in important ways from the treatment Fleetwood Walker and other African American players were given within the upper echelons of professional baseball. Although Chicago's Cap Anson was outraged at being forced to play with black players, he never aimed his racist vitriol at Nava for exclusion while the two played in the National League (1882–84).[51]

The journalistic practice of applying labels such as *Spanish* and *Cuban* to African Americans combined with the masquerading practices of the Cuban Giants to further illustrate the different positions into which Latinos and African Americans were slotted. After the 1880s, individuals from the Spanish-speaking Americas were understood as occupants of in-between positions as nonwhite others. This did not eliminate the possibility that a specific Latino had African ancestry. To the contrary, it compelled team and league officials to exercise diligence in ensuring that suspect players did not have African ancestry before admitting them to organized baseball.

3

Holding the Line
African Americans and Experiments with Racial Inclusion

My skin is against me. If I had not been quite so black, I
might have caught on as a Spaniard or something of that
kind. The race prejudice is so strong that my black skin
barred me.

Bud Fowler, *Sporting Life* (1895)

Organized baseball in the 1880s faced internal and external challenges
to the terms and conditions of inclusion. African Americans campaigned
for their inclusion as social equals at every professional level. Internally,
the first organized collection of big-league players waged a battle against
management, contending that they were highly skilled, professional men
who merited better treatment than being bought and traded like chattel.
In addition, a number of minor-league teams challenged the gentleman's
agreement, hoping to improve their squads by adding talented African
American players. These challenges to the terms of access, mounted primarily as distinct struggles to baseball's status quo, captured both the
promise and limitations of the professional baseball diamond as an egal-
itarian space where merit, in the form of athletic ability and performance,
was all that truly mattered.

Initiating these limited experiments with racial inclusion in the early
1880s were lower minor leagues located primarily in the Northeast and
Midwest. The experiments progressed up the minor-league ranks and
reached their zenith in 1887. That year the International League, an elite
minor league with teams in New York and Ontario (Canada), opened its

season with African American players on five of its ten teams. I characterize these signings as limited experiments for two reasons: they were not part of a league-wide effort, and they were not driven by unanimous agreement about racial inclusion as an ideal. Indeed, the signings of African Americans were test cases to gauge the resolve of league players, management, the press, and fans to maintain racial exclusivity. Collectively, the signings in different leagues demonstrated that at its core, integration involved a series of local experiments with racial inclusion that in the aggregate could transform an institution.

Through these experiments individual owners sought both to improve their teams by acquiring black players and to test the resolve of fellow owners and league officials. Vincent Nava's participation in the National League and the American Association from 1882 to 1886 can be understood as part of this testing of the limits of racial and ethnic tolerance. His entry into organized baseball, moreover, portended the approach individual team management would pursue in signing nonwhite players. The results in the mid-1880s were clear: talented African American players joined minor-league teams that had not previously included blacks. By 1887, seven African American players had risen through the ranks to join the International League. On the surface, the International League's experiment with racial inclusion seemed on the verge of success; an opportunity for an African American to perform in the National League no longer seemed beyond the realm of possibility.

Yet experiments with racial inclusion in the elite minor leagues came to a calamitous end by 1889, and baseball historians have debated the causes of this outcome ever since. Some blame the 1886 collapse of the Southern League, which made available its primarily southern-born players to sign with higher-level leagues throughout organized baseball.[1] The entry of former Southern Leaguers increased racial tensions, according to this argument, as most strongly opposed an integrated league.

A number of historians have focused on the contributions of Chicago White Sox player Adrian "Cap" Anson to the implementation of baseball's color line. In his *History of Colored Baseball*, Sol White assailed Anson, an Iowa native, for making "strenuous and fruitful opposition to any proposition looking to the admittance of a colored man into the National League." White, an African American player, team manager, and journalist in black baseball from the 1880s through the 1930s, noted that Anson's protest stretched back to 1883, when he adamantly refused to permit his team to play against Fleetwood Walker and the Toledo club, "until he was told he could either play with Walker on this team or take his nine off the field."[2] Thwarted in this attempt to impose a color line, Anson nevertheless made his position clear: according to published reports, he said, "We'll play this here game, but won't play never more with the nigger in."[3] Anson succeeded four years later in blocking the National League's New York Metropolitans from acquiring two black players. By then with New York, former Providence standout Monte Ward attempted to integrate the Metropolitans by acquiring George Stovey and Fleetwood Walker from Newark's International League team. White wrote, "Arrangements were about completed for [their] transfer from the Newark club, when a brawl was heard from Chicago to New York."[4] Anson's protest proved effective. New York opted not to break the National League's gentleman's agreement.

Examined as part of a wider process that culminated in Jim Crow segregation, Cap Anson's role appears less significant. Anson was clearly not alone in protesting the experiments with racial inclusion. Racial incidents occurred in the lower minor leagues as well as in the big leagues. Moreover, professional baseball did not exist, and has never existed, in a social vacuum. The path to Jim Crow baseball involved more than any one man's campaign to segregate the national pastime. Focusing on Anson overly individualizes the color line's impact and neglects the institutional character of professional baseball's racial barrier.

African Americans who aspired to a career in professional baseball faced a different challenge than those engaged in individual athletic pursuits, as noted African American intellectual James Weldon Johnson recognized. "The difficulty starts with prejudice against his becoming a team member," Johnson writes. "He never gets so fair a chance in those forms of sport or athletics where he must be a member of a team as in those where he may stand upon his own ability as an individual."[5] Nor did troubles end once a contract was secured. Wherever African Americans played, they struggled constantly to win and maintain the support of fellow players, fans, and the media.

The difficulty of securing stable employment in organized baseball motivated African Americans to form all-black professional teams such as the Cuban Giants and their own leagues. Launched in 1887, the National Colored League (NCL) operated less than a week before the undercapitalized venture collapsed. The short-lived circuit did receive an invitation to join the National Agreement. A seemingly positive gesture, the invitation fit the assumptions of segregationists, who supported the NCL's admission in the belief that no team within organized baseball desired to sign black players.[6] Opponents used this same belief to argue against the league's admission. An April 1887 *Sporting Life* editorial stressed the "pointlessness" of admitting the NCL since the National Agreement provided "undisturbed possession of its players" and "there is not likely to be much of a scramble for colored players."[7] The *Sporting Life* editorial belied the fact that several minor leagues, including the top-level International League, were undertaking experiments with racial inclusion in 1887.

Few were as familiar with the obstacles African Americans faced in nineteenth-century baseball as John "Bud" Fowler. From the late 1870s through the 1890s, professional baseball took Fowler throughout the United States, exposing him to the diverse people who played America's game. He performed in a number of integrated settings, and on at least two occasions—Guelph, Ontario (1881), and Binghamton, New York (1887)—pressure from teammates forced him off integrated teams.[8] Fowler's expulsion illustrated the tenuous position of African Americans and affirmed the inescapable truths of race and power in America's game. Talent might sway an owner to sign an African American player in the hope of fielding a competitive squad. But the racially motivated protest of players, fear of adverse reactions from fans or the press, or concern about fellow owners could easily weaken an owner's resolve. The power to change organized baseball's discriminatory practices lay in the hands of league executives, team management, and fellow players. These issues all came to a head during Fowler's single season in the International League in 1887.

THE NEW TROUBLE

The International League started the 1887 campaign as organized baseball's most integrated circuit. Five of the league's ten teams included African Americans on their rosters, totaling seven players in all. Economic hardships hampered league operations by midseason, causing two teams to fold and the league to release one of its black players. Some viewed the circuit's bold experiment with racial inclusion as the problem. In a June editorial, the *Sporting News* labeled "the importation of colored players" a "new trouble" that "seems to have done more damage to the International Association than to any other we know of."[9] By July the racial climate had indeed changed, and the league's board of directors gathered to consider whether to institute a color line.

The league's most experienced African American player, Bud Fowler was performing near his career peak and ranked among the circuit's leading hitters, with a robust .350 batting average. Although enjoying a strong season, Binghamton teammates protested his presence on their squad. Management decided to appease its white players and granted Fowler a release. Circumstances surrounding the decision did not surface until two months after his departure in early July. In August the *Binghamton Daily Leader* reported: "The players of the Binghamton Baseball Club were fined $50 each by the directors because six weeks ago they refused to go on the field unless Fowler, the colored second baseman, was removed."[10] This report came well after another Binghamton paper printed a public letter from Fowler that purportedly explained his petition for a release:

> Binghamton, July 2, 1887
>
> To the Public:
>   I take this occasion to announce that I have this date respectfully peti-
> tioned the Board of Directors of the Binghamton Base Ball Association
> for my release, which has been kindly granted. My reason for this step is
> that I received a flattering offer from the management of the Cuban Giants,
> which I am desirous of accepting. I desire to thank the Board of Directors
> for the gentlemanly treatment displayed toward me since becoming a mem-
> ber of the above organization, and to state that I entertain the pleasantest
> regard for them. Thanking the baseball public of this city for their kind
> and courteous treatment of me at all times, I am respectfully,
>   *John W. Fowler*[11]

The timing of Fowler's public letter and of his July departure suggest he was alerted to the changing attitude toward the circuit's experiment with racial inclusion. Fowler met with Binghamton team officials a week before the International League's board of directors convened to discuss the racial climate. Local papers did not divulge details of what Fowler and team officials discussed, though one Binghamton paper declared a movement was afoot among "many of the best players in the League" to leave unless the league ended its color experiment.[12] The league's board of directors acquiesced to the threat. In a five-to-three vote, which matched the ratio of all-white to integrated clubs, the board directed the league secretary "to approve of no more contracts with colored men."[13] Perhaps pressured by the clubs about to lose their black ballplayers, the board later partially rescinded its ban, permitting blacks already in the circuit to remain for the 1888 season.[14] The league's color line would force out the remaining black players by 1889, however. Fowler's 1887 release agreement with Binghamton, which precluded him from signing with any other International League team, bore the imprint of what was to come.

The threatened walkout represented an array of tactics International

League players used to deal with the "new trouble" within the circuit. Racial enmity prompted attempts to injure talented black players, according to Ned Williamson, veteran of more than a dozen major- and minor-league seasons spanning the 1880s and 1890s.[15] Another International Leaguer described such violent tactics: "While I myself am prejudiced against playing on a team with a colored player, still I could not help pitying some of the poor black fellows that played in the International League," he observed. "[Fowler] knew that every player that came down to second base on a steal had it in for him, and would, if possible, throw the spikes into him."[16]

Players disenchanted with the league's racial experiment also engaged in nonviolent forms of protest. Some staged baseball's version of a work slowdown by "laying down" on the field—purposely not performing to their full abilities, such as by running at less than full speed after a fly ball so that it landed safely for a base hit. The Syracuse Stars' black pitcher Robert Higgins fell victim to this tactic during the 1887 season. In a June game against Toronto several Syracuse teammates who had expressed their reservations about Higgins decided to "lay down."[17] The tactic upset some observers, who complained that the halfhearted efforts besmirched the game's reputation. The players' action had its intended effect, demonstrating extreme displeasure with being forced to share the field with an African American pitcher as their equal.

Protest actions also occurred outside of game action. A few days after the Toronto game fiasco, Syracuse pitcher Dug Crothers refused to sit for the team's annual portrait when informed it would include Higgins. A few other Syracuse teammates joined Crothers. Although the other Syracuse teammates relented, Crothers remained adamant in his refusal and had a physical altercation with the Syracuse manager. Clearly, the stakes were personal and racially significant. Sitting for a team portrait with a black teammate signified equal status—black and white teammates dressed in professional uniforms or sometimes formal attire. Reproduced and distributed for public consumption, the portraits gave longevity to this shared status. The image of respectable men gathered together also implied that both white and black players acquiesced to sharing a professional status. Management's reaction also informs the significance attached to the team portraits. Reproduced on postcards and placards for use as part of a team's advertising campaign, the portrait accompanied the team's schedule of games and exhibitions in different towns. Management therefore wanted the whole team represented, in hopes of attracting as many spectators as possible.

Disciplined for insubordination, Crothers nonetheless drew sympathy from some quarters of the sporting world. A July 2 editorial in the *National Police Gazette* strongly supported him: "The general impression is that Crothers was about right when he refused to have his picture taken in a group with Higgins, the 'Coon.' This thing of ringing niggers in with them is beyond common decency, and Crothers deserves great credit for showing his manhood." Moralizing the issue of racial inclusion further, the editorial continued: "If Syracuse wants a colored club there are plenty of niggers t[o] be had, but this thing of having their teams made up of half black and half white, like many of the International League clubs, is really disgusting and, if anything, degrading."[18] The *Gazette* editorial powerfully verbalized the sentiments of those who opposed racially integrated teams. As indicated by those who admitted the National Colored League into the National Agreement, some within organized baseball were amenable to including completely segregated, unmixed teams.

The Syracuse and Binghamton episodes capture how player productivity mattered little when it came to racial identification and job security. The small, fourteen-player roster intensified job competition as players jockeyed for position. The protests of white players demonstrated that when they retreated behind the wall of white privilege, merit and accomplishment mattered less than their claims of whiteness. Their protest thus fit a pattern of claiming of whiteness exhibited among the more recent generations of European immigrants from Ireland and those beginning to arrive from southern Europe. Rather than focusing on "their protracted competition with other whites," as historian David Roediger notes, the Irish working class asserted its status by focusing "much more forcefully on [its] sporadic labor competition with Blacks . . . [who were] so much less able to strike back, through either direct action or political action."[19] As seen in the International League, African Americans were in a much more vulnerable position than recently arrived European Americans who themselves were battling Americans of northern European ancestry for recognition as fellow whites. This vulnerability was especially keen when management balanced the protests of the squad's white players against the contributions of the one or two black players.

FROM MEN TO MASCOTS

The color line did not bar all blacks from the major-league scene. A telling sign of the times' racial and gender ideology, black mascots gained wide-

1. Ryan.
2. Williamson.
3. Farrell.
4. Pfeffer.
5. The Mascot.

Jos. HALL, Photo., Brooklyn, N. Y.

CHICAGO BALL CLUB, 1888.

6. Capt. Anson.
7. Van Haltren.
8. Borchers.
9. Burns.
10. Daly.

3. The 1888 Chicago Ball Club with its black mascot, Clarence Duval. Behind Duval is the club's captain, Adrian "Cap" Anson, a vocal opponent of black inclusion in the major leagues. (National Baseball Hall of Fame Library, Cooperstown, New York.)

spread popularity among segregated major- and minor-league teams at the same time that experiments with racial inclusion were facing mounting opposition. Black mascots affirmed popular ideas about race and social position in Jim Crow baseball. Each group had its proper place. The choice for African American men was either outright exclusion from organized baseball as players, or participation as team mascot.

The infantilized black mascot embodied stereotypes of black men as childlike beings who were governed by their passions and lacked the capacity for professional, respectable behavior. The description of the New York Giants' mascot in an August 1885 *National Police Gazette* article conveyed this perception: "The *colored boy,* the exchanges speak of as Buck Ewing's mascot, *is an infant* about 6 feet tall, and in the neighborhood of forty years of age."[20] The sole representative of black masculinity in segregated leagues, mascots reinforced the idea that European American and African American men did not share the same intrinsic gender characteristics; they were not fellow men. This belief in racially differentiated masculinity had been advanced in certain quarters since slavery, and stood at the center of Redemption campaigns in the South and fears of black males as sexual predators. The belief that black men showed innate childlike qualities, were unable to reign in their passions, and yet possessed natural athleticism served to justify excluding black players and denying them equality with whites.[21]

Diminutive, odd-looking, and often bearing some physical deformity, black mascots were the embodiment of black men as imbeciles, brutes, or dandies. In sharp contrast to the attributes teams looked for in a bat-boy (that is, a fresh-faced, precocious youngster), white segregated teams sought out black men whose physical appearance was "the reverse of beautiful."[22] This is what the Toledo club in the American Association accomplished in 1888 with its "diminutive" mascot.[23] A black mascot's unattractiveness indicated his "supernatural" abilities. According to superstition a mascot with grotesque features or a physical deformity could cast a curse on his opponents. If a diminutive mascot had supernatural ability, went the logic, a diminutive cross-eyed black mascot who was bow-legged and walked with a limp had all the more capacity to cast hexes.[24]

Clarence Duval developed a national following for his work as the mascot for Chicago's National League club and for his performance on the vaudeville circuit. Duval as Chicago's black mascot provided a visual reminder of why black men did not deserve to be placed on equal footing with white men. A Chicago newspaper's description was steeped in the familiar stereotypes the mascot embodied: "His grin is broad, his legs limbre and his face as black as the ace of spades. . . . Whenever anything goes wrong, it is only necessary to rub Clarence's wooly head to save the situation, and one of his celebrated 'double shuffles' to dispel all traces of care, even on the gloomiest occasion."[25]

Duval's act was known beyond Chicago's city limits. When the Chicago team came east to play the New York City clubs in 1888, a *New York Clipper* columnist predicted that Duval "will be a great favorite here. . . . He can sing like a lark and has committed to memory all the plantation melodies."[26] Duval's routine on the vaudeville circuit harkened back to the romanticized plantation life of simplified race relations—a time where everyone knew his place. Duval, however, sometimes forgot his place in the view of Chicago's Cap Anson. Never on cordial terms with his captain, Duval's midseason departure to perform on the vaudeville circuit infuriated Anson. About to embark on a world tour in the winter of 1888 that would take them to Australia, Asia, and Egypt and then through Europe, Chicago players wrangled with Anson to ensure Duval would accompany the team. Damaged relationships had to be repaired before this would meet Anson's approval. The captain relented to his players' demand; it was a long trip, and a black mascot could provide much needed entertainment.[27]

Although Duval's inferior position never seemed to have been in doubt, a contingent of European American players actively reasserted their racial superiority. Their actions during a stopover in Egypt, as reported in a Chicago newspaper, clearly demonstrate white men constructing a different masculinity for black men. "Several ballplayers forced [Duval] to wear a catcher's mask and glove and then paraded [him] about the Cairo railway station, tethered by a rope, 'as if he was some strange animal let loose from a menagerie.'"[28] Parading Duval like a captured beast illustrated how the touring players viewed their mascot—not their social equal, not even human. One can scarcely imagine these players subjecting a white teammate to the same dehumanizing treatment.

HOLDING THE LINE

The treatment of black mascots in conjunction with protests against experiments with racial inclusion underscored the wide-ranging efforts in professional baseball to keep blacks in their place. Bud Fowler and other African Americans who fell victim to the International League's drawing of the color line were well acquainted with the ways that race, labor, and masculinity overlapped in Jim Crow baseball. The actions of Cap Anson, Dug Crothers, and other players expressed their beliefs about who should be allowed to enjoy the privileges and benefits of playing in organized baseball.

The complex issues that factored into individual or group positions on racial inclusion were not always clear-cut, nor did they remain static; they changed with the times. At various times, European American players embraced racial and class ideologies that derailed experiments with racial inclusion.[29] In certain instances, players placed their position as white men above their team's goal of building a winning club. At other times, players collaborated with management and pushed for exclusion of individuals who harmed the sport's respectability by either association or direct action.

Although not every professional league fought the battle over inclusion and the color line, the localized battles had far-reaching repercussions. In a number of cases, team owners opted against further experiments with racial inclusion, seeking to avert negative reactions from players. Agreement between players and management to maintain a color line resolved a critical labor issue by ensuring that black players could not be used as strikebreakers, and made a racially exclusive playing field a basic element of white privilege in organized baseball. With the color line implemented, the game reflected the temperament and character traits ascribed to white men.[30] In addition, the white player could command a higher salary for his services, precisely because he was white and not black, and was an independent, professional working man, not a lazy, dependent, childish boy.

Professionalization changed how labor and management approached their economic relations. Playing professional baseball meant no longer playing for fun like boys. Rather, as professionals in an industrializing America, ballplayers had to produce like men whose activities and output were under management's intensified scrutiny.[31] A racially mixed labor force would diminish the ability of European American players, regardless of their ethnic stock, to openly agitate for better treatment as highly skilled "white" male professionals. Emphasis on racial identification, masculinity, and respectability to distinguish themselves from others seeking entry into organized baseball became a key element in their campaign against mistreatment at the dominating hands of management. The masculine discourse that big-league players employed in this campaign was similar to the rhetoric used in the printing industry between 1830 and 1920. As historian Ava Baron documents, male journeymen printers used the idea of masculinity to defend their jobs when master craftsmen began switching to more advanced technology, the linotype, and hiring increasing numbers of boys. Concerned about losing their status as independent skilled laborers, journeymen printers defended their place in the industry by arguing that proper performance of the job's responsibilities required a man (versus a young boy).[32] Similarly, when teams in organized baseball began to experiment with racial inclusion, white players redoubled their efforts to delineate differences between themselves and others seeking access.

ADVANCING THE PLAYERS' CAUSE

Industrialization permitted baseball management to set the professional game on a firmer economic foundation. Industrial work brought greater numbers of people into urban centers, while its regimented schedule contributed to an increase in the amount of leisure time for the laboring classes. Urban boosters and local politicians joined forces to attract (and retain) big-league franchises. Baseball magnates worked closely with these civic leaders to build transportation infrastructure and locate ballparks to make games accessible to the new urban dwellers.[33]

The evolution from independent producers to proletarianized laborers heightened concerns among the laboring classes about their plight individually and collectively. Industrial barons' heavy-handed approach to organized labor radically altered labor relations. Baseball management drew inspiration from the labor discipline that Andrew Carnegie and John D. Rockefeller imposed on workers and the monopolistic tactics they used to ward off or take over competitors. In a similar spirit, baseball magnates unilaterally extended the reserve system, seeking to impose their will on the game's "laborers."

The changing labor conditions within organized baseball inspired players to form their first labor organization, the National Brotherhood of Base-Ball Players, and to later organize their own cooperative, the short-lived Players League.[34] National Leaguers grew despondent with the reserve system's restrictions on their mobility and salary escalation. Initially formed in August 1885, the Brotherhood's membership surged to almost 90 percent of all National League players by the following season.[35] Frustration grew with the open-ended option that owners held on a player's services, and with management's unilateral extension in 1887 of the reserve list to cover an entire team's roster. According to Monte Ward, management's manipulations transformed the player into "a mere chattel. He goes where he is sent, takes what is given to him, and thanks the Lord for Life."[36]

Ward made an eloquent defense of the players' cause in his article "Is the Base-Ball Player a Chattel?" Appearing in the August 1887 edition of *Lippincott's Magazine,* the manifesto outlined management's abuse of the reserve system. Ward associated the National League (white) players' plight with the terror that captured fugitive slaves endured in antebellum America: "Like a fugitive-slave law, the reserve-rule denies him [the ballplayer] a harbor of a livelihood, and carries him back, bound and shackled, to the club from which he attempted to escape." The law school–trained Ward then delivered a biting critique of the National League contract. "We have then, the curious result of a contract which on its face is for seven months, being binding for life, and when the player's name is once attached thereto his professional liberty is gone forever."[37]

The concerns expressed by Ward and other Brotherhood leaders linked issues of labor, race, and masculinity. Their claim that the reserve clause system was tantamount to wage slavery racialized the player's condition and attempted to garner the sympathies of the common man. The Brotherhood's emphasis on big-league players' status as white, highly skilled professionals addressed an audience experiencing the alienating conditions of wage work within the emergent industrial order. Big-league fans would, the Brotherhood hoped, appreciate the privileges inherent to whiteness and understand that slavery was a *black* condition intolerable for any *white man* to suffer. Baseball's color line allowed players who were recent European arrivals or first-generation European Americans to assert a *white* American identity by objecting to the presence of blacks on the professional diamond. Race-based exclusion thus created a professional arena where white players could validate their demand for higher salaries precisely because they were white and not black.[38]

With its references to white wage slavery, the Brotherhood drew on the worst fears of white workers in industrial America. Whether one was a professional player, skilled craftsmen, or common laborer, chattel slavery represented "the ultimate expression of the denial of liberty," the absence of self-possession. Slavery transformed a human being into a piece of property that could be possessed by others; it was a condition that could afflict blacks, Asians, and other nonwhites, but no longer could conceivably extend to those socially accepted as whites. According to historian David Roediger, the version of white republicanism that so many European immigrants embraced in conjunction with Anglo-Americans "suggested that long acceptance of slavery betokened weakness, degradation and an unfitness for freedom."[39] Hence, players needed not only to defend their economic position from capital exploitation but also to protect their status as white men. To do otherwise would justify their economic enslavement and make precarious their claims to whiteness. The Brotherhood's position therefore did little to abate the growing support for racial segregation within the national game. Their claims about mistreatment depended on clearing the playing field of those who carried the mark of slavery in their skin color, African Americans.

SPANIARD OF SOME KIND

Ownership's expanded search for talent beyond the Northeast and South and into the West and Southwest increased tensions over organized baseball's terms of inclusion. The failure of the experiments with racial inclusion and the protests against African American players during the 1880s established unequivocally that blacks were not to be included as equals. Questions remained as to whether some of the "new" people whom major leaguers encountered out West or in the Caribbean were racially eligible.

Although protest short-circuited the New York Metropolitans' 1887 attempt to sign George Stovey and Fleet Walker, teams in the high minor leagues and a couple of major-league managers still considered challenging the racial terms of inclusion. In the 1890s, teams began to openly approach some players previously viewed as racially ineligible. In so doing, these teams played on the fine distinctions within racial understandings about who was white, who was black, and who fit elsewhere along the color line. The entry of players with southern European ancestry and of Native Americans such as Louis Sockalexis tested the lines of inclusion during the 1890s, and while Italians gained increasing social acceptance as fellow whites, "red" players allowed into organized baseball were constantly reminded that they were not white and that their inclusion remained tenuous.

Although Esteban Bellán and Vincent Nava made inroads, their racial positioning as "Spaniards" meant players were not strictly viewed as white or black. Awareness of the full spectrum of locations along baseball's color line enabled black players and entrepreneurs to devise different strategies for maneuvering through the revamped terrain of America's game. As explained in chapter 2, in the absence of native-born Cubans or Cuban Americans in U.S. professional baseball, the performance of African Americans as "Cuban" Giants, along with the journalistic practice of applying Spanish and Cuban labels to African American players, increasingly associated Cuban identity with nonwhite status. Masquerading as Cuban or Spanish mollified racial antagonism toward African Americans, but by no means did it guarantee entrance into white segregated leagues, or social acceptance. Bud Fowler was fully cognizant of the opportunities he was denied as a black player in a profession that increasingly embraced Jim Crow. He told *Sporting Life* in 1895: "My skin is against me. If I had not been quite so black, I might have caught on as a Spaniard or something of that kind. The race prejudice is so strong that my black skin barred me."[40]

The nineteenth-century careers of Latino and African American players give meaning to different positions along the color line. Cumulatively, their experience as racialized subjects from the mid-1880s onward illustrates that in between the black and white poles of baseball's color line were, not shades of gray, but red (Native Americans), brown (U.S.- and foreign-born Latinos), and yellow (Asians and Asian Americans).[41] This shift to a five-color race schema—white, black, red, yellow, and brown—

occurred approximately three decades before political discourse in the United States and Europe moved away from romantic racialism's notions of fifty or more races toward the idea of five grand races that divided people according to skin color.[42] This simplification of racial categorization worked to justify segregation. On one hand, it grouped players of European ancestry under the common cloak of whiteness that enabled them to defend their inclusion in organized baseball as professional, white men. On the other hand, the five-grand-race schema differentiated among nonwhites in a hierarchical manner that approximated popular beliefs about racial difference. This system allowed those within organized baseball to extend participation to those ranked higher in the hierarchy while continuing to exclude others, mainly African Americans.

Attempts to broaden the terms of racial inclusion within professional baseball continued to meet resistance as the nineteenth century drew to a close. For players, racial inclusion signified equality and meant opening the playing field to more labor competition. Indeed, the battle to garner greater respect and a better salary depended on developing seemingly concrete answers to the question of who, based on his racial standing, had the capacity to act as a professional and merited protection from capital domination. Conversely, player attempts to set strict limits on inclusion were antithetical to the goal of filling a team's roster with the most talented players. Resolving this tension would take time. Team owners' continuing search for new players would eventually extend beyond U.S. borders, as the United States stretched its interests beyond the North American landmass into the Caribbean and Pacific at the end of the nineteenth century.

PART TWO

LATINOS AND THE RACIAL DIVIDE

4

Baseball Should Follow the Flag
Incorporating Nonwhite Others
in the Age of Empire

Ever since its establishment in the hearts of the people as
the foremost of field sports, Base Ball has "followed the
flag." . . . It has followed the flag to the Hawaiian Islands,
and at once supplanted every other form of athletics in
popularity. It has followed the flag to the Philippines, to
Puerto Rico and to Cuba, and wherever a ship floating the
Stars and Stripes finds anchorage to-day, somewhere on
nearby shore the American National Game is in progress.

A. G. Spalding, *America's National Game* (1911)

MORE THAN A GAME

In 1911 sporting-goods mogul A. G. Spalding authored a history of baseball that celebrated the rise of "America's national game" and advocated
its spread in the "American colonies." Spalding described the expansion
of the U.S. national pastime into the outposts of the new American empire as a positive development and proudly proclaimed baseball was already being played throughout Cuba, Puerto Rico, Hawaii, and even the
Philippines. For Spalding, colonialism and the military were responsible
for the game's spread into these new lands: "our soldiers and sailors"
introduced baseball wherever they set foot.[1]

North American newspapers also enthusiastically reported the game's
adoption by Cubans, Filipinos, and Hawaiians. In July 1899, little more
than six months after the U.S. flag was raised over Cuba, the *Sporting
News* assessed baseball's popularity there. "Our national game has taken

a strong hold in Cuba, having been played on the island since 1874 [*sic*]."[2] Two years later, under the headline "Baseball's Spread throughout the Spanish-speaking Americas," *Sporting Life* hailed the success of the project in San Juan, Puerto Rico, stating, "Uncle Sam's New People Learning the National Game."[3] These enthusiastic reports gave hope to those like Spalding who urged baseball to follow the flag.

Spalding rightly acknowledged the presence and even popularity of baseball in the outposts of the emerging American empire. Baseball had indeed established roots in a number of locations where the U.S. military had set up quarters following the War of 1898. Attributing the game's popularity in the Spanish-speaking Americas to the new U.S. presence, however, ignores baseball's arrival in Cuba in the early 1860s and in other parts of the Spanish-speaking Americas before the U.S. flag flew over these lands. The game's popularity in the Spanish-speaking Caribbean arose not from U.S. military action but from cultural exchange, commercial activity, and labor migration within the region before 1898.

Even before the United States' intervention in the Cuban War for Independence, North Americans had envisioned baseball as part of an intercultural exchange that would influence North-South relations. Popular support for Cuba Libre in the mid-1890s prompted U.S. political leaders to intervene in Cuba on behalf of the nationalist insurgents. Some called for the U.S. intervention in Cuba as part of a new "civilizing mission" that would reinforce the work of American institutions by inculcating American cultural practices among the local populace. It was in this spirit that A. G. Spalding joined a chorus of North American moral reformers who saw baseball's spread as part of a cultural project that accompanied the U.S. colonial presence in the Caribbean and Pacific.

For many North Americans who lived in the outposts of the new American empire, baseball had just these associations. Most North Americans arrived in the Caribbean imbued with the belief that the United States had a civilizing mission and that the islands' natives were less civilized than they and were incapable of self-rule.[4] Style of dress, food, and marital traditions, among other cultural practices, were seen as indicators of the islanders' inferiority, evidence of the need for the United States to undertake what President McKinley labeled "benevolent assimilation."[5] North Americans therefore appointed themselves moral and cultural authorities in teaching cultural practices to their new charges.

Baseball's popularity among the new subjects in the Spanish-speaking Caribbean worked hand in hand with the imperial project. The game's longer history in the Spanish-speaking Caribbean meant that inhabitants had already infused the game with meaning about nation, gender, and race. That history distinguished the Caribbean scene from the Philippines and the Pacific theater.[6] In both cases, the baseball diamond evolved into more than an athletic arena; it also became a cultural battleground for discourses about citizenship, respectability, and racial equality.

The call for baseball to follow the flag reflected the cultural investment made in the U.S. national game. Widely viewed as the sport most representative of American culture, baseball was vested with important socializing functions. Moral reformers and colonial officials contended that the sport instilled values that prepared young children and immigrants for their role as U.S. citizens. The game taught players individual responsibility to the larger community (teamwork), a work ethic (playing hard), and the importance of collaborating for the greater good (winning as a team versus individual achievement). For some, a colonial subject's ability to play baseball (and understand its "democratic principles") predicted the degree to which he could become Americanized.[7]

This belief in baseball as a tool of assimilation for the nation's recently arrived immigrants and following generation(s) gained increasing favor in the early 1880s. Americans who descended from what were previously viewed as the lesser European races—colonized peoples such as the Irish and southern Europeans such as the Italians—demonstrated the assimilative powers of America's game. The ascent of Irish Americans Charles Comiskey, Connie Mack (Cornelius McGillicuddy), and John McGraw into the game's elite was read like a Horatio Alger story, proof positive that individuals who worked hard could achieve their dreams in U.S. society.[8] The wider inclusion of these newer European Americans did not alleviate the hardening of the color line in U.S. professional leagues.

The opportunity to break into organized baseball remained unequally available to those deemed nonwhite. After the failed experiments with racial inclusion of black players in the 1880s, teams in organized baseball continued to test who exactly the color line excluded. Here the story of Native Americans overlapped with that of Latinos. In both cases, exposure to the assimilative tools of mainstream society, whether schools or baseball, clarified questions about the racial eligibility of specific Native American and Latino players.[9] In this way, organized baseball's racial system began to be recast as team and league officials gained knowledge from interaction with Latinos and as the place of Native Americans within U.S. society shifted. In the 1890s Native Americans would participate in greater numbers, and in the 1900s the game would be reopened to Latinos.

BUILDING TRANSNATIONAL LINKS

In articles about the game's development in the Spanish-speaking Caribbean, the sporting press in the United States and the Caribbean documented the formation of a transnational baseball circuit. Henry Chadwick's *New York Clipper* columns provided the earliest comprehensive coverage of Cuban baseball, reminding fans of recent associations with formerly New York–based Latino players, informing them about National Leaguers heading south to play in Cuba, and even including box scores from the Cuban professional league's inaugural 1879 season.[10] From its inception in 1884, Philadelphia-based *Sporting Life* reported on U.S. professional teams touring Cuba in the winter. The St. Louis–based *Sporting News* did the same when it started publishing in 1886. These periodicals not only informed fans about transnational links between Cuba and the United States but also cultivated their own connections by hiring Cuban baseball men as columnists, exchanging information with Cuban journalists, and sending sportswriters to cover U.S. barnstormers in action.

Cuban sporting papers highlighted the connections with North American baseball. Cuban periodicals reported on action in organized baseball and black baseball circuits in the United States, paying particular attention to Cuban participants. *El Sport, El Score, El Pitcher,* and other Cuban periodicals regularly excerpted published stories from North American periodicals, thereby transmitting North American racial understandings to their Cuban readership.[11] Readers of *El Sport* found reports of Cap Anson's hitting or Mike "King" Kelly's base running in the same columns that described the exploits of Frank Grant, Fleet Walker, and other *jugadores de color* (players of color). This coverage informed Cubans about the marginalized status of black players in U.S. professional baseball while also drawing a sharp distinction between Cubans and North American blacks. A September 1887 column in *El Sport,* "Juego de Cuban Giants: De los Estados Unidos" (Cuban Giants' Game: From the United States), clearly distinguished between Cubans and the Cuban Giants by referring to the North American club as "*etiopes,*" Ethiopians—that is to say, not real Cubans.[12]

Exchanges between U.S. and Cuban baseball transferred technical knowledge that contributed to the development of the Cuban game. A January 1887 article in *El Sport* noted major leaguer Billy Taylor's contribution to Cuban baseball: "In general, our *pitchers* have adopted the system introduced in this country by the famous American *pitcher* Billy

Taylor in 1885 [*sic*], and that permits them to pitch the ball freely, be it *overhand, underhand,* stationary, running, jumping, or executing all the movements that a *pitcher* believes convenient."[13] The Cuban sporting paper's use of English terms (italicized in the quote) to describe pitching techniques introduced by Taylor illustrates the transfer of knowledge within the transnational circuit. Anything from everyday expressions, baseball terms, and playing techniques to ideas about race were transferred by individuals traveling the circuit and by publications documenting events within the circuit.

U.S. sporting journals solidified the links between North American and Cuban baseball by hiring notable Cuban baseball men Carlos Ayala, Louis Someillan, and Abel Linares as columnists. These sportswriters helped lay the groundwork for baseball's transnational circuit. Ayala, the publisher of *El Sport*, one of Cuba's earliest baseball periodicals, had cofounded the Fé Base Ball Club, served as the secretary of the Cuban Professional League in the early 1890s, and organized barnstorming tours for three U.S. teams visiting Cuba, a role for which he had drawn praise in the *Sporting News* in a February 1893 article.[14] The *Sporting News* took advantage of Ayala's experience by hiring him as its Cuban baseball correspondent in the mid-1890s. *Sporting Life* hired Louis Someillan as its Cuban correspondent in 1893. Someillan's writing stint, which overlapped with Ayala's tenure at the *Sporting News,* came to an abrupt end in 1895 when Spanish colonial authorities arrested him as an insurgent collaborator as part of their heightened surveillance of nationalist activity in Cuba. Cognizant of baseball's association with nationalists, this campaign included the prohibition of U.S. teams from barnstorming the island and the termination of the Cuban league's 1894–95 season.[15] Much to the Philadelphia-based journal's disappointment, Someillan met an unsympathetic justice system and was sentenced to a North African prison with others convicted of treason.

Abel Linares bridged the different eras of Cuban baseball, his involvement starting in the Spanish colonial era, when the game was under constant surveillance, and continuing after Cuban independence and the beginning of open exchange with North American baseball. Linares penned the "Cuba's Chapter" column as a correspondent for *Sporting Life* from 1902 to 1904, after he had organized the first team of Cuban professional players to tour the United States in 1899, less than six months after the War of 1898 ended.

The columns written by the Cuban correspondents informed North American readers about the meaning Cubans attached to baseball. They

also revealed the different racial character of Cuban professional baseball, an integrated league many of whose top stars were Afro-Cuban.
News of these players' exploits alerted North Americans to the available
Cuban talent. Racial eligibility would be addressed in the context of U.S.
expansion, with discourses that racialized the new subject people as neither white nor black.

Questions about racial eligibility in organized baseball were exten-
sions of broader societal anxieties about the racial stock of natives from
Cuba, Puerto Rico, and the Philippines. U.S. colonial authority in these
lands shaped popular perceptions about the racial status of the islands'
residents. The ability to self-rule, as Matthew Frye Jacobson demonstrates
in his examination of U.S. immigration and naturalization policy, has long
been a prerequisite for naturalization (acquiring U.S. citizenship).[16] That
these people were under U.S. colonial authority made them suspect. Anxieties about the new subject peoples, moreover, were exacerbated by the
failure of familiar, black-white racial categories to accommodate them:
many, from President Taft to the print media, regularly referred to the
new colonial people as "little Brown brothers."

Tensions between organized baseball's desire for new, cheap talent and
for a racially exclusionary system mirrored questions about the incorporation of nonwhite others into the United States. Jacobson argues that
debates about the incorporation of Puerto Ricans, Filipinos, and Cubans
were influenced by the "philosophical revisions of the concept of citizenship" following the failed project of Reconstruction and incorporation of African American males as full citizens. These debates about the
desirability of incorporating subject people from the United States' new
possessions occurred within the context of continued U.S. industrial and
economic development. "American integration into the world economic
system in this period of breathtaking industrialization," Jacobson notes,
"exposed a rather profound dependence upon foreign peoples as imported workers for American factories [and farms] and as overseas consumers of American products."[17]

Precluded from signing African Americans by its gentleman's agreement, organized baseball encountered a self-created dilemma. Admitting
these foreigners to the field involved revisiting organized baseball's color
line and popular racial understandings. Specifically, officials had to
weigh their desire to acquire new talent against the consequences of appearing not to uphold exclusionary racial practices.

The entreaties made to Cuban player Antonio María García reveal
that John McGraw, for one, contemplated challenging the orthodoxy of

baseball's racial policy.[18] A frequent visitor to Cuba throughout his professional career, McGraw first toured Cuba in 1891 as a player with Ocala, a minor-league team from Florida. During this initial trip García piqued his interest. A lighter-skinned Cuban nicknamed El Inglés (the Englishman), García had briefly studied in the States before starring in the Cuban circuit. Always quick to seize an advantage, McGraw approached García about going North to join him in playing for Baltimore's American Association club. According to Cuban sporting papers, García turned down McGraw's offer, saying he "was being paid better—$500 per month throughout the year—than what the Orioles offered."[19]

García's decision postponed the revisiting of the racial eligibility question for Cubans. Those hoping to maintain organized baseball's racial policy would likely have questioned his claim to whiteness. As North American whiteness evolved, it retained a close association with northern European ancestry. García might claim Spanish ethnic heritage, but having southern European ancestry and coming from a people still under colonial rule made one's claim to whiteness tenuous.

GOING NATIVE (AMERICAN)

Segregation and labor strife led several big-league organizations to turn to racialized communities that were not black-identified as an alternate talent pool. Although this strategy met resistance on and off the playing field, the first two decades of the twentieth century saw Indian (Native American), Cuban, and Mexican American players break into organized baseball. The strategic turn to Latinos during the Jim Crow era developed into a more enduring practice than the use of Native American talent. The incorporation of Latinos into organized baseball's racial system reaffirmed U.S. racial understandings and the elevation of whiteness.

Louis Sockalexis, a Penobscot Indian, made his National League debut in 1897 to much fanfare.[20] Much as Providence team officials had publicized Vincent Nava's arrival fifteen years earlier as the "Spanish catcher of the Providence Club," Cleveland widely advertised Sockalexis as the National League's first Indian player. The sporting press likewise marked Sockalexis as a racial curiosity whose mere presence could draw fans. Cleveland home attendance doubled in 1897 from the previous season. In what became a popular trend nationwide, crowds followed wherever Sockalexis played—to observe in person as the "noble savage" performed.

In the minds of countless Americans, the end of the Indian wars and changes in federal policy, such as the Dawes Allotment Act, had vanquished the old Indians. This significant shift toward assimilating Indians into mainstream culture sparked a fascination with Indians as subjects of museum displays, academic studies, and, most popular of all, Wild West shows. Personal encounters were part of the lure of Wild West shows starring Buffalo Bill Cody and real Indians, and they were what attracted fans to Cleveland games to watch Sockalexis perform.[21] As historian Philip Deloria notes, the performance of Indians on the athletic playing field "offered white audiences spectacles of a lost time of natural physicality and strength."[22]

Sockalexis's drawing power extended beyond male fans, attracting a significant number of women to Cleveland games, whom the *Sporting News* labeled "Soc's pale-faced maidens." Sockalexis's presence made Ladies Days at Cleveland's League Park a grand success. Women fans turned out in other big-league cities holding placards or "wearing single feathers like Indian squaws."[23] The practice of European Americans "playing Indian" was not unusual for the times. This performance of the Indian past resonated as a powerful marker of distinction between whites and Indians as the federal government and such educational institutions as Carlisle, Dickinson, and Dartmouth aggressively pursued a policy of assimilating Native Americans into the U.S. mainstream.[24]

Sockalexis had attended boarding schools as a youth and, later, the College of Holy Cross in Worcester, Massachusetts. Having been educated in these mainstream, assimilationist institutions and wearing the time's fashionable clothes and hairstyle, he was nonetheless constantly reminded of his Indianness. Sockalexis acknowledged as much in a June 19, 1897, interview: "No matter where we play I go through the same ordeal, and at the present time I am so used to it that at times I forget to smile at my tormentors, believing it to be part of the game."[25]

The sporting press consistently marked (and remarked on) Sockalexis's Indianness. "Indian garb" often served as a visual reminder of his racial Otherness. One published cartoon, "Sockalexis Breaking for Third," portrayed him in uniform but replaced his baseball cap with ceremonial feathers.[26] Fellow players also provided such visual markers. Before a June 1897 game against Cleveland, Baltimore's John McGraw appeared wearing "a full Indian war bonnet with feathers." At subsequent Cleveland-Baltimore games and later at other league parks, fans greeted Sockalexis wearing their own "war bonnets" and letting out war whoops.[27]

Responses on and off the field captured the tensions involved in the incorporation of Indians into the American mainstream. Future Hall of

Famer Ed Delahanty expressed strong reservations about Sockalexis's entry into the big leagues, commenting to a sport periodical: "The League has gone all to hell now that they're letting *them damn foreigners* in."[28] Perceptions of foreignness would also affect Sockalexis off the baseball diamond. In May 1898 he was caught up in the wave of anti-Spanish sentiment that accompanied the push for U.S. intervention in Cuba. *Sporting Life* reported a physical altercation that occurred on a train when several U.S. soldiers misidentified Sockalexis and "told the Indian what they thought of Spain." Sockalexis tried to leave the railroad car when one of the soldiers physically accosted him. After defending himself, Sockalexis reportedly stated it was "hard enough to be taken for a Spaniard, without being estimated a weakling."[29]

The incident illustrates that acquiring racial knowledge is an uneven process, contingent as it is on an individual's exposure, direct or indirect, to racialized groups. The army recruits in the May 1898 altercation used their (limited) racial knowledge to (mis)interpret Sockalexis's physical appearance as that of a Spaniard. Team and league officials in organized baseball also used their racial knowledge during this period as they explored the possibilities of signing Indian players. In 1897 the signing of Sockalexis was the test of racial tolerance. As the twentieth century opened, the incorporation of players from the Spanish-speaking Americas served as the experimental laboratory for testing tolerance and policing baseball's color line.

CUBA LIBRE AND BASEBALL

Cuba attained a unique place in the minds of U.S. politicians and capitalists and the American public. The struggle to liberate Cuba from Spain's colonial clutches became a regular topic in political and popular circles. Encapsulated in the term *Cuba Libre* (Free Cuba) popular support for a free Cuba in the United States was not necessarily built on the ideological principles of José Martí and Cuban nationalists. The cause of Cuba Libre in the North American mind was largely inspired by the sensationalistic coverage of William Randolph Hearst's *New York Journal* and Joseph Pulitzer's *New York World*. Labeled yellow journalism by their detractors, these newspapers' coverage mobilized American sentiment against Spain. The sporting world would not go unaffected.[30]

The mainstream and sporting press ran articles siding with the Cuban nationalists. The articles played on popular views of Spain as a backward, despotic nation and urged the United States to intervene, liberate, and civilize Cuba. North Americans who had previously toured Cuba spoke out on behalf of the nationalist cause. In a January 1897 *Sporting Life* interview, Frank Bancroft described the lasting impact his encounters with Spanish colonial rulers had on him and his fellow barnstormers from the 1879 Hop Bitters. "Several of the team have since passed away, but it is dollars to doughnuts that those who are living are dyed-in-the-wool rooters for the Cubans in their struggle for independence from Spanish tyranny."[31] Bancroft's reflections signaled the depth of sentiment against Spanish rulers within U.S. professional circles. After all, Spanish colonial rulers had been the main obstacle to unfettered movement of baseball talent within America's transnational circuit.

Cuban insurgents launched their (third) War of Independence in late February 1895. Although the U.S. Congress waited a year before passing a resolution recognizing the Cuban belligerency, popular North American support for the insurgents continued. Like much of the American public, prominent major-league figures advocated for U.S. intervention in the Cuban struggle. The sinking of the USS *Maine* while sitting in Havana harbor provided the necessary justification for the U.S. intervention, and on April 25, 1898, President McKinley asked for and got a declaration of war against Spain. The U.S. intervention changed the stakes of the Cuban War of Independence: for North Americans the fight in Cuba had become an American struggle, the Spanish-American War.

Support for Cuban nationalists also had a basis beyond national politics: economics. Like other U.S.-based industries, sporting-goods manufacturers anxiously awaited the cessation of hostilities in the Caribbean so that they could energize the followers of America's game on the islands. The prospect of a Cuba opened to trade sparked optimism. Albert Spalding for one hoped that economic activity in the newly liberated territories would revive the faltering sporting-goods industry. A *Sporting Life* correspondent described another sporting-goods dealer who remained hopeful for "a record-breaking base ball season next year" after the "small decline" in business caused by the war. In making a case for optimism, the dealer noted that the same conditions had predominated right after the U.S. Civil War when "everybody seemed to have plenty of money and sports boomed from ocean to ocean."[32] The prospect of free trade with Cuba led Frank Bancroft and other baseball promoters to draft plans to tour Cuba even before the war ended. Bancroft's plan called for a barnstorming team composed of National League stars to land in Havana for a series of games with Cuban clubs after the city was under U.S. control on January 1, 1899.[33] For these promoters, a friendly government in Cuba offered assurance that profits from their economic ventures would not be limited by hefty taxes, as they had been during the Spanish colonial era. And the U.S. military government that presided over Cuba in the war's immediate aftermath (1898–1901) proved their optimism for better economic conditions to be well founded.

The arrival of the All Cubans team in July 1899 marked a turning point for Cubans attempting to reclaim their name in the U.S. playing field. In anticipation of this first U.S. barnstorming tour, the *Sporting News* alerted U.S. baseball enthusiasts to the difference between the visiting Cuban team and the more familiar Cuban Giants. "This [Cuban] team is the first and only club that ever contemplated a visit to the States and is the only native born Cuban Giants in existence."[34] The clarification reminded U.S. fans that the teams that normally played under the Cuban Giants name were composed of African Americans, not actual Cubans.

Although other Cuban teams had traveled to Florida to play teams in Key West and Tampa in the 1890s, the All Cubans' tour had a different purpose and travel itinerary. This team was headed for New York to begin a two-month barnstorming tour that would include games against local, semiprofessional, minor-league, and black teams throughout the Northeast and Midwest.[35] Composed of players drawn from all the Cuban professional-league teams, the All Cubans met with mixed success on the baseball diamond. Despite mediocre on-field results, the club's 1899 tour set into motion the annual practice of Cuban professional teams barnstorming through the United States after the close of the Cuban league season.[36]

Initiated in the euphoria of the U.S. victory in the War of 1898, Cuban barnstorming tours aroused the interest of North American baseball fans, particularly those who had rallied behind the cause of Cuba Libre. These fans came to see what they perceived as a triumph of American culture among those recently freed from Spanish colonialism. To them, few things were more American than baseball, and few activities better symbolized the new freedoms extended to their Cuban brothers than Cubans playing baseball with their "liberators."

The barnstorming tours plotted by Linares and the Cuban organizers following the 1899 All Cubans' tour highlighted the transnational link between Cubans on the island and those residing in the United States. The tours during the 1900s and 1910s typically made strategic stops in towns with Cuban or Latino enclaves, such as New York, Chicago, New Orleans, and Tampa. In these towns, Cuban émigrés renewed connections with compatriots around the sport Cuban nationalists had long embraced as part of their national culture.

The tour schedule Linares established after 1899 ran from late March through September. The squad usually arrived in March for spring training, docking in Key West, Tampa, or New Orleans. In preparation for their northern and midwestern engagements the team played games throughout the segregated South. These annual treks familiarized Cuban players with the whims of Jim Crow segregation in baseball and everyday life. Southern teams would often agree to play the Cubans sight unseen, having made contact only with Linares in making the arrangements. The team's composition—ranging from the lighter-skinned Antonio María García and medium-toned Luis Padrón to the darker-skinned Gervasio Gonzales—sometimes surprised opponents and fans when the Cubans appeared at their ballpark. It was not uncommon for southern teams to cancel exhibition games as soon as word was received that the Cuban club was racially mixed. Some who canceled their games claimed they were unable to secure grounds to host an integrated game or were unwilling themselves to take the field with players who, if not black, were too racially ambiguous for their own comfort.

Arriving in New York by mid-April, Cuban squads often found a more accommodating environment. The Cuban tourists lined up games against black professional, white semipro, and other local clubs with much less turmoil. The Midwest swing included brief stops in small towns to play collegiate, semipro, and lower-level minor-league teams, with longer stays (up to a week) in major cities such as Indianapolis to play against top-tier minor-league clubs and black professional teams. The Cubans' main goal, however, was arriving in Chicago by Memorial Day for that city's holiday double-header, which after 1909 included at least one game against Rube Foster's American Giants. The midwestern leg lasted into July, when the team started its return East that culminated with the Labor Day twin billing in New York City at the close of its annual tour.[37] These tours exposed North Americans to talented Cubans who would one day perform in organized baseball or the Negro leagues.

A COLOR EXPERIMENT OF ANOTHER KIND

The issues involved in securing entry for Latinos in organized baseball were distinct from what officials faced in signing Sockalexis and other Indian players. The majority of the first wave of Indian players had benefited from exposure to assimilation-geared educational programs.

A significant proportion of the Indian players who followed Sockalexis were of mixed parentage, resulting in a range of physical characteristics. Their entry was viewed nonetheless as a possible opening in organized baseball's racial policy. If "Red" players like Sockalexis were permitted to enter, could "Brown" players follow?

The prospect of securing an exceptional talent by manipulating racial understandings proved too enticing for Baltimore Orioles manager John McGraw. In 1901 Baltimore signed infielder "Chief Tokahoma," hoping to take advantage of the opening created by the entry of Sockalexis and other Indian players such as Charles Bender and Elijah Pinnance. The talented second baseman, however, was in actuality Charlie Grant, an African American who had previously played on several black semi-pro teams in the Midwest.[38]

Grant's masquerade as Tokahoma was the brainstorm of John Mc-Graw, whose professional travels had given him insight into the workings of baseball's complicated racial system. McGraw planned the scheme after he observed Grant play with other African American players near the Orioles spring training camp in Hot Springs, Arkansas. Inspired by Grant's performance, McGraw told the ballplayer, "Charlie, I've been trying to think of some way to sign you for the Baltimore club and I think I've got it. On this map there's a creek called Tokahoma. That's going to be your name from now on, Charlie Tokahoma, and you're a full-blooded Cherokee."[39] Otherwise forbidden from performing in the segregated league, Grant agreed to the scheme.

A part-time resident of northern Florida who lived in proximity to the state's Seminole population, McGraw attempted to take advantage of the age-old overlap between Native American and African-American communities in parts of the South and West. In the antebellum era, enslaved African Americans who fled their bondage often found sanctuary in Native American nations, such as the Seminole, Cherokee, and Creek, located in Georgia, Florida, and later, Oklahoma. In some instances, Native Americans held African American slaves, which, as scholar Tiya Miles has documented, further complicated the relationship and overlap between these communities.[40] The incorporation of African Americans, free or enslaved, into these communities and their intermixture produced offspring who could claim ancestry as Black Seminole or Black Cherokee, among other mixtures. Forced relocations of Native Americans to the Great Plains territories of Oklahoma and Arkansas would produce additional contact with African Americans. The identity that John McGraw bestowed on Charlie Grant thus referenced a long history; Tokahoma would not be the first "Indian" whose ambiguous physical features reflected inter-actions between Indians and African Americans.

Because McGraw was attempting to circumvent the association be-tween skin color or physical features and exclusion, the success of Toka-homa's masquerade depended on the collaboration of whites. Although the entry of racially ambiguous ethnics in the 1890s had widened the category of whiteness, few league or team officials expressed interest in making a mockery of the color line by permitting players widely per-ceived as black to enter as Indians.

Baltimore's experiment demonstrated the economic potential of racial integration as throngs of fans came out to cheer on Baltimore's Chero-kee infielder during his spring training outings. In fact, black newspa-pers contended that Baltimore's plot might have succeeded if not for the overzealous response of black fans. "Nobody would have been the wiser," a *New York Age* article suggested, "if the team hadn't made the trip to Chicago to play Anson's White Stockings and the colored folks in Chi-cago's South Side hadn't lined up six deep along State Street with an Elks marching band to welcome the 'Indian' Grant."[41] Though this was likely a colorful overstatement, the enthusiastic response black fans lavished on Baltimore's new second baseman clearly made him suspect in the minds of opposing league and team officials.

Informed by his own sources about McGraw's attempt to manipulate the racial barrier, Chicago's Charles Comiskey sharply criticized Balti-more. "I'm not going to stand for McGraw ringing in an Indian on the Baltimore team," Comiskey informed reporters after a contest against Baltimore. "If Muggsy [McGraw] really keeps this Indian, I will get a Chinaman of my acquaintance and put him on third." Comiskey ex-plained he had been informed that "the Cherokee of McGraw's is really Grant, the crack Negro second baseman from Cincinnati, fixed up with war paint and a bunch of feathers." Complaints from American League team officials ended Baltimore's ploy, and Grant returned to the black baseball circuit.[42]

The pioneering cohort of Indian players faced a particular set of chal-lenges in breaking into the major leagues and organized baseball. Cer-tainly, many European Americans saw these players as intimate outsiders. That is to say, Indians were familiar but did not exactly occupy the same location as whites along the color line. Native Americans were constantly reminded of this difference. "I don't think it looks right for these for-eigners to be breaking into the game," commented a major leaguer about Philadelphia's two Indian players, Charles Bender and Elijah Pinnance.

The comment, which appeared in a September 1903 *Philadelphia Inquirer* article, powerfully testifies to the conflation of Indianness with foreignness that placed Native Americans outside the nation, foreigners in their own land.[43]

The reception that fans and the press extended to catcher John T. Meyers captured the public ambivalence toward Indians who were fan favorites. Described as a member of the "old tribe of Spanish Mission Indians of California," Meyers signed with McGraw's New York Giants in 1911 and quickly developed a following. Whenever he stepped to the plate, the New York faithful greeted him by letting out a "war-whoop," although Meyers "probably never emitted a war-whoop in his life or heard one except on the stage or in a wild west show." Despite this acknowledgment, the sportswriter nonetheless added, "at the same time he knows that the war-whoop has the same relation to an Indian as water has to ducks."[44]

The racialization of Native Americans included the seemingly innocuous act of assigning them the nickname "Chief," as occurred with Bender and Meyers. "Chief" had entirely different connotations than such endearing nicknames as "Babe," "Cap," or "Lefty" that other ballplayers received. Applied indiscriminately to all Indian players, "Chief" stripped Indian players of their individuality. Just as significant, the nickname trivialized the significance of an actual chief and also racialized Indian players as foreign.[45]

LATINOS BREAK THROUGH

The gradual opening of the major leagues to Native Americans helped teams within organized baseball make a case for signing Latinos. As a group that had been viewed as racially ineligible, Indian players set a precedent for the entry of other nonwhites. Major-league team officials imparted an important lesson in the process: they possessed the power to construct whatever racial categories they deemed necessary to distinguish between blacks and other nonwhites while still maintaining a color line that excluded African Americans. A few Latinos benefited from the loosening of organized baseball's racial policy. Their incorporation involved many of the same figures that facilitated the entry of Native American players.

A year after Baltimore's failed attempt to pass Charlie Grant off as a Native American, the Philadelphia Athletics signed Colombian-born infielder Louis Castro without fanfare or reported controversy.[46] Discovered by Connie Mack, Castro had been playing for Manhattan College's varsity team less than two years before.[47] Given the unenviable task of replacing Philadelphia's recently departed star second baseman, Napoleon Lajoie, Castro drew sharp criticism. When the Athletics started slowly, a *Sporting Life* columnist wrote bluntly, "The trouble with the Athletics is that Castro can't fill the bill at second base." After an inauspicious first month, Castro's performance improved as the Athletics rebounded to claim the American League pennant and win the 1902 World Series title, a triumph the Philadelphia-based *Sporting Life* celebrated on its October 2 cover. Castro's stint with the Athletics, however, was brief. Set loose by Philadelphia after the 1902 campaign, he signed with the Class A Eastern League's Rochester.[48] Although he would continue in organized baseball into the 1920s, Castro would never again appear in the majors.

The first recognized player from the Spanish-speaking Americas to perform in the majors since Vincent Nava in 1886, Castro set the profile of Latinos who entered the major leagues in the early twentieth century. Most were lighter skinned, had perceptible European physical features, and came from their native country's propertied elite, and many had attended a U.S. educational institution. Born in 1877 into an elite Colombian family, the light-skinned and U.S.-educated Castro personified this description: his father was a federal judge in Colombia, his uncle Cipriano Castro was the president of neighboring Venezuela.[49] This combination of characteristics motivated the North American press to stress Castro's "Spanish" background. A July 1902 column in the *Sporting News* referred to him as "a Spaniard by birth."[50] Identified as Spaniards, lighter-skinned Latinos like Castro secured admittance in organized baseball, but this passage to acceptance did not necessarily translate into being accepted as a fellow white.

The reappearance of Latinos in the majors started anew six years after Castro's release by Philadelphia. In the midst of a rash of injuries to its pitching staff in 1908, the Boston Red Sox dipped into the talented Pacific Coast League to sign pitcher Frank Arellanes. After his signing, *Sporting Life* referred to him as Mexican American, Mexican, and "of Spanish extraction."[51] Featured on the cover of *Sporting Life*'s December 12 issue, Arellanes's photo bore the caption "a descendent of the Spaniards who settled in southern California some three generations ago."[52] The publication thus distinguished Arellanes from most Latino residents of California, who were of Mexican descent and perceived by most people in U.S. society as having mixed racial ancestry. Arellanes soon learned that strong on-field performance did not exempt Latino pioneers from being the subject of public racialization. The same caption that accompanied Arellanes's front-page photo attributed his pitching success to his "true Spanish stubbornness."[53] The caption reminded fans that although the "Mexican" pitcher of "Spanish extraction" performed in the segregated big leagues, he did not wholly reside in the same racial camp as his fellow major leaguers.[54]

Colombian native Louis Castro and Mexican American Frank Arellanes were the first of a new wave of players from the Spanish-speaking Americas to break into the majors. Cubans, however, would compose the largest pool of Latino talent that would enter in the early twentieth century. Although Arellanes was the sole Latino major leaguer in 1908, other Latinos were performing in the minor leagues. Minor-league teams in the Northeast and West tapped into the Latino talent pool more than others. Teams in the New York State League, Connecticut League, Atlantic League, Texas League, and Pacific Coast League all signed Latino players in the mid-1900s. The same year Arellanes debuted with Boston, a number of Latinos were performing with minor-league clubs throughout the United States, including four players on the New Britain entry in the Connecticut League, a Class B minor league.

The incorporation of Latinos into organized baseball in the early twentieth century brought to the fore the complex issues involved in determining racial eligibility while maintaining black exclusion. Attempts to broker the entry of Latinos would introduce new ethnoracial categories, such as Castilian, into U.S. baseball circles to differentiate between eligible Latinos and the majority deemed racially ineligible to participate in the major leagues. In so doing, the process of including players from the Spanish-speaking Americas would mirror the concerns arising from the incorporation into U.S. society of colonial people from newly acquired territories.

5

"Purest Bars of Castilian Soap"
Cubans Break into Organized Baseball,
1908–1920

An odd thing about the makeup of the Cuban teams is the
fact that the best catchers and pitchers are black, while the
crack infielders are generally white men. Most of the outfield-
ers are dusky chaps, Marsans of the Reds not rating as an
outfielder in Cuba. . . . Almeida . . . Cabrera . . . and Romanach . . . are all as faultlessly Caucasian as Walter Johnson
or Duffy Lewis. The mixture of white races in Cuba is almost
as remarkable as in the United States. Marsans is a Spaniard,
Almeida is a Portuguese, Cabrera is a Canary Islander, and
Romanach, I believe, is a Basque.

William Phelon, "Baseball among the Magnates," *Baseball Magazine*
(February 1912)

BARNSTORMING *EN LAS AMERICAS*

Between 1900 and the early 1920s a transnational baseball circuit
emerged that linked New York, San Francisco, and Chicago with Havana, San Juan, and Santo Domingo. This period saw teams from organized and black baseball make regular tours of Cuba and other parts of
Latin America. Big-league teams started annual barnstorming tours in
1900. Two years later, African American teams began to tour Cuba, and
by 1907 African American players were formal participants in the Cuban
league. It would be another five years before Detroit Tigers Matty McIn-
tyre became the first major leaguer to play on a Cuban league team.[1]

Representing multiple locations within the Americas and various levels of race mixture, Latinos who participated in baseball's transnational circuit exposed others to the complexities of the racial systems of different regions in the United States and the Spanish-speaking Americas. Travel within the transnational circuit proved critical to the roles that Frank Bancroft, John McGraw, and Clark Griffith played in opening up access to the major leagues for Cuban players. The major-league organizations' discriminatory pursuit of Cuban talent illustrated the power organization officials wielded in determining racial eligibility. But these officials were not the only ones who used racial knowledge in negotiating (or manipulating) racialized lines of difference. Cubans and other Latinos would form a variety of strategies to combat the impact of segregation on their professional careers, enabling a few to cross lines that seemed impassable to others.

Reinforced with African American players in 1907 and after, Cuban teams competed against barnstorming big leaguers and eventually prompted organized baseball's leaders to change their stance regarding barnstorming tours. Composed of players from American and National League teams, the barnstorming All Leaguers won only five of their eleven contests against Cuban teams Almendares and Habana during their winter 1907 visit. The following winter, the Cincinnati Reds mustered only six wins in thirteen games against Cuban league teams. The Reds' lackluster performance upset Cincinnati team president August "Garry" Herrmann. A late-December article in *Sporting Life,* "No More Trips," detailed why Herrmann now opposed barnstorming by big-league squads. Winter ball tours gave Cincinnati Reds fans "the impression that the men are going back whenever a defeat is chalked up against them," Herrmann explained. Additionally, the tours wore his players down "to such an extent that they cannot go full pace keyed up to the highest notch the next season." But there was also a racial component to his stance. "I find that the Reds are playing against certain men in Cuba against whom there is an unwritten law in the big leagues," he declared. "That is another reason why I am opposed to any future games in Cuba."[2]

Despite Herrmann's declaration, major-league teams—almost intact, not all-star—continued to barnstorm Cuba. The American League champion Detroit Tigers toured the following winter and, perhaps unaware of the improved abilities of their Cuban host, arrived without their two top players, Ty Cobb and Sam Crawford. The Tigers squad won only four out of twelve games. The lesson to be drawn from Detroit's horrendous performance of 1909 was clear to sportswriter Joe Jackson. Cuban teams were gaining on their North American counterparts, and one thing the series "emphatically" demonstrated, according to Jackson, was that "it is impossible to bring down a short-handed club and kid the Cubans."[3]

Big-league barnstormers enjoyed mixed success the next winter. Although they arrived with the great Sam Crawford in tow, the Detroit Tigers struggled to split their first eight games in this return engagement in Cuba. Team officials cabled back to the States and convinced the team's star Ty Cobb to join his teammates. Cobb's arrival lifted the club to three straight victories to finish with seven wins against four losses. The 1910 American League champion Philadelphia Athletics also came calling that winter. Although they won 102 regular-season games, the Athletics suffered six defeats in ten games against Cuban teams. After the Athletics' disastrous visit, American League president Ban Johnson issued a decree prohibiting league teams from barnstorming the island as intact squads. Johnson's dictum made it clear that these games, though played in a foreign land, had taken on racial meaning. "We want no makeshift club calling themselves the Athletics to go to Cuba to be beaten by colored teams."[4]

The following winter two National League clubs barnstormed Cuba. The Philadelphia Phillies, a midlevel National team, fared a little better than their cross-town counterparts the Athletics had in 1910, winning five closely contested games out of nine played. John McGraw's New York Giants followed the Phillies to the island in the 1911–12 winter. McGraw's team, unlike the Detroit Tigers the previous two years, arrived with a full roster of players and reasserted major-league supremacy by winning nine of twelve games.

The inability to consistently assert outright superiority over the racially integrated Cuban teams perturbed major-league officials. Herrmann and Johnson attempted to regulate the terms under which big leaguers barnstormed in Cuba. Such an attempt was especially important since big-league officials could not control perceptions of their competition when the print media, major leaguers, or contributing fans reported game results and described the play of talented black and Latino players. Losing a game was perhaps less embarrassing in itself than losing to Cuban teams most of whose Cuban and *all* of whose African American players were racially ineligible to participate in the major leagues. The competitive games in Cuba contradicted the assumption underlying Jim Crow baseball that a lack of talent justified excluding these groups.

Officials who organized Cuban barnstorming teams faced their own set of issues in dealing with the complexities of the U.S. playing field. Organizers had to establish good working relationships with North American baseball promoters, including Rube Foster and Ed Lamar in the Midwest and Nat Strong in the East. These baseball men assisted Cuban baseball entrepreneurs in taking care of such tour details as drafting itineraries and securing accommodations. Their contributions were indispensable since they were in a better position to book venues and schedule exhibition games that had strong revenue potential.[5] Just as significant, they helped Cubans develop familiarity with local customs and racial norms in different parts of the United States. For it was not enough to know whether a town was segregated; team officials needed to know which establishments would serve Cubans though they refused service to African Americans.

Cuban team officials also had to comply with U.S. immigration laws and other federal policies in order to secure entry for their teams. Prior to leaving for the States, Cuban team officials had to secure U.S. visas for their players. Organizers were required to post bonds with U.S. immigration officials to gain travel clearance. The bonds assured the U.S. government that the visiting Cuban team members had sufficient funds to return to their native country and would not remain in the States and become public charges.

Much like the visa issues that occur with current Latino major leagues organizations at spring training each year, complications arose regularly when Cuban teams traveled to the United States. Players did not always get their visas processed on time. Medical conditions delayed others. All had to deal with shifts in immigration policies and their enforcement. Such was the case in 1910 when Cuban Stars pitcher José Méndez was denied entry by U.S. immigration officials because he had had trachoma—a chronic contagious bacterial conjunctivitis that would later contribute to his poor health and early death in 1926. Fellow Cuban Armando Cabanas was also delayed that spring. His case exposes how U.S. racial understandings guided the active U.S. border policing to which individuals were subjected. Cuban newspaper *La Lucha* reported that U.S. immigration officials initially denied Cabanas entry because they suspected he was of Chinese descent. Suspicions about Cabanas's ancestry reflected the lingering impact of the Chinese Exclusion Act of 1882, and also intimated U.S. awareness of the migration of Chinese laborers to Cuba in the late nineteenth century.[6] Immigration officials eventually granted Cabanas entry. Ironically, no reports indicated that his Cuban Stars teammate Carlos Morán, nicknamed "El Chino" in Cuban baseball circles, encountered such difficulty securing entry into the States.

The vagaries of assigning race to Cuban players were powerfully displayed when Cuban players were signed by North American teams. For clubs inside and outside organized baseball, Cuban players were the latest untapped source. Intrigue surrounding these new entrants onto the U.S. playing field helped them become drawing cards. Yet Cubans still had to confront the way lines of inclusion and exclusion were chalked on the U.S. diamond. As would become quickly apparent, Cubans who had been professional teammates in Cuba or who had barnstormed together through the United States faced different destinies once they joined U.S. professional leagues.

A COLOR TEST IN CONNECTICUT

Victories won by integrated Cuban teams motivated organized-baseball team officials to take a serious look at Cuban players. A few minor-league teams rushed to outmaneuver one another in order to place Cuban players under contract. In 1907 Scranton (Pennsylvania League) and New Britain (Connecticut League) made competing claims on Cuban players Rafael Almeida and Armando Marsans. The interleague matter went before National Commission chair Garry Herrmann, who awarded the players' rights to Scranton; neither player reported.[7] The decision turned out a temporary setback for New Britain.

The following spring New Britain's pursuit paid off when it signed four Cubans for the 1908 season: Almeida, Marsans, Alfredo "Cabbage" Cabrera, and Luis Padrón. All four enjoyed strong campaigns in the Class B minor league, the equivalent of today's AA minor league. Padrón was the league's fourth-leading hitter, while Almeida and Marsans ranked eleventh and fourteenth, respectively. Their inclusion did not proceed without protest, and reaction to the Cubans' presence on the field occasionally took a bad turn.

Cuban players in the Connecticut League were the targets of knockdown pitches and attempted spikings by opponents, much as African American players in the International League had been in the late 1880s. Hartford pitcher Ray Fisher did not hide his contempt for the league's newcomers. A future pitcher for the New York Yankees, Fisher took "a great dislike to the Cubans." The first time Fisher faced New Britain, he knocked two Cubans out of the game, including Cabrera, who "was carried off the field unconscious."[8] Although Cabrera eventually recovered, Fisher had sent a clear message: not all Connecticut Leaguers were pleased with New Britain's decision to sign the Cuban players.

Verbal taunts from fans reminded the Cubans that some vehemently opposed their presence in the New England–based circuit. Several newspapers reported that fans in Hartford "ragged" New Britain's Cuban players. The jeering struck one sportswriter as ironic, given that one of the Cubans' New Britain white teammates "had such a dark complexion that he looked more like a Cuban than the visitors from Havana."[9] The observation underscores the capriciousness of racial perception: peers accepted this New Britain player as white, while his Cuban teammates were treated as racially suspect.

Protests prompted Connecticut League officials to reconsider the inclusion of Cubans following the 1908 season. Concerns about the Cuban players' racial background had been published as soon as New Britain had announced their signing. The *Springfield Union* alluded to these concerns in the weeks preceding the 1908 campaign: "Manager Humphrey is getting what looks like a good team together. He has signed up to four Cuban players. . . . It will not be surprising if a drive is made against them in organized base ball on the ground that they are negroes, and it is well known that the colored brethren are not welcome in organized ball."[10] At the league's postseason gathering, officials decided to forbid teams to contract "black" players. Since no African Americans participated in the league, the change specifically called into question the racial ancestry of Cubans.

Concerned with the league's revised policy, New Britain's new manager, Billy Hanna, traveled to Cuba to secure documentation that verified the racial eligibility of his Cuban players. Hanna returned to the States with mixed results. According to a published report, he discovered that all the players were "real Cubans" except Padrón.[11] New Britain would have to play its 1909 season without its second-leading hitter and arguably its best pitcher.

For Padrón, the disappointment of being forced to leave New Britain was a sobering end to the 1908 season. The year had opened with the versatile Cuban at the Chicago White Sox's spring training camp for a tryout. Although he reportedly impressed owner Charles Comiskey, Chicago's top executive ultimately decided Padrón was too dark—others would surely protest that Chicago was too ambitious in testing the color line. Unsigned by Chicago, Padrón joined New Britain for the 1908 regular season. Padrón's expulsion from the Connecticut League underscored the limitations most Latino players confronted when they entered the U.S. playing field. Off-field factors dashed their hopes of fully profiting from their place among top Latino players. Exiled from organized baseball, the immensely talented Padrón joined the majority of Latino players, who were with barnstorming teams or in the independent black professional circuits.

Padrón's continued strong performance with the Cuban Stars the next several seasons placed him among the best Cuban players coming north annually.[12] Although his performance for the Chicago-based team sparked the interest of minor-league teams in the Midwest, the *Sporting News* reported in August 1911 another sorry season ending for Padrón in organized baseball: "Louis Padron, the Cuban with New Britain several years ago and in the early part of the season with Mansfield, . . . was released in the interest of 'harmony' because some players objected to his presence."[13] Two years later Padrón was back in organized baseball as a member of the Long Branch Cubans, with a chance to break into the majors seemingly in the works.

A Class D New York–New Jersey League team, the Long Branch Cubans typified the form of racial inclusion permitted by organized baseball during the Jim Crow era. Composed entirely of Cuban players, the Long Branch roster ranged from the lighter-skinned Angel Aragon to the more racially ambiguous Padrón.[14] Despite its diversity, Long Branch was allowed to participate within what was otherwise an entirely white minor league. The team's membership in the New York–New Jersey League thus recalled the National Colored League's entry into the National Agreement in 1887. In both cases, nonwhite teams were permitted to enter the National Agreement because they did not pose a direct threat to the jobs of white players.

The 1913 Long Branch Cubans proved that this form of inclusion could indeed threaten the positions of white Americans. In August the *Havana Post* reported that the Long Branch players had so impressed the National League's Boston Braves that the Braves purchased Padrón's contract along with those of Adolfo Luque, Angel Aragon, and Angel Villazon.[15] Luque and Aragon made their big-league debut the following year. Despite big leaguers' accolades, Padrón's major league aspirations were forestalled again by racial perceptions.[16]

"PUREST BARS OF CASTILIAN SOAP"

Much careful planning went into getting Cubans into the majors. Family history had to be scrutinized; team officials had to produce "proof" of racial eligibility. To break into the major leagues, or even to perform in the minors, a player needed verification that he was not black. Frank Bancroft engineered the opening of opportunity's door to Cuban players. In December 1910 Bancroft traveled to Cuba with the Philadelphia Athletics, having agreed to lead the American League champion team during its Cuban tour as a favor to Connie Mack. The two-week visit gave Bancroft a chance to survey the Cuban talent.[17] Cuban infielder Rafael Almeida especially impressed Bancroft. Excited with the young Cuban's performance, Bancroft included a brief scouting report on Almeida in a letter to Garry Herrmann, telling the Cincinnati Reds' president, "Wish we had him. He is not colored."[18]

Bancroft's letter set in motion the process whereby the Cincinnati Reds would sign Almeida and also land fellow Cuban Armando Marsans. Within days of receiving Bancroft's letter, Herrmann dispatched letters inquiring about Almeida to journalists throughout New England. The response of J. F. Sullivan, sports editor of Springfield newspaper the *Union*, captured the resistance Cincinnati would confront in its attempt to incorporate Cuban players. Sullivan wrote, "Were he a white man, he might be good for the big show. He is Cuban, all right, not a nigger. But I find the presence of these Cubans breed [*sic*] discontent here and I think it would do so even more on a major league club." Sullivan concluded, "Like the other Cubans on the team, he is good when they are winning, but there is no fight in any of them when they are losing."[19]

The letter contained several red flags that might have deterred most major-league organizations from pursuing the signing any further. First, Sullivan warned Herrmann about the divisiveness the Cuban presence had caused in the Connecticut League and its potential to cause a similar reaction among major leaguers. Second, the reply reiterated the perceived racial differences between whites, blacks, and Cubans. Sullivan's description clearly differed from Bancroft's. Whereas to Bancroft, Almeida was "not colored," to Sullivan he was not a "white man." Sullivan's concluding statement referenced a familiar (U.S.) discourse about masculinity and race, particularly as it pertained to rigorous athletic competition.[20] According to the era's popular application of social Darwinism and eugenics to athletic competition, mental abilities had a racial character. Followers of this pseudoscience placed Cuban players in the same category as African American athletes, who, it was believed, lacked the fortitude of whites to withstand adversity and pain in the midst of intense competition.

Cincinnati's defense for signing Rafael Almeida and Armando Marsans emphasized their social status and ethnic heritage in a manner that resonated with the workings of racial systems in Latin America. By Cuban social tradition, social class and wealth combined to effectively lighten how others perceived an individual's skin color and racial status. The distinction Cincinnati team officials made in justifying their signing of Almeida and Marsans hinged on this racial knowledge, which surely must have been the brainstorm of Frank Bancroft, who had working relationships with several Cuban journalists he had met on his many winter visits to Cuba.[21]

Team officials and sportswriters who supported the Reds' signing stressed that Almeida and Marsans came from the island's elite and that their ethnoracial ancestry placed them well above typical Cubans. Their parents reportedly had descended from the elite of Portugal and Spain. North American periodicals identified Marsans as "a pure Havana feller of Castilian parentage," having "more Spanish blood in him than Cuban."[22] Sporting papers identified Almeida's father as a "Portuguese merchant" and his mother as a "Cuban of Spanish parentage—the old Castilian stock."[23] One sportswriter further distinguished Almeida's ancestry, explaining that he was a "direct descendent of a Portuguese marquis" and "not actually of Cuban ancestry."[24] In distinguishing among members of a group perceived by most North Americans as a homogenous lot, league officials and sportswriters partook in the creation of a hierarchy of ethnoracial types for Latinos. It was a process that made Castilians out of Latinos of various national origins who possessed the right blend of talent, physical features, and ancestry.

Family background allowed Marsans and Almeida to substantiate claims of racial eligibility to perform in the segregated major leagues. Members of the island's commercial elite, both their families enjoyed greater social and geographical mobility than the average Cuban had. The Marsans family, like many other supporters of the Cuban insurgent movement, had fled to New York in the 1890s "to keep out of the way of American and Spanish bullets in war time." His time in New York reportedly gave Armando Marsans "a bit of knowledge of the American pastime."[25] The Almeida family enjoyed a loftier position in Cuba. The family's significant wealth enabled their son to attend the University of Havana before he pursued a professional baseball career in the States. "Independently wealthy," in the words of one writer, Almeida played baseball more "for the pure love of the sport than for the salary attached to it."[26] Class status enabled him to stand up to the power that team management usually wielded over players. Early in 1911, Almeida reported late to New Britain's spring training camp, "because an uncle [had] died and left him a fortune of $200,000" and Almeida chose to wait for the estate to be settled.[27]

Even before the Cubans appeared in Reds uniform, local and national sportswriters discussed the ramifications of their signings for the color line. On June 22 the *Sporting News* described the obstacle Cincinnati faced: "Of course there is no rule in the National Agreement that prevents a club from employing *colored or partially colored* players. At the same time, nothing darker than an Indian ever has been tolerated in fast society, and it is not likely that either Marsans [or] Almeida will be permitted to perform in the big league if it is found that either has African blood in his veins." A *Cincinnati Enquirer* column appearing a day later cited Cuban sportswriter Victor Muñoz's letter to Reds president Garry Herrmann as further validation of Almeida and Marsans's racial eligibility. "Both of these men are pure Spaniards, without a trace of colored blood."[28]

After much coverage in local and some national sporting periodicals, the two Cubans made their big-league debut on July 4, on the road against the Chicago Cubs. Since Cincinnati was often an also-ran in the National League, speculation arose that the signing was a publicity stunt plotted by Frank Bancroft to "bolster up battered gate receipts." "From a box office view it was a mighty poor move to arrange [the] first appearances of the Cuban pair—Almeida and Marsans—on the road," *Sporting Life*'s Cincinnati correspondent countered.[29] Others also speculated about the Reds' decision to launched their Cuban experiment on the road. Was the team trying to hide something?

Shortly after the Cubans' debut several large urban newspapers, including the *Detroit Free Press* and the *Philadelphia Enquirer,* published a full-page story with a photograph of the Reds' new additions.[30] Their appearance in print unsettled some readers; evidently, the photo rendered the players' "race" visible and revealed physical features that alarmed some concerned with maintaining the racial barrier. In response, a few local sportswriters attempted to educate North American fans about the importance of recognizing racial difference among Latinos. Veteran sportswriter Bill Phelon warned North Americans about indiscriminately lumping Cubans together. "The Cubans are rated, by too many otherwise educated Americans, as a race of mixed whites and negroes. . . . This tires the white Cubans extremely," he explained, "for they are a proud sort of people, who can show pedigrees of purest Spanish strain, and a negro cross is regarded with the same sentiment as in the United States."[31] A *Cincinnati Enquirer* writer took a different approach, offering a grand introduction for the two Cubans: "Ladies and Gentlemen, we have in our midst two descendants of a noble Spanish race, *with no ignoble*

African blood to place a blot or spot on their escutcheons. Permit me to introduce two of the *purest bars of Castilian soap* that ever floated to these shores, Senors Alameda [*sic*] and Marsans." Other publications followed the lead of the *Cincinnati Enquirer*. In short order, publications ranging from the *New York Times* to the *Sporting News* began referring to Almeida and Marsans not simply as Cubans but also as Castilian and of northern Spanish ancestry.[32]

BROWN AND BLACK OTHERS

All players from the Spanish-speaking Americas underwent a process that uniquely positioned them in the racial system of U.S. professional baseball. Darker-skinned Latino players who went on to star in the Negro leagues bore a special burden, for they had to endure the triple impact of their color, race, and ethnicity. Even players like Almeida and Marsans were not automatically admitted into the fraternity of whiteness. To the contrary, their skin color and other physical features were viewed through a U.S. racial gaze and filtered by an ethnic lens.

"Adding Bronze to the Red," as a columnist characterized Cincinnati's experiment, reflected the evolution of major league baseball's racial system. Bronze and brown as racial categories located Cuban and Latino players in an intermediate space along professional baseball's color line. Popular perceptions of Cubans as nonwhite were slow to change. Less than two weeks after Almeida and Marsans had made their debut, the *New York Times* reported the "surprise" of New York fans "who expected to see Cuban ball players looking like Pullman porters."[33]

The Cincinnati signings sparked a glimmer of hope in African American circles that the successful entry of Cuban players would ultimately lead to the dismantling of the racial barrier. As *New York Age* columnist Lester Walton wrote in September 1911, "With the admissions of Cubans of a darker hue in the two big leagues it would then be easy for colored players who are citizens of this country to get into fast company." "The Negro in this country has more varied hues than even the Cubans," the African American journalist explained, "and the only way to distinguish him would be to hear him talk." Walton's advice: "Until the public got accustomed to seeing native Negroes [i]n big leagues, the colored players could keep their mouths shut and pass for Cubans."[34]

In spite of the hope expressed by Walton, no tangible change to major-league racial policy resulted. Even though a few racially ambiguous Cubans like Luis Padrón occasionally landed a minor-league position,

Cubans of a darker hue continued to find no opportunities to break into organized baseball. Instead, league officials continued to adhere to racial supremacy (white over black) and exclude those they perceived as black.

The opening of the major leagues to lighter-skinned Latinos in the 1910s inspired a number of plots to manipulate racial understandings and sneak an African American player into organized baseball. Black baseball lore contains many accounts of plots involving a team official or scout approaching an African American player with a proposal: if the player would travel to Cuba, Mexico, or elsewhere in the Spanish-speaking Americas, play for a season, and learn Spanish, on his return to the States, the club would sign him as a Cuban or a Spaniard.[35] Rumors of plots to surreptitiously sign a black player occasionally made their way into newsprint. The *Chicago Defender* reported in 1917 that a New York State League team offered Negro league pitching star John Donaldson $10,000 to go to Cuba, adopt a Spanish surname, and return to the States as a Cuban.[36] Donaldson refused, opting to continue playing in the black baseball circuits in the United States. A decade later, according to Negro-league historian Donn Rogosin, a scout approached Negro-league catcher Quincy Trouppe with a similar offer. The scout suggested Trouppe "go to a Latin country and learn Spanish, explaining that if he could speak the language, he would have a good chance to play organized baseball."[37] Determining whether such plots were carried through or were successful is beyond the realm of this study. That these plots were discussed in newsprint and in baseball circles reflects the impact that circulation of racial knowledge throughout baseball's transnational circuit was having in professional baseball, affecting how people thought about race and place, locally and transnationally.

U.S. racial understandings continued to limit prospects for most Cuban ballplayers even after the entry of Marsans and Almeida. "The racial problem is a hard thing to deal with in regard to the Cuban ball players," Phelon explained in a May 1912 *Baseball Magazine* article. "Most of their men are black, jet black, and their star battery performers are nearly all African of the darkest shade." Black Cubans such as José Méndez, Cristobal Torriente, and Gervasio "Strike" Gonzalez may have been "A1 performers," but because they were so visibly black, their prominence in Cuba's professional ranks, some contended, "block[ed] the path of the Cuban teams to full recognition and proper welcome in the States."[38]

With major-league organizations increasingly willing to sign Cubans, envy and a desire to get even more Cubans into the majors combined to produce proposals to restructure Cuban professional baseball, even on racially defined terms. In the winter following the big-league debut of Almeida and Marsans, a movement arose to transform Cuba's professional league operation and to consider imposing a color line.[39] Prior to the 1912 season, the circuit's cooperative system distributed 60 percent of attendance revenues among the players and 40 percent to promoters, team owners, ballpark owners, and others. Cuban-league officials and team owners disliked the system as it gave players too much control.

Those who advocated the restructuring clearly valued the increased opportunity the change would create for lighter-skinned Cubans. Cuban baseball was hardly immune from the legacy of the island's racial ideology, which subordinated the aspirations of Afro-Cubans to those of Cubans who came from a higher economic class or had more European ethnic heritage or a lighter skin color.[40] The proposal was clearly aimed at undermining the prominent position of Afro-Cubans who, detractors complained, "controlled the system to such an extent that it failed to develop young players." "The black players sort of monopolized the juicy lemon, and limited the teams to about 15 men each," a Cuban baseball official told a *Sporting Life* writer. The official added, "The fewer players the more money each made."[41] The desire to restructure Cuban baseball placed some Cuban team officials in a peculiar position. Eugenio Jimenez, for one, remarked longingly to Bill Phelon, "I wish . . . some big league team would whip us ten straight games. That would reduce the heads of the black players, make them listen to reason, and also give a better chance for white men to succeed them on the local teams."[42]

The campaign to change the Cuban league ultimately replaced the cooperative system with a contract system, giving owners greater control over team operations. Afro-Cuban players continued to dominate the Cuban professional scene, although they were still excluded from the island's amateur circuit. Lighter-skinned Cubans did continue to break into organized baseball, and their numbers in the minor leagues increased throughout the 1910s. By contrast, the Negro leagues would remain the primary destination for the majority of Cubans who went north to play professionally in the United States.

"KNOW[S] NO RACE"

The U.S. sports media boasted of organized baseball's widening talent base that incorporated Native Americans and a new contingent of ethnic European players. Early in the 1911 season, *Sporting Life* proclaimed that baseball "Know[s] No Race" and that baseball had become a place where, through "the stress of a contest," race prejudice was combated and participants were transformed into fellow Americans. Four months before Rafael Almeida and Armando Marsans made their major-league debut, the article already claimed that in America's game "all nationalities merge and race prejudices are forgotten, as every fan remembers only that he is an American watching his favorite play the game of games." The acceptance of the swarthy Indian and the southern European, according to the sporting sheet, signified the continuing progressive nature of America's game.[43]

Celebration of baseball's inclusiveness ignored what individuals of African descent encountered on the U.S. playing field. The broadening terms of inclusion made the reality of the color line all the more poignant for those excluded. To the African American community, the power and hypocrisy of those who policed organized baseball's racial divide were abundantly clear. *New York Age* columnist Lester Walton remarked, "There is an unwritten law against Negroes playing in the major baseball leagues which appears more incongruous when one recalls that some colored players, such as Indians and Cubans, are not discriminated against on the account of color."[44] For Walton and other African Americans, the entry of Indians and Cubans of various shades revealed that an individual's skin color alone no longer translated into exclusion.

Baseball enthusiasts viewed the entry of various ethnic Americans into the majors as confirmation that the game acted as a "melting pot" that forged Americans out of disparate groups of immigrants. In a 1928 *Baseball Magazine* article, "Baseball the Game 'of All Nations,'" sportswriter Stetson Palmer extolled the diversity of the 1928 World Series champion New York Yankees—which included Polish, German, Italian, and Irish players—as a prime example of the assimilative power of America's game. "Nor is this condition peculiar to the New York club," Palmer exclaimed, "although [the] team is the leading exponent of the new tendency in baseball."[45]

Press members on both sides of baseball's racial divide acknowledged this ethnic diversity within the major leagues, but with different interpretations of its significance. "Time was when the Dolans, Moriartys, Kellys and others of Erin's hue dominated, and a few good German-American names like Wagner, Zimmerman, Lobert, and Schulte were prominent," observed a columnist for the *New York Age*. "Now you find on the Giants Mancuso and Cuccinello, Brooklyn has a Cuccinello, Philly has Chiozza and Camilli, Pittsburgh a Lavagetto. This places the spaghetti twisters on seven out of eight National League clubs." Descendants of immigrants from England, Scotland, and Germany, among other northern European nations, were thus joined by southern Europeans who had once been perceived as swarthy, dark, and racially suspect.[46]

The metaphor of baseball as a melting pot held out the prospect of an attainable American identity for the recently arrived. Although extension of this metaphor to the segregated major leagues suggested an attainable whiteness for the circuit's new entrants, such was not exactly the case for Native American or Latino players. New York Giants catcher John Meyers remembered the treatment given Indian players. "In those days, when I was young, I was considered a foreigner. I did not belong. I was an Indian."[47] Players such as Frank Arellanes and Rafael Almeida were viewed as little different from Indians. Entering organized baseball as Castilians or Spaniards so as to be distinguished from blacks meant that Latinos, even if U.S.-born, retained an element of foreignness and ensured that they would not secure the same status as white Americans or Americanized European immigrants.

Rafael Almeida and Armando Marsans were the first fruits of Major League Baseball's opening up to "meltable" ethnics in the 1910s. The expanded terms of inclusion did not alter organized baseball's racialized hierarchy, however. The signing of Latino players was driven by the desire to secure better talent at an affordable price. Cincinnati management's insertion of race in a salary dispute with Armando Marsans in 1913 demonstrated the intersection between economic and racial concerns in the turn to the Spanish-speaking Americas.

Knowing his worth as a talented player after two solid big-league seasons, Marsans held out for a contract that would pay him what a North American player earned. When the Reds balked at meeting his salary demands, Marsans threatened to jump to the Federal League, an upstart rival major league. Cincinnati made several attempts to coax their wayward player back to its camp. At one point, the Reds even called on Cuban sportswriter Rafael Conte to "retrieve" Marsans. When that failed, Cincinnati sent Frank Bancroft to Cuba, hoping he could entice Marsans back. Neither side equivocated. Cincinnati management informed the sporting press of its position on paying Cuban players: "We will not pay any Honus Wagner price for a pair of dark-skinned islanders."[48] Marsans stood firm and jumped to St. Louis when the Reds failed to match the salary the Federal League team offered him.

Armando Marsans's strong stance is an exception on two accounts to the general vulnerability of Latino players. First, the offer from a rival major league gave him a fallback if the Reds refused his demands. Rival major leagues, however, did not arise often in the twentieth century—the Federal League's challenge was crushed after several seasons. Second, Marsans came from a privileged social class in Cuba. In this sense he needed baseball much less than did ballplayers who were discovered in the island's sugar mill leagues. Indeed, their status as foreign-born talent in conjunction with their class position left most Cuban players who entered organized baseball highly vulnerable to management exploitation.

PRODUCING THE FIRST WAVE

The signing of foreign-born Latinos continued to provoke concerns among major-league organizations that not all teams were abiding by the same racial policy. Cincinnati's successful incorporation of Rafael Almeida and Armando Marsans emboldened other major-league clubs to engage in their own "color study." Over the next few years the Boston Braves, New York Giants, New York Highlanders (later Yankees), Philadelphia Athletics, and Washington Senators all explored signing Cuban players. New York Giants manager John McGraw, who had first visited Cuba as a player, made regular visits to the island for both business and pleasure. Following the Giants' 1911 visit, McGraw signed lighter-skinned Cubans Emilio Palmero and José Rodríguez. Other organizations followed suit. The Boston Braves signed Miguel Angel González and Adolfo Luque, among other Cuban prospects. After former Cincinnati Reds manager Clark Griffith took over the managerial helm of the Washington Senators in 1912, he put his imprint on the organization by actively pursuing Cuban talent, signing Merito Acosta, Jacinto Calvo, and other Cubans over the next four decades; the Senators would be the most active major-league team in acquiring Latino talent.

The issue of whether a particular Latino player presented the proper mix of talent, physical features, and ancestry arose time and again. A player's entry into the minor leagues did not guarantee his racial qualification to play in the majors. A number of players perceived as racially eligible by one major-league organization had previously been rejected by another as too "swarthy," "dark-skinned," or racially ambiguous. The inconsistencies of racial perceptions complicated matters.

Defending the signing of Latino players such as Miguel Angel ("Mike") González, Emilio Palmero, and José Rodríguez based on their physical appearance and ethnoracial ancestry was not overly complex. One Boston scribe upheld the Boston Braves' 1912 signing of González, describing the team's new catcher as "a white man, North Spanish in ancestry, and not the big black Gonzalez who catches the great [José] Mendez." The February 1917 issue of *Baseball Magazine* expanded on this description of González, who had by then joined the St. Louis Cardinals, stating that his family was "of pure Spanish blood, not of the mongrel Indian or Negro mixture that has barred many a star of 'The Pearl of the Antilles' from major league company."[49]

Physical appearance, even more than talent, opened opportunities for Latinos to sign with a big-league organization. Emilio Palmero benefited from this reality when he joined the New York Giants in 1913. John McGraw had first learned about the Cuban left-hander earlier that year during the Giants' tour of Cuba. Although Palmero's performance in the Cuban league and against barnstorming major-league and minor-league clubs impressed McGraw, the Cuban pitcher's physical appearance made his signing easy to defend. Describing him as having "reddish blond hair and light complexion" or "light hair, blue eyes and ruddy complexion," sportswriters quipped that no one would ever "take [Palmero] for a Cuban" since he "bears none of the facial characteristics of the Cuban" and "does not look like the swarthy, raven-haired, black-eyed Cubans."[50] Acceptable to those who monitored the major leagues' color line, Palmero's physical appearance could not replace talent and on-field performance. He spent the majority of his North American career pitching in the minors, appearing with four big-league clubs in five seasons between 1915 and 1928.

Fellow Cuban José Rodríguez received a harsher reception than Palmero. After signing him, the New York Giants assigned Rodríguez to play in the Connecticut League. As happened repeatedly as the first wave of Latinos was incorporated into organized baseball, the young Cuban encountered hostility. "They Say They'll Get Cuban," declared a 1916 article that described "an understanding" among Connecticut League players "to 'get' Rodriguez at the first opportunity and put the Cuban out of the game."[51] The understanding contradicted the Connecticut League's reputation (dating back to 1901, when the Philadelphia Athletics sent Louis Castro to the circuit) as a safe place to send Latino players. Several white players made enough of a clamor that their threats to hurt Rodríguez reached print. Although the sportswriter personally placed "no credence" in the rumors, such threats, whether carried out or not, intimidated Latino players and demonstrated their tenuous location along the color line, dangerously close to deportation from organized baseball.

Close association with Latinos at times caused misidentifications of players, as in the case of Bert Gallia, a Texas native of Czech descent. A member of the 1913 Washington Senators, the club's only non-Latino who spoke Spanish, Gallia befriended the team's two young Cuban players, Jacinto Calvo and Baldomero "Merito" Acosta. This association led some to assume that Gallia was himself Mexican. The assumption followed him when he was sent to the minors to pitch for Kansas City during the 1913 season. After one particularly strong pitching performance, a local paper hailed him as the "Mexican Hurler Invincible" and as "Chief Gallia, bronze-skinned Señor from the land of Madero."[52]

These 1913 episodes of misidentification were not the first for Gallia. Three years earlier Gallia had played with Cuban and Mexican players on the Laredo team in the Class D Southwest Texas League. Located on the border with Mexico, the Laredo team had long signed Mexicanos and Tejanos. A local paper that covered the circuit, the *Victoria Advocate*, noted that Laredo engaged in this practice although "chocolate colored players" were probably ineligible to perform in organized baseball.[53] The Southwest Texas League's racial policy worked much like that of the major leagues when it came to Latinos: signing a racially ambiguous player "was left optional with the various clubs to play whomsoever they please."[54]

Cultural factors were at times as crucial as playing skills in determining which Latinos progressed to the majors. Because language was often Latinos' most noticeable characteristic, major-league teams devised a couple of strategies to deal with the language barrier. Some hoped that their Latino player would prove a quick study in mastering English. Other organizations took a more hands-on approach, attempting to teach their coaches to speak Spanish or signing a bilingual or Spanish-speaking catcher to handle pitchers. After signing Almeida and Marsans, Cincinnati Reds manager Clark Griffith required that his coaching staff take primers in Spanish—a plan they later abandoned. Lacking a Latino catcher, the New York Giants turned to their Native American catcher, John Meyers. A stalwart behind the plate, Meyers was conversant in Spanish, which enabled him to communicate with Latino pitchers and also to translate for his teammates and Giants manager John McGraw.[55] These efforts put the Cincinnati Reds and the New York Giants ahead of their time since most organizations gave no consideration to cultural factors that might affect the success of their Latino players. The inability to overcome cultural difference meant that most Latinos who entered organized baseball spent their entire U.S. professional careers performing in the minors.

PAVING THE WAY

The first generation of Latino players who entered the black baseball circuits in the United States learned the brutal reality of race and America's game. Winning games in the Negro leagues or excelling against major leaguers in exhibitions mattered little for those who lacked the right racial characteristics. José Méndez clearly had the talent, but not the racial pedigree. On seeing the great Méndez pitch in Cuba, New York Giants manager John McGraw was sold. Aware that race limited his ability to sign players based strictly on talent, McGraw reportedly told a New York City sportswriter that if "Méndez was a white man he [McGraw] would pay $50,000 for his release from Almendares."[56]

Méndez stood tall among his peers in the baseball circuit that linked Havana, New York City, Chicago, Tampa, and a host of other cities. A Latino pioneer who excelled against the best talent in major-league and black baseball, Méndez exemplifies the talent and skill that existed outside organized baseball. His annual trips north starting with the 1908 tour of Abel Linares's Cuban Stars were highly anticipated. The *Sporting News*'s announcement of his first return visit in 1909 reviewed his prior feats but also described the limitations he and the Cuban Stars encountered in the States. "In the party will be pitcher Méndez, who repeated[ly] beat the Reds and once held them down to a single hit in nine innings. This fellow is coal-black, *being a native Cuban, with no Spanish blood,* and several of the other players are dark as to their complexion, but as skillful on the field as any white team."[57]

Lacking any telltale of whiteness, or the racially ambiguous appearance of his compatriot Luis Padrón, Méndez made the best of the opportunities to compete against major leaguers in exhibition games. The Cuban hurler's assortment of pitches became a familiar source of misery for white major leaguers barnstorming in Cuba. At one point he compiled a scoreless streak of twenty-five innings pitching against the Cincinnati Reds (1908) and the Detroit Tigers (1909). In a 1908 game he held Cincinnati batters hitless into the ninth inning before settling on a one-hit, extra-innings shutout.

An assortment of major-league officials, players, and sportswriters lauded Méndez's abilities and proclaimed his big-league credentials. Athletics catcher Ira Thomas witnessed the Cuban's prowess firsthand during Philadelphia's 1911 tour and later wrote about facing Méndez in *Baseball Magazine.* "More than one big leaguer from the states has faced him and left the plate with a wholesome respect for the great Cuban star,"

Thomas wrote. "It is not alone my opinion but the opinion of many others who have seen Méndez pitch that he ranks with the best in the game."[58] The Phillies' John "Honus" Lobert echoed Thomas's assessment in the *Sporting News* following Philadelphia's December 1911 visit: "Méndez is some pitcher, and here on the island they call him 'Mathewson in the Black,' and if we could paint him white we surely could use him on the Philly team next season."[59] Sportswriter Bill Phelon lauded Méndez after he dominated another group of big-league tourists in 1912: "Méndez is a big league pitcher, there is no doubt about it. He has the goods. . . . The man is every bit as classy as [Washington Senators pitcher] Walter Johnson."[60] But the major leagues' racial barrier meant that in the United States, Méndez would make his mark in the black baseball circuit.

A member of the pioneering generation of Latino Negro leaguers, the Cuban ace took on a new role in 1920 when Kansas City Monarchs owner J. L. Wilkinson handed him the team's managerial reigns. Up to this point, only barnstorming Cuban teams had employed a Latino at the managerial helm. The Monarchs were thus the first Negro-league team composed primarily of African American players to hire a Latino manager. Pitcher Chet Brewer reflected on Méndez's ability to negotiate the cultural divide: "He spoke English pretty well. . . . Some words would tie him up, but he spoke well enough. He was a shrewd manager and really a good teacher of baseball."[61] Although English was his second language, the Cuban native proved a highly capable manager. He directed the Monarchs to two consecutive Negro league World Series in 1924 and 1925, the former triumph making him the first Latino manager to capture a title in either the Negro or major leagues. Managerial credentials added to an already impressive résumé. Ballplayer turned historian Sol White ranked the Cuban pitching ace at the head of black baseball's pantheon of stars in a March 1929 *Amsterdam News* column, placing Méndez "far in the lead as the greatest colored pitcher of all times."[62]

Cristobal Torriente, the era's hitting counterpart to pitcher Méndez, heads a long list of Latino players whose physical features excluded them from the majors. The gifted Cuban outfielder's career started with his mercurial rise from the baseball diamonds in Havana to stardom in the Negro leagues, but came to a tragic ending—his lonely death in New York City in his early thirties, reportedly due to alcohol-induced cirrhosis. The hard-hitting Cuban first ventured north as a nineteen-year-old rookie in 1913 as a member of Linares's Cuban Stars, and in short order he established a reputation as one of Cuba's best offensive imports. Cuban Hall of Famer Martin Dihigo assessed Torriente's talents and place in baseball history: "We have never given Torriente the credit he deserved; . . . he did everything well, he fielded like a natural, threw in perfect form; he covered as much field as could be covered; as for batting, he left being good to being something extraordinary."[63]

The Cuban outfielder's clutch performances in the Negro leagues and Cuban league intrigued major-league clubs—as was often the case when word first got out about a Cuban player who vastly outperformed his peers.[64] His talent was clearly major league, but obviously, getting signed by a major-league club took more than performance. Torriente occupied an ambiguous racial position, however, due to his nationality, skin color, and physical features. Kansas City Monarchs pitcher Chet Brewer, for one, described Torriente as having "Indian color," which in the 1920s could have garnered him a tryout from a major-league club. Floyd "Jelly" Gardner, a teammate of Torriente's with the Chicago American Giants, witnessed firsthand the interest a New York Giants scout expressed in Torriente in 1920. According to Gardner, the Cuban's play impressed the scout but something held him back. In his view, Torriente would have gone "up there but he had real bad hair . . . he would have been all right if his hair had been better."[65] Given his physical appearance, ushering Torriente past the guardians of the color line posed an almost insurmountable task. Major-league teams' manipulation of existing racial understandings and notions of ethnic identity could broaden access to the segregated leagues only slightly.

COLOR ADJUSTMENTS

José Méndez and Cristobal Torriente, among other darker-skinned Cubans who starred in the Negro leagues, first plied their skills in barnstorming teams such as the All Cubans and the Cuban Stars. The pioneering Cuban Stars squads of Abel Linares left a lasting impression on the memory of black-baseball fans. A *New York Age* sportswriter fondly remembered these early Cuban teams in a December 1924 column: "The first really first class colored team which I remember was the Cuban Stars of fifteen years ago. They carried twelve of the greatest ballplayers that ever left Cuba."[66] But, as Torriente and other Latinos who performed on this side of U.S. professional baseball's racial divide became all too aware, a player's hair, skin color, or facial features could warrant his exclusion. Racialized perceptions of physical features thus forestalled the major-league aspirations of a host of Latinos. No matter how powerful their swing, fleet their steps, or light their complexions, Latino ballplayers could not escape the effect of racial ideology and the limits of racial understanding in the U.S. playing field.

Organized baseball's incorporation of the first wave of Latinos in the early twentieth century demonstrated that racial eligibility depended primarily on team and league officials' perceptions of individual ballplayers. The racial knowledge of these officials was transformed by the increased movement of talent and information within baseball's transnational circuit, movement that was accelerated when Cuba and later Puerto Rico were opened up to North American commercial interests after the War of 1898 ended. Along these commercial avenues traveled barnstorming teams, exposing the talented Cuban players to North American audiences and opening a South-North talent flow.

The sporting press shaped perceptions of this first wave of Latinos significantly. As the twentieth century progressed, North American press coverage of Cuban baseball increased, detailing U.S. professional tours as well as the Cuban winter circuit. Sports columns assessed not just the players' skills but also their racial eligibility. Sports journalists were influenced in their writing by organized baseball's experiments with racial inclusion and the lessons learned from incorporating players of southern European and Native American descent. As borne out in press coverage, the experience of the first wave of Latino signings contradicts the claim that these major-league newcomers were viewed or accepted as fellow whites. No such claim was offered to explain the racial status of Native Americans who preceded Latinos into the segregated major leagues.

In this first phase of incorporating Latinos in organized baseball, team and league officials devised new ways to differentiate between blacks and other nonwhites, demonstrating the evolution of racial understanding that resulted from increased North-South interaction. The ethnoracial labels used by the Cincinnati Reds and their supporters in justifying the signing of Almeida and Marsans effectively demonstrated the power that these officials had at their disposal. Initially, these officials applied the label *Spaniard* indiscriminately because few players from the Spanish-speaking Americas were entering the major leagues. They focused not on Latino players' national origins but on their ethnic ancestry. Distinctions along national lines did not gain importance in the United States until the late 1910s and, moreover, were not enacted into law until passage of the 1924 Immigration Act, which emphasized "national origins" in determining an individual's race and eligibility to immigrate to the United States.[67]

For organized baseball, these changes in U.S. racial understanding did not disrupt the central purpose of its color line. Segregation persisted, white continued to rule over black, and the power to determine the terms of inclusion and exclusion remained squarely in the hands of major-league owners and league officials. It was up to major-league organizations to "prove" whether a Latino ballplayer was black or not black. Such determinations grew increasingly difficult to abide by as big leaguers observed the vast talent performing on the other side of baseball's racial divide.

6

Making Cuban Stars
Alejandro Pompez
and Latinos in Black Baseball

Color alone kept such Cuban stars as Chacón, Joe Mendez, Torrienti [*sic*], Dihigo, Oms, Mesa, Baro, Oscar [Levis], Montalvo, Fernandez, Fabre, and Padrone [*sic*] out of the episode.

Negro-league commissioner W. Rollo Wilson, 1934

MAKINGS OF A CUBAN AMERICAN GIANT

The story of Latinos and America's game is incomplete without a discussion of their long participation in Negro-league baseball. Nor can this story be told without acknowledging the dynamic presence of African Americans who participated at the Latin American points within baseball's transnational circuit. From the turn of the early twentieth century in Jim Crow America, before there were formally organized Negro leagues, to after the Negro leagues had disintegrated in the 1950s, African American players were sought after and secured for their skills by Latin American baseball entrepreneurs in Cuba, Mexico, Puerto Rico, and elsewhere in the Spanish-speaking Americas. Conversely, the professional teams and leagues of black baseball extended a much kinder welcome to Latinos than did the white baseball establishment. In contrast to organized baseball's institutionalized racial exclusion, black baseball circuits were open to all Latinos based on their talent, not their skin color or nationality.

Abel Linares, Alejandro (Alex) Pompez, and other pioneer Latino entrepreneurs cultivated the links between Latino and black baseball. From the 1900s to the 1930s this linkage went from informal barnstorming relationships to formal memberships in the Negro leagues. As they traveled the black baseball circuit, Latinos would encounter directly the brutal reality of Jim Crow segregation. Their experience quickened their awareness of the U.S. racial landscape and increased their racial knowledge: they learned that others perceived Latinos as people of color (nonwhite) yet differentiated them from African Americans primarily due to their different cultural practices.

If Latino players have been overlooked in celebrations of baseball's best, the role of Latino entrepreneurs in the development of America's transnational baseball circuit is even more underappreciated. Team operators such as Pompez, Linares, and Agustin "Tinti" Molina widened the world of black baseball by introducing to the Negro leagues the best of Latino talent and creating opportunities for African Americans to play in Latin America. Pompez's greatest contribution to black baseball occurred off the playing field. His work as a team owner, Negro-league executive, and talent scout places him alongside Rube Foster, Gus Greenlee, J. L. Wilkerson, Effa Manley, and Cum Posey as one of black baseball's most significant executives. Considered within baseball's transnational circuit, his longevity and contribution stand alone. He was present at the creation of Negro-league baseball and was there at its end, and as a major-league scout, he helped shape its historical legacy.

As the owner of Negro-league teams and as a scout for the Giants, Pompez introduced the greatest number of talented Latinos to U.S. professional baseball. The first wave of players he signed performed primarily in the Negro leagues. Among those he signed for his Cuban Stars and New York Cubans teams were all-star-caliber players Martin Dihigo, Alejandro Oms, Horacio Martínez, and Juan "Tetelo" Vargas and, in the 1940s, future major leaguers Orestes "Minnie" Miñoso, Edmundo "Sandy" Amoros, and José "Pantalones" Santíago. He also opened up the Negro leagues to talent from outside Cuba, introducing the first players from the Dominican Republic, Puerto Rico, and Panama.

In many ways, the story of Alex Pompez encapsulates those of Latinos generally in America's game. He looms in the shadows of baseball history, a figure whose contributions to the internationalization of U.S. professional baseball remain mostly hidden to the game's followers. Most fans know little about the Cuban American trailblazer who helped build organized black baseball in the late 1910s and ended his career as a key scout for the San Francisco Giants in the early 1970s. Available accounts consist of fragments of larger stories about his participation in the Negro leagues, his work as the Giants' director of international scouting, and his involvement in Harlem's numbers racket from the 1910s through the mid-1930s. Integrated into one history, these fragments illuminate the work of transnational actors who were products of overlapping migrations within the Americas and who used the transnational circuit of information, labor, and economic exchange to forge new forms of group identification, to recreate community wherever they lived, and to alter racial understandings to better their own lives. In Pompez's case, his involvement in the Negro leagues, the numbers racket, and other business ventures reflected attempts to negotiate the U.S. racial landscape as someone who was both black and Latino and had been raised in the Jim Crow South and cosmopolitan Havana before settling in New York City as an adult.

That Alejandro Pompez immersed himself in the world of cigars, numbers, and baseball is hardly surprising considering the place of baseball in Cuban national culture and his own family history. An avid supporter of the Cuban independence movement, José Gonzalo Pompez, Alejandro's father, arrived in Key West in the 1870s, where he could more freely pursue his politics. He thus participated in the Cuban migration to towns in Florida as well as New York, Philadelphia, and New Orleans. At these locations, baseball, cigar factories, and mutual aid societies provided émigrés critical sites for exchanging ideas about nation, race, and group identification, an exchange that influenced what it meant to be Cuban, Latino, and a Negro.

A lawyer by training, José Gonzalo Pompez opened a cigar factory in Key West and entered the local political scene in support of Cuban independence. In 1892 he joined the Key West chapter of the Partido Revolucionario Cubano as a founding member. A year later, he was elected to serve as one of Monroe County's representatives in the Florida State Assembly. While Pompez and his wife, Loretta Pérez Pompez, resided on Key West (just ninety miles north of Havana), they gave birth to Alejandro (March 13, 1890) and at least one of his siblings. Enticed by an offer of three building lots and $1,000 from a local development company to relocate his cigar factory and family, the Pompez family moved in 1894 to West Tampa, located two miles west of Tampa's first cigar-making district, Ybor City.[1] A year after the move, José Pompez successfully ran for city clerk for West Tampa. Tragedy struck the family in 1896, when José Pompez died unexpectedly. Committed to the Cuban independence movement, Pompez bequeathed his entire estate to the cause, which required that his cigar factory and home be sold and proceeds go to insurgent forces. The powerful gesture left Loretta Pompez and her children to depend on the largesse of the local Cuban community, and contributed to their decision to return to Havana in 1902 after the end of the island's first U.S. military occupation.[2]

Life in Tampa and Havana exposed Alex Pompez to the worlds of cigars, baseball, and the Cuban community and the ways that race mattered in each. Baseball had a long history among Tampa's Cuban residents. The city's first recorded "colored" game between the Tampa and Ybor City clubs had taken place in October 1888. By 1894 Afro-Cubans in Tampa had organized a club that traveled to other towns to face black teams. While Pompez lived in Havana, according to a 1947 interview in *Puerto Rico Deportivo,* he was "infected with baseball's atmosphere that was ingrained in the [Cuban] Republic."[3]

Growing up in Tampa and Havana made it difficult for Pompez to see himself as anything other than a person of color and a transnational Cuban. Life for a Cuban who was not phenotypically white was made increasingly difficult as Tampa underwent its own version of Jim Crow segregation in the early twentieth century. The presence of a vibrant Cuban community in Tampa complicated matters. Cubans had been vital to the building of Tampa's economy, in the cigar-making industry and as founders of Ybor City and West Tampa, both later annexed to the city of Tampa. Residents therefore had to account for difference in more than black and white terms.

Division of the Cuban social world along the color line developed greater significance after Cuban independence was secured in 1899. The patriotic struggle that had bound all Cubans together no longer existed, anthropologist Susan Greenbaum points out, and the "racial boundaries between Cubans [that had been] deliberately obscured" came back to the fore. Thousands of émigrés returned to Cuba, hoping to rebuild their war-ravaged country. Those who remained in Tampa turned their attention to more immediate concerns. Racial matters in Florida and throughout the South had changed. The Supreme Court decision in *Plessy v. Ferguson* (1896) sanctioned the idea of "separate but equal," transforming racial segregation from local social custom to law. The fractures within the Cuban community in Tampa became evident as Cuban social clubs, formerly united in the struggle for nationhood, split along racial lines. The most telling of these splits was the disintegration of El Club Nacional Cubano in October 1900, which ultimately led Afro-Cubans to form La Union Marti-Maceo.[4]

Tampa in the early twentieth century was already marked by informally segregated neighborhoods. Since the 1880s African Americans had had their own neighborhood, the Scrub. The living situation for Cubans created its own form of segregation that, though not as rigid, was no less powerful. Susan Greenbaum notes that the wage scale for cigar workers "depended on skill rather than color" and that the master plan for housing in Ybor City "had no provision for a Negro section."[5] Despite this lack, over time a section emerged where darker-skinned Cubans predominated, as Evilio Grillo vividly describes in his memoir, *Black Cuban, Black American*. By the 1910s these Cubans often attended "black" schools, whether public or private, and worshiped at different churches than lighter-skinned Cubans. Despite increased interaction between Cubans and African Americans, ethnic boundaries were "deliberately sharpened," according to Greenbaum. Cubans learned where the lines existed from both personal experience and from the collective knowledge passed down by relatives and neighbors. They thus learned to live what Greenbaum labels "double-hyphenated lives" as Afro-Cuban-Americans.[6]

Alex Pompez returned to the familiarity of Tampa by 1910. Now in his late teens, he found work making cigars and joined La Union Marti-Maceo in 1910. Later that year he left Tampa for New York City. Twenty years old when he arrived, Pompez again secured employment as a cigar maker, earning $20 a week. Shortly thereafter he opened a cigar store from which he reportedly started operating his numbers bank.[7] He also established a relationship with Nat Strong, the largest booking agent in the New York metropolitan area.

Well-positioned within the eastern baseball scene, Nat Strong controlled the booking of sporting events at major-league stadiums (Yankee Stadium, Ebbets Field, and the Polo Grounds) and most of the better venues in New York City. Strong, an Irish American, was often criticized by black baseball owners and Negro-league officials for placing his financial interest above black baseball's future growth. Critics suspected that through his booking operations Strong hoped to monopolize control of the eastern baseball scene. As evidence of his grand design, black baseball officials pointed to the exorbitant fees Strong charged for booking Negro-league events at major-league parks and other venues.

Unlike most of his Negro-league peers, Pompez found a way to use his relationship with Strong to his own advantage. In his 1947 interview, Pompez explained how he formed a mutually beneficial relationship with the much maligned Strong.[8] The young Cuban American possessed access to an untapped market, New York City's Latino community as well as the Caribbean—in both of which Strong had failed to establish a significant presence. Working with Pompez enabled Strong to develop ties with Latino baseball, and Strong's tutelage prepared Pompez for a career as a sports promoter and baseball team owner.

Like other baseball entrepreneurs in the East, Pompez initially relied on Strong to secure bookings at the New York City parks where the best semipro and independent clubs performed—Brooklyn's Dexter Park, the Bronx's Catholic Protectory, and Manhattan's Dyckman Oval. Yet, because his Cuban Stars played games in the Caribbean, Pompez established connections beyond Strong's control that later enabled him to exercise greater independence. Pompez's transnational positioning of his baseball operations was readily apparent in the Cuban Stars' inaugural campaign. Prior to the start of the U.S. professional regular season in 1916, his Cuban Stars toured the Caribbean, including stops in Cuba, the Dominican Republic, and Puerto Rico. The trip enabled Pompez to promote his team, scout new players, and establish a presence in baseball's transnational circuit.

MAKING CUBAN STARS

The Cuban Stars marked Pompez's initial foray into professional baseball. In launching his franchise, he took advantage of his unique status within professional baseball—a U.S.-born Latino intimately familiar with the United States and Caribbean. From the outset, the Cuban Stars performed as a year-round outfit, playing in the United States, Cuba, Puerto Rico, and the Dominican Republic. The team's travels thus linked the different points of the Cuban American's personal migrations.

Pompez's formation of a second "Cuban Stars" team that would perform in the U.S. black baseball circuit infuriated fellow Cuban baseball entrepreneur Abel Linares. At the height of his leadership in Cuban professional baseball, Linares took enormous pride in having brought the first Cuban team to barnstorm the United States in 1899. But more important for Linares, "the Cuban Stars" was his team's name, whose good reputation he had worked hard to build in U.S. baseball circles. When Puerto Rican baseball promoters informed him that Pompez's team was scheduled to play on the island under the Cuban Stars name, the elder statesman of Cuban baseball in the States sent the Puerto Rican officials an irate cable, claiming "that the authentic 'Cuban Stars' were his, that they were the same [team] that played in the Cuban championship and who traveled to the United States every year."[9] Quick to take advantage

4. Alex Pompez's 1921 Cuban Stars. *Back row, left to right:* Pelayo Chacón, José Rodríguez, Barcelo, José Junco, Alejandro Pompez, Pablo Mesa, Isidro Fabre, Juan Padrone. *Front row:* M. Borrotto, Recurvon Teran, Tatica Campos, Juanelo Mirabal, Alejandro Oms, Oscar Levis, Julian Fabelo (National Baseball Hall of Fame Library, Cooperstown, New York.)

of an opportunity to make more money, the Puerto Rican promoters extended Linares an invitation: let the two Cuban Stars teams battle it out on the playing field for the rightful claim to the name. Linares, ever confident as a veteran team owner, accepted the invitation.

Advertisers framed the face-off as one between the "authentic" Cuban Stars and "the imposters." Linares's team arrived in Puerto Rico with its full allotment of players: José Méndez, Adolfo Luque, Gervasio "Strike" González, Cristobal Torriente, Bienvenido Jímenez, Tatica Campos, and Luis Padrón. But Linares soon regretted accepting the invitation. Pompez's upstart team defeated Linares's club by a 3–2 score in the March 1916 game. Adding to Linares's frustration, Pompez flatly refused him a rematch. "Not enough time," Pompez explained; his triumphant Cuban Stars had to set sail for the States to begin their 1916 campaign.[10]

Pompez's Cuban Stars initiated a new era of Latino participation in black baseball. The organization of independent black baseball teams into formal professional leagues created more stable opportunities for Latinos. Operating out of Chicago, Linares's team joined the Negro National League as a charter member in 1920. Based in New York City,

Pompez's Cuban Stars participated in the eastern-based independent circuit until it joined the Eastern Colored League (1923–28). Together, the two Cuban Stars clubs introduced nearly all Latino players to the Negro leagues as they extended black baseball's talent net beyond Cuba into new Latino territory.

Abel Linares enjoyed a tight hold on Cuban talent participating in the U.S. professional circuit until the appearance of Pompez's club in 1916. From his start in 1899, Linares introduced to the U.S. playing field future major leaguers Rafael Almeida, Armando Marsans, and Adolfo Luque and black baseball standouts Luis Bustamente, José Méndez, and Cristobal Torriente. Competition for Cuban players first developed in the late 1900s when teams from organized baseball began to pluck lighter-skinned players off his Cuban Stars. Linares's hold deteriorated further when J. L. Wilkinson signed Méndez away for his All Nations team in 1914. The formation of Rube Foster's Negro National League emboldened black baseball teams to sign top Cuban players. As a result, Méndez, Torriente, and other former Cuban Stars appeared on other teams when the Negro National League was founded.

Pompez posed the most enduring challenge to Linares. The two battled constantly to sign the most talented Latino ballplayers and regularly signed players off each other's roster. The competition for Cuban players from other Negro-league teams prompted Linares and Pompez to abandon the strategy of filling their club rosters exclusively with Cubans. Pompez's greater ability to find talented players outside Cuba eventually distinguished his eastern-based squad from Linares's midwestern team.

Led by all-star-caliber players Martin Dihigo and Alejandro Oms, Pompez's Cuban Stars proved stronger on-field competition for its foes in the Eastern Colored League (ECL) from 1923 to 1928 than Linares's squad was in the Negro National League (NNL) from 1920 to 1931. The eastern Cuban Stars compiled a winning first league season, finishing in second place—a feat that Linares's club never accomplished. The following years were less successful for the eastern squad, motivating its Cuban American owner to branch further out in search of Latino talent. With new players Alejandro Crespo and the Negro leagues' first Dominican, Pedro San, his Cuban Stars rebounded to respectability in 1926, securing their first winning season in three.[11]

Among the Negro leaguers discovered by Alex Pompez, Martin Dihigo was clearly the centerpiece of Pompez's 1920s Cuban Stars. The versatile Dihigo excelled at several positions in the field, including pitcher, and always posed an offensive threat at the bat. His ultimate accomplishment

5. Martin Dihigo of the 1935 New York Cubans. A player of exceptional versatility, Dihigo was the first Latino from the Negro leagues to be enshrined in the U.S. National Baseball Hall of Fame. One of the most respected players in black and Cuban baseball who on several occasions managed Pompez's team in the Negro leagues, Dihigo is also enshrined in the Cuban, Venezuelan, and Mexican Halls of Fame. (National Baseball Hall of Fame Library, Cooperstown, New York.)

was unmatched by any other player in either the Negro or major leagues: enshrinement in the Hall of Fame of four different countries—the United States, Cuba, Mexico, and Venezuela.

Dihigo broke into the ECL in 1923, when as an eighteen-year-old rookie he earned a spot in the Cuban Stars' starting lineup and had his first exposure to the U.S. brand of racism. By mid-June the tall, sinewy right-hander was playing first base. Off the field, the young Cuban's first direct encounter with the various permutations of Jim Crow left him bewildered. "My first contract with the Cuban Stars was $100 a month," Dihigo informed a Cuban interviewer, "but more than all that, I began to experience firsthand the hatred of 'gringos,' going through lots of hardships and vexations, and having to struggle daily for subsistence." These experiences sharpened Dihigo's awareness of the impact the U.S. racial system could have on a ballplayer who was black and Cuban. There were, he said, "all types of double discrimination, for being black and for being of Latino origin."[12] Societal conditions perturbed the proud Cuban. "Those gringos were such cretins that in many hotels, if they, by chance, admitted us, they would go to the extreme of denying us water to bathe. The food, the mess hall, the waiter, it was all the same." And it was not that Dihigo had not attempted to learn the customs or language. Negro leaguer Frank Duncan observed that Dihigo "learned how to speak English quicker'n anybody you've ever seen."[13] Dihigo thus mastered the challenge of cultural adjustment as someone who was black and whose first language was Spanish.

Pelayo Chacón, a Cuban Stars teammate of Dihigo in the 1920s, also learned the perverse ways racial understandings curtailed the big-league prospects of Latinos. The smooth-fielding shortstop left a lasting impression on black baseball fans. A 1919 *Chicago Defender* column proclaimed Chacón "a brilliant player" who was "the equal" of New York Yankees shortstop Peckingpaugh. Aware that other racially ambiguous Cubans had secured tryouts and signed with teams in organized baseball, the columnist wondered why Chacón had not been signed by a big-league club. Major-league teams apparently did take notice. Two years later, word circulated in the black press that several big-league scouts were following Chacón.[14] Although the major-league clubs' reasons for opting against signing the shortstop cannot be ascertained, Chacón probably did not register the right mixture of talent, physical features, and pedigree to warrant signing him.

Pelayo Chacón enjoyed a long professional career (1909–31) largely out of the U.S. baseball public's view. Prevented from employment in organized baseball and with limited opportunities in black baseball, Chacón, upon retiring from his playing career in 1931, headed to Venezuela and worked as a coach in that country's still-developing professional baseball circuit. His decision fits a larger pattern of migration among Latino laborers who moved within the Spanish-speaking Americas or to the United States due to their lower position within the Americas' segmented labor structure.

Laborers from the Caribbean moved throughout the Americas in the early twentieth century, filling the labor needs of U.S.-based corporations. West Indian and Latino migrants worked on the United Fruit Company's banana plantations in Central America, in the American Sugar Company's cane fields in Cuba or the Dominican Republic, and as construction workers on the Panama Canal. The search for work and improved economic prospects also brought tens of thousands of Latino and Afro-Caribbean immigrants to New York City, Chicago, Tampa, and other U.S. cities during the interwar period. Through such travel, migrants learned firsthand about the different jobs available to whites and nonwhites as well as the wage differential. In Panama such practices took clear racial form, with North American companies paying West Indians and other black workers on the canal with what became known as "Panama Silver," while white Americans were paid in gold; thus blacks were not only paid less but were paid in a less valuable currency.[15] A similar story transpired in U.S. professional baseball where the major leagues' racial barrier denied those excluded from enjoying the higher salaries and social benefits of a professional career in organized baseball.

The story of Pelayo Chacón and his family captures the shifting racial realities in U.S. professional baseball. After the racial barrier was dismantled, Chacón's son earned the chance never afforded his father. Nearly three decades after his father retired as a player, Venezuelan-born Elio Chacón made it into the big leagues, playing parts of three seasons in the majors (1960–1962), including playing in the 1961 World Series with the Cincinnati Reds. The Chacón story sheds light on the multigenerational legacy created through the contributions of Latino players in the Negro leagues. Latinos who followed Pelayo Chacón into the U.S. playing field—and one notable player who did not, Pedro "Perucho" Cepeda—would also see their sons perform in the major leagues. Such was the legacy that Chacón, Cepeda, Luis Elefterio "Lefty" Tiant, and a handful of other Latino ballplayers created as they blazed a trail through the black circuit and in Latin America.

BUILDING THE "LATINS FROM MANHATTAN"

The comparative success of the eastern Cuban Stars stemmed in large part from Alex Pompez's skillful evaluation of Latino talent and fierce defense of his claim to that talent. Effective recruitment required a network of scouts and contacts in the sports world who alerted Pompez to emerging talent. His current players, such as José María Fernández and

Martin Dihigo, served as informal scouts, recommending players who might interest Pompez for the upcoming North American season. Sportswriters who covered local professional circuits in the Caribbean were additional sources of information about up-and-coming players. But the Cuban American entrepreneur did not leave the work to his players and press contacts. Each winter Pompez would travel to the Caribbean to personally observe new talent in winter league action.

Squabbles over the right to sign Latino players in the Negro leagues reveal Pompez's logic in defending his "exclusive" rights. Controversies arose in 1926 and 1927 over the signing of Pedro San and Esteban Montalvo, respectively.[16] In the Montalvo case, Pompez asserted a territorial basis for his claim to an exclusive market on Latino talent. The Caribbean and Latin America were his domain for scouting and acquiring players, whereas the other Negro-league team owners had the entire United States on which to draw. A May 21, 1927, *New York Age* article asserted that Pompez's objection to the Lincoln Giants' claim on Montalvo, and his motivation for keeping African Americans and Latinos on separate teams, was "based on racial prejudice." Contrary to the sportswriter's charge, Pompez's motives were more likely grounded in a competitive desire to field the best possible team while not allowing his fellow owners any advantage. Pompez's argument for an exclusive claim on Cubans was based on his annual scouting tours of Latin America. None of the other ECL owners was bilingual, familiar with Latino cultures, or capable of scouting through the Spanish-speaking Americas by himself. Pompez thus feared that his competitors would benefit from his unique abilities and effort, signing players he had scouted and introduced to the circuit, without his receiving due compensation for his efforts. This concern, the Cuban Stars owner claimed, had produced "an agreement with the other Commissioners of his League to the effect that they would not use Cuban players."[17]

Pompez's exclusive use of Latino talent in the ECL had previously drawn criticism. In March 1925 *New York Age* columnist John Clark criticized the extensive efforts Pompez made in locating talent. In complaining about the composition of Pompez's roster, Clark spotlighted the Cuban Stars owner's transnational search for Latino players. "Not only does manager Pompez intend to visit well known Cuba, but Porto Rico, San Domingo, and even the small elevated plots of St. Kits [*sic*] and St. Thomas may be combed by Senor Alex in quest of 'apple busters.'" The issue for Clark was that "the invading manager flatly refuses to use any of the boys who are natives of the 'States.'"[18] Despite such criticism, Pompez would continue to field an all-Latino squad as long as his Cuban Stars participated in the eastern-based circuit.

Black baseball came to a virtual standstill during the throes of the Great Depression. In the East, the ECL's collapse was followed by the brief appearance of several successors. After the East-West League ceased operations following the 1932 season, no league operated in the East in 1933. The Negro leagues reorganized the following year as two leagues, reopening employment opportunities for Latinos. And while the number of Latinos in the major leagues grew from 1935 to 1945—over half of all Latinos who performed in the majors during the Jim Crow era made their debut in this period—it is in the Negro leagues that Latinos made their greatest mark. This would become the era of the "Latins from Manhattan," headlined by Dihigo, Tiant, Miñoso, Silvio García, and Horacio "Rabbit" Martínez. Their efforts vaulted the New York Cubans toward black baseball's upper echelon on three occasions and twice put the team in position to secure a Negro-league championship (1935 and 1947).

The year 1935 represented a turning point for Pompez and black baseball in New York City. Nat Strong's death in January emancipated team owners from having to work through Strong's booking agency. Granted an official franchise at the NNL owners' meeting held later that month in Harlem, Pompez signed a three-year lease for Dyckman Oval with the New York City Parks Department, an arrangement that allowed him to operate outside the control of white booking agents. Pompez spared little expense on Dyckman Oval's transformation into a modern professional ballpark, reportedly spending $60,000 on renovations that increased seating capacity to ten thousand and modernized the grounds. "New style seats have been installed, a new cover has been placed over the grand-stand; box seats have been erected," the *New York Age* reported in May 1935, adding, "there is no comfort that the fans can crave undone by Pompez Exhibition Co., Inc."[19] Pompez even installed floodlights for night games.

The renovated Dyckman Oval gave Harlem sports fans their own multipurpose sports facility. For the next three years, Dyckman served as a gathering place for Harlemites to retreat to, a place where they could escape the indignities of racialized treatment in wider society and celebrate their own. In addition to baseball games, it hosted football games, wrestling cards, and boxing matches that included African Americans and Latinos. Among the notable bouts Dyckman hosted were an August 1935 championship match featuring Puerto Rican Sixto Escobar in his first stateside match and fights of Cuban boxers Kid Chocolate and Kid Gavilan and local Puerto Rican favorite Pedro Montañez. "Dyckman Oval is rapidly gaining the right to the title of Manhattan's amusement center," wrote *New York Age* Lewis Dial. "Every branch of sports from races to cricket have been exhibited at Pompez's beautiful miniature stadium."[20]

Besides fielding competitive baseball clubs and a range of sporting events, Pompez also endeavored to provide Harlem's sports enthusiasts with entertainment. The impresario's promotional flair led to game-day promotions such as raffling off a new car and bringing in celebrities and politicians. In 1935 Pompez invited heavyweight champion Joe Louis and baseball great Babe Ruth for special appearances. Louis threw out the ceremonial first pitch for a Cubans game in August.[21] Bringing Ruth to Dyckman for a September doubleheader exhibition was a true marketing coup. The recently retired star brought his Babe Ruth All-Stars, a white barnstorming team, to face the New York Cubans shortly after the Negro-league campaign ended. The doubleheader was an all-around success, drawing a reported ten thousand fans. Harlem fans got to watch the Babe perform on their turf, and their Cubans swept the two games by scores of 6 to 1 and 15 to 5.[22]

Although New York City's black weeklies popularly claimed the New York Cubans as "Harlem's Own," the team's home field was located outside Harlem. Despite its location in upper Manhattan at 204th Street and Nagle Avenue—north of Washington Heights and south of the Bronx's Riverdale section—the events held year-round at Dyckman Oval clearly made it part of Harlem's cultural world. At a time when Harlemites could not enter the Cotton Club or other entertainment establishments in Harlem unless they were members of the band or performers, going to Dyckman took on special meaning for Harlemites.[23] A home park in close proximity to Harlem, accessible by automobile just off the Harlem River Parkway or by elevated train at the end of the recently opened IRT Lenox Avenue line, helped to increase fan interest. A roster that reflected Harlem's own diversity gave Harlem baseball fans further incentives to head north to Dyckman.

From the New York Cubans' 1935 debut to their demise in 1950, Pompez worked tirelessly to field a competitive team and create a venue worthy of the Cubans' place in the hearts of Harlem's fans. In his third decade operating teams in black baseball circuits, Pompez adopted a new approach to filling the Cubans' player roster, a move that reflected the widening of his worldview and Harlem's own diversity. Unlike its pre-

6. The 1943 New York Cubans. Indicative of owner Alex Pompez's revised signing practices, the New York Cubans' 1943 squad was composed of African American and Latino talent. *Back row, left to right:* José Fernández, Pedro Díaz, Javier Pérez, unidentified, Barney Morris, Dave "Showboat" Thomas, Rodolfo Fernández, Carranza "Schoolboy" Howard. *Middle row:* Bill Anderson, Ameal Brooks, Juan "Tetelo" Vargas, Francisco "Pancho" Coimbre, Rogelio Linares, Horacio Martínez, unidentified. *Front row:* Louis Louden, Roosevelt Cox, Charlie Rivera, David Barnhill. (National Baseball Hall of Fame Library, Cooperstown, New York.)

vious incarnation, the newly christened New York Cubans included U.S.-born African Americans and Latinos on its roster. From 1935 onward one could find southern-born African Americans such as Dave "Showboat" Thomas, northern-born Johnny "Schoolboy" Taylor, native New Yorker (and Puerto Rican) Charlie Rivera, island-born Puerto Rican Francisco "Pancho" Coimbre, Dominican native Juan "Tetelo" Vargas, or West Indian Pat Scantlebury in the New York Cubans uniform.

Pompez's revamped approach paralleled the demographic changes Harlem was undergoing in the 1930s. Between 1900 and 1930 the number of foreign-born blacks who settled in Harlem grew along with New York City's overall black population. In 1900 the city's African American population totaled 60,000, including 5,000 foreign-born blacks. Three decades later, and still in the midst of the Great Migration, the city's black population skyrocketed to 328,000. The majority of these blacks (224,000) lived in Manhattan, and slightly less than one-fifth

(40,000) of those residents were foreign-born; the majority of both of these groups settled in Harlem.[24]

This influx set in motion Harlem's radical transformation from a middle-to-upper-working-class neighborhood of primarily white European American residents in the 1910s to a predominantly black working-class neighborhood in the 1930s. Harlem's new residents came from all over the Americas: the American South, the West Indies, and the Spanish-speaking Caribbean. Uneasy around these new arrivals, many whites fled Harlem. Composed of African Americans, West Indians, and Latinos, Harlem embodied a newly imagined black community that challenged previous notions of blackness. A broader understanding of the struggles of black folk everywhere helped drive the formation of Harlem's black community as what historian Irma Watkin-Owens labels an "intra-racial ethnic community."[25]

Consisting of English- and Spanish-speaking fans, the stadium crowds at the New York Cubans' home games reflected Harlem's diverse population, revealing a community much more culturally and ethnically diverse than what most people today visualize when they hear the terms *Black Harlem* or *Harlem Renaissance*. The Harlem that was home to the New York Cubans was not just African Americans but also Antiguans, Trinidadians, Puerto Ricans, Dominicans, and Cubans. Harlemites shared more than the geographical area that constituted Harlem: their intra-racial ethnic community served as a creative center for black culture. Harlem's poets and writers such as James Baldwin and Zora Neale Hurston, its entertainers and artists such as Harry Belafonte and Augusta Savage, its historians and public intellectuals such as John Henrik Clarke and Arturo "Arthur" Schomburg, and its ballplayers such as Rodolfo Fernández or Charlie Rivera blurred the distinction between home and diaspora. After all, migrants and immigrants did not leave one society and replace it with another, but rather lived in both, sometimes uncomfortably, and certainly confusingly, but never with the disjunctions often read into the past.

Community building did not proceed without its own series of conflicts: West Indians battled with U.S.-born blacks over leadership of local political parties; Puerto Ricans and other Latinos were at times portrayed as a social problem or as the "Spanish menace"; southern blacks were scoffed at by native black New Yorkers and Afro-Caribbean immigrants for their lack of sophistication. Yet together these "new" blacks added to Harlem's diversity and contributed to its cultural milieu, as is evident in the musical, artistic, and literary production of the Harlem Renaissance and beyond. It was from among these residents of Harlem that Pompez's teams drew their fan base.

The development of a "Spanish section" in East Harlem exacerbated concerns about opportunities for Harlem's native-born blacks. Already dealing with exorbitant rents and a restricted housing market, black Harlemites complained of the preferential treatment Latinos received from landlords. On September 20, 1927, Harlem resident Edward Ryan wrote the *Amsterdam News:* "In my rounds of flat hunting I have discovered something new. From 112th to 118th streets are to be found several vacancies, but when you apply you are told 'only for Spanish.' It does not matter what the complexion of the prospective tenant is, so long as he speaks the lingo it's all right." "This is rank discrimination against the native Negro," Ryan continued, "which I consider dangerous, as it puts the same race of people against each other merely on the grounds of a difference in language."26 In verbalizing his concern, Ryan not only exposed a practice that contributed to the emergence of a Spanish section in Harlem but also called on blacks to unite across lines of national origins to resist the fractures accentuated by rank discrimination.

Whether the change in Pompez's hiring practices for his baseball teams directly reflected complaints such as Ryan's or earlier criticisms of Pompez is not known. The New York Cubans entered the NNL with a roster featuring stellar African American and Latino players, and would later add West Indians. In so doing Pompez acted more boldly than fellow Negro-league teams had previously. Since Rube Foster had launched the original Negro National League in 1920, teams had experimented with their rosters by including one or two Latinos with the African American players. Pompez's 1935 team roster, in contrast, equally balanced English-speaking black players and Latinos. Such a roster meant players would have to negotiate lines of difference that some claimed could not produce a winning combination.

Debates about the composition of the New York Cubans, while mainly about baseball, acted as a proxy for concerns about how best to incorporate individuals from the Spanish-speaking Americas into Harlem's black community. The discussions brought to the fore many of the same questions that Harlemites confronted in their everyday interactions. Could blacks and Latinos work together? Build community? Among Harlem's local sportswriters who covered the Negro leagues, both the lack of ethnic diversity on Pompez's Cuban Stars of the 1920s and the diverse composition of his New York Cuban teams produced contention. The arguments extended beyond player signings and retention to questions of race and social experimentation. Critics such as sportswriter John Clark pondered why Pompez opted against manning his 1920s teams with African American players. A decade later the debate focused on whether the Cubans could really work together to win a Negro-league pennant.

Perhaps projecting their own anxieties, a few followers of the New York Cubans feared that Pompez's experiment with diversity would hamper the team's on-field success. *New York Age* reporter Lewis Dial noted the fan murmurings that attributed the team's rocky 1935 start to internal divisions. "The New York Cubans look like a real classy outfit, man for man, but for some reason or other, they fail to jell," Dial began. "It is rumored among fans that the Cubans and the Americans don't seem to pull together." Aware that Pompez operated more than one club out of New York—the Havana Cuban Stars served as an unofficial farm team—Dial proposed a solution: split the players on the squads into two distinct clubs, one entirely composed of Latinos and the other disproportionately African American.[27] Guided perhaps by his knowledge of the way players of diverse backgrounds had worked together in the Caribbean winter leagues, and by his own sense of the complexities of racial, ethnic, and national identification, Pompez did not follow Dial's advice. His inclination proved correct as the Cubans rebounded from a slow start and built a winning streak that propelled them within a game of claiming the NNL title.

From a talent perspective, the 1935 matchup between the Pittsburgh Crawfords and New York Cubans was among the greatest championship series in black baseball. The Crawfords' line-up featured future Hall of Famers Satchel Paige, Josh Gibson, James "Cool Papa" Bell, and Oscar Charleston, along with other notable Negro leaguers Sam Bankhead, Jimmy Crutchfield, and Leroy Matlock. Directed by player-manager and future Hall of Famer Martin Dihigo, the Cubans' squad boasted its own collection of talented players, including Ramon Bragaña, Horacio Martínez, Alejandro Oms, Lazaro Salazar, and Lefty Tiant.

The 1935 series upset those who expected the Crawfords to overwhelm the Cubans. Pompez's club took the first two games in New York, 6–2 and 4–0, before the Crawfords shut the Cubans down in game three 3 to 0. With New York ahead two games to one, the series shifted to Pittsburgh. On their home turf at Greenlee Field, the Crawfords claimed game four 3 to 2, but the Cubans snapped up a 6–1 victory in game five to take a three-games-to-two series advantage. The promise that the Cubans would clinch the NNL pennant in their inaugural campaign took a disastrous turn in game six. Playing under the lights in Philadelphia, the

Cubans took a 6–3 lead into the ninth inning, but Oscar Charleston's three-run homer off Martin Dihigo led a determined Crawfords comeback that resulted in a 7–6 victory, tying the series. The action returned to Dyckman Oval for the deciding seventh game. The hard-hitting contest featured three extra-base hits by Chester Williams, home runs by his Pittsburgh teammates Josh Gibson and Oscar Charleston, and homers by the Cubans' Clyde Spearman and Paul Dixon as the Cubans took a lead into the eighth inning. The ninth inning again proved the Cubans' downfall when the Crawfords managed to rally, taking an 8–5 lead. The Cubans mounted a comeback of their own, but fell short, dropping the decisive seventh game 8 to 7.[28]

The 1935 NNL championship series showcases the choices that followers of black baseball faced in deciding which teams to root for in the Negro leagues. Owned by a U.S. Latino, the New York Cubans had a mixed roster of Caribbean-born Latinos and U.S.-born African Americans. By contrast, Gus Greenlee's Pittsburgh Crawfords included only African Americans. Harlem baseball fans could either emphasize racial and national identification with African Americans and align themselves with the Crawfords, or they could place their allegiance with Pompez's diverse squad, which reflected Harlem's diversity. This was a choice that was possible only in the black baseball circuit, which had, unlike the major leagues, welcomed Latino entrepreneurs into its executive operation and Latino players by the score onto its teams.

HARLEM'S NUMBERS KING

There was no owner within Negro-league baseball better prepared to negotiate this complex terrain than Alex Pompez. The baseball entrepreneur learned as a child while growing up in Tampa the power of the racialized perception that divided white from black in a Jim Crow town and even in the Cuban community. He also knew all too well, as someone who counted himself among "people of the darker races," that the policing of these divisions was made doubly complex by someone who was both Latino and black: no dividing line could be drawn through him.[29] His world was multilingual and full of difference, yet it was also filled with people waging similar struggles to maintain their human dignity in a society where they were constantly reminded that race mattered.

Movement between the United States and the Spanish-speaking Americas, and involvement in both cultural worlds throughout his professional career, conditioned Pompez to the realities of race and segregation. His participation in baseball's transnational circuit and Harlem's numbers racket highlights different strategies devised by those who originated in the Spanish-speaking Americas to counteract racism and segregation. Such individuals were shaped by their immediate experience in the United States as well as by the racial knowledge passed down from their parents and older members of their communities and shared by neighbors. In places like Tampa where Jim Crow reigned, the challenge of being twice different—a black person and a Spanish-speaking Latino—affected more than the first generation. Although the experience was different for New York's Cuban and Latino community, since Jim Crow was not a legal system in the urban North, Latinos there faced challenges as nonwhite individuals who engaged in different cultural practices.

The business world in which Pompez operated was another location where opportunity was influenced by racial understandings. Segregation in professional baseball and most of New York's entertainment industry affected everyone from the performers to club owners and executives. Participation in the "underground" entrepreneurial sector was part of Pompez's strategy for coping with the limitations imposed by racial discrimination in the sporting world and in everyday life.[30] Pompez made his initial wealth within the underground economy. Thus, like fellow Negro-league team owners such as Gus Greenlee (Pittsburgh Crawfords), Abe Manley (Newark Eagles), and James Semler (New York Black Yankees), Pompez funneled earnings from his numbers bank operations to finance his baseball operations.[31] Wealth from the numbers also allowed him to live in Harlem's most exclusive areas, from Strivers Row in the 1920s to the top of Sugar Hill at 409 Edgecombe in the 1930s and 1940s. The policy business also jeopardized all of his other enterprises whenever law enforcement and elected officials attempted to control vice in Harlem.

Pompez was part of the generation that introduced to New York City what evolved into the numbers game. Barbershops and other storefront businesses, including the Seventh Avenue cigar store Pompez opened in 1910, were the launching points through which the numbers game arrived in Harlem. By the mid-1920s Pompez had emerged as one of the numbers kings who controlled the majority of the bets placed in Harlem. By 1932, according to testimony Pompez gave in a 1938 trial, his bank's daily gross averaged between $7,000 and $8,000, well over $2 million a year.[32] Newspaper accounts reported higher estimates of his daily gross, proclaiming his combined bank with "Big Joe" Ison as Harlem's biggest numbers operation in 1935, grossing around $5 million.[33]

Harlemites played the numbers not just for leisure but also to cope with the economic and social realities that segregation imposed on their everyday lives. Because of discriminatory hiring practices at the department stores they frequented on 125th Street, few if any of their own worked there. The high rent they paid did not guarantee that landlords maintained their housing. It was not the Jim Crow South, where laws forbade equal access and opportunity to blacks and shattered any illusions of social equality, but the impact of such social practices and of de facto segregation was nonetheless harsh.[34] Although the dreams of many Harlemites were deferred (to paraphrase poet Langston Hughes), Harlem streets were filled with protests, pickets, and parades, along with more informal actions. Activists campaigned against discriminatory practices in several ways. Some enlisted in the NAACP, the Urban League, or other mainstream organizations and mounted protest campaigns such as the "Don't Buy Where You Can't Work" campaign. Others joined Marcus Garvey's Universal Negro Improvement Association or the Communist Party and pressed for a more radical agenda. These were the Depression years, and economic conditions and opportunities were even worse for most of Harlem's residents than for the rest of the city's working-class poor.

Harlem's residents took to playing the numbers, especially during the Depression, because the outlawed game offered the opportunity of landing an economic windfall. The numbers game operated much like a modern pick-three lottery. Bettors selected a number from 000 to 999 and wagered from as little as a penny to as much as several dollars (a sizable bet that not all bankers took). Pulled from a variety of prearranged published sources such as the last three numbers in the stock market's closing quote to a player's printed batting average, winning numbers paid off at a rate of 600:1. The remaining money went to the bank to cover operating costs—employees' wages, protection money to police and city officials—and as profit.[35]

The numbers racket provided jobs to scores of individuals who otherwise would not have found employment, especially during the Depression. The numbers employment structure included runners who carried messages between the bank and other employees; slip collectors, who took in the bets (policy slips); lookouts who watched for police or for enforcers from other banks; enforcers (the "muscle"), who ensured that employees were not cutting into the money collected or being paid out and that other numbers bankers were not encroaching on their employer's territory. A trusted few worked directly in the banks, counting money taken in and doling out winnings. Pompez's numbers operations employed a diverse workforce of men and women, U.S.-born and foreign, Spanish and English speaking. Among the trusted lieutenants for his bank were none other than his former ballplayers Juanelo Mirabal and Oscar Levis.[36] Just as significant, the numbers bank kept much-needed capital in circulation in Harlem during the Depression and afterward.

Pompez and other Harlem numbers bankers enjoyed a relatively free run into the late 1920s. Things began to change when Dutch Schultz, New York's gangster kingpin, learned about the numbers racket's profit-making potential and started to muscle his way into Harlem's gambling scene.[37] Schultz's violent campaign scared many numbers bankers into retirement and pressed others into service for his syndicate. Historian Rufus Schatzberg, a retired New York City police detective, claims that Schultz's brutal intimidation tactics introduced a level of violence not previously seen in Harlem's numbers scene, radically replacing the working understandings between bankers about respecting territory with violent competition and policing of boundaries.[38]

Able to dodge Schultz's entreaties until late in 1932, Pompez reluctantly joined Schultz's outfit when the Dutchman delivered a personal ultimatum. Their arrangement was no partnership but rather a demotion for Pompez. No longer in control of his bank, he was now a controller for Schultz's syndicate, paid a salary ($250 monthly) and a percentage of the profits from his former bank—which somehow never produced a profit while under Schultz's control.[39]

The free reign Schultz still seemed to enjoy in operating his numbers syndicate upset Harlem residents and drew the attention of New York City's special prosecutor Thomas Dewey. Harlemites worried that the bloodshed caused by Schultz's outfit would go unpunished. Driven by his political ambitions and a desire to root out vice, Dewey organized a campaign aimed at regaining control of Harlem streets and ending the corruption of the Tammany Hall Democratic machine. Rivals murdered Schultz in October 1935 before Dewey could fully exercise his legal authority and dismantle Schultz's criminal empire. Schultz's death freed Harlem's numbers bankers to resume operations. Combining forces with Big Joe Ison's bank, Pompez returned to the top of Harlem's numbers racket, a rapid recovery that troubled Dewey, who redoubled his efforts to bust the racket.

Scandal rocked the New York Cubans in 1937 when the recently elected district attorney Thomas Dewey won an indictment against Pompez. The news made front-page headlines. The cover of the *New York Age* declared: "Alexander Pompez of 409 Edgecombe avenue, owner of the New York Cubans basebal[l] team and lessee of Dyckman Oval, was reported indicted Monday on the testimony of alleged 'numbers' collectors as a 'banker' in the policy racket." Instead of opting to stay and fight the charges, Pompez fled. The hasty departure caused the New York Cubans to cease operations for the 1937 season, forcing his players to find new employment.[40]

The Latino numbers king evaded capture until law enforcement officials in Mexico City arrested him in March 1937. Pompez fought extradition for six months before he negotiated a deal with Dewey to turn state's evidence and returned to New York on the last Friday before Election Day in November. In exchange for testifying against Tammany Hall Democratic judge Jimmy Hines, Pompez would receive two years' probation. His testimony given at Hines's 1938 trial and 1939 retrial detailed his start in the numbers business, Schultz's violent takeover, and the protection Schultz's outfit received from Hines.[41]

Harlem raged against the well-placed Democratic city officials, local judges, and police officers who had shielded Schultz's syndicate from the full brunt of the law. Harlemites viewed Schultz and his protectors as outsiders who had violently taken over Harlem's numbers game and then refused to reinvest the money in Harlem. They had a different reaction to Pompez's role in the numbers, his legal woes, and his turning state's evidence. He was one of their own; a "stand-up" guy who demonstrated a commitment to Harlem through business ventures that employed a diverse group of Harlemites and kept capital circulating within the local economy. This was certainly the stance taken by the African American press. "We have known him for over a period of more than 15 years," *New York Age* columnist William E. Clark wrote, "and have always found him a square-shooter in his dealings with his players and the public. . . . To our way of thinking his crimes are no worse than those of bookmakers who accept bets on horses."[42]

Pompez suffered no backlash in Harlem or in Negro-league baseball. His reacceptance into Harlem's sporting world and social circles following the Hines trials compensated for the loss of much of his wealth, which was seized as part of his prosecution and plea agreement. He also lost Dyckman Oval when the City Parks Department rescinded his lease and razed the structure for a proposed parking lot in 1938.[43] Law enforcement and judicial authorities could seize his wealth, but his social capital and network were still largely intact. Questioned by the press after his testimony at the Hines trial, Pompez told reporters he would abandon the numbers racket and focus his energies on baseball. "There may not be as much money in it . . . but it's safer."[44] Fellow Negro National League owners accepted Pompez's Cubans franchise back into the circuit in 1938. No longer possessing a home park, the New York Cubans once again depended on booking agents to secure grounds for home games, until 1942, when Pompez negotiated an agreement with the New York Giants to use the Polo Grounds for home games.

JIM CROW ENCOUNTERS IN THE URBAN NORTH

Pompez's business dealings reveal interconnections between Harlem's black and Latino communities, for the payrolls of his various businesses, as well as his network of friends and associates, included African American, West Indian, and Latino Harlemites. These interconnections may clearly be seen in the housing arrangements he made for his players.

When pitcher Rodolfo Fernández departed his native Cuba for the first time in 1932, he arrived in New York with his housing taken care of. Like other teammates who were single and unfamiliar with the city, the Cuban pitcher benefited from Pompez's assistance, which placed him in a home near the barrio Latino and the team's home field. Fernández believed these arrangements helped him endure the cultural isolation that young ballplayers and many immigrants encountered upon arriving in the States. Fellow New York Cubans Armando Vásquez, Ray Noble, and Charlie Rivera benefited from the multiethnic network that Pompez had established by the early 1930s.[45] This web of African American and Latino households—both recently arrived and native-born—located throughout Harlem enabled Pompez to strategically place his players in homes that exposed them to English, provided access to familiar cuisine and cultural life, and fostered connections with Harlem's Latino community.

Latino players maintained contact across the racial divide despite the major leagues' putative forcible separation of members of the Latino baseball fraternity. Rodolfo Fernández remembers maintaining his friendship with fellow Cubans Adolfo Luque and Miguel Angel González in the 1930s. The trio performed on opposite sides of baseball's racial divide. Fernández recalls: "When I first arrived to the United States Luque played with the New York Giants and Miguel Angel played with the Cardinals. During that time major-league teams only played day games, and after the games Luque would come from the Polo Grounds and . . . stop in to visit." González would also visit Harlem's "Spanish" barrio to renew acquaintances, talk baseball, and have dinner with Fernández.[46] In addition to maintaining bonds of friendship, these reunions allowed the trio to swap information on players, make signing recommendations, and network to advance their postplaying careers as coaches and managers.

For Latinos in New York and other cities in the Americas, baseball provided a cultural bond that transcended national boundaries and physical geography. Indeed, on New York City streets, ragtag teams of children played stickball, dreaming of their ascent into *las grandes ligas* (the big leagues), while in city parks their fathers, relatives, and neighbors played on such teams as the Borinquen All Stars, Ciudad Trujillo, or the Black Puerto Rican Stars. Participation in Harlem's baseball scene left memorable impressions on countless Latinos who settled or were raised in New York City. Born to a Cuban father and a Puerto Rican mother at Harlem Hospital in 1938, Puerto Rican poet Piri Thomas learned early on the significance of baseball's color line. As a youngster he would often travel to watch his father, John Thomas, play semipro baseball for the Black Puerto Rican Stars and other local teams. Yet, for Latinos who possessed both talent and a darker skin tone that muted any semblance of racial ambiguity, games played in the local semipro circuit did little to advance their big-league dreams.

Games between Latino and black teams throughout the city were more than weekend outings; they signified the re-appropriation of public space as a place to re-create home, to meet with fellow blacks, Latinos, and Puerto Ricans. All these aspects of the games permeated Thomas's recollections. "But most, most were the World Series in Central Park," he recalled, "because teams thought that this was ours. They [the major leagues] didn't allow us to go in theirs, but we made our World Series. . . . And just like any World Series, there were selling going on, but it was *cuchifrito* [Puerto Rican fritters] not very much hot dogs."[47] Other Harlemites who came from different locations within the African diaspora to settle in Harlem have similar memories. Everard Marius, a West Indian who was born in Harlem, recalls that baseball replaced cricket as the sport of choice for him and his siblings. Playing baseball represented an important part of his identity formation, his "Americanization," and also allowed him to bond with his African American and Latino neighbors as they played in the streets or attended New York Cubans games.[48]

For Latinas, games played in Central Park and elsewhere in the city provided a chance to create a distinctly Latino/a space. The foods they brought to the game, which reflected the traditional fares of the islands, gave the setting a particular flavor. But they performed more than the traditional gender roles. Some women collected bets on the action on the field. Others umpired. A few ventured onto the field and played alongside the men. And perhaps others avoided the scene entirely, using the time to tend to other matters.[49] Women too would head to the Polo Grounds, wearing their Sunday best to watch their New York Cubans. Thus, whether as fans or as players, participation in the baseball scene cultivated a sense of commonality among Latinos and helped assuage the toll that physical relocation, economic exploitation, and racialization took in the United States. Sports, then, combined with food, music, and other leisure pursuits, allowed ordinary folk to recuperate from the demands of their wage-earning jobs and to recreate themselves in communion with others.

Throughout the twentieth century, blacks and Latinos observed and learned from interactions among European American groups who, grudgingly at first, made room for newer European immigrants in the fraternity of whiteness. Slavs, Italians, and eastern and southern European Jews essentially became whiter and whiter as the century advanced. The broadening of the legal definition of whiteness and the social acceptance of new ethnic groups as white did not eliminate the powerful effects of race on the lives of Harlem residents. To the contrary, Harlemites who grew up rooting for New York's professional baseball teams, whether the New York Cubans or the New York Yankees, could recognize the ironic truths of race and the process of manipulating racial understandings in their own everyday experience.

Sporting figures as well as everyday residents who came from points throughout the African diaspora learned to manipulate, if not master, the poetics of racial knowledge to their own advantage. Albertus "Cleffie" Fennar, an African American ballplayer, and his team manager, former New York Giants player José Rodríguez, engaged in a bit of chicanery to protect Fennar's amateur status when he joined Pompez's Havana Cuban Stars in 1934. "They changed my name to Dario," Fennar recalls. "José Rodríguez told me, let's see, he said, I am going to put your name as Dario, he was a good second baseman in Cuba."[50] To carry out the masquerade, Fennar learned to speak a little Spanish, thereby expanding his cultural repertoire while also meeting others' expectation of "Dario," the Cuban ballplayer.

Harlem residents attempted to manipulate popular understandings of race and foreignness by their use of language. Everard Marius frankly admitted, "In fact, language would (not as much as today) but language at one time could get you across as not being an ordinary Negro. Some of my relatives used to take advantage of that, speaking creole and all of that business."[51] As Marius explains, linguistic abilities had the power to transform an ordinary Negro into an "extraordinary Negro," thus positioning him to extract social benefits denied those who spoke only American English.

The place of Spanish-speaking Latinos of African descent in an English-speaking place in the diaspora exposed the complexities of language and region as few other examples could. The dexterity of language, when attached to history and social perception, transformed meaning and understanding. Although most of these Latinos could not speak English and were not fully aware of the intricacies of U.S. racial understandings, they observed and learned ways to negotiate race. Examples can be drawn from their handling of the language barrier when ordering food. Many players ordered the same meal time and again when they first arrived. For some, it was always ham and eggs, or steak and eggs. Others simply pointed at what they wanted or echoed their teammate's order: "The same." However, as they gained more experience, they became more attuned not just to the English language but also to variation in racial understandings according to location and context.

Cuban Negro leaguer Armando Vásquez initially spoke very little English and was constantly denied service due to his black skin color. After his first year, he plotted a strategy that put him in a position to get what he wanted. Not speaking English sometimes worked to his advantage. "In certain places . . . I would arrive at restaurants where they would not serve black people, and I would arrive speaking in Spanish and they would serve me."[52] On recognizing that Spanish could serve as a marker of ethnoracial difference, Vásquez conveniently "forgot" whatever English he knew and spoke strictly in Spanish when he arrived at restaurants throughout the segregated South. This act often transformed him in the eyes of the server from black to "foreign." Aware of this tactic, Negro-league teams often drafted a Latino player to place their orders when entering restaurants known for denying service to blacks but for being more open to Latinos.

The manipulation of racial understandings, as by masquerading as Cuban, using a foreign accent, or speaking Spanish, was part of the collective racial knowledge held within black communities. Wherever their communities overlapped with those of Latinos, African Americans learned about the different opportunities offered to those who were darker-skinned but spoke Spanish. A native of Jacksonville, Florida, James Weldon Johnson regularly encountered segregation during his upbringing and through his travels as an adult. In his autobiography, *Along This Way*, Johnson describes several instances when speaking Spanish (masquerading) changed the treatment he received from conductors on Jim Crow trains or in other segregated facilities.[53]

On one level, the masquerade performances that Johnson describes parallel what Latino ballplayers and other Negro leaguers did in trying to get service at segregated businesses. At another level, the stakes involved in each situation were different. A talented ballplayer represented a desired commodity that teams in organized baseball sought to acquire. Often it was those who safely resided on the other side of the racial divide who solicited blacks to engage in acts of racial masquerade—such as a white team scout promising a position to an African American who would go to Cuba or Mexico and learn Spanish. The invitation to manipulate racial understandings and circumvent baseball's color line involved different power dynamics and resonated with the distinctive ways team officials in organized baseball brokered the entry of other nonwhites into their segregated organization.

Travels across baseball's racial divide and throughout the transnational circuit equipped Latino players with the knowledge of how race worked at different points within that circuit. Awareness of the ways race structured opportunity in professional baseball and affected everyday interactions off the playing field in the United States weighed heavily in the individual player's decision whether to participate in the Negro leagues. Darker-skinned Latinos with little hope of breaking into organized baseball had to decide whether a North American venture was worth the psychological toll that playing segregated baseball would exact. Black Latinos had to weigh more than the cultural dislocation they would endure. Unlike their lighter-skinned compatriots, darker-skinned Latinos were not as readily perceived as Latinos on first glance; North Americans were more likely to take them for African Americans.

Puerto Rican Pedro "Perucho" Cepeda, father of Hall of Famer Orlando Cepeda, is one talented black Latino who opted against playing in the Negro leagues due to social conditions in the States. Enshrined in the Puerto Rican Hall of Fame for his feats on the field, Pedro Cepeda starred in the Puerto Rican and other Caribbean baseball circuits in the 1930s and 1940s. The batting champion of the inaugural Puerto Rican Winter League season (1938) with a .485 batting average, he competed throughout his playing career with Negro leaguers and major leaguers imported from the United States. Playing with North Americans in the Caribbean allowed Cepeda to compare his abilities directly with theirs while they informed him about social conditions in the Jim Crow North.

Accounts shared by fellow players who performed in the Negro leagues provided secondhand information about life in a segregated profession. These encounters sometimes took the form of recruitment visits during which Negro-league players or team officials tried to convince a Latino player to join their team. Alex Pompez came closest to convincing Puerto Rican league standout Pedro Cepeda to come north, even listing the strong-hitting infielder on the New York Cubans' 1942 roster submitted to the Negro National League office. This came to naught, for Cepeda steadfastly refused to set foot in the U.S. mainland.[54]

Pedro Cepeda's decision not to play in the United States illustrates the options available to some Latinos. Cepeda was fortunate to have had a choice between holding a regular job in his native country that allowed him to continue playing during the winters, and playing professionally year-round in the Negro leagues and elsewhere. A local city job in his hometown of Ponce gave Cepeda both economic security and the flexibility of playing professional ball during weekends. (Caribbean winter leagues typically played games on Saturdays and Sundays, with an occasional midweek game scheduled in the hope of maximizing attendance.) His job thus kept Cepeda from having to depend on playing summer ball in the United States.

Employment status complicated the choices of Latino players slated to perform in the Negro leagues in the Depression era. Rodolfo Fernández, a teammate of Cepeda's during the 1937 Dominican season, remembers, "Then, if somebody had a really good job, he did not leave it to play baseball, because he could play every Sunday. Those people, they did not live off baseball." Fernández points out that talented players with good-paying jobs at times turned down professional opportunities in the States, choosing the security and stability of their situation in Cuba, Puerto Rico, the Dominican Republic, or elsewhere in the Spanish-speaking Americas.[55] Such decisions made the task of developing and maintaining a stable pool of players all the more difficult for Latino- and Negro-league team owners.

Alex Pompez used his unique position as a U.S.-born Latino entrepreneur who had also lived in Cuba to increase the Latino presence in the black baseball circuit. On and away from the playing field, he constructed a network that eased the process of cultural adjustment for the players he introduced to the U.S. playing field. The extensive work this involved earned him the gratitude of many of his players and others in Harlem. Cuban infielder Antonio "Pollo" Rodríguez passed up a chance in 1939 to sign with the New York Giants so that he could stay with the New York Cubans. "Pompez [is] my friend. He brought me here," the

Cuban explained through an interpreter to an *Amsterdam News* sports-writer. "With Pompez I can do a lot of things. I know the offer from the Giants might mean more money and greater fame, but I like playing with my own people and for Pompez."[56] Rodriguez thus preferred to remain in an institution and setting that Latinos had helped shape. Organized baseball might offer more money, but as a segregated institution it did not offer a welcoming work environment.

Organized baseball nonetheless posed an enduring challenge to Pompez's ability to attract Latino talent. In the 1930s minor-league teams and a handful of major-league organizations continued to test the resolve of their league rivals by acquiring racially ambiguous Latino players. The departures forced Pompez to scout new parts of the Americas to stay ahead of the talent drain. In some instances, Pompez helped arrange for his players to leave the Negro leagues for organized baseball. He did so knowing that America's game was not just about what happened between the white lines of the baseball diamond. His life experience made him exceedingly aware of the power plays involved in widening or limiting access to institutions and opportunities by either altering or maintaining racial understandings. The stakes in professional baseball were clear: inclusion in organized baseball meant access to a more secure livelihood, though in an alienating environment. What remained unclear was how this inclusion would change racial understandings about Latinos as a group, and to what extent the inclusion of Latinos would transform the working of baseball's racial system.

7

Becoming Cuban Senators

Take the position of the Cubans and South American players
on the Washington Senators. They have been subjected to all
sorts of abuses. Rival pitchers have been low enough to try
"beaning" them. In other instances, players on their own
teams have refused to room with them, and in dining cars
and other travel facilities discriminated against them.

Eddie Gant, *Chicago Defender* (July 25, 1942)

Griffith is one of the big leaguers who prefers to go outside
the borders of these United States and bring in players,
rather than hire American citizens of color. He has so many
foreigners on this team it is necessary to hire an interpreter,
and if you ever hear this conglomeration of personalities
talking to each other in the airport, you'd swear, you were
sojourning in Madrid, Lisbon, or Havana.

Wendell Smith, *Pittsburgh Courier* (February 27, 1943)

OPENING UP THE PLAYING FIELD

Throughout baseball's Jim Crow era, major-league team officials widened
the eligible talent pool by adopting labels that fused notions of race and
ethnicity yet preserved the overarching goal of black exclusion. Big-league
officials traced the national origins of players from the Spanish-speaking
Americas back to particular regions of Spain, or in a few cases Portugal,
to establish the racial eligibility of individual players they sought to sign.
This practice created the context in which Californian Vernon "Lefty"
Gómez, Tampa native Al Lopez, Mexican native Melo Almada, Cuban-

7. Adolfo Luque, whose 194 wins made him the winningest Latino pitcher in major-league history until he was surpassed by Dominican Hall of Famer Juan Marichal and, in 1998, by Nicaraguan Dennis Martínez. The fiery right-handed Luque pitched with the Boston Braves, Cincinnati Reds, Brooklyn Dodgers, and New York Giants in a playing career that lasted from 1914 to 1935. (National Baseball Hall of Fame Library, Cooperstown, New York.)

born Adolfo "Dolf" Luque entered the major leagues as suitable ethnics from the Spanish-speaking Americas.

The use of ethnic labels to convey European ancestry and status as nonblack Others eased concerns about attempts to circumvent the color line. The practice of emphasizing ethnicity to widen access to organized baseball did not originate with Latino players themselves. To the contrary, this emphasis resulted from major-league team officials pushing the limits of each others' racial and ethnic tolerance. An individual player could claim Castilian ancestry, but only a Washington Senator, New York Giant, or major-league official could legitimate such a claim and allow it to translate into inclusion in the major leagues.

The increased number of Latinos signed in the 1930s nonetheless fueled the perception that certain major-league organizations were indeed attempting to gerrymander the color line by admitting racially ambiguous Latinos. In seeking to acquire Latino players, the Washington Senators, Boston's two big-league teams, and the New York Giants extended the mechanism by which Italian Americans and other Americans of southern European ancestry had been incorporated in preceding decades. America's game was becoming more inclusive, and in a certain sense "Latin" players were simply another group major-league organizations signed to become more competitive.

Baseball enthusiasts and the sporting press saw another motivation in the active recruitment of Cuban and Latino talent. Led by the example of the Washington Senators, major-league organizations sought Latino players not just for their talent but also as a means to improve their own financial viability. Although the Latino players the Senators acquired occasionally raised concerns that the organization was circumventing the color line, Washington president Clark Griffith's interest in Cuba had little to do with integration or social justice. The Senators approached Cuban, Venezuelan, Mexican, and other foreign-born Latinos as a cheaper labor source than U.S.-born prospects offered. Their turn to Latin America was rooted in the racialized economy of organized baseball, in which foreign-born Latinos were much less expensive in terms of acquisition, player development, and salary if the Latino player panned out.

Latinos who broke into the majors were not necessarily accepted as racial equals. Their entry required manipulating the fine points of national origin, ethnicity, and skin color that distinguished racially eligible from racially ineligible Latinos. Not all of the players allowed to participate in the majors were racialized as white, nor did major-league organizations that signed them necessarily present them as such. Rather they adamantly insisted that these ballplayers were not black. The Latinos who entered after Rafael Almeida and Armando Marsans thus inherited the space first created to accommodate Vincent Nava in the National League in 1882—except they were no longer just "Spaniards" but were now the "purest bars of Castilian soap," "sons of Portuguese nobility," or Mexican but "more American" than their compatriots.

Coverage by the U.S. sporting press provides a glimpse of the qualitative difference between equality and inclusion. Actually, instances of the racial treatment Latino players endured on and off the playing field that reached print account for only a small portion of what these players actually faced—as oral testimony shared by the era's surviving players makes clear. Verbal taunts and harangues rarely made print, even when they sparked altercations. Moreover, the challenges the first generation of Latinos encountered were rarely the focus of the U.S. sporting press. Nor did they receive overly sympathetic coverage of their unique situation. Language difference was one impediment to getting their story told, but racialized perceptions were just as significant. The problem was not exclusive to one side of the racial divide. The overwhelming majority of North American sportswriters, white or black, knew little or no Spanish; interviews with Latino players in their native language were often out of the question. The names of Latino players appeared in the box scores, but their words were rarely printed in columns, and when they were, it was often with racialized accents. These factors contributed to an uneasy relationship with, and weariness regarding, the English-language press.

Although they generally escaped the harsher treatment dealt their darker-skinned compatriots, lighter-skinned Latinos who broke into the majors nevertheless underwent a process of racialization that differentiated them from whites. Cuban right-hander Adolfo Luque attested to the intense scrutiny Latinos underwent. Throughout his twenty-year big-league career, Luque endured press and fan treatment similar to the racist venom later encountered by African Americans. The racialization of Luque associated everything from his skin color to his temperament with his "Spanish" race. Opponents liberally hurled racial epithets at the Cuban pitcher, even though New York City papers initially characterized him as "a very light-skinned Cuban, in fact lighter than Marsans or Almeida, and look[ing] more like an Italian than a full blooded Cuban."[1] The most trying situations for these early Latino major leaguers occurred when white opponents openly questioned their ancestry (hence their inclusion) by taunting them with racial insults from across the field. Such verbal challenges reiterated that racial perception involved more than skin color; sometimes they sparked violence.

Racial taunting incited Adolfo Luque's 1922 attack on New York Giants player Casey Stengel. Tired of the insults directed his way from the Giants bench, Luque opted against his usual tactic of throwing brushback pitches at the opposing team's batters in favor of going right after the person whom he perceived as the agitator. Luque walked off the pitcher's mound and into the Giants dugout and punched Stengel, sparking a brawl. It was neither the first nor last on-field fracas in which Luque was involved, which contributed to his reputation as a hothead.[2] A 1933 newspaper retrospective on his big-league career recalled the abuse heaped on him. "Time was when life was not so calm for him. Players of earlier day frequently flamed [his] *hot Spanish blood* to boiling point with uncomplimentary remarks about his nationality. Taunts and goading caused him to lose temper. . . . Casey Stengel and many others have felt his wrath over innuendos [*sic*] and 'cracks' about blood."[3] The taunting reminded the Cuban that he was not viewed as a fellow white; press coverage suggested that the temperamental Cuban's reactions were rooted in biology, his "hot Spanish blood."

The sporting press used Luque's participation in the majors as a touchstone in discussing the politics of inclusion within organized baseball. More than two decades after Lester Walton hailed the "colored player" breaking into "fast company," *New York Age* columnist Buster Miller expounded on the continuing power of race despite the major leagues' newfound diversity. "It is true that the doors of organized baseball are open to Indians, Cubans, Porto Ricans [sic], Hawaiians, etc. but only if their skin, hair and features will pass muster as evidence of membership in the white race." Miller then extended a challenge: "This writer defies any member of the above mentioned national groups to obtain entrance into the major leagues with a black skin. Or even mahogany colored, lest he be hailed as a 'nigger' as was Adolfo Luque, swarthy Cuban pitcher of the New York Giants, by the 'sportsmen' when he made his first appearance on the mound in St. Louis."[4] Miller's reference to Luque and other Latinos showed that their lighter skin color and ethnic background offered only momentary relief in an institution that closely scrutinized ancestry for any telltale sign of a false racial claim. Although they may not have been discernibly black, few of their contemporaries viewed them as white. They lived between racial poles along the color line.

The in-between racial position occupied by Cubans and other Latinos served as a starting point in discussions about the manipulation of the major leagues' color line. "Much ballyhoo" had been made about "Negroes" performing in the big leagues, noted African American journalist Lewis Dial in a July 1934 column. An associate of his, he observed, "claims that a certain New York Giant ball player is colored, and it isn't Luque, the Cuban star, either." Dial's aside that Luque was not the player in question illustrated the point that any speculation about transgressors of the color line immediately involved Latino ballplayers. Just as significant, the rumor captured the difficult situation African American journalists confronted in reporting on players possibly passing. Their first impulse might have been to claim such a player as one of their own and to attribute his inclusion to the capriciousness of the major leagues' racial policy. On the other hand, they understood the ramifications for the player and his family of "outing" him—the player stood to lose his big-league career and all its benefits. Moreover, exposing him did not guarantee that the barrier would come tumbling down.[5] Major-league officials would very likely have continued treating "Negroes" as an undifferentiated mass while creating subtle distinctions among Latinos.

Players from the Spanish-speaking Americas were plagued by the press's misidentifying their national origins or by neglecting to acknowledge how individual ballplayers self-identified. Reporters' unfamiliarity with the origins of "Latin" players was partly to blame. Ignorance on the part of reporters irritated players less, however, than purposely minimizing differences of national origins and ethnic ancestry that the players considered significant. Just as bothersome was having one's family history misrepresented and being publicly misidentified as a noncitizen.

Al López was particularly irked at being referred to as a foreigner and reading inaccuracies about his family history. Early in his career, the press repeatedly identified the Tampa native, who lived his entire life in the United States, as a foreigner, a Cuban. In response, López asserted his American (U.S.) identity and Spanish ancestry by recounting his family history. López informed writers that his father, a man from Spain's "oppressed class," had migrated to Tampa after a brief residency in Cuba in the late nineteenth century. The maternal side of his family tree had even more impressive roots, according to López's account. His mother, although born in Tampa, was "of pure Castilian blood."[6] López was thus well positioned in the hierarchy of those from the Spanish-speaking Americas since his family came from European stock, not from the colonized Cuban masses. A few sportswriters heeded López and offered clarifications. The "Spanish-American Star," a 1930 article declared "is not, as many believed him, of Cuban descent. His family came from Spain. Lopez is one of the few Spanish players in professional baseball."[7] The formation of a "Spanish-speaking battery" when Adolfo Luque arrived in Brooklyn that year revived familiar descriptions. The "bronze-skinned individuals" popularly recognized as being "of Spanish descent," one writer insisted, were really Cubans.[8] The writer's insistence on knowing Luque's and Lopez's "real" identity captures the power journalists wielded in shaping the baseball public's knowledge and racial understanding.

The antics of Vernon "Lefty" Gómez while he was a tantalizing left-handed pitcher on the New York Yankees earned him the favor of teammates, the press, and fans who nicknamed him the "Goofy Castilian." The pitcher's surname gave away part of his ethnic background, which was Mexican and Irish.[9] Latinos throughout the United States came to see Gómez as one of their own, regardless of the extent to which he acknowledged a Mexican ethnic identity. A curious relationship developed between the unwitting Gómez and his "Spanish" fans. "Vernon Gomez still is receiving mail written in Spanish," a 1936 article informed readers, "a letter today, so far as he could make out, inviting him to address a Spanish society in Chicago." Popularity with such fans was perhaps rooted in their desire to associate with a successful public figure bearing a Spanish surname. The sportswriter tried to mute such claims: "The Irish in him has pretty much neutralized the Castilian, and, while he will reply with the gallantry of a don, he'll grin a big Irish grin as he writes it, hoping the recipient will be able to find an interpreter."[10]

Despite the press's familiarity with Gómez, he too encountered ethnic misidentification. The California native was "irked" at being misidentified as Portuguese, according to sportswriter Will Wedge, who explained that Gómez "is of proud Castilian stock, on the paternal side. His blood is a romantic mixture of Spanish, Irish, and English. . . . His four brothers and two sisters are dark like their father, who hailed from Madrid in sunny Spain." Drawing a straight line back to Spain, the explanation bypassed the route through Mexico trekked by the Gómez family and by most settlers of Mexican California. (Others sources revealed that his father had been born in California and Gómez's paternal grandfather had been born in Mexico.)

Castilian identity was inserted into the parlance of ethnoracial identification within organized baseball to alleviate concerns about possible indigenous or African ancestry that came with being labeled a Mexican American or Mexican national. Constructed as the negation of indigenous or African roots, Castilian identity became a powerful label that validated the inclusion of a limited number of players from the Spanish-speaking Americas.[11] Just as significant, the label reiterated the main principle of the color line—the elevation of whiteness associated with European ancestry and the denigration of blackness. Equally important, disassociation with indigenous or *mestizo* roots meant that "Castilians" would be located at a different point on the color line than Native Americans.

FROM MEXICAN STARS TO TEDDY *BEISBOL?*

For players from Mexico in the pre-integration major leagues, ethnicity and social class were used in combination to substantiate the claim of racial eligibility. Social class assuaged doubts raised by skin color or nationality in the minds of team and league officials. Asserting social class to distinguish an individual player from his countrymen proved ever critical as big-league teams extended their search for talent beyond Cuba to Mexico in the mid-1930s.

At a time when Joe and Dom DiMaggio and other Italian Americans from California were beginning to grab baseball headlines, many assumed that the Boston Red Sox's newest addition to its 1933 outfield, Melo Almada, was another Italian American breaking into the majors. Sportswriter John Drohan set the record straight. "While he is forced to disappoint a lot of fans who thought he was an Italian, [Almada] confesses that he's of Spanish descent, but born in Sonora, Mexico." Newspaper descriptions of Almada's physical appearance reveal why some individuals who supported the color line were conflicted about the first native son of Mexico to perform in the majors. A feature story in the *Sporting News* described the Mexican native as "the young, dark-skinned Boston Red Sox star." While one writer perceived a "dark-skinned" person, journalist Bill Cunningham saw a Mexican who, although "proud of his Mexican lineage and completely loyal to it, . . . doesn't even look like a Mexican, being taller, broader, and considerably fairer than most of the citizens of our sister republic."[12]

Almada was arguably the best-prepared Latino for the challenge of breaking into the Jim Crow major leagues. Raised from toddlerhood in Los Angeles, the son of a Mexican consulate officer, Almada was a fluent English speaker intimately familiar with U.S. racial understandings and social customs. Almada also learned to play baseball in Los Angeles, playing at Jefferson High School before joining a local semipro team, El Pasos.[13] The *Washington Post* celebrated Almada's Los Angeles connections and his ancestral lineage when he joined the Washington Senators in 1938.[14] The full-page article traced his "noble" lineage back to the fourteenth century through the conquistadors and gave Almada a different social class status from the Cubans who would join him in the Senators camp and from fellow Mexican native José "Chile" Gómez.

The sporting press's description of Gómez's identity as a Mexican stressed the hierarchy of Latinos. "Gomez is the first big leaguer to come directly from Mexico," explained one article, reminding readers, "Almada was little more than an infant when his parents brought him across the border."[15] The article further distinguished between the two by claiming that Gómez "is just as Mexican as Adolfo Luque is Cuban" and that he was "no relative of Senor Vernon Gómez . . . whose Spanish blood goes back several generations."[16] Lefty Gómez's mixed-race background and Melo Almada's elite social class status, along with their facility with U.S. social customs, put those within organized baseball at ease. But José Gómez had not been exposed to the assimilation-driven curricula of the U.S. educational system, in which students learned the three R's (reading, 'riting, and 'rithmetic) as well as how to be Americans. José Gómez was therefore viewed as the true *Mexican* pioneer and in the minds of many observers, as more suspect racially.

The professional experiences of Melo Almada, José Gómez, and Lefty Gómez were distinct from Hall of Famer and San Diego native Ted Williams. The son of a white U.S.-born father and a mother of Mexican descent, Williams never stressed the Mexican side of his roots during his big-league career. Societal views of Mexicans in the 1930s as uncivilized "greasers" and immigrants who could not be assimilated into mainstream U.S. society gave him little reason to publicly acknowledge this part of his ancestry. Nevertheless, the search for additional players who might have had "Spanish" ancestry has led some baseball historians, sportswriters, and fans to proclaim Williams as the greatest Latino ballplayer of all time.[17]

The debate about where to place Ted Williams within the history of Latinos, race, and the color line raises the larger issue of what constitutes Latino identity. Is it rooted in biology? Cultural practices? The place where one was born or raised? The controversy also raises the ethical question, and the methodological concern, of the appropriate means of acknowledging Williams's partial Mexican ancestry, given that he did not publicly self-identify.

Ted Williams's decision not to publicly acknowledge his Mexican ancestry during his career as player or manager matters in a historical sense. His choice attests to the dominant ideas of race and place that affected people from the Spanish-speaking Americas on U.S. professional diamonds and in the United States generally. Williams indicates awareness of these issues in his autobiography, *My Turn at Bat,* when he declares that his professional baseball career would have taken a different trajectory had others known of his Mexican ancestry. His mother, May Venzor, was born along the U.S.-Mexico border in El Paso, Texas, in 1893 and was of Mexican and French ancestry. "Her name was Venzer [*sic*]," Williams wrote, "and that's fate for you; if I had my mother's name, there is no doubt I would have run into problems in those days, the prejudices people had in Southern California."[18]

Born in 1918, Ted Williams grew up across the border from Tijuana in San Diego. Undoubtedly, Mexican and Mexican American culture was an inescapable presence. His mother, a Salvation Army worker, ensured that Williams would not escape the harsh reality of poverty—occasionally she brought him with her on visits to the slums of Tijuana. His 1988 autobiography gives no sense that Williams identified with the people his mother aided and proselytized, or with the Mexican Americans living in southern California. His concern about the impact his mother's maiden name could have had on him reveals awareness of the historical animosity Mexicans faced during the Depression, when tens of thousands of Mexicans were repatriated.[19]

The future major leaguer who earned the nickname "Splendid Splinter" for his masterful hitting did not grow up in a Spanish-speaking barrio in San Diego or in a household where Mexican culture was dominant. This cultural background distinguished Williams from Melo Almada, whose tenure in Boston ended two years before Williams's 1939 arrival. Almada's upper-middle-class upbringing in Southern California placed him in a much higher social position than Williams, who grew up in the working class. Although Almada's ancestry was indeed scrutinized to validate his inclusion in the major leagues, such strict scrutiny did not result in access denied. Lefty Gómez could neither hide nor escape his ancestry; it was in the family name. Gómez's tenure with the New York Yankees from 1930 to 1943 made it nonetheless clear that a U.S.-born Spanish-surnamed player who acknowledged "Spanish" ancestry from the Spanish-speaking Americas could participate in organized baseball.

That Williams's Mexican-born mother is now celebrated attests to a growing awareness in the late twentieth and early twenty-first century of Latinos in U.S. society and in baseball. That awareness does not, however, necessarily recognize the history of racialization in which individuals from the Spanish-speaking Americas were categorized as distinct from Caucasians, whites, and European immigrants who were undergoing Americanization. Certainly Williams was not racialized as Mexican while he performed in the major leagues. Nor did he flee to Mexico during the Jorge Pasquel–led Mexican League player raid of the late 1930s and early 1940s, when Latinos in organized baseball and the Negro leagues flocked south for better money, a more hospitable racial climate, and better working conditions.

By 1939, when Ted Williams made his big-league debut, organized baseball had developed a sophisticated racial system that centered on denying entry to blacks. This system did not, however, bar lighter-skinned

Latinos if they possessed the right combination of ancestry, physical features, and talent. The presence of Almada, Lefty Gómez, and dozens of other foreign-born Latinos who joined the Washington Senators and other major-league organizations in the 1930s shows that a space had already been made to accommodate them.

MAKING CUBAN SENATORS

The Washington Senators' interest in Cuba developed from team president Clark Griffith's prior experience as a barnstormer on the island and as the Cincinnati Reds' manager. The success of Cincinnati's Cuban experiment in 1911 convinced Griffith that there was available talent in Cuba and, equally significant, that a case could be made for their racial eligibility. When Griffith took the Senators' managerial helm in 1912, he attempted to acquire Rafael Almeida and Armando Marsans, who were engaged in disputes with Cincinnati. The Reds eventually resolved their dispute, so Griffith turned his attention elsewhere. The following season Griffith's Senators would have their own pair of Cubans, Merito Acosto and Jacinto Calvo.

Economics factored heavily in the Senators' turn to the Spanish-speaking Americas over the next three decades. Clark Griffith purchased part of the franchise in 1919, and his partners named him team president. He earned a reputation as a miserly executive who had little qualms selling top players to other teams to avoid paying high salaries. This was most clearly seen in 1934, when the Senators finished an extremely disappointing seventh place in the American League a year after having claimed the league pennant. Griffith dismantled his team's roster, selling away several star players. He then hired Joe Cambria as Washington's scout in Latin America, making the Senators the first major-league organization to have an official scout working the Caribbean beat. The Senators evolved into the era's most active major-league organization in Latin America, accounting for over 40 percent of the Latino players (thirteen of thirty) to debut in the majors between 1935 and 1945.

Griffith brought Cambria on board to save Washington money. Their agreement called for Cambria to receive a commission for each Cuban prospect who secured a roster spot with either the Senators or one of its minor-league teams. The arrangement gave Cambria incentive to sign as many prospects as possible—the more players who made the grade, the higher his commission. Over the next twenty-five years Cambria signed over four hundred Cubans.[20]

Cubans welcomed Washington's reliance on their players. Cambria's progress was followed closely on the island. It was national news whenever a Cuban made the Senators' squad. One of the few to criticize Cambria's scouting practices in Cuba was journalist Jess Losada. The Cuban sportswriter accused Cambria of outright exploitation and of signing players "without much concern about the prospect's ultimate chances of making the majors." Losada mocked Cambria as "Christopher Columbus of baseball."[21]

"Papa Joe," as Cambria would become known in Cuba, developed into organized baseball's most influential figure in Latin America during the Jim Crow era. His initial exposure to Cuban talent came when, as an owner of the Baltimore Black Sox, he met Alex Pompez while their teams squared off on the field. Cambria and Pompez formed a working relationship that created opportunities for Latinos to break into organized baseball and that would extend into baseball's integrated era.

After Cambria joined Washington, the two entrepreneurs brought several players from Pompez's Cuban Stars into the Senators organization. Their first such transaction revealed more attention to the cultural adjustment that foreign-born Latinos underwent than Cambria typically received credit for. According to an August 1932 *Washington Post* article, Cambria, after expressing interest in Ysmael "Mulo" Morales, agreed to have Morales continue playing with Pompez's team for the 1932 season "so that he could travel around a bit and pick up a little better English."[22]

Concerned that the New York Giants or the Brooklyn Robins (later Dodgers) would steal the Cuban prospect away, Griffith decided to sign Morales for the 1933 season and let him try out with the Washington Senators. An all-too-familiar problem arose that ultimately doomed Morales's major-league prospects: the *Washington Post* noted that on several occasions Morales was unable to communicate even with Washington's multilingual catcher, Moe Berg, during his brief August stay with the big-league club.[23] The following year Washington sent Morales down to the minors early in spring training; the Cuban would never appear in a major-league game. But the acquisition of Morales helped inspire the pennywise Griffith to bring the Italian American Cambria into the Senators fold.

Cambria and Griffith profoundly shaped the way the major leagues approached the Latin American baseball market. Attracted by the low cost of acquiring foreign-born Latino talent, the Senators signed Cuban players in bulk and came out ahead financially. To be sure, Washington's turn to Cuba and Latin America elicited sharp criticism. *New York World Telegram* sportswriter Joe Williams blasted Griffith for revamping the Senators' approach to filling its team roster. "By opening day Washington will probably be known as the Cuban Giants. . . . There was a time when old Griff used to try to build his club, but that time is gone."[24] Sportswriters for the *Daily Worker* called attention to the way Washington exploited the desire of foreign-born Latinos to break into organized baseball, noting Cambria and Griffith "pioneered in finding capable Cuban and Venezuelan stars, such as Carrasquel and Estalella, at no cost."[25] *Washington Post* columnist Shirley Povich echoed this assessment of Cambria's motivation for signing Cubans: "He has learned that in Cuba ball players can be had cheaply. He clinks a few pesos in their ears and they put their marks on a contract."[26] The tryouts the Senators offered these prospects confirmed the organization's desire to secure them at low cost and little financial risk. A player was typically provided with one-way transportation to Washington's spring training camp with no guarantee of a position in the organization. If the prospect failed, he would have to find his own way home.

PLAYING THE LINES

The case of Roberto Estalella further highlights the economic payoff involved in the Senators' scouting and acquisition of Cuban players. After two years with Cambria's minor-league teams, Washington called Estalella up to the big-league squad in 1935. The transaction, sportswriter Sam Murphy notes, provided an immediate financial payoff to all involved except the Cuban. Clark Griffith stood to gain a major leaguer after an initial investment of $75, the cost of Estalella's transportation to the States and accommodation. Cambria, who owned Estalella's contract, was slated to receive $10,000 for transferring his rights to the Senators.[27] Like the majority of Latinos who followed him into the Senators organization, Estalella received no signing bonus when he signed with Washington. He was, however, one of the few to make good on his chance to break into the majors.

Roberto Estalella's 1935 debut ended a thirteen-year absence of Cubans on the Washington squad. Cuban residents in the U.S. capital came out to Griffith Stadium to celebrate the achievement. As an indicator of the significance attached to a Cuban player's advent on the Senators, Cuba's ambassador to the United States, Guillermo Patterson y de Jauregui, attended the game in which Estalella made his debut and

8. Cuban native Roberto "Bobby" Estalella raised questions about the Washington Senators' signing of Latin American players and their commitment to maintaining the color line. Although the Senators would not have an *accepted* black player until 1954, when fellow Cuban Carlos Paula appeared, many fans, players, and journalists pointed to Estalella's presence on the Senators' roster as evidence that the team's management was toying with the color line. (National Baseball Hall of Fame Library, Cooperstown, New York.)

participated in a postgame celebration by posing with the young Cuban infielder.[28]

When, after three seasons spent mostly in the minors, Estalella returned to the majors in 1939, he drew the noticeable consternation of those who supported the strict policing of the color line. To hard-liners, the Senators had taken liberties with the loophole previously created to admit lighter-skinned players from the Spanish-speaking Americas into the major leagues. Estalella looked different enough from his Cuban predecessors to unsettle those committed to barring black players from organized baseball. Their protest was evidence to *Washington Post* columnist Shirley Povich that "there are many 200 per cent Americans in the big leagues" who "resent the presence of the Cuban ball players, particularly the swarthy ones like Estalella." These Americans included some of Estalella's Senators teammates. John Welaj, a 1939 teammate, recalled that most of the Senators' white players thought Estalella and other Cuban Senators were "black—and they were treated as such."[29] Another Washington teammate, Ossie Bluege, remembered that opponents expressed animosity despite Estalella's friendly demeanor, one teammate telling Estalella, "You might be Cuban, but you're still a nigger sonuvabitch to me."[30]

Suspicions about Estalella's racial status continued to draw comment long after he retired. Commentators relied on their racial knowledge to form their perceptions. "Bobby Estalella definitely was black," stated former *Washington Star* sportswriter Burton Hawkins. "I can't go into [his] heritage, but to look at [him], Estalella was black." Shirley Povich perceived Estalella similarly: "I would characterize [him] as black or seemed to me as black." Even Cuban contemporaries viewed Estalella as unquestionably non-white. Negro-league pitcher Rodolfo Fernández, who played against Estalella in the Cuban winter league, described his compatriot as a "*mulatto capirro*," a very light mulatto.[31]

Washington team officials offered mixed responses when questioned about the Cubans they signed, Estalella in particular. Calvin Griffith, nephew of Clark Griffith who eventually assumed the Senators' top post, invoked racial stereotypes in detailing perceptions teammates and team officials shared about Estalella. "We used to call him the Black Snake," Griffith informed historian Brad Snyder, demonstrating with his hands the size of the Cuban's sexual organ. Griffith thus intimated racial knowledge that the Cuban native indeed had black ancestry—one had only to take a close look. Calvin Griffith also divulged (to his biographer Jon Kerr) the organization's manipulation of racial understandings. "You had to have 'em mixed up. . . . You got a Cuban and you got a Castilian, they were white—true Spanish." "There's no question that some of the ballplayers Mr. Griffith signed had black blood," Calvin Griffith declared. "But nobody said anything about it. So why bring up questions about something that nobody asked about."[32] The retort that "nobody said anything" about the Cuban signings belied the fact that many white and black sportswriters questioned the racial status of most of the Cubans who donned the Senators uniform. A July 1942 *Daily Worker* column claimed Clark Griffith was a master manipulator of the color line, declaring the Old Fox "has already broken down the Jim Crow barrier. He has had Latin-American players who are Negroes on his team for several years."[33]

Sportswriters accused Washington of exploiting fellow big-league franchises' reluctance to confront the Senators about their signing of racially ambiguous Latinos. The Senators went unchallenged for several reasons. First, Washington's foreign-born Latinos were incorporated into organized baseball as nonblack Others. This status kept them from posing the threat African Americans did to the underlying logic and economic rationale of baseball's color line. Second, for most of the time Joe Cambria was scouting for Griffith, Washington was a second-division team that represented no competitive threat in the American League.

AMBIVALENT PARTICIPANTS

The first group of foreign-born Latinos whom Joe Cambria signed presented complications. Late in 1938 the Senators scout signed Alejandro Carrasquel, a tall Venezuelan pitcher in Cuba's professional circuit. Like other Latino players Cambria signed, Carrasquel entered the U.S. playing field unfamiliar and ill prepared to deal with life in the United States. Problems began for the Venezuelan as soon as he attempted to enter the United States in February 1939. Immigration officials, concerned that Carrasquel lacked proof of economic self-sufficiency, detained him for several days until Washington team officials posted a $400 bond.[34]

Matters did not improve much when Carrasquel arrived at the Senators' spring training camp. The Venezuelan pitcher surprised sportswriters not only with his pitching abilities but also with the announcement that he was changing his name. Cambria informed the journalists on hand that the pitcher was to be known as "Al Alexander." The "American name" conferred on the Venezuelan, Shirley Povich reported, was Cambria's attempt to smooth the rough path to acceptance for his latest Latino find.[35] The strategy failed miserably. Sportswriters mocked the effort and continued to call him Carrasquel.

The sporting press's ridicule of the attempt to anglicize Carrasquel's name was part of a broader interrogation of the Venezuelan's personality and physical appearance. The press and even his Senators teammates were hesitant to embrace Carrasquel, described as having "Spanish-Indian ancestry." His unusual physical appearance and unique sense of style constantly amused them. Povich struck a sympathetic tone in 1943 when he faulted Carrasquel's teammates. "They resented the presence of the South Americans. They were fedup [*sic*], in fact, with all the Latins the Washington club was importing." Conditions changed for Carrasquel only when Washington management stepped in and demanded that his teammates give the Venezuelan "some of the common courtesies" they extended to each other.[36]

Initially ambivalent, Senators manager Bucky Harris grew increasingly frustrated with the Cuban players management supplied him. Part of his frustration stemmed from having to devise ways to communicate with his Spanish-speaking players, particularly his Latino pitchers. New York Yankees manager Joe McCarthy witnessed firsthand the maneuvers Harris went through with pitcher Alejandro Carrasquel in a 1939 contest. With the Senators leading by only a run, Harris brought Carrasquel in from the bullpen to face the Yankees with the bases loaded and two outs. Instead of personally delivering the game strategy to his relief pitcher, Harris had to share instructions with third baseman Roberto Estalella, who then relayed them to Carrasquel. McCarthy found humor in the situation: "I don't know what he told him. . . . But, to me, it was the funniest thing that ever occurred in big-league baseball. Our great American game—and they had to have an interpreter to tell the pitcher what to do!"[37]

A tall, hard-throwing Cuban pitcher, Roberto Ortiz, got a quick introduction to the communication barrier in his first spring training with Washington (1940). Described by Joe Cambria as "faster than Walter Johnson and a longer hitter than Jimmy Foxx," Ortiz was asked by manager Bucky Harris what position he wanted to play. The Cuban responded with a blank look; he neither understood nor spoke English. Already frustrated by his previous experiences dealing with Roberto Estalella, Harris turned to Cambria. "You ask this guy whether he's a pitcher or an outfielder." But Cambria, of course, was of no use. "The best he could do was to shout the question in English, to which Ortiz could only respond with a bigger shrug and a blanker look."[38] The extracurriculars involved in communicating with Latino players frustrated Harris and sparked a tirade against them in 1940. "They're trash. They're doing no good and they ain't in place here. They don't fit. They've all got to show me something and show me quick or I'm cleaning out the joint. If I have to put up with incompetents, they better at least speak English."[39]

The hostile reception given Washington's Latino players generated sympathy from Senators fans. Shirley Povich sarcastically described opposing pitchers as being struck with "a great temptation to aim their pitches at the heads of the Islanders" whenever a Cuban Senator stepped into the batter's box.[40] Bucky Harris applauded Washington fans for their support in a May 1942 interview, explaining that theirs "had been the friendliest of greetings to our Cuban and Mexican players," even though Washington was considered "something of a Southern city." Fans were particularly supportive of "Bobby Estalella," who although "quite dark," developed into a fan favorite and for whom they showed "real indignation" whenever they believed an opposing pitcher had purposely hit Estalella with a pitch.[41]

Opposing players made clear to Cuban Senators that entry did not equate with acceptance. In September 1944, over a year before the Brooklyn Dodgers signed Jackie Robinson, players of the St. Louis Browns conveyed this message during a game. St. Louis bench jockeys persistently abused Washington's Latino contingent verbally, claiming that the Cuban players "were of African, rather than Latin, descent."[42] Tired of the season-long insults, the Senators' Roberto Ortiz confronted St. Louis catcher Tom Turner, whom sportswriter Arthur Patterson described as "one of their most aggravating tormentors," in the midst of the pregame batting practice. The six foot, three inch Ortiz planted himself in front of the Browns dugout and called Turner out. The two came to blows, and a full brawl erupted. Ortiz missed several weeks of action after breaking his right thumb in the fight, but the Cuban won the respect and support of his Senators teammates.[43]

The bench jockeying by Browns players made evident that they did not view Ortiz or his Latino teammates as fellow whites. That Ortiz's confrontation with a white player occurred in a segregated institution in a Jim Crow town suggested that he did not exactly occupy a *black* racial position, either. In the Jim Crow South, few deeds were more strictly tabooed than a black man aggressively confronting and physically assaulting a white man—such actions often resulted in mob retaliation. The point here is not that a race riot could have occurred, but that inclusion within organized baseball meant a player occupied something other than a black position on its color line. Ortiz's ability to publicly and physically retaliate captured the intermediate position he and other Latinos held.

MANAGING DIVERSITY

The Washington Senators and Joe Cambria benefited from baseball's ongoing development at the amateur and professional levels in Cuba. Like his Negro-league counterpart Alex Pompez, Cambria constructed a network of contacts who alerted him to potential prospects. This network included Pompez and the first Cuban player Cambria acquired from him, Ysmael Morales. After spending the 1934 season playing with Cambria's Albany minor-league team, Morales alerted Cambria about Roberto Estalella, then performing with the Hershey Plantation team in Cuba's Sugar League.[44] This network grew with each player Cambria signed and with each trip the scout made to Cuba. Word of Cambria's scouting ventures inspired Cuban players to believe they could achieve their dreams of playing in the big leagues.

Upon arrival in the United States, however, Cuban prospects found a system arrayed against them. The baseball diamonds they played on might have had well-manicured fields and modern amenities, but the cultural playing field was strewn with bumps and divots. Latinos had not only to perform on the baseball diamond but also to overcome the cultural challenge. Historian Brad Snyder contends that the Senators and Cambria were largely indifferent to this challenge, subjecting their Latino players to racially hostile environments in the South. Although able to sneak questionable players past the guardians of baseball's color line, Washington team officials still had to find segregated housing for these players in order to comply with local segregation laws in Florida during each spring training and in minor-league towns such as Charlotte, Chattanooga, Panama City (Florida), and Selma.[45]

Institutionally, the Senators were unprepared to deal with the influx of Spanish-speaking Latino players that their scouting activities in Latin America produced. No executive or team official spoke Spanish. Nor did any of the team managers employed from 1935 through the 1950s. That simple fact complicated the incorporation and development of Latino talent. The Latino player's feeling of isolation was immediate. Unable to speak the language on arriving in the United States, he had little or no meal money and had to travel on Jim Crow trains or buses to spring training or to Washington, D.C., to report to the team. Estalella recounted his angst-filled initial trip to Washington, clutching his ticket, fearful of missing his destination, and not yet knowing how to order food. In making his first trip north, Alejandro Carrasquel faced immigration officials in Tampa without a Senators official or translator to guide him through the customs inspection.[46] These players arrived from countries, moreover, that had different racial systems where both physical features *and* social class determined racial positioning. They encountered the various permutations of U.S. racial understanding without any guidance from the Senators—no one in the organization could communicate these lessons to the Cubans in their native tongue. Ysmael Morales had the advantage of a year in the Negro leagues that familiarized him with some of the workings of Jim Crow. Most of the other Latino Senators were not as fortunate.

The Senators eventually implemented a few stopgaps to address the language barrier and aid cultural adjustment. When Cambria arrived at Washington's spring training camp in Orlando with Roberto Ortiz, the Senators called Boston Braves catcher Al López to assist them with the Spanish-speaking pitcher. Although the Senators did not hire bilingual coaches, the team did occasionally acquire catchers who spoke Spanish. In the early 1940s the Senators brought in Italian American Angelo "Tony" Giuliani, a reserve catcher who was able to bridge the language divide in catching for Carrasquel.[47] When Bucky Harris returned for a third stint as Senators manager, he insisted that Washington reacquire Cuban catcher Fermin "Mike" Guerra, who was conversant in English and Spanish. "I simply have to get this Guerra to run my Spanish-speaking pitching staff," Harris informed sportswriter Dan Daniel. "I have no Spanish beyond 'si, si' and there is no English among [Senators pitchers] Sandalio Consuegra, Conrado Marrero, Julio Moreno and the rest of my Cuban-Castilian cast." After the Senators took Guerra back, the Cuban catcher translated for Harris whenever the manager visited a Latino pitcher on the mound or needed to speak with Spanish-speaking players off the field.[48]

Latino players did receive a reprieve once Cambria showed up at spring training camp. Shirley Povich noted that Cambria took the players to dine at Spanish restaurants and bought the "latest rumba records" to keep Carrasquel from being homesick.[49] On the other hand, the organization made no structural changes that would better their Latino prospects' chances of making it through the minors and to the big leagues. Nor did the Senators relocate any of their southern minor-league affiliates to cities that were not segregated. In the end, Washington team officials placed the onus on the Latino players themselves to make cultural adjustments by becoming one another's best resource in learning to live in the world of Jim Crow baseball.

The Senators took advantage of the vagaries of U.S. racial understanding and the indifference of fellow major-league organizations to closely scrutinizing the Latino players whom Washington signed. Cambria's scouting practices ensured that Latin America was constantly represented within organized baseball. In the early 1940s, the Cincinnati

Reds, Brooklyn Dodgers, and New York Giants joined the Senators in acquiring and developing their own handful of Latino prospects. Although not every Latino would make it to the majors, their growing presence in the minor leagues promised greater numbers in the future.[50] Their participation in organized baseball, including the majors, during World War II would continue to provoke the question of why organized baseball maintained a color line in the face of wartime player shortages and the presence of more racially ambiguous Latinos in the circuit.

8

Playing in the World Jim Crow Made

It is no secret that players of suspected Negro parentage have
appeared in big league games. . . . They were presented as
Indians, Cubans, Mexicans, and you name it. Despite the
generally accepted notion that some blacks had passed as
white to enter organized baseball, no proven instances of this
phenomenon exist.

Joe Williams, sportswriter, 1945

IN THE SHADOW OF JIM CROW

Latinos enjoyed their greatest level of participation in U.S. professional
baseball in the 1930s and 1940s, prior to the dismantling of the racial
barrier. The thirty players from the Spanish-speaking Americas who made
their major-league debut between 1935 and 1945 unsettled supporters
of segregation. The Latino presence on either side of baseball's racial barrier, and especially the handful of players who moved back and forth between the Negro leagues and organized baseball, clouded the associations among skin color, race, and exclusion. Those who supported racial
integration pointed to the entry of more racially ambiguous Latinos into
the majors as a positive development, hoping that resistance to integration was diminishing. Those disturbed by the blurred line of exclusion
called for renewed policing of the in-between space along the color line.
This focus on Latinos showed that the segregationists' most salient concern was not that blacks were passing as white but rather that they were
entering organized baseball as Spaniards, Mexicans, or Cubans. The line
between white and black was much clearer for team and league officials
to police than that between a "Negro" and a "bronze-skinned" Cuban.
   Questions about their racial status followed Latinos wherever they

went in organized baseball. Speculation, bench-jockeying, and racial taunting greeted them in the minor-league towns where they gained their first professional stateside experience. But that was tame compared to the openly hostile treatment Latinos confronted on the baseball diamond from those who remained steadfast in opposing their admission to organized baseball. Opposing pitchers hurled brushbacks at them, while other players peppered them with racial epithets from across the diamond. It made for a rough introduction to the big leagues.

The growing presence of Latinos made observers, regardless of their position on the integration question, dubious that all major-league team officials were equally committed to maintaining the color line. Further questions were raised about this commitment when the Senators, Cincinnati Reds, Chicago Cubs, and other organizations turned to foreign-born Latinos to compensate for the player shortage caused by World War II. Organizations that lost major- and minor-league players to military service and defense work protested that teams that used Latin Americans gained an unfair advantage. Others charged that these organizations were overly aggressive in acquiring talent from the Spanish-speaking Americas, claiming that the complexions of the Latino newcomers were noticeably darker. This complaint revealed how suspicions moved from an individual's possible deception—a Latino player attempting to pass for white—to the possible complicity of major-league officials.

Latino participation on either side of baseball's racial divide signaled the continued development of Latin American baseball. New professional leagues in the late 1930s flourished in the Dominican Republic (1937) and Puerto Rico (1938), while the summer schedule of the Mexican League (1937) put it in direct competition with the Negro leagues and the majors. The formation of these leagues marked a shift in North-South baseball relations. Formal participation in the Latin American leagues supplanted the short barnstorming trips in the Caribbean as the primary way North American players played in Latin America. As Latin American leagues began to compete for these players' services, the stakes involved in maintaining segregated baseball in the United States were altered.

For many North Americans, the first recognizable "wave" of Latinos entered the major and Negro leagues in the mid-1930s. Interest in Latino talent increased as the United States mobilized for entry into World War II. All aspects of the nation's economy radically reorganized as factories converted to wartime production of tanks, airplanes, and warships. The federal government called for the rationing of goods and natural resources and, perhaps most significant, drafted U.S. citizens into military service and prioritized available labor for defense industries. The mobilization pressed professional ballplayers who were U.S. citizens into the military or shifted them to defense plants. Major- and Negro-league teams turned to Latin America to replace these departed players, resulting in previously unforeseen levels of Latino participation.

African Americans and Latinos combated Jim Crow's powerful impact on professional baseball, as has been shown, by participating extensively in baseball's transnational circuit. The level of participation in this circuit reveals that the segregation of America's game was more than a national story. Games in Havana, Veracruz, and San Juan had repercussions in Chicago, Philadelphia, and New York and resonated on either side of the racial divide in U.S. professional baseball. Managers, team owners, and league executives marked what transpired in Latin American leagues, especially when these leagues tried to sign away talented African American and white players from the North American leagues.

The Mexican and Caribbean professional leagues served as safe havens for African Americans and others excluded from organized baseball. Here Satchel Paige pitched against talented Negro and major leaguers and Caribbean stars. On these diamonds Martin Dihigo took the mound to face white and black North Americans in games that counted toward league championships, not just the glory of excelling in barnstorming exhibition games. These were showcase contests where Monte Irvin, Max Manning, and Ray Dandridge became local heroes who stood alongside Latino stars Dihigo, "Pancho" Coimbre, Juan "Tetelo" Vargas, and others. In the shadow of Jim Crow, Willie Wells earned the nickname "El Diablo" for his intense play and powerful hitting. Also in that shadow, Wells felt his dignity as a man restored. "I am not faced with the racial problem in Mexico," Wells told *Pittsburgh Courier* sportswriter Wendell Smith. "When I travel with Vera Cruz we live in the best hotels, we eat in the best restaurants and can go anyplace we care to." Comparing life in the Jim Crow North with that in Mexico, Wells concluded: "I've found freedom and democracy here, something I never found in the United States. I was branded a Negro in the States and had to act accordingly. Everything I did, including baseball, was regulated by my color. They wouldn't give me a chance in the big leagues because I was a Negro, yet they accepted every other nationality under the sun."[1]

The vibrant baseball culture created in Cuba, Puerto Rico, and the Dominican Republic built on longstanding social, political, and economic ties between the Spanish-speaking Americas and members of the African diaspora throughout the Americas. Interactions on and around the base-ball diamond mirrored broader imaginings of blackness being forged in the jazz clubs of Havana, New Orleans, and Harlem. The collaboration between Latinos and African Americans on professional teams forged bonds that transcended national boundaries and led some to embrace a transnational blackness, a diasporic consciousness that moved blacks throughout the Americas to join Cubans in their anti-colonial struggles in the 1890s, form organizations such as the Universal Negro Improve-ment Association (UNIA), or enlist on behalf of Ethiopia in the Italian-Ethiopian War (1935).[2] The new imaginings of blackness that these dif-ferent struggles shared challenged narrow definitions of membership while calling for action against entrenched power interests that restricted claims to citizenship on the basis of racial ideologies.

SOUTH FOR THE WINTER

South of the U.S. border the battle against Jim Crow continued. African Americans defied the nefarious "separate but equal" system that afflicted the national game and much of U.S. society by taking their talents to the Mexican League and to Caribbean winter leagues. Latinos likewise dem-onstrated their unwillingness to perform in the Jim Crow baseball cir-cuits by staying south. Together in Latin America blacks and Latinos re-alized dreams denied them elsewhere. The Latin American professional leagues provided them not only a relatively good livelihood but also en-tertainment and relief, even if fleeting, from the slights and indignities imposed by Jim Crow. This is not to say that African Americans or Afro-Latinos did not encounter racism in Latin American points within base-ball's transnational circuit. There were hotels and social clubs in Havana, Santo Domingo, and Mexico City, among other places, where blacks were not welcome regardless of their nationality or social status. The profes-sional leagues, however, welcomed all comers, and success brought glory and money not available in the Jim Crow baseball world.

Involvement in Latin American baseball changed the stakes of par-ticipating in America's game on two fronts. Claims that players outside organized baseball lacked talent were contradicted through firsthand ex-posure. Forced to perform on opposite sides of the racial divide in the United States, white and black North Americans competed together as teammates in Latin America's integrated leagues. Their on-field experi-ence debunked the common justifications for segregation in the States — that whites would refuse to play under black managers, that black catchers would be unable to command white pitchers, or that the quality of play would suffer in an integrated setting.

Opportunities to play in Latin America curtailed the control North American team and league officials exerted over the careers of Negro leaguers. African American ballplayers had been regular participants in Cuba's winter scene since the early 1900s. The professional leagues established in Mexico, the Dominican Republic, Puerto Rico, and Venezuela (1946) provided African Americans the option to perform year-round in Latin America and avoid subjection to the everyday manifestations of Jim Crow in the United States.

The Latin American scene evolved into an African American player's market due to the competition created by the *refuerzo* system.[3] League rules prescribed the number of roster spots earmarked for foreign players (*refuerzos*), typically between two and five per team. As Latin American teams aggressively pursued the best available foreigners, African American players became a highly valued commodity. The *refuerzo* system and the shorter seasons gave Latino baseball greater intensity than the longer U.S. seasons. A *refuerzo* did not have the luxury of working his way out of a prolonged hitting or pitching slump; it was literally "produce or go home." A host of talented Negro leaguers, as pitcher Wilmer Fields and others recall, made hasty departures back to the States when they did not produce.[4] A reputation established while playing in the North created the opportunity; lack of production quickly took it away in the South.

Relationships forged during the Negro-league season provided critical connections that could result in a Latin American wintertime position for African Americans. Latino teammates and team managers helped promising players find a spot on a winter-league team. Joe Black, a hard-throwing right-handed pitcher who started playing in the Negro leagues in 1943, was one of dozens of African American players whose reputation grew through participation in Latino baseball. After serving in World War II, Black emerged as a top hurler with the Baltimore Elite Giants. His first chance to play in Cuba came when New York Cubans pitching coach Rodolfo Fernández, who managed a team in the Cuban League, recommended Black to another Cuban league team when a roster position opened. Thereafter, Black became a regular participant (and a desired commodity) in the Latino winter circuits, pitching in a Caribbean World Series and representing the champion teams of different leagues.[5]

The practice of recommending players introduced new talent at different points within the transnational baseball circuit. Those like Fernández who moved within the circuit had the advantage of learning first-hand about up-and-coming talent. Work coaching or managing in the winter league allowed Latinos and African Americans to recruit promising players. Negro leaguer Quincy Trouppe took full advantage of this opportunity while he was manager of Caguas in the Puerto Rican winter league in the late 1940s. Trouppe signed several young Latino players (Bienvenido Rodríguez, Roberto Vargas, and Rafaelito Ortiz) to the Chicago American Giants, the Negro-league team Trouppe managed. After the Negro National League folded, Trouppe continued to sign promising Latinos whom he managed in the Puerto Rican league, taking an eighteen-year-old Vic Power with him to the Provincial League (Canada) for the 1949 campaign.[6]

The reasons African Americans were attracted to playing professionally in Latin America remained essentially unchanged from the start of the twentieth century. Latin American teams recruited them based on their ability. The money was good, and there was no Jim Crow. Bill Cash made this point clear in reflecting on his years in the Mexican League. "You would be real thirsty and see a water fountain and look above it for the 'White Only' sign and there was none. Water never tasted so good."[7] Freedom from the everyday encounters with Jim Crow endured while participating in the Negro leagues attracted black baseball's best and brightest players to head south.

TWO DIFFERENT FRONTS

Starting in 1937, the Mexican League mounted player raids that challenged the hold the Negro and major leagues had on the sport's top talent. With Mexican oil tycoon Jorge Pasquel coordinating, the Mexican League first raided the Negro leagues, then used the same successful tactics in 1943 to raid major-league teams. Latino players from both sides of the racial divide jumped to Mexico. From the Negro leagues came Martin Dihigo, Silvio García, and Manuel "Cocaina" Garcia, among others. Latino major leaguers Luis Rodríguez Olmo, Roberto Estalella, Roberto Ortiz, and a dozen of their contemporaries joined the Negro-league "jumpers" in Mexico. Indeed, half of the thirty Latinos who made their major-league debut between 1935 and 1945 answered the Mexican League's call.

Intensified competition to acquire the best North American talent translated into higher salaries for African Americans. The lack of a reserve clause to inhibit player movement meant the Negro leagues were hit harder by the Mexican League raid than were the major leagues. Negro-league defections began as soon as the Mexican League adopted a summer schedule in 1937. By April 1941 the Negro leagues had lost thirty-six players to the Mexican League, including future Hall of Famers Josh Gibson, Willie Wells, Monte Irvin, Ray Dandridge, and James "Cool Papa" Bell.[8] Negro-league attempts to enforce a blacklist that penalized players for jumping to the Mexican League backfired. The blacklist kept African Americans and Latinos who had "jumped" south of the border since the salaries Mexican League teams paid easily surpassed what Negro-league owners were either willing or able to pay. Newark Eagles third baseman Ray Dandridge reaped this financial windfall in 1939 when he joined the Mexico City Diablos Rojos for a salary that was reportedly four times more than what Newark paid. Two years later Josh Gibson left the Negro leagues to sign with Veracruz for $6,000, $2,000 more than what the Homestead Grays offered the power-hitting catcher.[9]

Latinos jumped to the Mexican League, in part because they no longer had to engage in the politics of equal pay for play. The lucrative offers from Mexican League teams were a welcome departure from the acrimonious contract negotiations Latinos often had with major-league team officials. Mexican League teams paid Latino major leaguers on par with what they offered white major leaguers based on ability and expected performance. In contrast, major-league officials openly refused to pay Latinos what their white American teammates were paid. This mentality prompted Puerto Rican Luis Rodríguez Olmo to leave the Brooklyn Dodgers after the 1943 season, during which he led the National League in triples and had the highest batting average among Dodger regulars. Brooklyn general manager Branch Rickey was nonetheless adamant in turning down Olmo's contractual demands. Rickey, according to sportswriter Dan Daniel, offered the Puerto Rican outfielder a "ridiculous" annual salary of $7,500 when Olmo was "worth better than twice that." Rickey's offer made the decision to jump to the Mexican League easier; Olmo signed a three-year contract that would reportedly pay US$40,000 over its duration.[10]

The politics of equal pay for play revealed the ethnocentrism that at times guided major-league officials in their contract negotiations with Latinos. These officials avoided paying Latino players the economic value their performance merited. Instead they emphasized the opportunity these "foreigners" were granted by the big-league organization, a negotiating tactic rooted in the notion that foreign-born players should be grateful for this opportunity. The insertion of the player's "foreign" identity in contract negotiations unmasked this ethnocentrism. It was a tactic that other major-league players occasionally encountered in contract negotiations, but without the invocation of their citizenship or ethnoracial status.

Money was not the only factor influencing Latino players' decision to head to the Mexican League. In addition to higher salaries, Mexico provided a more welcoming social climate than what Latino players typically encountered in the United States. There was no segregated train to take to spring training, no need to sleep on the team bus because a Jim Crow hotel refused them a room. Nor did Latinos have to endure the extreme cultural adjustment required to play in the United States; Mexico was a Spanish-speaking country with a familiar cuisine and cultural practices that put these players much more at ease. Responding to the more welcoming environment, Cuban big leaguers Roberto Estalella, Roberto Ortiz, and Gilberto Torres took their entire families to Mexico when they jumped from the major leagues—something they had not done while playing for the Washington Senators.[11]

The Second World War and the Mexican League raids were economic boons for Latino ballplayers. Open roster spots abounded on major-league and Negro-league teams as U.S.-born players departed for military service and work in defense plants. Over seventy major leaguers answered the call for military service in the first year of U.S. military involvement in the war. The following year, 1943, the number more than tripled to more than two hundred. The Mexican League raid further depleted the big-league rosters. The Washington Senators were particularly hard hit, losing Roberto Ortiz, Gilberto Torres, and Adrian Zabala, along with several of their Latino minor leaguers to the Mexican circuit. The New York Giants also suffered losses as Cuban Napoleon Reyes and three of the team's European American players (Sal Maglie, Roy Zimmerman, and George Hausman) departed for Mexico.[12]

The flight of the Mexican "jumpers" was viewed as more injurious since they left for economic reasons rather than to fulfill a patriotic duty. Latino players drew criticism for heading to the Mexican League and, in the case of those who were not U.S. citizens, for not having to serve in the war. The hazing that Latinos typically faced worsened during the war, according to sport historian Phil Hoose. "Not only were they not white and not American," Hoose observes, "but they were considered cowards as well; they were playing while Ted Williams was fighting."[13]

Wartime departures made an impact on both sides of the racial divide. Negro leaguers left the financial insecurity of black baseball for the stability of jobs in defense plants. African American stars Leon Day,

Monte Irvin, and Larry Doby, along with several dozen other Negro leaguers, joined the U.S. military, serving in segregated units stateside and overseas in the European, North African, and Pacific theatres.[14] Negro-league teams turned to Latin America to replace their departed players, resulting in the highest number and widest participation ever of Latinos throughout the black circuit.

Many within the major leagues persistently asked whether it was fair for certain organizations to rely on foreign-born players who were ineligible for military service. These teams, opponents complained, enjoyed a stable player roster while the majority of major-league organizations suffered drastic hits to their major- and minor-league squads. More to the point, protesters contended that supporting the war effort should not place an organization at a competitive disadvantage. Initially, neither the major-league commissioner nor the federal government responded favorably to the protests.

The federal government finally took action in April 1944, after Senators scout Joe Cambria declared the team's Latin American players who entered the United States on six-month visas "immune to any draft regulations in this country." Cambria's declaration rekindled the outcry about the military draft's unequal impact. The Selective Service Commission clarified its policy shortly thereafter, classifying Latin Americans who entered the United States to play professional baseball as "resident aliens" who faced the choice of registering for the draft within ten days of their arrival or leaving the United States when their six-month work visas expired.[15] The policy clarification had its most significant impact on the Senators, who opened their 1944 spring training camp with sixteen Latino players vying to make the roster: eleven Cubans, two Puerto Ricans, two Mexicans, and a Venezuelan. The possibility of being pressed into a foreign country's military service proved incentive enough for three Cuban players (Fermin Guerra, Roberto Ortiz, and Gilberto Torres) to immediately return to Cuba.[16]

FILLING THE SHORTAGE

The peculiar status Latinos occupied in U.S. society and professional baseball became increasingly significant as the world war continued. Acquired to replace players who had been drafted into the war effort, the Chicago Cubs' Spanish-speaking battery of Puerto Rican pitcher Hiram "Hi" Bithorn and Cuban catcher Salvador "Chico" Hernández would develop into a curiosity. Shared identity as Latinos was part of the repertoire for the pair, who had previously teamed up as members of the Pacific Coast League's Los Angeles Angels. Chicago manager Jimmy Wilson tried to capitalize on their public familiarity by inserting Hernández behind the plate whenever the Puerto Rican pitcher took the mound during the 1942 and 1943 seasons.

Cultural practice set the pair apart from most major leaguers, their act of openly conversing in Spanish on the field making them the subject of fan and press curiosity. A boxed item, "Castilian Signal Code," that accompanied a May 1943 story on Hernández in the *Sporting News* translated the signals and instructions the Cuban catcher used with the Puerto Rican pitcher.[17] The Cubs' Latino pair learned that different tactics were required when an opposing team included Spanish-speaking players or coaches. When the Cubs faced the New York Giants, manager Mel Ott decided to insert Adolfo Luque as the Giants' third-base coach, knowing Luque could translate the pitches Hernández called out from behind the plate and relay them to Giants batters.[18]

Unlike the majority of the era's Latino major leaguers, Hiram Bithorn entered the U.S. playing field as a U.S. citizen—a status conferred on island-born Puerto Ricans through the Jones Act of 1917. Thus eligible for the U.S. military draft, the Puerto Rican pitcher faced greater pressure than foreign-born Latinos did to join the war effort. In December 1943 Bithorn answered the call by enlisting in the U.S. Navy, where he would serve for two years.[19] Bithorn's departure left the Chicago Cubs with little need for a Spanish-speaking catcher. Cut loose by the Cubs, Hernández headed to the Mexican League rather than return to the minors. After two seasons in Mexico, he signed with the Negro leagues' Indianapolis Clowns in 1945, joining the small list of Latinos who performed on both sides of the racial divide in the Jim Crow era.

Whereas Hernández later performed in the Negro leagues, Bithorn was the subject of suspicions and racial taunting while in the National League.[20] Matters reached a boiling point during a 1942 game against Brooklyn. *New York Age* reported that "colored spectators" who attended the game heard Dodgers manager Leo Durocher shout "black," "Negro," and worse at Bithorn after the "swarthy Puerto Rican" pitcher threw a couple of "bean balls" at Dodger batters. When the Cubs manager pulled Bithorn out of the game, the Puerto Rican went into "a frenzy of indignation" and threw a ball into the visitor's dugout. Given the racial overtones and the ongoing war, the incident demanded comment from league officials. In a move to perhaps mute ongoing tensions about the increased presence of Latinos, major-league commissioner Judge Kennesaw Mountain Landis felt compelled to declare, as he would on numerous occasions, that there was "no ban in organized baseball against the use of colored players, either by rule or by agreement or by subterfuge."[21]

A season after sparking the ire of Hiram Bithorn, the Dodgers had their own Puerto Rican in uniform, outfielder Luis Rodríguez Olmo. Like his Puerto Rican compatriot, Olmo's appearance in the big leagues unsettled some baseball followers while delighting those who pressed for integration. The reception the Dodgers gave Olmo at the 1943 spring training camp pleased sportswriters at the *Daily Worker*. "The Dodgers, much to their credit, have taken Olmo as an equal, without giving much thought to the fact that his skin is colored," the paper reported on March 30. Their optimism sparked by Olmo's acceptance, the *Daily Worker*'s integration crusaders assured readers: "Certainly Olmo's example is enough to give impetus to the drive to get Negroes into the major leagues. Great Negro stars would be as welcome on the Dodgers as Olmo. That is a dead certainty."[22]

Those who policed the major league's racial borders curbed such enthusiasm. By August of Olmo's rookie year the sportswriters at the *Daily Worker* had changed their tune, complaining bitterly that "the whole business, in fact, smells of hypocrisy." The *Daily Worker* blasted Dodgers officials who "feign ignorance" about the race matter while the organization signed Olmo out of the Puerto Rican league, "which was composed of brown-skinned people and Negroes [and] Olmo himself is brown-skinned."[23] The paper's comment on Olmo's racial status shows that the category "brown" justified the inclusion of suspect Latinos in organized baseball yet also worked to maintain black exclusion.

Unshaken, the *Daily Worker* continued an aggressive campaign against organized baseball's hypocritical racial policy. The newspaper published the mailing addresses of major-league commissioner Judge Landis and team officials so that fans could write and press for integration. Other sportswriters and publications increased the pressure on big-league teams by invoking the spirit of the *Pittsburgh Courier*'s Double V campaign—"Victory at home, victory abroad." Journalists resorted to new pressure tactics to secure tryouts for black players. On April 6, 1945, African American sportswriter Joe Bostic appeared at the Dodgers' spring training camp at Bear Mountain, New York, with Negro leaguers Terris McDuffie and Dave "Showboat" Thomas and demanded that Brooklyn try the two out. Brooklyn complied but offered the two no contracts. Political pressure from Boston city councilman Isadore Muchnick and African American sportswriters produced another set of tryouts in

Boston on April 16. The Red Sox passed on signing the three Negro leaguers brought by the press: Jackie Robinson, Marvin Williams, and Sam Jethroe. The barrier to African Americans remained firmly in place.[24]

As made evident in the *Daily Worker*'s comments on Olmo and the Cubans on the Washington Senators, the campaign to integrate organized baseball was partly inspired by the inconsistent, if not hypocritical, inclusion of Latino players. The brevity of Tomás "Tommy" de la Cruz's big-league career generated much speculation about whether the Cincinnati Reds had circumvented the color line in signing a Latino player with African ancestry. Certainly the Cuban right-hander was not so light-skinned as the majority of Latinos who preceded him. Cubans were well aware that the family backgrounds of de la Cruz and fellow Cuban Roberto Estalella included relatives with African ancestry.[25] Speculation about de la Cruz's racial eligibility was not unwarranted. Although sporting papers described him as being "of Spanish descent," de la Cruz got his professional start in the United States in 1934 with Alex Pompez's Havana Cuban Stars.[26] After the 1934 season, he left Pompez's club to join Joe Cambria's Albany minor-league team. The pitcher would languish in the minors for nine seasons, making only brief spring training appearances with the Senators and the New York Giants.[27]

No big-league team would risk bringing up de la Cruz until the wartime player shortage. When the Cincinnati Reds signed the Cuban pitcher, he compiled a decent 1944 season, splitting eighteen decisions and logging the fourth-highest number of innings pitched for the third-place club. His 1944 season ended early when, according to newspaper reports, he returned to Cuba in mid-August to serve in the Cuban Army.[28] When Cincinnati's 1945 spring training camp opened, de la Cruz was not among those attending. The Cuban right-hander had decided to jump to the Mexican League; he would not return to the majors again.

BLURRING THE LINE

The end of World War II resulted in overhauls of major-league team rosters. Players who had served in the military or taken defense jobs returned to claim their roster spots. Their return made expendable the majority of Latino players who had entered the majors during the war. Although major-league officials did not openly recognize it as a concern, the looser criteria by which certain organizations had signed Latinos to fill their rosters could potentially breed conflict on the postwar major-league teams. African Americans had already raised the issue of fairness during the war. Proclaiming their U.S. citizenship, patriotism, and military service, a chorus of African American sportswriters protested the hypocrisy of major-league owners in signing so many foreign-born Latinos while still excluding blacks. This was the issue for *New York Age* sportswriter Buster Miller, who sounded off against the "patriotic ownership" of big-league clubs that fielded an "unprecedented number" of Latin Americans "rather than break their own private jim-crow agreement against hiring Negro players."[29]

The official denials of any restrictive covenant to bar blacks from the big leagues provoked calls for honesty. On one hand, observers witnessed Tommy de la Cruz hurling for the Cincinnati Reds, Roberto Estalella batting for the Senators, and dozens of other Latinos performing in big-league uniform. Visually, it seemed the line between inclusion and exclusion had continued to shift throughout the war. New York sportscaster Art Rust Jr., a teenager living in Harlem during the war, recalled that the Washington Senators' teams during 1930s and 1940s were "loaded with Latin players of a darker hue," who got away with it "because they spoke Spanish."[30] Other African American columnists shared this perception that Clark Griffith had sneaked in Cuban players with African ancestry. "Sepia sportsmen contend that Negroes have been playing in the big leagues for some time," claimed a July 1942 *New York Age* column, listing Estalella, Alejandro Carrasquel, and Hiram Bithorn among the suspicious entrants.[31] That their skin color did not exclude these questionable Latinos prompted supporters of integration to question the obvious inconsistency. Why would the major leagues exclude a talented player like Roy Campanella, who was half African American and half Italian and not dark-skinned, while permitting de la Cruz, a Cuban native of similar skin color, to enter the major leagues? The relative privileged status extended to Latinos during the war even drew comment from integration pioneer Jackie Robinson after his playing days ended. "Few of them could speak English and none of them had been American citizens for any length of time," Robinson remarked, "but Clark Griffith for some reason considered them more acceptable than North Americans."[32]

The machinations that major-league teams performed to legitimize the incorporation of darker-skinned Latinos left a lasting impression on baseball insiders. Howie Haak, a longtime Pittsburgh Pirates scout who combed the Spanish-speaking Caribbean for talent over four decades, expressed suspicions about de la Cruz many times. According to Haak, major-league teams devised a form to circumvent the color line and defend their signing of questionable Latinos. Yet while the form stated

"Latin" players were of "white ancestry," it could not hide the truth as Haak saw it: "Tommy De La Cruz [sic] was as black as they came."[33]

The unresolved issue of the Mexican League player raids made relations between Latin American professional baseball and the major leagues acrimonious. Major-league officials labeled the Mexican circuit an "outlaw" league—a label "long distasteful to Mexicans, especially when applied by Americans," noted *Washington Post* columnist Shirley Povich. The refusal of major-league commissioner Albert "Happy" Chandler to negotiate with Mexican baseball officials puzzled observers who pointed out that the Mexican League might have raided the major-league rosters, but it was not without precedent among executives in U.S. professional baseball. "The same sort of tactics were used by the American League in its war with the National early in the century," Povich pointed out.[34] Negro-league owners and executives were perhaps just as perplexed by Chandler, especially given his public position, when the Brooklyn Dodgers raided the Kansas City Monarchs' roster to sign Jackie Robinson in October 1945.

The major leagues minimized the racial issue, even as they reached into Latin America for talent to replace their departed players. When Latin American leagues reached north to acquire talent, it sparked a battle that would have postwar repercussions on baseball. The major leagues formed a multilevel response to the Mexican League's encroachment on their talent pool. At the individual level, the major leagues blacklisted all players from organized baseball who jumped their contract to play in Mexico. Chandler attacked the raid on an organizational level as well when, after the 1946 regular season, he extended the blacklist to include all those who performed in any professional game against ineligible players.

Chandler's expansion of the ban perplexed Cuban baseball officials. The major leagues' revised policy prohibited the Cuban circuit from hiring its native sons who played summers in the Mexican League. The policy also prevented Cubans who played organized baseball during the regular season from participating in the Cuban winter circuit if it included blacklisted Latinos. The major leagues' position represented a stark reversal of the way Cuba had made its baseball talent available to the majors just a few years earlier. "We in Cuba feel that baseball was perfectly willing to use our 100 Cuban players during the war, when there was a manpower shortage," Cuba's national director of sports, Luis Orlando Rodríguez, complained, "but now that the war is over they are through with us."[35]

While the front offices warred, blacklisted players who wanted to return to organized baseball had to find new places to play until the ban was lifted. One of the first Mexican jumpers, Danny Gardella, challenged the blacklist by filing a lawsuit against Chandler and major-league baseball to be reinstated. Other blacklisted players joined barnstorming teams that competed against local clubs throughout the United States. A number of players headed north to Canada to play in the Quebec Provincial League. Latinos had additional options, although not all of them paid as well as the majors. Former Chicago Cubs catcher Sal Hernández headed for the Negro leagues, where he joined returning Latino Negro leaguers Silvio García, Alejandro Crespo, and others during the following seasons.

Upon their return, players discovered that the terms of participation in the U.S. playing field had begun to change. The Mexican League player raid had exposed vulnerabilities in the Major Leagues' Jim Crow policy. The action that had taken place in the Mexican League and in the Caribbean winter leagues had showcased the abundant talent available outside organized baseball, and the flight to the Mexican League demonstrated that some white major leaguers were quite willing to perform in integrated settings. The signing of Jackie Robinson opened the possibility that these players could again perform in integrated leagues, but this time it would be in the United States.

PART THREE

BEYOND INTEGRATION

9

Latinos and Baseball's Integration

When I played baseball, I was neither white nor black, and
the white fans loved me, but after the game I was just another
colored guy in town.

Vic Power

Minnie Minoso is to Latin ballplayers what Jackie Robinson
is to black ballplayers. He was the first Latin American
baseball player to become what in today's language is a
"superstar."

Orlando Cepeda

LATINOS AS INTEGRATION PIONEERS?

When integration is revisited with the understanding that it was a process and not a moment of instantaneous change, the important precedent established through the signing of Latinos comes into sharper focus.
Assuredly, major-league team officials contemplated, if ever so briefly,
signing African American players before Branch Rickey signed Jackie
Robinson. Rickey's willingness to break from the gentleman's agreement
separated him from his peers in major-league front offices. But the history Rickey drew on in making his decision to break from convention
remains a critical consideration in assessing the process of integration.
Such an assessment requires considering how contemporaries in baseball circles viewed the transformation of America's game: who did they
perceive as participants in its transformation, what did they view as the
most significant obstacles, and what antecedents did they draw on in integrating the game? This approach yields an appreciation of how players from the Spanish-speaking Americas acted as test subjects in a bat-

tle over the color line's exclusionary point in the almost half century leading up to baseball's "great experiment."

Integration initiated a significant shift in the social relations of all
Americans. The story of baseball's integration has justifiably focused on
the 1947 campaign and the drama of Jackie Robinson. As historians Jules
Tygiel, Howard Bryant, and Bruce Adelson, among others, have documented, the path toward integration was neither swift nor smooth. For
most Latino ballplayers, however, integrated baseball was not a novel
experience. Professional leagues in the Caribbean and Mexico were all
racially inclusive, and most foreign-born Latinos developed their skills
while participating in these integrated leagues prior to entering the U.S.
playing field. This experience gave Latinos an advantage that most North
American players, white or black, lacked. It also shaped their expectations about what playing professionally in the States would be like once
the racial barrier was dismantled.

The official start of racial integration created new opportunities while
posing unique challenges to Latinos. Integration allowed all Latinos to
enter straightway into organized baseball. This placed a number of them
in the role of racial pioneer—the first player of color to integrate minor-
league teams in towns such as Lake Charles, Louisiana; Kokomo, Indiana; and Walla Walla, Washington—or in the cases of Minnie Miñoso,
Nino Escalera, Carlos Paula, and Ozzie Virgil, as integration pioneer on
major-league teams. In the following list of integration pioneers, names
of Latino players are italicized.

Year	Team	First Black Player
1947	Brooklyn Dodgers	Jackie Robinson
1947	Cleveland Indians	Larry Doby
1947	St. Louis Browns	Willard Brown, Hank Thompson
1949	New York Giants	Hank Thompson
1950	Boston Braves	Sam Jethroe
1951	Chicago White Sox	*Minnie Miñoso*
1953	Philadelphia A's	Bob Trice
1953	Chicago Cubs	Gene Baker, Ernie Banks
1954	St. Louis Cardinals	Tom Alston
1954	Pittsburgh Pirates	Curt Roberts
1954	Cincinnati Reds	*Nino Escalera*

1954	Washington Senators	*Carlos Paula*
1955	New York Yankees	Elston Howard
1957	Philadelphia Phillies	John I. Kennedy
1958	Detroit Tigers	*Ozzie Virgil Sr.*
1959	Boston Red Sox	Pumpsie Green

The idea that Latinos were integration pioneers broadens who exactly participated in this process. Interrogation of the meaning that contemporaries attached to Latino participants challenges modern assumptions that Latinos were tangential to the process. Long before Jackie Robinson signed with the Dodgers, African American journalists had pointed to the presence of racially ambiguous Latinos in organized baseball as indicative of big-league officials' racial hypocrisy and unfair policing of the color line. Indeed, many Latinos had endured the trials of being the first player of color on minor- and big-league clubs prior to 1947. Similarly, after Jackie Robinson had begun dismantling the racial barrier, black Latinos like Minnie Miñoso and Vic Power continued to confront the racism that was part of the legacy of Jim Crow baseball.

Miñoso and Power and the black Latinos who followed them broke into organized baseball not only as black men but also as Latinos, requiring cultural adjustments that further complicated their place in this integration generation. Their cultural practices and ethnic backgrounds added another dimension that teams, the sporting press, and those involved in the local scene took into account. The experiences of Vic Power, Minnie Miñoso, and other darker-skinned Latinos demonstrate that the conclusion of this integration process was not guaranteed or highly anticipated. Just as significant, Latinos who participated as integration pioneers after 1947 continued to face many of the same cultural constraints encountered by those who preceded them into the majors, and also mirrored what everyday Latinos faced in their interactions in U.S. society.

The collective profile of the fifty-five players from the Spanish-speaking Americas who entered the majors before the official start of racial integration (see the appendix) reveals that the Caribbean was the most popular source of talent. Given baseball's long history in Cuba, it is not surprising that Cubans constituted the majority (thirty-nine) of pre-integration Latinos in the big leagues. In total, these major leaguers represented six different countries: eight U.S-born players (whose ancestors were from Mexico or Spain), three Mexican natives, two Puerto Ricans, two Venezuelans, one Colombian, and one player born in Spain but raised in Cuba.

9. Osvaldo "Ozzie" Virgil in his New York Giants uniform. The Dominican-born Virgil's family migrated to New York, where he attended high school before signing with the Giants. In September 1956 Virgil became the first Dominican native in the majors. Traded to the Detroit Tigers organization, he pioneered racial integration in the Motor City, appearing as the team's first black player. (National Baseball Hall of Fame Library, Cooperstown, New York.)

The regional character of Jim Crow and local racial customs did not influence which organizations acquired these players. With their predilection for foreign-born Latinos acquired on the cheap, the Washington Senators—despite being based in a segregated city—led organized baseball in the incorporation of players from the Spanish-speaking Americas. Out of the fifty-five Latinos who appeared in the majors during the Jim Crow era, nearly one-fourth made their debut with the Senators. Cincinnati followed with six Latinos making their initial appearance with that club. In total, thirteen of the sixteen major-league organizations that existed between 1902 and 1947 had at least one Latino debut in their uniform. Surprisingly, only twenty-two players (40 percent) started their major-league careers on teams from "the North"—in this case, New York, Boston, Philadelphia, and Pittsburgh. Nearly as many players began their careers with southern-based teams: twenty between Washington and St. Louis, twenty-five if Cincinnati is included.

Talent alone did not guarantee a Latino an opportunity to play in the majors in the pre-integration era. Without question, the more talented Latinos were playing outside organized baseball during this earlier period. Indicative of their sheer numbers and their greater ability, over twenty different Latinos appeared in the East-West Classic in the Negro leagues between 1933 and 1947, while only Al Lopez (twice) and Lefty Gómez (seven times) appeared on major-league all-star teams. The black baseball circuit, moreover, featured Hall of Famers from the Caribbean José Méndez, Cristobal Torriente, and Martin Dihigo, while only Adolfo Luque established himself as a significant big-league contributor. The majority of Latinos who appeared in the majors were primarily reserves or players who enjoyed brief call-ups. Approximately a third (eighteen) appeared in only one season.

CAMPAIGNING FOR INTEGRATION

As the war came to a close, the sporting press and advocates of racial integration gave increased attention to Latino participation in the major leagues and their affiliated minor leagues. Shirley Povich, Lester Rodney, and the *New York Daily News'* Jimmy Powers, among other white sportswriters, wrote about the Latino presence in discussing the unfairness of organized baseball's continued exclusion of black players. Such black sportswriters as Sam Lacy, Wendell Smith, and Dan Burley pointed to the wider inclusion of Latinos in calling for integration. Collectively, they wondered why major-league officials from Commissioner Landis on down to team officials allowed a seemingly more diverse group of foreign-born Latino players into the majors, maintaining all the while that no rule or agreement, formal or otherwise, barred African Americans. Locally, sportswriters counteracted the leagues' official stance by pressuring major-league teams. In New York City, sportswriters openly suggested that if the Brooklyn Dodgers and New York Giants signed African American players such as Buck Leonard, Josh Gibson, Ray Dandridge, and "Wild" Bill Wright, their stagnant franchises would be revived. In so doing, they argued for integration based on an economic benefit analysis, in addition to social justice.[1]

The pressure exerted by civil rights activists, sportswriters, and fans on New York City's major-league teams built on the wartime contributions of African American citizens to the Allied effort. The black press lauded the courage and wartime achievements of African American soldiers. Yet it also continued to prick the national conscience with the contradictory images of African American soldiers courageously fighting for victory abroad while serving in segregated units, and of African American migrants at home meeting resistance in the urban North as they sought entry to shop floors, scarce public housing, or residential neighborhoods. The power of these images compelled integration supporters to renew their efforts on behalf of the Double V campaign. The campaign was therefore simultaneously local, national, and international. And the national pastime was a forum in which the inconsistencies in American discourses on racial equality, and the lived reality of race riots and segregation, would become glaringly obvious.

A big-league official's role in the acquisition of Latino talent prior to 1947 did not necessarily indicate his role in baseball's integration. Although both Clark Griffith and Branch Rickey had previously signed Latino players, the two firmly planted themselves on opposite sides of integration. Griffith condemned Rickey's pursuit of integration. Publicly Griffith called for allowing the Negro leagues to build themselves up as professional operations and for African Americans to "lend all of their efforts to developing their own National and American leagues." "If properly organized and officered," the Negro leagues could, he predicted in 1943, eventually "take their place in the annals of baseball." This position, historians have rightly argued, was no doubt influenced by the money the Senators earned by renting Griffith Stadium to the Homestead Grays and other Negro-league teams. Calvin Griffith later acknowledged that these rentals "kept us [the Senators] in the game. We used to make, back in those days, thirty-five, forty thousand dollars a year maybe off of 'em."[2]

Clark Griffith presented himself as a defender of the Negro leagues while he publicly supported the continuation of segregation. Negro-league owners were in an unenviable position. They disapproved of Rickey's approach to integration while not necessarily opposing integration itself. Griffith publicly took up the Negro-league owners' cause. "While it is true that we have no agreement with Negro leagues—National and American—we still can't act like outlaws in taking their stars," Griffith informed reporters. "If Brooklyn wanted to buy Robinson from Kansas City, that would be all right, but contracts of Negro teams should be recognized by organized baseball." Two days after the historic 1945 signing of Robinson, Rickey provided an entirely different portrayal of the Negro leagues in response to Griffith's criticism of the "ethics" of obtaining players from another league. "The Negro organizations in baseball are not leagues, nor, in my opinion, do they have even organization. As at present administered they are in the nature of a racket."[3] With this depiction Rickey attempted to vindicate himself in the court of public opinion for not compensating the Kansas City Monarchs for the talented Robinson.

The questionable status of the Cubans whom Griffith had previously signed was also inserted into the verbal skirmish between the two stalwart baseball officials. In the face of Griffith's continuing public opposition to Rickey's signing of Robinson, the Dodgers general manager accused Griffith of having already used "Negroes" on his Senators ball club. "Griffith had already hired blacks," Rickey remarked in a 1945 exchange with veteran sportswriter Red Smith, adding sarcastically, "Hiring Negroes was nothing new to Clark Griffith." Red Smith inferred from Rickey's remark that "there was a Senegambian somewhere in the Cuban batpile where Senatorial timber is seasoned." Giving a new twist to an old saying, Smith expressed what many had long suspected: Clark Griffith's team had ushered in at least one Cuban player with African ancestry into the major leagues.[4]

Accusations that Griffith's Cuban Senators had encroached on the racial forbidden zone were also made in the *Daily Worker* throughout the 1940s. Relentless in advocating for integration in their columns, sportswriters Lester Rodney and Nat Low pointed to Clark Griffith's track record of signing Latino players. A September 14, 1942, column declared that Griffith had manipulated the major leagues' racial system by admitting "at least one and perhaps two Cubans of Negro descent on his team."[5] Griffith, not surprisingly, disagreed, insisting that these Cubans were not black.[6] In the case of Roberto Estalella, the Senators' top executive insisted that the Cuban infielder was born of "Spanish" parents. This claim countered those who, reading the telltale signs in his physical appearance, would argue that he also had African ancestry.[7]

Branch Rickey himself might have drawn some inspiration from Griffith's signing of Cuban players. Rickey, according to anecdotal accounts, briefly contemplated signing a darker-skinned Latino when he was formulating his integration plans. Spring training stints in Havana in 1941 and 1942 piqued Rickey's interest in Latino players while familiarizing him with talent performing outside organized baseball. By October 1942, under Rickey's administration the Dodgers had begun to sign lighter-skinned Latinos—Puerto Rican native Luis Rodríguez Olmo would later become the first of these prospects to make the Dodgers squad. But it was Afro-Cuban star infielder Silvio García who reportedly interested Rickey as a potential pioneer to dismantle baseball's racial barrier. Well known in black baseball circles as a member of Alex Pompez's New York Cubans, García's strong performance as a centerpiece of the Cuban All-Stars during their spring training encounters with the Dodgers in 1943 confirmed Rickey's scouting reports that García had major-league talent.[8]

Baseball historians have developed a number of explanations for the Dodgers' decision not to sign García. Peter Bjarkman contends that Rickey was probably dissuaded by García's advanced age and an investigation into his lifestyle and personality, which revealed a "considerable affinity for night life and the hated demon rum." The most apocryphal explanation focused on the Cuban infielder's temperament. According to Cuban journalist Edel Casas, Rickey held a one-on-one meeting with García in which the Dodgers executive allegedly asked the Cuban star how he would respond in a physical confrontation with a white American player. García's reported response: "I kill him."[9] Casas's account indicates that García lacked not only the right skin color but also the right personality to deal with the virulent racism entrenched in the majors. Playing integrated baseball was nothing new to García, a proud man who had faced off against white American players in Cuba and Mexico. To him and other Latinos who developed their skills in integrated settings, racial insults on the diamond were intolerable. On and off the field, cultural difference thus distinguished García and other darker-skinned Latinos from Jackie Robinson. As a college-educated, U.S.-born African American, Robinson had encountered the slights and insults of Jim Crow many times, and for him, such affronts were part of growing up in a society divided by de facto and de jure forms of Jim Crow.

Importantly, signing a darker-skinned Latino like García would not have obliterated the racial ideas that had sustained the most persistent function of baseball's color line—exclusion of African Americans. Although García was clearly black, his Cuban nationality would only have reinforced the ambiguity major-league organizations like the Washington Senators and Cincinnati Reds had established by signing players from the Spanish-speaking Americas. More particularly, it would have only partly debunked the commonplace justification for the presence of Latinos such as Roberto Estalella and Tommy de la Cruz that these players were Cuban, not black.

TALENT DRAIN

The Dodgers' signing of Robinson launched a frontal assault on organized baseball's segregationist practices. By agreeing to become the twentieth century's first African American major leaguer, Robinson consented to facing the hostility of segregationists, dealing with institutionalized racism in professional baseball and U.S. society, and enduring media and fan scrutiny. His ascent from the minors to the Dodgers in April 1947 introduced a level of racial proximity and intimacy not previously encountered in major-league circles. Countless Americans entered a new realm of social experience as Robinson's arrival inspired thousands of black fans to attend major-league games throughout the National League circuit, a scene that would be repeated with Larry Doby's entry into the American League later in 1947. Increased black attendance initiated both a shift toward interracial crowds at major-league stadiums and a transformation of the public culture of attending sporting events.

The experience of signing players from the Spanish-speaking Americas provided a blueprint for approaching racial integration. Expanded access during the Second World War meant that Latinos who a generation earlier may have been barred were appearing with major-league teams. Just as significant, although Branch Rickey and Clark Griffith might have disagreed about the appropriateness of pursuing racial integration, the two nonetheless followed the same approach when it came to Griffith's signing of questionable Latino players and Rickey's 1945 signing of Robinson. The two did not secure prior approval from officials from other clubs before making their signings—they just did it.

Rickey purposely timed the launch of baseball's great experiment. It came almost a year after Commissioner Landis's death in November 1944. Ever emphatic that the major leagues had no rule or agreement barring blacks, Landis had been viewed as the biggest obstacle to racial integration. *Daily Worker* columnist Lester Rodney insisted that Landis, whether through direct mandate or conscious inaction, prevented the majors from pursuing integration. "If you ask any honest sportswriter, he will tell you Landis was a racist," Rodney told baseball historian Larry Lester in an interview. As commissioner, Rodney said, Landis could at any point have declared, "Something is wrong with this game. As Commissioner I am going to change it." Sportswriter Wendell Smith took the same stance following Landis's death. "Perhaps he was exactly what he appeared to be—a Gibraltar of Honesty. But I cannot help feel that Mr. Landis never set his teeth into the question of Negroes in the majors with the same zest that he did other problems which came under his jurisdiction," Smith wrote candidly in December 1944. "The fact remains he never used his wide and unquestionable powers to do anything about the problem."[10]

Robinson's 1945 signing with the Dodgers organization opened opportunities for African American and Latino players to enter organized baseball. The talent drain caused by shifts in organized baseball's practice of signing Latinos was a familiar problem for Alex Pompez. Since the early 1930s the Cuban American entrepreneur had arranged the transfer of players into organized baseball through his dealings with Joe Cambria. Since 1938 his New York Cubans had also dealt with Mexican League teams signing away players. Seeing the major leagues tap into his primary source of talent frustrated the veteran team owner months before the Dodgers launched their integration experiment. In June 1945 Pompez publicly expressed his annoyance with the evolving signing practices of major-league clubs: "The big league teams are taking most of them now, and I have a very small field to pick from. There was a time when I could get all I wanted, but theese [sic] Cincinnati Reds, Washington Sen-atoors [sic] and minor league teams are taking them like anything."[11]

Negro-league teams that extended their reach into the Caribbean were the first to feel the impact of the major leagues' changed signing practices. Due to his prominent role in signing Latino players, Alex Pompez's New York Cubans would be the most affected of the Negro-league teams. Hit with player losses, Pompez responded in typical fashion, intensifying his scouting efforts throughout the Caribbean and Latin America in order to keep the New York Cubans competitive. His success in acquiring, and in some cases reacquiring, Latino players helped his club surge to the top of league standings. Among the young talent he added to the Cubans' roster were infielder Orestes Miñoso, pitcher José Santiago, catcher Rafael "Ray" Noble, and outfielder Edmundo "Sandy" Amoros; all four would later perform in the major leagues. Pompez also convinced talented Latino players Claro Duany, Lorenzo "Chiquitín" Cabrera, Silvio García, and Alejandro Crespo to leave the Mexican League and join the New York Cubans. The Cubans thus featured a revamped roster in 1947 with returning players from Mexico and fresh talent from the Caribbean.

The 1947 season was a historic one on a number of levels for Latino ballplayers and fans. In addition to the launch of baseball's integration, the year also saw the high-water mark for Pompez and his New York Cubans. Competitive from opening day, the Cubans finished the first half of the Negro National League in second place behind the Newark Eagles but surged in the second half to claim the NNL pennant and qualify to face the Negro American League champs Cleveland Buckeyes for the Negro League World Series.

The Cubans' dream season featured incredible pitching, with the ageless wonder Lefty Tiant going undefeated (10–0) in regular-season action, and fellow left-hander Pat Scantlebury enjoying his best Negro-league campaign, garnering all-star consideration while winning ten games. Given the excellent pitching of Tiant, Scantlebury, and longtime ace David Barnhill throughout the 1947 regular season, some observers awaited a low-scoring series with the Buckeyes. But the New York Cubans' big three did not pitch up to expectations as Pompez's aggregation sought to claim its first Negro League World Series championship.

The Cubans' quest for the NLWS flag opened at the Polo Grounds. The opening game ended in a rain-shortened 5–5 tie with Cleveland roughing up Barnhill, who left the game trailing 5 to 0 in the second inning. The big bats Pompez had acquired came through as Cabrera's run-scoring double led a three-run outburst that tied the game in the fifth inning, before torrential rains prompted the umpire to call the game in the sixth.[12] Cleveland took an initial advantage with a 10–7 victory in the series' first completed game, where the Cubans' pitchers again faltered. In the following game, Cubans pitcher Barney Morris finally gave a performance in which the team could take pride, hurling a five-hit shutout, while New York put six runs across the plate in the ninth inning.[13] Barnhill followed with his own strong pitching performance, and the Cubans' offense was sparked by catcher Ray Noble's grand slam, which struck the left-field roof at Philadelphia's Shibe Park.[14] Pitching woes apparently behind them, the Cubans took game four 9 to 2, seizing a three-to-one series advantage. Although Tiant faltered again in game five, the Cubans took full advantage of Cleveland's shoddy defense to mount a late-inning comeback. With the Cubans entering the eighth down one run, Noble came through again, slamming a two-run double that put New York ahead 6 to 5. New York finally had a Negro-league champion.[15]

Across town the Brooklyn Dodgers were putting together their own championship drive. The Jackie Robinson–led team propelled themselves to their first Major League World Series in six years. Although the Dodgers dropped the exciting seven-game series to the New York Yankees, the season was a success on and off the field. African American and other baseball fans flocked to see Robinson and the Dodgers wherever they played. The vastly increased attendance motivated two more major-league organizations to join in the integration experiment and sign their own black and Latino players. Meanwhile attendance at Negro-league games dropped precipitously during the 1947 and following seasons, giving Negro-league team owners less working capital with which to pay their players and keep their teams in the financial black.

The protests of Negro-league owners, calls for continued fan support, and redoubled scouting efforts did little to stem the flow of talent into organized baseball. Newark Eagles owner Effa Manley did negotiate the sale of a few prized players to major-league organizations. In July 1947 Manley sold the contract of second baseman Larry Doby to the Cleveland Indians. Manley's business dealings with Cleveland departed from what had transpired two years earlier when Branch Rickey simply signed Jackie Robinson without purchasing his contract rights from the Kansas City Monarchs—Rickey had claimed Negro-league contracts lacked a reserve clause, thus making Robinson a "free agent." "The ambiguity of Negro-league contracts notwithstanding," historian Jules Tygiel recounted, Cleveland owner Bill Veeck "was determined to buy Doby's contract from the Eagles." Although, like Clark Griffith, Veeck disagreed with Rickey's approach, Veeck decided to act quickly and to integrate his American League franchise by acquiring African American and Latino talent. The Cleveland owner thus took a different tack than either Rickey or Griffith had taken and acquired Larry Doby, whom many considered the best Negro-league prospect given his playing skills, age, temperament, and military service.[16]

Effa Manley had initially attempted to sell Larry Doby's contract to the New York Yankees, based on the Newark Eagles' long-standing relationship with the Yankees. The Yankees lacked interest and passed on Doby. So when Bill Veeck offered the Eagles $10,000 to purchase Doby's contract, Manley was pleased that a major-league team owner was not trying to steal one of her prized players, but she also knew that Veeck's offer was an appallingly low figure. Before agreeing to the sale, Manley told Veeck what everyone in professional baseball knew: "If Larry Doby were white and a free agent, you'd give him $100,000 to sign as a bonus."[17]

Veeck pursued integration with the advantage of having witnessed the dramatic unfolding of Branch Rickey's carefully plotted strategy after October 1945. Veeck therefore devised a different strategy. "I'm not going to sign a Negro player and send him to a farm club," he informed an African American journalist. "I'm going to get one I think can play with Cleveland." Just a day after Cleveland announced its acquisition of

Doby at a July 5 press conference, Doby was in uniform for Cleveland's game against the White Sox; the integration of the American League was under way.[18]

Jackie Robinson and Larry Doby marked the beginning of the talent drain from the Negro leagues into organized baseball. Major-league officials took advantage of racial integration's overwhelming support within the African American community and Negro-league owners' weakened ability to protect their players. Major-league owners put Negro-league officials in an unenviable position by signing away the best black and Latino prospects without compensating or by vastly underpaying for the players. This approach to integration effectively zapped the energies of Negro-league owners and team officials who had scouted, signed, and developed the talent. Often positioned as "race" men and women, black baseball officials could not protest too vehemently that the major-league teams were taking their best players. The public and the sporting press might easily have interpreted such protest as black baseball owners' placing their own financial interests ahead of the civil rights cause that baseball integration represented.

Black baseball owners faced the possibility of being publicly labeled obstructionists for holding out for better offers that hampered the pace of integration. Even before integration began, black baseball's East-West Classic had drawn the interest of big-league scouts. The 1947 game proved no different. *Chicago Defender* sportswriter Fay Young reported the prospective signings of Lorenzo "Piper" Davis, Sam Jethroe, and Luis Márquez, among others, in his August 2 column. Young also reported that Orestes Miñoso was slated to leave the New York Cubans for the Brooklyn Dodgers. However, as he had done previously with the Mexican League, Alex Pompez warded off the Dodgers and retained the services of his talented infielder for the duration of the 1947 season.[19] A year later, following the East-West Classic, the headline dreaded by Negro-league executives appeared in the *Chicago Defender*: "Negro Club Owners Fail to Deal Fairly with Major Leaguers." The accompanying article lambasted Pompez and other Negro-league owners for demanding purchase prices that exceeded the value of the prospects they sought to sell to major-league organizations.[20] The paper's charge increased the pressure on Negro-league owners to accelerate rather than hinder the pace of integration.

Integration hastened the decline in fan attendance at Negro-league games. Black baseball owners continued selling talented players to get their teams' financial ledgers out of the red. A year removed from winning the Negro-league championship, Pompez's New York Cubans franchise struggled to survive the 1948 season. Pompez was holding out on selling two of his top prospects, Miñoso and pitcher José Santiago, waiting for the right offer. Again it was Bill Veeck who expressed interest. The Cleveland owner haggled with Pompez over the purchase price, and negotiations stretched into August. The *Chicago Defender* again criticized Pompez for the drawn-out deal making and in early September accused him of asking too much for what the sportswriter labeled Class C players—an assessment disproved by Miñoso's major-league debut less than a year after the sale.[21]

The *New York Age* interpreted the lengthy negotiations differently, acknowledging the impact that racial integration and the flight of black fans to the major leagues had wrought on the New York Cubans and Negro-league baseball. The *Age* reported that Pompez's 1948 club was in the red for $20,000 and that the sale of Miñoso and Santiago, reportedly a transaction worth $15,000, would help the Cubans' owner cover most of his financial losses.[22] When his franchise's financial straits continued, Pompez established a working agreement with the New York Giants. Thereafter the Cubans would operate as a farm team for the Giants, the parent club having first option on Cubans players, and the sales offsetting some of the team's operating losses. In 1949 Pompez sold Ray Noble, Ray Dandridge and Dave Barnhill to the Giants; the following year it was left-handed pitcher Raul Lopez.[23] The transactions got Pompez's club closer to being in the black, but it did little to ebb the tide: Negro-league teams were swimming in a sea of red. The continued departure of the most talented African American and Latino prospects, combined with the intransigence of major-league owners against incorporating the Negro leagues into organized baseball, signaled that Negro-league teams would lose the economic struggle to survive in baseball's new era. The Negro National League folded in 1949. A few Negro-league teams would continue operations into the late 1950s, but the glory days of Negro-league baseball had ended.

A LATINO JACKIE ROBINSON

The presence of Latinos on both sides of baseball's racial divide during the Jim Crow era and their participation as integration pioneers complicate our understanding of the main cast of actors in baseball integration. Revisiting baseball's various eras—the consolidation of Jim Crow (1880s–1900s) and the testing of racial lines (1910s–1947) reveals that a two-tone racial order simply did not exist. The pre-1945 testing of the exact point of exclusion along baseball's color line in order to accommodate Latino players represented one of the ways organized baseball operated as a laboratory for racial ideas.[24] The important contributions these Latinos made continue to be among the game's infrequently told stories.

The declared start of racial integration brought Latinos out of the shadows and into sharper focus. Minnie Miñoso, Vic Power, and Roberto Clemente and the Latinos who appeared after 1947 performed in a different context than had Roberto Estalella, Alejandro Carrasquel, and the Latinos who played in the pre-Robinson era.[25] Assigned to teams throughout the United States, Miñoso, Power, Orlando Cepeda, and Felipe Alou, as well as those who never made it to the majors, arrived in towns that had neither a Latino nor a sizable African American community. Here they endured extreme isolation and cultural dislocation, in addition to dealing with the racist persecution and institutional neglect that Jackie Robinson had confronted earlier.

Orestes Miñoso personally experienced the promise and limits of integration. Miñoso first entered the U.S. playing field in 1946 when signed by Alex Pompez to play third base for the New York Cubans. Over the following three seasons, he paced the Cubans' offense primarily as its leadoff hitter, started at third base for the eastern squad in the 1947 and 1948 East-West Classics, and was a vital member of the Cubans squad that captured the 1947 Negro League World Series. Ranked among the most promising Negro leaguers at the time integration started in 1947, he was sold to the Cleveland Indians in late August 1948.

Miñoso became the first black Latino to play in the majors when he made the Indians' club right out of spring training in April 1949. The Cuban struggled in his limited appearances, however, and was demoted to San Diego in the Pacific Coast League, where he remained through the end of the 1950 season. The racial glass ceiling in baseball created by the slow pace of integration cost Miñoso and other members of the integration generation years in the majors. Cleveland's active role in integrating baseball in a certain sense hurt Miñoso's chances for sticking with the big-league club. The first American League team to integrate, Cleveland aggressively pursued black and Latino talent. From 1947 to 1951 the Indians' efforts resulted in the emergence of Larry Doby, Luke Easter, and Harry Simpson as well as Mexican Roberto "Beto" Avila. Traded to the Chicago White Sox, Miñoso pioneered that club's racial integration during the 1951 season, making Chicago only the third American League club to integrate.

Although their careers overlapped, Miñoso and Roberto Clemente represent two different baseball generations. Miñoso was part of the transitional generation of players who began their careers in the pre-integration Negro leagues and later pioneered the integration of the major leagues. With Jim Crow no longer in place, Clemente's generation of Latinos entered organized baseball directly. Like Jackie Robinson, Miñoso's contribution extended beyond on-field performance, his success opening new opportunities for darker-skinned Latinos who followed.

As a black Latino who was an integration pioneer, Miñoso endured the double impact of race and ethnicity. He thus blazed a slightly different path than Jackie Robinson and Larry Doby had before him. African American teammates sometimes reminded him of the difference he embodied. Teammate Harry Simpson even accused him of not being black. Admittedly, Miñoso approached the racial situation differently than his Cleveland teammate. "When I first came here, if it was against the law for a person of color to go to a certain place, I would say, 'That's the law and I will respect it.' Something like that wasn't going to hurt me."[26] Miñoso was puzzled that this approach to the racial situation somehow disqualified him as a black man. "When I came to the United States," he told historian Lisa Brock in 1993, "I was surprised and a bit amused to hear some black ballplayers tell me that I didn't understand prejudice and discrimination because I was Cuban, not black." The lack of awareness about conditions in Cuba astonished Miñoso, who reminded others that Cuba was no racial paradise. "What nonsense! . . . Just as in the United States, there were many sections of Cuba, and many neighborhoods, where you only saw white people. And here in this country, the signs in restaurants and buses prohibiting blacks applied as much to me as it did them."[27] But Miñoso could not just simply turn to his Latino teammates during these early years to find comfort, understanding, or true empathy about the challenges he faced. He was black and Latino, the first such player ever to wear a major-league uniform.

The manner with which Miñoso responded to social conditions challenged the popular stereotype of the "hot-blooded Latin." The English-language press often poked fun at Miñoso's accent. On the diamond he dealt with beanballs, bench jockeying from opposing teams, and jeers from fans who remained opposed to integration. Orlando Cepeda's reflections underscore the challenges, now mostly forgotten, that Miñoso overcame as the first black Latino. "This is not meant to be a complaint, but the language barrier back then was so difficult. . . . Players today who come from Venezuela, Panama, and other Spanish-speaking countries

10. Orestes "Minnie" Miñoso *(left of unidentified officer)* and Luis Aparicio. The two Latino stars led the "Go-Go Sox" of the 1950s. In 1984 Aparicio would become the first Venezuelan elected to the Hall of Fame. Miñoso made history as the first black Latino to perform in the majors. (National Baseball Hall of Fame Library, Cooperstown, New York.)

don't seem to realize that. They have no idea. That is too bad, because it diminishes a part of what Minnie has meant to so many of us."[28] Miñoso's example of fighting back without anger made it easier for Latinos to later speak out against those who denigrated their place in U.S. society. More specifically, as a black Latino who pioneered integration, Miñoso made it possible for Roberto Clemente, Felipe Alou, and Carlos Delgado to speak more freely as men fiercely proud of being black and Latino.

Events held to commemorate the fiftieth anniversary of the dismantling of major-league baseball's racial barrier largely ignored the participation of Latinos like Miñoso in the integration of America's game. The oversight sparked a wave of protests from active and retired Latino players. Particularly upsetting was that no Latino player was initially invited to sit on a special panel on race and sports convened as part of President Bill Clinton's Initiative on Race, held in Houston. Other commemorative events demonstrated a similar blindness to the impact of integration on Latinos and to Latino contributions to the process.

The centerpiece of the Robinson commemoration occurred April 15 at New York's Shea Stadium, where major-league baseball retired Robinson's uniform number (42) in recognition of his role as a civil rights pioneer. Journalists and fans lamented that the 1997 Dodgers roster featured only one African American player. Although critics castigated the Dodgers for having backslid from their trailblazing role, they failed to acknowledge the international ramifications of Robinson's success as an integration pioneer. The 1997 Dodgers featured three darker-skinned Latinos with visible African ancestry: Raul Mondesi, Wilton Guerrero, and Ramon Martínez. These players and the hundreds of Latinos who now play in the majors are also part of Robinson's legacy.[29]

Robinson demonstrated that integration could succeed; yet organized baseball did not integrate overnight. Twelve years would pass before every major-league team had a black player performing in a game. Others had to persevere to ensure the integration experiment's full success. The barriers that Miñoso, Vic Power, and Pumpsie Green encountered were no less real because they came after Robinson. Beanballs kept coming; epithets kept flying; threatening letters continued to be mailed; team management continued to find reasons to defer the big-league dreams of black players. Collectively, integration pioneers—whether playing on a diamond, moving into a segregated neighborhood, or breaking down the barrier at a segregated school—demonstrated that the creation of an integrated society is not a natural occurrence.

Racial integration changed more than the color of the major leagues. Following the Dodgers' success, other major-league teams had license to sign players from throughout Latin America. Although coming too late for Martin Dihigo, Cristobal Torriente, and Lefty Tiant, the success of Robinson, Doby, and Miñoso created a new era for all Latinos. The wave of signings during this era produced immediate results. In the two decades that followed Robinson's debut, players such as Vic Power, Luis Aparicio, Juan Marichal, and Orlando Cepeda stood alongside prominent African American stars such as Hank Aaron, Willie Mays, Ernie Banks, Bob Gibson, and Don Newcombe. Together, these players pioneered integration at the minor- and major-league level, in the process taking most of the game's yearly laurels, including Most Valuable Player, the Cy Young Award, and Rookie of the Year.

10

Troubling the Waters
Latinos in the Shadow of Integration

With the exception of a few—for example, Felix Mantilla
and Juan Pizarro of Milwaukee—Latin Negroes do not
willingly mingle with American Negroes. The reason is
simple and painful . . . to be a Negro in the United States
is to be socially inferior. Therefore, Latin Negroes are not
Negroes, at least as far as they are concerned.
Robert Boyle, *Sports Illustrated* (March 21, 1960)

STARTING OVER IN AMERICA'S GAME

Denied entry into the majors a generation earlier, black Latinos were no
longer restricted to performing in Latin America and in the Negro leagues
or subjected to being summarily bounced from organized baseball for
having African ancestry. For the first time in the history of Latino participation in organized baseball, darker-skinned Latinos could openly acknowledge their black and Latino identity. Although the racial barrier
that restricted access was being dismantled, the powerful beliefs that had
long sustained segregation lived on. Vic Power, Felipe Alou, and the
dozens of other Latinos who pioneered integration in minor- and big-
league towns learned that these racial beliefs persisted in the hearts and
minds of many fans, the local press, white players, and management.
White major leaguers' concerns about integration's unfairness and alleged tendency to result in reverse discrimination revealed how racial privilege had become engrained in the minds of individuals who had enjoyed
unquestioned access. "I fought my way through the minors for five years,"
complained an anonymous player in a July 1947 article in the *Sporting*

News. "I rode buses all night for three of those five years, so that I could get a chance in the Majors." "If we are to have Negroes in the Majors," the ballplayer continued, "let them go through the long preparation the white player is forced to undergo. Let us not discriminate against the white player because he is white."[1] Conveniently disregarding the conditions Negro leaguers endured due to organized baseball's racial policy, the complaint revealed his flawed notion of "earning" one's way into the majors.

The collapse of the Negro leagues marked a downside to baseball's integration experiment. In the first decade of integration, opportunities were scarce for blacks and Latinos within organized baseball, whether in on- or off-the-field capacities. Organizations that signed previously ineligible players often bypassed established Negro-league stars for younger players who showed promise. Even fewer opportunities emerged for black business managers, team trainers, umpires, or others who had been employed in off-the-field capacities in the Negro leagues.

A few Negro-league figures such as Buck O'Neil, Quincy Trouppe, and Alex Pompez adjusted well to the transition by parlaying the skills honed in their years in black baseball into scouting jobs with major-league organizations. As scouts these men influenced the pace of major-league integration. For the Chicago Cubs, O'Neil signed future Hall of Famers Ernie Banks and Lou Brock as well as Eugene Baker, who along with Banks, integrated the Cubs in 1953. A catcher who briefly appeared with the Cleveland Indians in 1952, Quincy Trouppe first exhibited a keen eye for talent while managing in the Negro leagues and the Puerto Rican Winter League, where he helped develop future big leaguer Vic Power. Upon retiring as a player, Trouppe became a St. Louis Cardinals scout and signed Tom Alston (who integrated the Cardinals in 1954) and pitcher Brooks Lawrence. Building on his established relationship with the New York Giants, Alex Pompez became the most significant Negro-league figure to affect the incorporation of black and Latino talent after the start of integration. (See the appendix for a list of the first Latinos to play on major-league teams.)

MAKING LATINO GIANTS

In the late 1950s the Giants supplanted the tight-fisted Washington Senators as the top importers of Latin-American talent. The two organizations pursued different scouting philosophies. With Joe Cambria and Clark Griffith at the helm, the Senators had signed Latino prospects as much for their affordability as for their promise. After the start of integration, the Giants took a different approach, hiring experienced Latino baseball expert Alex Pompez to guide their scouting of Latin America.

Hiring Pompez was a departure from the way most big-league organizations incorporated Negro-league and Latino players. Giants executive Horace Stoneham decided that his team could maximize its scouting activity in the Latino market and most effectively acquire African Americans by leaning on Pompez's already developed expertise. Years before the demise of the Negro leagues, Pompez had established a working relationship with the New York Giants, leasing the Polo Grounds to serve as the New York Cubans' home grounds starting in 1943. Once integration began, Stoneham turned to Pompez for recommendations about which Negro leaguers the Giants should pursue; in 1948 the Giants also entered into an agreement for the New York Cubans to operate as a farm team. Pompez's personal recommendations spurred Stoneham to sign Monte Irvin and, according to Armando Vásquez, he almost landed Henry Aaron—only a disagreement over the purchase price between Stoneham and Indianapolis Clowns owner Syd Pollock scotched the deal.[2]

The New York Giants recognized early that racial integration not only made African Americans available but also opened up all of Latin America. In a 1984 letter to the *Wall Street Journal,* John "Jack" Schwartz, the Giants' director of scouting, detailed the genesis of the organization's involvement in Latin America. "We realized there was a huge talent pool that hadn't been tapped," Schwartz explained. "We were fortunate enough to be able to hire Alex Pompez . . . to scout for us." Schwartz continued, "He traveled to the Dominican Republic with Frank (Chick) Genovese to pass judgment on the players, and persuaded a former shortstop of the New York Cubans to show them the best players in the Dominican Republic."[3] An adept talent evaluator, Pompez presented an unmatched combination of professional experience and interpersonal skill as a bilingual Latino. Over the next twenty years his responsibilities with the Giants evolved; ultimately he became its director of international scouting.

Hiring his former shortstop Horacio Martínez ranked among Pompez's most significant decisions. A six-time selection to the East-West Classic, Martínez helped develop the Dominican Republic as a baseball hotbed for the major leagues. The varsity baseball coach at the University of Santo Domingo after he retired, Martínez alerted Pompez to Felipe Alou, Juan Marichal, and other talented Dominican prospects.[4] Their collaboration opened the Dominican talent to the majors; the ensuing influx of talent into the Giants organization helped transform the Giants into a first-division National League team.

The contributions of Alex Pompez and Horacio Martínez to the making of Latino Giants illuminates the cloak of invisibility that often enveloped Latinos who participated in the majors prior to the 1980s. Respected across the Dominican Republic as one of the game's elder statesmen, Martínez in scouting for Pompez laid the groundwork for what would be the major leagues' most significant source of foreign-born talent by the end of the twentieth century. In U.S. baseball circles, however, Martínez's contribution remains largely unknown. Indeed, one can extend Marcos Bretón's description of the story of Dominican baseball as having "been *lost in the translation from Spanish to English*" to the larger story of Latinos in America's game.[5] That larger history remains lost in translation, submerged beneath a black-white narrative that renders the contributions of Latinos as inconsequential to the story of race in organized baseball.

The revamped scouting operation that introduced Latino and African American talent into the organization helped the Giants in the 1950s and 1960s compete with the Dodgers and St. Louis Cardinals for the National League pennant. According to the *New York Times* in August 1959, Pompez was the "key" to the flow of this talent into the Giants' organization. Pompez had his scouts "roam[ing] everywhere," looking for African American talent in the States and for Latino prospects throughout Latin America. The roster of talent evaluators Pompez organized proved an extremely proficient lot, procuring all-star players such as Monte Irvin, Willie McCovey, Orlando Cepeda, Juan Marichal, and the Alou brothers.[6]

In team clubhouses, front offices, and league administrations, the challenge of integrating Latinos reproduced conflicts about the meaning of inclusion and difference. Institutionalized practices proved difficult to eradicate. How best to deal with players who were black and Latino perplexed team officials, especially when it came to assigning such players to teams within their farm systems. By the late 1950s, the Giants were sending African American players to minor-league affiliates in the South. Team officials, however, decided against assigning darker-skinned Latinos to southern-based leagues out of concern that exposure to segregation "might sour a foreign Negro" on life in the United States.[7]

The Giants maximized the services of Alex Pompez by giving him responsibility for aiding foreign-born Latinos in their cultural adjustment and for watching over the team's black and Latino players at spring training.[8] To alleviate culture shock, he supervised the players' living quarters, made roommate assignments (initially assigning Dominicans with other Dominicans, Cubans with Cubans, and so forth), and imparted cultural lessons to prepare players for their encounters with the media and public. A 1960 *Sports Illustrated* article detailed how a seventy-year-old Pompez mentored the organization's Latino prospects in negotiating the intricacies of segregation in the United States. "When they first come here they don't like it," Pompez explained. "Some boys cry and want to go home. But after they stay and make the big money, they accept things as they are." The well-traveled Pompez offered them advice that harkened back to his own encounters with the law as a numbers king: "My main thing is to help them. They can't change the laws."[9]

In placing Pompez in charge of their Latino prospects, the Giants recognized that cultural adjustment was a significant factor in these players' ultimate success. The organization wisely positioned Pompez as a cultural translator, a U.S. Latino who understood the cultural backgrounds from which these players came and could interpret U.S. social norms and cultural practices for them.

A COMPLICATED PATH

With the influx of players from different racial and ethnic backgrounds, integration entailed new locker-room dynamics. In a reflection of contemporary thinking about race and group identification, Latinos were often confronted with the choice of whether or not to identify as a "Negro," regardless of their individual family history or physical appearance. A constant source of friction was the accusation that Latinos were denying their *colored* identity. Latinos, particularly darker-skinned ones, were often perceived as not wanting to associate with African American teammates. "I don't think I'm any better than they are," stated one African American big leaguer, "but I'm not any worse either. They think they're better than the colored guy."[10]

Cultural difference combined with job competition reignited smoldering feelings between African Americans and Latinos. These ballplayers often competed for roster spots regardless of whether they played the same positions. In the nascent years of integration, major-league teams often hesitated, if they did not refuse, to carry an odd number of "colored" players—whether black or Latino. Similarly, white players also expressed a general unwillingness to room on the road with a black teammate. In many instances, the personal preference was moot because of Jim Crow laws and social customs in many of the hotels that big-league teams used for spring training and in towns such as St. Louis and Washington, DC, during the regular season.

The slow pace of integration furthered antagonisms and competition among players of color. Five years after the Dodgers initiated baseball's integration, only five other major-league organizations had joined Brooklyn by integrating their big-league squads. In 1959, when the Boston Red Sox became the last team to integrate, African Americans represented less than 10 percent of all major leaguers. Foreign-born Latinos were less numerous than African Americans, with thirty-five players appearing on the spring training rosters, or about 5 percent of those in spring training, an average of two per team.[11] This number, however, misrepresents the preferences of certain organizations. The Washington Senators had long demonstrated a preference for Latino over African American players. Slow to sign African American talent, the Senators had five Latinos perform on its 1959 squad and only one African American. Even the Senators' first black player, Carlos Paula, who appeared in 1954, was Cuban; the Senators' first African American player appeared three years later, when Joe Black briefly joined the club.[12]

Questions of individual identification were at the center of sportswriter Robert Boyle's article "The Private World of the Negro Ballplayer." An interrogation of how major-league player culture changed with racial integration, Boyle identifies fractious relationships that developed on big-league teams, as well as coping strategies adopted by black and Latino players to deal with life within a formerly segregated institution. In so doing, Boyle sheds light on the cultural misunderstandings that fed tensions.

African Americans were much more familiar than foreign-born Latinos with navigating the idiosyncrasies of and regional variation in racial practices in the United States. They were angered when darker-skinned Latinos shunned them inside or outside the clubhouse, or when Latinos did not turn to them for guidance in their cultural adjustment. A few African American players took these actions as an affront, believing Latinos were trying to avoid identifying as "colored" players. One African American player offered a cool response when informed that some "Latin Negroes . . . cry when they encounter segregation for the first time." "I don't cry," he responded. "We [African Americans] don't cry, and we have it a hell of a lot worse than they do." Reflecting on their different backgrounds, the player offered, "But we're conditioned, I guess."[13]

The double bind of cultural difference and racial standing in the United States sharpened the awareness of Latinos. Their social interactions off the diamond educated them about racial segregation and the inconsistent policing of the color line. Often puzzled by local variations in racial practices, Latinos learned one had to be ever cautious in social settings since the rules were not always the same.

Latinos encountered segregation immediately since most big-league clubs held their spring training in Florida. Upon joining the New York Giants in 1951, Puerto Rican pitcher Rubén Gómez stayed in segregated spring training facilities in Florida. In moving about the town, Gómez noticed that restaurants selectively enforced the segregation laws. Coming upon a "whites only" restaurant, he decided to enter, but an African American teammate opted to stay outside. Much to his surprise, the owner greeted Gómez when he entered the establishment and served him. Observing the treatment Gómez received, his black teammate decided to enter. But the staff refused him service. Perplexed, the Puerto Rican Gómez commented, "How crazy the whole question of race is in America—if you speak Spanish you're somehow not as black."[14]

African American players were often acutely aware of the different treatment team officials extended to Latinos, whether it was finding accommodations for Latinos outside the whites-only and "black" hotels in the segregated South, or allowing a few lighter-skinned Latinos to stay in the regular hotels. This was not to say that Latinos were immune to the vagaries of racial perceptions. Puerto Rican Carlos Bonilla encountered the power of shifting racial perceptions while in training with the Brooklyn Dodgers. Initially, as historian Jules Tygiel found, Bonilla stayed at the same hotel as his white Dodgers teammates. A couple of weeks working out in the Florida sun changed matters. Bonilla's skin darkened to the point that his perhaps ambiguous racial status had become clarified; Dodgers reassigned him to live with the black teammates.[15]

Vic Power was intimately familiar with the impact that racial perceptions continued to have on nonwhites after the dismantling of the racial barrier. An Afro–Puerto Rican, Power saw his major-league career limited to twelve seasons (1954–1965) due to the recalcitrance of New York Yankees team officials. His experience as a Latino pioneer shows integration to have been a complicated process that involved overcoming racial beliefs in white supremacy and dissolving institutionalized practices geared to maintaining segregation.

A strong-hitting, slick-fielding first baseman, Power languished with the Yankees' top minor-league affiliate for three years waiting for a chance

11. Vic Power *(right)* with Al Lopez. Power languished in the New York Yankees' farm system in the early 1950s, waiting for the chance to become the first black player for the Yankees and drawing the support of civil rights protesters and fans who campaigned for his promotion and for racial integration. Traded to the Philadelphia Athletics in December 1953, Power made his big-league debut on April 13, 1954, and went on to appear in four all-star games. He revolutionized first-base play, winning seven consecutive Gold Glove awards. (National Baseball Hall of Fame Library, Cooperstown, New York.)

to become the first black player to don the fabled Yankee pinstripes. A leading hitter in the International League in 1952, he received a call from the Yankees only in late September. Hopes that he would appear with the Yankees were quickly dashed; the purpose of the call-up was to protect the team's claim on him in advance of the 1953 season. In reality, although Power was one of the organization's top hitters in the minor leagues, batting .331 in 1952 and .343 in 1953, the Yankees' top executives had no plans for him to play with the parent club. Power did not represent the "right kind of Negro." Yankees general manager George Weiss revealed this position to the local media, informing reporters that the Yankees would not be pressured into bringing in a black player and that "the first Negro to appear in a Yankee uniform must be worth having been waited for."[16]

Vic Power posed problems to the team's management that had little to do with his playing abilities. His personality was markedly different from that of the quiet, grateful player George Weiss envisioned the pioneering black Yankee to be. The black Puerto Rican ran counter to the genteel black southerner or the corporate player who abided by the rules. Much to the organization's dismay, Power was gregarious and unafraid to speak out about racial slights, and enjoyed being a jokester. These traits in combination with his flair for playing first base disqualified Power for the role of integration pioneer in the eyes of the Yankees' front office. He played the game differently, not just in terms of baseball, where he helped initiate the one-handed catching style at first base, but also in the way he approached living in the United States. His most egregious behavior as a young black man was to openly date white women and lighter-skinned Latinas, in flagrant violation of 1950s racial sensibilities. This behavior pointed to an unstated but nonetheless significant issue: how Power's sexuality as a black man was perceived.

Power was aware of his ethnoracial difference as a black Puerto Rican, and of the sexual politics of his actions. In an era when interracial unions were illegal in many states, Power possessed a dangerous sexuality. He admitted as much in later reflecting on the attention his dating habits drew. "Maybe if I had driven a Volkswagen and told them I was after a big, fat colored girl, they would have said, 'Oh, he's a nice guy, see how beautiful he is!'" But there was little that was conventional about him. During his playing days in Kansas City, he drove around town in his new car with his lighter-skinned Puerto Rican wife, who often wore a blonde wig. It was an offense for which he was pulled over on numerous occasions, one that did not typically incur penalties once the police officer recognized him: routine traffic stop, Power was informed, but he knew the larger issues at play.[17] Pioneering black players were expected to strictly adhere to social custom and to make their personality or pride noticeable.

Vic Power developed into a cause célèbre as organized labor and civil rights activists joined the campaign to pressure the Yankees to integrate. The popular belief that inclusion meant progress mobilized people who in turn perceived the presence of black players in the major leagues as symbolizing improved racial relations. Their protest and picketing outside Yankee Stadium situated the baseball diamond in the struggle for civil rights and social justice.

Despite the pressure from civil rights activists, Yankees management remained steadfast. Team officials went so far as to produce a scouting report that described Power (a future seven-time Gold Glove winner) as "a good hitter, but a poor fielder."[18] Victory seemed assured in September 1953, when the Yankees added Power to their roster for the forthcoming season, but then the Yankees disappointed Power's supporters again. Less than two months later, New York traded the International League's 1953 batting champion to the Philadelphia Athletics as part of a multiplayer exchange; Power would not pioneer integration in Yankees pinstripes. In a postcareer interview, Power spoke facetiously about what it would have taken for him to crack the Yankees' roster. "They were waiting to see if I could turn white, but I couldn't do it. . . . I had to make fun and joke so I could survive in the game."[19]

In a way, the professional baseball diamond served as an oasis from America's racial problems for ballplayers who were part of the pioneering generation. Vic Power noted the peculiar position in which he and other players of color were placed. "When I played baseball, I was neither white nor black, and the white fans loved me, but after the game I was just another colored guy in town."[20] The elevated status that came with wearing a major-league uniform could not be easily transported beyond the playing field. Once the cheering ended, Power and other players of color were likely to be pulled over for "routine" traffic stops or to be prevented from moving into the "wrong" neighborhoods—personal affronts that minimized the class mobility their professional peers enjoyed. Their darker skin color and accents gave them away, to the police officer patrolling the neighborhoods with nicely manicured lawns and to the real estate agent steering them into the "right" neighborhood. The sting of such experiences lasted decades. Puerto Rican pitcher Julio Navarro and his wife did not forget being denied in their effort to rent a house in Detroit when the owner perceived them as black. The landlord changed his mind when he learned Navarro played for the Detroit Tigers, but the initial refusal left a bitter taste that compelled the Navarros to continue their search.[21]

The controversy over the Yankees' failure to bring up Vic Power illustrates how Latinos were essential actors in baseball's integration drama. An impressive group of Latinos that included Miñoso, Power, Orlando Cepeda, Roberto Clemente, and Felipe Alou entered the majors during the twelve years it took to "complete" baseball's integration (see the appendix). Like Jackie Robinson, these Latinos encountered old-line segregationist practices and racial beliefs. Unlike Robinson, however, they faced the challenge of participating in the game's integration with the added weight of their cultural difference.

TROUBLING THE WATERS

Organizations that actively scouted and signed previously ineligible players troubled the calm waters of complacency. Each time the New York Giants, Cleveland Indians, or Brooklyn Dodgers signed and developed a black player, other organizations appeared to increase their resistance to social change. A close look at the teams that signed Latino and African American players early in the process of integration reveals that racial knowledge affected critical aspects of the organizations' operations, including interactions among teammates, management decisions, and ideas about how integration should advance, at what pace, and why.

Integration required team management to devise strategies for dealing with the changing diversity of their rosters and to negotiate language and cultural difference. After acquiring Larry Doby, Cleveland signed a handful of Latino players in the late 1940s, including Miñoso, José Santiago, and Mexican-born infielder Roberto "Beto" Avila. Young second baseman Avila arrived at the 1948 spring training camp speaking no English. Cleveland's travel secretary, Harold Goldstein, recommended Avila buy a Spanish-English dictionary, and, perhaps more significant, he assigned Mike García, a Mexican American pitcher from California, as Avila's roommate to help the Mexican native acclimate to big-league life in the States.[22] The Senators took a similar approach in the 1950s, using whichever of their Latino players had best picked up English to serve as interpreter.[23] The Dodgers also used their players as a resource to bridge the language gap. When Cuban outfielder Sandy Amoros joined the club in 1952, Brooklyn relied on African American players Joe Black and Roy Campanella, who had picked up some Spanish while playing in Latin America, to act as translators.[24]

Communicating in the same language was part of the issue, but at times language difference masked much larger issues. While the Negro leaguers whom major-league teams acquired were typically seasoned veterans, the prospects who were signed out of the Caribbean were usually still teenagers. These Latino prospects went through their residency in the United States without the guidance of team officials who spoke Spanish or who were capable of fully dealing with the ballplayers' cultural adjustment. The Giants were exceptional in this regard, with Alex Pompez assigned to mentor the organization's Latino prospects. However, even the Giants encountered problems in managing their diverse rosters and marshalling their talented club's potential for another successful championship drive after their 1954 World Series triumph.

12. Orlando Cepeda *(left)* and Juan Marichal. The Giants boasted perhaps the best contingent of Latino ballplayers during the 1960s, thanks to their director of international scouting, Alex Pompez. (National Baseball Hall of Fame Library, Cooperstown, New York.)

Discovered by Horacio Martínez and signed by Alex Pompez, Juan Marichal arrived in the United States from the Dominican Republic in 1958 and ascended rapidly through the Giants organization, which had relocated to San Francisco that year. After making his big-league debut in 1960, Marichal quickly assumed a place among the National League's top hurlers and earned the nickname "Dominican Dandy" for his style on and off the baseball diamond. Although English was his second language, he also developed a reputation for bench jockeying, unnerving opponents with his comments from the Giants' dugout during games when he was not pitching.

The San Francisco pitching ace created a maelstrom in a memorable if regrettable incident during the 1965 pennant stretch run. With the Giants hosting the archrival Los Angeles Dodgers for a four-game series that would go a long way in determining the National League pennant, Marichal took his turn on the mound for the August 22 contest. In previous games, Marichal's banter had agitated Dodgers players. Tired of Marichal's antics, Dodgers catcher John Roseboro informed Giants outfielder Orlando Cepeda the night before the altercation "that if he [Marichal] had the guts to tangle with me, fine, but if not, to quit hiding behind fat [Giants manager] Franks and 'wolfin'' at me."[25] Roseboro's promise to get back at Marichal put the Giants pitcher on edge.[26] Things erupted in the third inning during Marichal's turn at bat. The Dominican took offense at Roseboro's return throws to Dodgers pitcher Sandy Koufax, believing the throws were coming too close to his head. Marichal retaliated, striking the Dodgers' African American catcher over the head with his bat, setting off a bench-clearing brawl that ended with a bloodied Roseboro being escorted off the field by the Giants' Willie Mays and several Dodgers.[27]

Marichal's claim of self-defense did little to assuage the outrage his act caused. The blame lay squarely on Marichal's shoulders, according to *New York World Telegram* Larry Fox. Marichal overreacted and, unable to keep his emotions in check, broke the informal masculine and professional code regarding behavior in the heat of competition. "Riding each other" from the bench was part of baseball culture, Fox explained. "The theory is, of course, if you can't take a riding from your friends, how are you going to take it from your enemies?" Bench jockeying was indeed an exhibition of masculinity, testing other players' composure while performing. Nothing was sacred, Fox informed readers. "Racial, religious and family slurs are common in the dugout and in the clubhouse. . . . When the players get on the field, it's no holds barred and intimidation is a weapon."[28] Indeed, bench jockeying helped create a hypermasculine space where players proved their masculinity through physical displays of athleticism, attempts to unsettle their opponents with their words, and control of their own emotions.

Sportswriters pointed to tensions within this generation of African American and Latino players as another contributing factor. The "true problem," according to *New York Daily News* columnist Dick Young, was that "American Negroes and the Latin Negroes in baseball do not like each other—not even a bit."[29] Young contended that tensions between San Francisco's African American and Latino players was the Giants' main problem, not the lingering legacy of Alvin Dark's tenure as Giants manager. Dismissed before the 1965 season, Dark had proven incapable of uniting the diverse club that featured future Hall of Famers Willie Mays, Willie McCovey, Gaylord Perry, Orlando Cepeda, and Marichal. Rather than quell tensions during his four seasons as manager, Dark created a hostile workplace for Latinos, banning them from speaking Spanish and publicly questioning their drive on the field.

13. Felipe Alou *(right)* and his brothers Mateo (Matty) and Jesús *(left)*. (National Baseball Hall of Fame Library, Cooperstown, New York.)

Alvin Dark thought he knew the root of the Giants' problem. In a 1964 interview, Dark told a New York–based sportswriter that the "trouble" with the Giants resulted from having "so many Spanish-speaking and Negro players" and that these players "are just not able to perform up to the white ball players when it comes to mental alertness." Offering a compelling example of how racial knowledge could impact a club's operations, Dark managed the Giants with the belief that "you can't make most Negro and Spanish players have the pride in their team that you get from white players." Orlando Cepeda clashed with Dark over his method of managing the team's diverse roster. Dark instituted his English-only policy in 1962, even though the Giants entered spring training with eleven Latinos, and though Latinos would represent over half the regular season's starting lineup.[30] Dark's policy infuriated Cepeda, who stormed into his manager's office. "Listen," he told Dark, "I'm Puerto Rican and I'm proud of my language. I would feel foolish if I talked to [José] Págan in English. First of all we won't be able to communicate because we don't speak [English] that well and secondly, I'm Puerto Rican and I'm going to speak my language." Felipe Alou explained that the club's Latino players did not speak Spanish in order to alienate their non-Spanish-speaking teammates. "They feel that the moment we begin speaking in Spanish that we are talking about them. This is not so." Speaking Spanish, Alou explained, "free[s us] of the uneasiness that so often bothers us when we continually have to think about which word is right or wrong in English."[31]

Cultural pride and masculinity were inextricably involved in negotiating the politics of language. Dark's policy put Cepeda and his Spanish-speaking Latino teammates in an awkward position, denying them use of the language in which they were most fluent. The policy angered Cepeda, who believed Dark was also attacking his position as a leader and his commitment as a team player. "Dark thought I was trying not to play," Cepeda stated. "He treated me like a child. I am a human being, whether I am blue or black or white or green. Dark did not respect our differences."[32] Forbidden to communicate in their native tongue, those who were less fluent in English were forced to fumble for words when talking to teammates, the coaching staff, and the press; they no longer sounded like men able to speak for themselves.

MEN WITHOUT A COUNTRY

In contrast to African Americans, foreign-born Latinos were not incorporated into organized baseball within the context of a civil rights campaign calling for equitable treatment and inclusion based on U.S. citizenship. Rather, many viewed Latino inclusion more as an outgrowth of expanded scouting for talent than as an aspect of integration. Consequently, the significant role Latinos played as integration pioneers rarely entered into public discussion, nor did the impact of cultural adjustment, team rules, and league policies on Latinos receive full consideration.

Latinos, especially the foreign-born, often suffered from major-league policies that directly infringed on their bonds of shared identity and culture. Coming from countries with their own rich histories of professional baseball, Latinos entered the U.S. playing field with their own cultural practices and expectations about the place of baseball and community. The perceived arbitrariness of team rules and league policies developed into a regular topic of conversation among Latino ballplayers. Latinos called on team and league officials to recognize their unique circumstances in organized baseball—calls that typically went unheeded.

Contention had tinged the relationship between Major League Baseball and Latino baseball since the Mexican League player raids of the mid-1940s. Seeking to isolate the Mexican League, major-league officials instructed players and Latin American–league officials not to compete against or sign any player who left for the Mexican League. The penalty for noncompliance was banishment from organized baseball. Miguel Angel González, the longtime St. Louis Cardinals coach who also owned the Havana Reds, ran afoul of the major leagues' dictum by signing players for his Havana club who had performed in the Mexican League. In July 1947 *New York World Telegram* sportswriter Dan Daniel reported that Commissioner Chandler had expelled González for "harboring Mexican Leaguers and other ineligibles."[33] The majors eventually rescinded their ban after the Mexican League had been neutralized as a rival major league. But all was not forgotten.

Ten years later, González once again upset major-league officials. Interested in asserting the major leagues' supremacy while establishing a more formal and hierarchical relationship, newly selected commissioner Ford Frick convened a meeting between the executives of organized baseball and the Caribbean leagues. Prior to the meeting, rumors circulated that the North Americans were going to propose a new system in which they would appoint a czar over Latin American baseball. González spoke out against the proposal. Portrayal of his response by the U.S. sporting press powerfully illustrated the process of intellectual disfranchisement. "No need to tole some-boddy else how to run heez beez-ness. Maybe in con-tree where baseball ees new, but I speak for Cuba an' I know we need noboddy to supervise," the *Sporting News* quoted González as saying in its July 24, 1957, edition. "We have same rule you have . . . that why we no need beeg boss to come down there."[34] The *Sporting News* article clearly prodded readers to perceive the proud Cuban as lacking intelligence and as inarticulate. Stripped of its phonetic veneer, González's response to the major-league plan reveals an astute Latino businessman seeking to defend Cuban baseball's autonomy: "No need to tell somebody else how to run his business. Maybe in [a] country where baseball is new, but I speak for Cuba and I know we need nobody to supervise. We have [the] same rule you have . . . that [is] why we [don't] need [a] big boss to come down there."

Contemporaries of González were cognizant of such scripted acts of intellectual disfranchisement. Sportswriter Daniel said as much in referring to González's earlier battle with major-league officials over signing blacklisted players from the Mexican League. Reporting on the conflict between González and the commissioner's office, Daniel offered a much different assessment of González's critique of league officials: "Divested of its bilingual nuances, Mike's ensuing dissertation was an eye-opener."[35] For Daniel, how González talked mattered less than what he said about his right to sign Latino ballplayers.

From the perspective of Latin American baseball, Commissioner Ford Frick's tenure resembled a foreign leader pursuing an imperial agenda. Frick worked diligently to establish formal agreements that would subsume the operations of Latin American winter leagues under the dictates of organized baseball. The agreements established tough eligibility standards under which talent from organized baseball would be permitted to participate in Latin American leagues, thus restricting the talent pool available to Latin American leagues. Just as significant, these restrictions also applied to Latino players seeking to perform outside their native country in the 1960s, sparking protests about the unfairness of Frick's policy. In the end, Frick achieved his goal of integrating the most important Latin American leagues within the hierarchy of organized baseball, but not without dissent.

Political instability in Cuba and the Dominican Republic in the early 1960s threatened to disrupt the participation of Latinos throughout organized baseball. The turmoil worried many big-league officials because it endangered their main supply of foreign-born talent: the percentage of Latinos in the major leagues nearly doubled between 1959 and 1969 to 9 percent.[36] Frick's response to political events in the two Latin American countries in conjunction with his role in other controversies affecting Latinos during his fourteen-year tenure (1951–65) added to the tensions Latinos experienced in adapting to life in baseball.

The Cuban Revolution, a crucial turning point in U.S.-Cuban political relations, was perceived as an immediate threat to the relationship between Cuban and U.S. professional baseball. Given baseball's long history on the island and its place in Cuban national culture, Fidel Castro's newly installed government attempted to maintain the prominence of the national game despite the cooling of relations with the United States. The U.S. imposition of an economic embargo in October 1960 signaled a break in bilateral relations. On November 11, 1959, the *New York Times* declared, "Baseball Is Dying in Castro's Cuba." The accompanying article described the Cuban government's urgent call for baseball fans to continue supporting the Cuban winter league, which was suffering from declining attendance and losing money.[37] The *New York Times* turned out to be right, to a certain extent. Shortly after the article appeared, Fidel Castro declared the end of Cuban professional baseball and converted the circuit into an amateur national league, *serie nacional.*[38]

The impact of the U.S. embargo on the major leagues was not immediately clear. Cuba had become organized baseball's most significant
source of foreign-born talent in the 1930s. The embargo forbade the major leagues from continuing to engage in economic activity either with
the Cuban baseball league or with Cuban players who maintained their
residence on the island. Concerned about Cuba's political instability, Ford
Frick defied Fidel Castro and Cuban baseball officials and engineered the
midseason transfer of the Havana Sugar Kings franchise to Jersey City.
Later that year, citing security concerns, Frick prohibited U.S.-born players from participating in the 1960 Cuban winter league season.[39] Deteriorating U.S.-Cuban relations called into question the availability of
Cuban players for the major leagues. Early in January 1961, the Cuban
government reassured major-league officials that the sixty Cuban players in organized baseball, including twenty big leaguers, would be
granted visas to leave the island and continue their careers. The U.S. role
in training and funding the failed Bay of Pigs invasion of Cuban insurgents in April 1961 further deteriorated bilateral relations and again jeopardized the movement of players between the United States and Cuba.[40]

Political turmoil over the next several years sent big-league team
officials scrambling to secure travel clearances so that their players could
leave Cuba. After the Bay of Pigs debacle, the U.S. government continued to closely monitor developments in Cuba as part of the Cold War.
Tensions skyrocketed in October 1962, when spy-plane photographs
uncovered the installation of Soviet missiles in Cuba. President John F.
Kennedy negotiated a settlement with Soviet Union leader Nikita Khru-
shchev that resulted in withdrawal of Soviet missiles from Cuba in exchange for the U.S. removal of missiles in Turkey and, most significant
for Cubans, a promise by the United States not to invade Cuba.

The turbulent political climate made a trying time even more difficult
for Cuban professional ballplayers. Orestes Miñoso, Tony Taylor, Mike
Cuellar, and dozens of Cuban players faced the difficult, life-changing
decision of whether to stay in Cuba and give up their U.S. professional
career, or leave the island without knowing whether they would be able
to return. San Francisco Giants infielder Tito Fuentes experienced firsthand the difficulties of continuing to travel between Cuba and the United
States. In charge of ensuring entry into the United States for the Giants'
Cuban players, Alex Pompez worked overtime to clarify passport matters for Fuentes. In 1963 Pompez used his international contacts to
arrange for Fuentes's safe passage out of Cuba via Mexico. As for other
Cubans, after he left in 1963, years would pass before Fuentes again saw

some of his family members or his native Cuba.[41] They would see their lives became increasingly entangled in the broader political and ideological battles between the United States and Cuba.

LATINOS DIS-UNITED

Major-league policies that prevented players from opposing teams from socializing produced further isolation and anxiety among Latino players, given their small numbers and the political events transpiring in the Caribbean. While African Americans typically found a vibrant black community in big-league cities, Latinos were not so likely to find an established Latino community everywhere they performed. Thus the ballpark became a space where Latinos could renew acquaintances and discuss how players were coping with circumstances back home. Ever aware of fellow Latinos who were dealing with the changes going on in Cuba, Alou reached out to Cuban native Orlando Peña before the Giants squared off against the Cincinnati Reds in 1961. This was viewed as an infraction of the league's fraternization rule, and the National League fined Alou. Two years later Alou was again fined for fraternization, this time for talking with his brother Mateo (Matty), who was a member of the Pittsburgh Pirates. The fines upset Alou, who protested that the fraternization policy unfairly affected Latinos, especially the foreign-born who were away from home throughout the long regular season. Alou declared publicly that representation would help remedy the problem of league rules' effects on Latinos. "We need somebody to represent us who knows what goes on in Latin American countries," Alou informed sportswriter David Arnold Hano.[42]

Events during the 1962 off-season reaffirmed the need for an advocate within the major-league commissioner's office. With Cuban–U.S. relations at an impasse, Cuban players worried about their ability to re-enter the United States if they spent the winter in Cuba. As a result, few Cubans considered playing the winter season in other Latin American leagues. Commissioner Ford Frick decided to enforce the previously adopted policy prohibiting players from participating outside their native country during the off-season. Cubans bore the brunt of this policy since the Cuban winter league was no longer professional.

By prohibiting Cuban big leaguers from playing winter ball or exhibition games during the off-season, Frick's policy prevented such players as Pedro Ramos, Minnie Miñoso, and Camilo Pascual from supplementing their regular-season salaries. Ramos, for one, protested the unfair impact of the league's policy, explaining that off-season opportunities for Cubans were much more limited than those available to U.S.-born players. "The American boys can get jobs during the winter. They work in their hometowns," Ramos explained. "Me, I'm a stranger. I cannot get the same job an American can. My job is playing baseball in the winter."[43] Ramos and other Cuban players attempted to get a reprieve in October, but Frick declined to make an exception to his policy. A handful of Cuban players challenged Frick's policy in January 1963 by participating in exhibition games in the Dominican Republic that featured players from throughout Latin America. When Frick received word of the major leaguers who played in the games, Dominicans Felipe Alou, Julian Javier, and Juan Marichal were fined for participating in "unauthorized" contests in Santo Domingo against "ineligible men." The "ineligible" men were none other than Pascual, Ramos, and Joe Azcue, Cuban players who had played in the exhibitions to earn some winter income.[44]

Frick's fines underscored the need for an advocate for Latinos within the executive offices of Major League Baseball. The January 1963 games in the Dominican Republic had been organized as goodwill exhibitions to provide relief to a nation reeling from political instability following the assassination of dictator Rafael Trujillo nineteen months earlier. Hoping to participate in the contests, Alou, Marichal, and a few other Dominicans went through the formality of asking Commissioner Frick's permission to participate in the games. Perhaps to their surprise, Frick denied their requests, positioning himself (and the major leagues) against the desires of Dominican leaders who had invited the Dominican big leaguers to play. Frick's stance insulted Felipe Alou and other Dominican ballplayers, who viewed it as their patriotic duty to play in the goodwill series. Upset with the commissioner's ruling, Alou opted not to comply, explaining the pressures Dominicans faced. "These are our people and we owe it to them to play," he explained. "Juan [Marichal] and I were big names. We had just played in the World Series. How could we say no?"[45] Latinos who called for an advocate would have to wait until after Ford Frick left the commissioner's office in 1965.[46] Frick's successor, William Eckert, appointed Bobby Maduro, former owner of the Havana Sugar Kings, as a liaison between the commissioner's office and Latino players.

RETURNING TO LIFE IN THE SHADOWS

Cuban ballplayers encountered an ever-changing set of issues in adjusting to life as exiles in the United States. The closing off of the circuit's link to Cuba meant fewer employment possibilities. Cuban major leaguers were unable to return home and play winter ball. Retired players who had become coaches in the Cuban winter league, such as former Negro leaguers José María Fernández and his brother Rodolfo Fernández, lost jobs and critical work experience that might have helped them secure positions in organized baseball. Isolated from family and forced to make their lives anew in the States, Cuban players could not fully share the joys of their success with their friends and loved ones. A number of Cubans would suffer during this period of adjustment, which was particularly hard in their first few winters away from Cuba.

Edmundo "Sandy" Amoros experienced extreme highs and lows in America's game. He is most famous for his spectacular catch of a Yogi Berra line drive in the seventh game of the 1955 World Series, a feat that enabled the Brooklyn Dodgers to finally defeat their arch-nemesis. Though hailed a World Series hero in 1955, Amoros would never again enjoy the same international spotlight in a big-league career that lasted five seasons.[47] One of the few Cuban players who went back to the island in the days following the Cuban Revolution, Amoros received a job offer from Fidel Castro to manage one of the teams in the newly formed *serie nacional*. The former big leaguer turned Castro down, citing his lack of managing experience. The decision might have sealed his fate. Amoros would later state that his original intention in returning to Cuba after the revolution was to retrieve his wife, children, and other family members. Instead, they were all forced to remain in Cuba another five years.

Amoros returned to the United States in 1967 as part of the sixty-four thousand Cubans who participated in the Freedom Flights arranged by the Cuban and U.S. governments.[48] Although the two had been separated by their countries' widening political gulf, Amoros had maintained his friendship with Armando Vásquez, whom he had met during their playing days in the Cuban and Negro leagues. Unlike Amoros, Vásquez had remained in the States, settling in New York City. When Amoros decided to leave Cuba, he turned to Vásquez, who sponsored Amoros's visa application and helped the Amoros family get settled once in the States.[49] The previous five years had been hard for Amoros; adjusting to life in the United States as a predominantly Spanish-speaking black man would also prove challenging. A week shy of qualifying for a major-league pension, Amoros was put on the Dodgers roster for seven days as a favor to the player who had helped the team win a World Series title a decade earlier. In December, however, Amoros and his wife divorced; his next ten years in New York City would be rocky.

Traversing the path many Afro-Cubans before him had blazed, Amoros moved to Tampa in 1977. He was collecting a major-league pension and living in Tampa's historic Cuban center of Ybor City, when his health quickly deteriorated and he had his right leg amputated due to a diabetes-related infection. He lived the rest of his days unable to work and out of the public eye, except for an occasional article reminiscing about his Brooklyn playing days.[50] In June 1992 the proud Cuban died in Miami at age sixty-two, feeling that Castro's revolution had taken everything from him: "He took my money, my house, but most important he took my love. If he takes $100,000, it's nothing. But he took my life away from me, what I love more than anything in the world."[51]

Part of the first generation of darker-skinned Latinos who entered directly into organized baseball, Zoilo Versalles was one of the few Cuban prospects signed by Joe Cambria who became an all-star. In the mid-1960s Versalles helped propel the Twins to the top of the American League. His greatest success came in 1965, when he was named the American League's Most Valuable Player. But Versalles would also deal with the severe emotional toll caused by his separation from Cuba and his parents. This emotional battle, along with injuries sustained on the field, extended beyond his playing career; in 1995 Versalles died at the age of fifty-five, penniless and alone.[52]

The sad fate that Amoros and Versalles met captures the isolation and mental affliction that some Cuban players suffered. Their stories signal how creation of a stronger community of Latinos was critical to overcoming the personal and collective toll taken by political realignments and community reconfiguration. Connections within the baseball world and links to the Cuban exile and broader Latino community in New York City helped Rodolfo Fernández make the necessary adjustment. Fernández, for one, had already retired from pitching when integration began, and had worked as a pitching coach for the New York Cubans and as a manager in the Cuban league, helping to develop the next generation of black and Latino pitchers and taking great pride when one of them made it into the majors.[53]

Memories shared by former Negro leaguers Rodolfo Fernández, Armando Vásquez, and Ray Noble attest to the power of bonds established during their playing days to facilitate creation of a lasting community. Cut off from Cuba and facing the diminished employment opportunities left by the demise of the Negro leagues and Cuban winter league, the ballplayers coped with the hemispheric political changes by relying on this community. In affirmation of their membership in a transnational community, this group conducted a series of reunions in the 1970s and 1980s. Held in Union City, the reunions featured baseball games, concerts, and other social events.[54] The participants, from both the segregated and the integrated eras of U.S. professional baseball, included Cubans Ruben Amaro and Adrian Zabala, who had played exclusively in the major leagues, and others who had performed their entire careers in the Negro leagues, such as Cuban natives Manuel "Cocaina" Garcia and Rodolfo Fernández. More than a space for Cuban exiles, these reunions were inter-Latino gatherings that even included African Americans. Fernández recalled non-Cuban players who were regular reunion participants such as Puerto Ricans Jose "Pantalones" Santiago and Vic Power, Mexican native Roberto Avila, and African American Sam Jethroe.[55] The drawing power of these reunions even went beyond the baseball fraternity, bringing out Cuban and Latino entertainment stars, such as *gran salsera* Celia Cruz, not only to perform but also to join in the celebration of community. Historically, the reunions provided a space for players to affirm their identity; these commemorations demonstrated the participants' ability to build and maintain community.

Cuban native "Lefty" Tiant did not attend these reunions.[56] Tiant had enjoyed a successful professional career from 1930 to 1947 that took him to Cuba, Mexico, the Dominican Republic, and the United States. After his playing career ended, the Cuban hurler returned to his native land to raise his family. When diplomatic relations with the United States soured, Tiant remained on the island. As a result, the former Negro-league star would remain an outside observer as his son Luis Tiant Jr. embarked on a journey that the father had been denied by Jim Crow practices, including a chance to perform in the majors.

After each season, Luis Tiant faced the difficult choice of whether to return to Cuba. Still not assured of making it as a professional ballplayer, he worried that he might be permanently separated from his family if his career flourished. Tiant at age seventeen had informed his parents of his decision to become a professional ballplayer. "My father said no," Tiant recalled, "because he felt there was no place in baseball for a Black man. But my mother finally got him to let me try." In 1961 the younger Tiant left his native Cuba; it would be another fourteen years before he would see his father again.[57]

Denied an exit visa from Cuba since the 1960s, Luis Tiant Sr. finally made a return visit to the United States in 1975 to observe his son pitch for the Boston Red Sox in the World Series. Still sporting the skinny legs that were his trademark during his playing days, "Lefty" tossed the opening pitch at the October 11 game and then watched his son perform for the first time as a major leaguer. After the first game Tiant pitched, a 6–0 shutout victory, reporters gathered around the Tiants. Asked whether he had encouraged his son to pursue professional baseball, the former Negro-league ace replied in the negative. "I didn't want Luis to pitch. . . . I didn't want him to come to America. I didn't want him to be persecuted and spit on and treated like garbage like I was."[58] The father's words exposed the emotional scars that Jim Crow had left on him, preventing him and countless other Latinos from demonstrating their talent in the major leagues prior to integration.

LATINO ACCENTS AND ACCENTING LATINOS

The challenge of cultural adjustment for Latino players was further complicated by interactions with the English-language sporting press. Rather than publicizing their grievances and concerns, the press often posed another hurdle in Latinos' adjustment to life in organized baseball and participated in their racialization. Focusing on Latino players' Spanish accents or accentuating their pronunciation in sports columns or broadcasts reminded fans of the difference these players embodied. These practices purposefully shifted readers' focus from words as communication to language and accents as markers of ethnoracial difference and thereby contributed to the intellectual disfranchisement of Latino participants. These actions reinforced popular perceptions of Latinos as unintelligent, inarticulate, and unworthy of being treated as intellectual peers.

Positioned as intermediaries between fans and players, journalists enjoy a level of access to ballplayers and team officials few fans ever experience. In producing informative accounts about on-field action, management decisions, and other matters that affect the game, these intermediaries are influenced by racial knowledge. Their writings help facilitate certain stereotypical depictions of the game's on-field participants—whether it is the "hot-blooded" Latino, the "racist southern" ballplayer, the "naturally athletic" black superstar, or the hustling, hardworking white utility player. Given sportswriters' power to transcribe the player's words and recount his actions, it is little surprise that Latinos who speak Spanish as their primary language often weary of the English-language press. In baseball's early integration era, Latinos devised strategies for dealing with the press and counteracting racial perceptions that affected everyone from the star Latino to the reserve infielder. The range of tactics used to negotiate the linguistic divide between English and Spanish reveals a complex understanding of the politics of language, race, and place.

The practice of writing copy by manipulating Latino players' accents shows that economics was also a factor in the perpetuation of racialized images. Sportswriters built their reputation on turning clever phrases, obtaining good quotes, and collecting vital information (the scoop) about a player or a team's management. Achieving stardom did not protect Latino players, and journalists did not learn Spanish just because a team's top players had greater fluency in that language. Nor did sportswriters stop drawing on old stereotypes because a Latino had become an all-star performer. Superstars Juan Marichal, Roberto Clemente, and Orlando Cepeda voiced their discontent about journalistic practices that adversely affected public perceptions of Latinos either as individuals or as a group.

Popular portrayals negated Latino cultural nuances, recasting Latino ballplayers as exotic, inarticulate, and unintelligent. This is not to deny that Latino players whose first language was Spanish did speak English with an accent. To the contrary, examples abound of Latino players' statements being misunderstood due to their accents. This occurred early in Vic Power's career while he was playing with the Kansas City Athletics. The Puerto Rican first baseman caused a firestorm after a radio interview during which listeners believed they heard Power describe opposing pitchers as "sons of bitches" rather than "some of their pitches."[59] Fearing a recurrence, the local radio station decided against conducting any more on-air interviews with Power.

The issue of language and accents distinguished the power dynamics involved in press relations with Latinos from those involved with other groups in organized baseball.[60] On one hand, Latino players shared with other ballplayers similar complaints about the press: "I was quoted out of context"; "I never said that"; "I was misquoted." On the other hand, language as communication was employed quite differently in Latino versus European American interactions with the press. U.S.-born players, whether African American or European American, were interviewed in their first language. By contrast, when interviewed by the English-language press, foreign-born Latinos were usually attempting to communicate in a second language.

Dominican player Rico Carty clearly understood the way journalistic practices affected Latinos. "When you cannot express yourself the way you want to, you get frustrated," Carty explained, noting that when Latino players became openly upset about the press, they were labeled "hot-headed, hot-blooded Latins." Tired of being misunderstood and even taken advantage of by the English-language press, Carty learned English. "Now that I can speak the language I can defend myself with words," the Dominican native said after gaining proficiency, "but when you can't, all you have left is to fight to defend yourself."[61]

Public image figured large in the often tense relationship between Latino ballplayers and the English-language press. Latinos' feeling that they were being manipulated made them wary and prompted many to avoid speaking with the press. To them, not appearing in print was better than being publicly mocked, which was considered an affront to their masculinity. The ability to speak and verbally defend oneself in an eloquent manner, *a defender el lenguaje,* had long been viewed as a reflection of one's cultural pride and as part of one's masculinity: men stand up and speak for themselves to defend their honor. This notion of masculinity had evolved from a patriarchal system of male and family honor rooted in Spanish colonialism.[62] Distinct from facile understandings of *machismo*—the specific masculine behaviors that sustained patriarchal domination—the masculinity asserted on the diamond combined both popular and baseball-specific notions of masculinity. Because of its history in Caribbean Latino communities, baseball was associated with the inculcation of important social values, such as teaching teamwork, building community, and helping turn boys into men. The baseball diamond was therefore a space for performances of masculinity, where men defended their individual and collective honor while engaging in displays of manly athleticism.

Intellectual disfranchisement did not diminish with the end of Jim Crow. The practice of emphasizing (or exaggerating) the Latino players' English pronunciation endured in various media forums as cultural practices were interpreted in U.S. terms. This journalistic usage demonstrates the power differential between the sporting press and Latino players in crafting a public image in the United States. The renaming of Latino ballplayers further illustrates this power differential. Sportswriters, radio broadcasters, and even baseball card company officials anglicized the Spanish names of a host of Latino players. Attempts to mute cultural difference and to project an image of assimilated Latinos to the baseball public, the name changes were often opposed by the individual players. Certainly, many U.S.-born Latinos like Mike García (birth name Edward Miguel García) entered organized baseball with anglicized names, acquired during their upbringing or after they entered professional baseball. In other, notable cases, however, name changes were imposed on foreign-born Latinos, such as when "Jesús Alou" became "Jay Alou."

The imposed name change for Roberto Clemente was immediate. Sportswriters began to refer to the proud Puerto Rican as Bob against his wishes even before his 1955 major-league debut.[63] The change also appeared on Clemente's baseball cards. After his Topps-issued cards appeared with the name *Roberto* in 1955 and 1956, every regularly issued player card from 1957 to 1970 came with the anglicized *Bob*. Clemente's 1959 Topps card bore the imprint of the imposed name, featuring a facsimile "Roberto Clemente" signature while the name below read "Bob Clemente." The Puerto Rican's increasing outspokenness about press treatment perhaps prompted the baseball card company to revert to labeling his card "Roberto Clemente" from 1970 until his premature death in 1972.

Fiercely proud of being both black and Puerto Rican, Clemente recognized the powerful role the press played in the creation of public image. His status among the game's elite did not prevent sportswriters from referring to him as "the dusky flyer," the "lashing Latin," or the "chocolate-covered islander."[64] Ever aware of the way the press racialized him, Clemente once stated to renowned author Roger Kahn, "Me, I'm a double nigger because I'm black and a nigger because I'm Puerto Rican."[65]

Notorious for his strained relationship with the press, Roberto Clemente recognized the politics involved in dealing with sportswriters. "Lots of times I have the feeling people want to take advantage of me, especially writers," stated the Pittsburgh Pirates outfielder.[66] The tense relationship showed in reactions on both sides. In one instance, Clemente learned of a sportswriter's alleged criticism secondhand and lashed out at the journalist. Clemente later apologized when he found out that the writer's column actually complimented him for his performance. Pittsburgh teammates understood his guardedness. "Some writers put words in your mouth and that's what they did to Roberto," longtime Pirates teammate Bill Mazeroski explained. "They tried to make him look like an ass by getting him to say controversial things and they wrote how the 'Puerto Rican hot dog' was 'popping off' again," Mazeroski continued in his teammate's defense. "He was learning how to handle the language, and writers who couldn't speak Spanish tried to make him look silly."[67]

The sportswriter's goal of creating good copy meant emphasizing for readers the lines of cultural and racial difference. A Pittsburgh newspaper column captures what Mazeroski and Clemente complained about while vividly illustrating the intellectual disfranchisement of Latino players. After Clemente suffered a slow start, a sportswriter quoted the Puerto Rican's explanation for his early season ineffectiveness as: "I no play so gut yet. Me like hot weather, veree hot. I no run fast cold weather. No get warm in cold. No get warm, no play gut. You see." The column infuriated Clemente. "I never talk like that; they just want to sell newspapers," he fired back, adding that he was not the only one to get such treatment. "Anytime a fellow comes from Puerto Rico, they want to create an image. They say, 'Hey, he talks funny!' But they go to Puerto Rico and they don't talk to us. I don't have a master's degree, but I'm not a dumb-head and I don't want no bullshit from anyone."[68]

Despite his understanding of the press's power, Clemente spoke frankly with the media, whether about his injuries, his views on race relations, or the paternalistic beliefs held by some of those he encountered while playing America's game. Clemente believed that he did not ultimately play for the press's approval, but rather for the admiration and approval of fans. "I live two lives," Clemente explained to journalist Luis Mayoral. "In public life, I belong to the fans. That's why I should maintain myself in the best physical condition to do well on the field." As for his other life, Clemente expounded, "I am black and Puerto Rican. I have to behave well. Perhaps I have more responsibility than others."[69] This self-defined responsibility guided Clemente's actions on and off the playing field. On the field, in the minds of some sportswriters, he carried this sense of responsibility to extremes; the Puerto Rican outfielder was not embarrassed to sit out a game if he felt he could not play at full capacity. His forthrightness in sharing his assortment of maladies prompted some sportswriters to label him a hypochondriac and others to question his work ethic. Off the playing field, Clemente worked extensively to help the less fortunate, setting a model for all his fellow players in charitable activities and generosity. Clemente's tragic death on New Year's Eve in 1972, while en route to Nicaragua with relief supplies for earthquake victims, marked a transition in Latino baseball history: the close of the pioneering generation of Latinos.

Thrilling performances from Latinos helped define the period from the mid-1950s through the early 1970s. Minnie Miñoso and Luis Aparicio transformed the Chicago White Sox into the "Go-Go Sox." Vic Power revolutionized first-base play with his one-handed catching style. The heavy hitting of Orlando Cepeda, Tony Oliva, and Roberto Clemente lifted their teams to World Series titles, while the pitching of Juan Marichal, Juan Pizarro, and Rubén Gómez kept batters on their toes. A look at the all-star team rosters reveals the abundance of Latino talent—including Aparicio, Cepeda, Clemente, Miñoso, Marichal, Oliva, Power, and Versalles—alongside African American stars Hank Aaron, Ernie Banks, Mays, McCovey, and Frank Robinson. Together these players changed the face of America's game.

11

Latinos and Baseball's Global Turn

The demand for new players accelerated the globalization
of the sport. Baseball was no different from Gillette or Nike
in this respect; it was the age of free trade, and the game
was on the lookout for new, relatively cheap labor.

Steve Fainaru and Ray Sanchez, *The Duke of Havana*

The academy is the baseball counterpart of the colonial
outposts, the physical embodiment overseas of the parent
franchise. It operates . . . like the subsidiary of any other
foreign country: it finds raw materials (talented athletes),
refines them (trains the athletes), and ships abroad finished
products (baseball players).

Alan Klein, *Sugarball*

STEPPING ONTO HALLOWED GROUND

Roberto Clemente's death rocked the baseball world as the sport and
Puerto Rico lost one of their most recognizable Latino stars. Recognition of Clemente's historical significance came much more quickly for
him than it did for Martin Dihigo and other Latino pioneers in the Negro leagues. In an unprecedented move, the Baseball Writers Association
of America (BBWAA) waived its five-year waiting period and elected
Clemente for enshrinement as part of the 1973 induction class.

Credit for renewing interest in Negro-league greats belongs, in part,
to Ted Williams, who used his 1966 induction acceptance speech to call
for recognition of Negro-league stars. Williams praised the game for
giving "every American boy a chance to excel. Not just to be as good as
anybody else, but to be better. This is the nature of man and the name

of the game." The Boston Red Sox great continued, "I hope some day Satchel Paige and Josh Gibson will be voted into the Hall of Fame as symbols of the great Negro players who are not here only because they weren't given the chance."[1] Williams's speech spurred the National Baseball Hall of Fame into action. Within a few years the Hall began to formulate plans to honor Negro-league greats. Initial plans for a separate gallery dedicated to black baseball and its stars were scrapped. Instead, the Hall formed a blue-ribbon panel that voted on Negro-league candidates worthy of enshrinement. Formed in February 1971, the panel included African American sportswriters Wendell Smith and Sam Lacy, retired Negro leaguers Monte Irvin and Judy Johnson, and former league officials and team owners Frank Forbes, Eddie Gottlieb, and Alex Pompez. Satchel Paige was the first inductee in 1971, followed by Josh Gibson and Buck Leonard (1972), Monte Irvin (1973), James "Cool Papa" Bell (1974), Judy Johnson (1975), and Oscar Charleston (1976). The family of Martin Dihigo received word of his selection in 1977, making Dihigo the first Latino Negro leaguer inducted into the National Baseball Hall of Fame.

The overdue recognition of Negro-league greats by the Hall of Fame initiated the process of addressing the daunting legacy of organized baseball's gentleman's agreement. Conspicuous by their smaller presence in the new accounts of the Negro leagues were Latinos. Dihigo, Pompez, Cristobal Torriente, and José Méndez, among others who performed in the Jim Crow era, are baseball history's forgotten men. In popular versions of baseball's history of race, these men are still dealing with the double bind of their race and nationality. Their connection to a broader history of Latino participation remains obscured by the perpetual status of "foreigner" that comes with being Latino in the U.S. playing field.

The inductions of Roberto Clemente and Martin Dihigo were part of a series of events that marked the end of the generation of Latino integration pioneers. A Latino legend retired from the big-league diamond in each of the four years between Clemente's and Dihigo's induction: Luis Aparicio (1973), Orlando Cepeda (1974), Juan Marichal (1975), and Tony Oliva (1976). The departure of these Latino stalwarts created a void in the visibility, if not the quality, of Latino participants in the majors, in contrast to the continued development of African American talent in the 1970s. Several factors contributed to a less noticeable Latino presence. Political events, especially the deterioration of relations with Cuba, altered the availability of foreign-born talent. The transformation of baseball's labor relations in the 1970s with the rise of free agency would also impact the approach that major-league organizations took toward the acquisition of Latino talent.

The cessation of U.S.-Cuban diplomatic relations closed Cuba off as a source of talent to the major leagues by the mid-1960s. The loss of Cuba, baseball's main source of foreign talent since the 1930s, forced major-league organizations to look elsewhere in the Spanish-speaking Americas. Over the next several decades, they turned to Puerto Rico, the Dominican Republic, and Venezuela as sources of fresh talent. The shifts produced tangible results. In the 1970s Puerto Ricans replaced Cubans as the majors' largest group of Latin American–born players. The Dominican Republic surpassed Puerto Rico the following decade. The inclusion of Puerto Rico in baseball's amateur draft in 1989 helped the Dominican Republic to retain its position as the major leagues' largest supplier through the end of the twentieth century.[2]

Changes in baseball labor relations compelled organizations to look to Latin America. In 1976, the Major League Players Association finally won the right to free agency with the elimination of the reserve clause. Free agency ended the exclusive lifetime claim baseball management had enjoyed since 1879. The new labor terms meant organizations were now fully subject to market demands in signing players who had fulfilled the terms of their initial contracts. The change resulted in more lucrative contracts for established big leaguers. Thus, a few organizations turned to Latin America to minimize the cost of procuring young prospects to develop. This strategic turn was inspired in part by major-league rules that made amateur players born outside North America ineligible for baseball's amateur draft but eligible to be signed directly by an organization at the age of sixteen.

SCOUTING THE AMERICAS

Shifts within the Latin American scouting operations, along with player development strategies used by major-league organizations, worked to re-create difference between Latinos and other participants within professional baseball. Scouting practices raised new and sometimes lingering questions about the terms of Latino inclusion. Did Latinos enter organized baseball on equal terms with other prospects, whether U.S. or foreign-born? Was Latin America a cheap labor source full of talented youngsters who willingly signed for lower signing bonuses to get a shot at their American dreams? To what extent were the major leagues responsible for oversight of the scouting practices that developed in the Dominican Republic and Venezuela?

These questions were part of the legacy of scouting practices employed in Latin America during segregation. The Washington Senators set the precedent for acquiring Latino players for low or no signing bonuses. Joe Cambria's complaint to sportswriter Bob Addie in March 1958 about the increased signing bonuses Cuban players were demanding underscored the Senators' approach. "That's the trouble with the Cuban kids today. They are like Americans now and want a bonus. Imagine giving a Cuban kid $4000. . . . That's what some big-league scouts are offering now."[3] Cambria rationalized his treating Cubans and other foreign-born Latinos differently when it came to signing bonuses. "I don't believe in bonuses," he insisted. "I open the door to opportunity for ball players. But they have to have ambition to make it to the majors. Bonuses make them too satisfied."[4]

Much to the chagrin of Cambria and the Senators, the onset of integration increased competition for Cubans and other Latinos and drove up signing bonuses. Greater competition meant changing scouting practices. Concerned that other scouts might sign Cuban prospects, Cambria explained his revised scouting strategy in an October 1962 article. "I've got to get the ballplayers while they're still young kids about 14 or 15. I can't wait for them to develop."[5]

New York Giants scout Alex Pompez took a different approach, which highlighted his status as a Latino. Pompez emphasized the care he would provide in giving assurances to the parents of the Latino player he was interested in signing. Pompez told a *Sports Illustrated* journalist in April 1965, "I go to the mothers and fathers and I say, 'Every team has money to offer. But no team has a man like me! Your boy go with the Giants, and I will look after him. Your boy gets sick, I see he get better. With the other clubs no one speaks Spanish.'"[6] As a scout and, later, the Giants' director of international scouting, Pompez pursued a more expansive approach to finding Latin American talent, creating a network that covered Cuba, Puerto Rico, the Dominican Republic, Venezuela, Panama, and the Virgin Islands. However, Pompez's death in March 1974 and new immigration restrictions would compel the Giants and other big-league organizations to reorganize their Latin American scouting operations.

In 1974 the U.S. Labor Department imposed a quota that limited the number of work visas allotted to each major-league organization to between twenty-six and twenty-eight. The quota covered the entire organization, from the big-league club to its lowest minor-league affiliate.

Organizations had to refine their scouting, evaluation, and player development processes in order to optimize their visas. They no longer enjoyed a free reign as Joe Cambria had.

Acquisition of Latin American prospects as a cheap labor source figured prominently in Major League Baseball's global turn in the 1980s. Many scouting practices harkened back to baseball's segregated era, when the Senators, Cincinnati Reds, and New York Giants looked to Cuba for talent. Now even more major-league organizations have turned to the Dominican Republic, Venezuela, and other parts of Latin America to sign young prospects as cheaply as possible to offset the high cost of developing players selected in the amateur draft and, even more costly, signing high-priced major-league free agents.

At the forefront of acquiring African American talent since the signing of Jackie Robinson, the Dodgers extended their scouting operations to the Dominican Republic and just across the U.S. border to Mexico in the 1970s. These expanded operations culminated in the opening of a baseball academy, Campo Las Palmas, in the Dominican Republic in 1974. The academy created a talent pipeline that would produce such all-star players as Pedro Guerrero, brothers Rámon and Pedro Martínez, Raul Mondesi, and Alejandro Peña. Just as significant, in 1979 the Dodgers signed a young, talented, Mexican phenomenon, Fernando Valenzuela. His signing revived interest among Latino fans throughout the country, particularly those of Mexican origins, and helped the Dodgers attract a larger segment of Southern California's Latino market.

The Dodgers and Toronto Blue Jays led the way among major-league organizations refining their scouting operations in the Dominican Republic. Both organizations established baseball academies that gave coaches and organizational talent evaluators the chance to work directly with up-and-coming talent. The baseball academies provided not only sites for developing and evaluating players but also basic English-language instruction for the young Dominicans, as well as cultural lessons about life in the United States. The academies paid great dividends for both organizations. Led in part by their Latino contingent, the Dodgers appeared in two World Series during the 1980s, while the Blue Jays' productive farm system was part of the reason Toronto won consecutive World Series titles in 1992 and 1993. Other major-league organizations joined the Dodgers and Blue Jays in establishing a strong presence in the Dominican Republic. Establishing baseball-training complexes allowed the Atlanta Braves, Montreal Expos, and Cleveland Indians to continue signing Dominican talent while containing costs. Their academies enabled these organizations to more carefully screen which players to send to the United States, thus avoiding wasting valuable visas on players with marginal prospects.

WAGES OF LATINO FOREIGNNESS

Interest in scouting in Latin America was not driven by the simple goal of locating the best player regardless of cost or any altruistic desire to provide players a chance to break into the majors. It was, as Samuel Regalado and other baseball scholars have documented, about getting "Latin players on the cheap." The amounts organizations spent on signing players selected through the amateur draft and on acquiring undrafted Latino free agents are telling. In 1975, according to calculations by baseball scholar Kevin Kerrane, major-league organizations gave U.S.-born players selected in the amateur draft an average signing bonus of $60,000. By contrast, signing bonuses for foreign-born Latinos acquired as undrafted free agents averaged $5,000. This disparity continued to widen over the next thirty years. The discrepancy in expenditures also extended to player development funds. In the case of the Philadelphia Phillies— who scouted and signed talented Dominican players such as Julio Franco and Juan Samuel in the early 1980s—the organization's player development funding in 1981 for their Latin American prospects was $25,000, compared to $355,000 for North American players.[7] The Phillies were not unique in taking this approach. Foreign-born Latinos have been incorporated into organized baseball under various financial terms since the days of Joe Cambria and the Washington Senators. Importantly, the inequities in the terms of inclusion illustrate an economic toll that Latinos pay for their foreignness and for securing a chance to pursue their big-league dreams.

In contrast to North Americans, foreign-born Latinos remain ineligible for the major-leagues' amateur draft. Instituted in 1965, the amateur draft was envisioned as a mechanism to ensure competitive balance by systematically distributing the sport's best amateur prospects among the different organizations. Previously, all amateur players had been signed as free agents, providing an advantage to organizations with more money or greater prestige. Until 1989 the amateur draft included only North American players. Before this change, Puerto Ricans were the only group of U.S. citizens excluded from reaping the financial rewards of the amateur draft and from enjoying the legal protections guaranteed by the major leagues. The Texas Rangers and San Diego Padres took the greatest advantage of Puerto Ricans' free-agent status. Texas signed future all-star performers Juan González and Ivan Rodríguez, among others who would perform in the majors, while the Padres developed their own group of Puerto Rican stars that included Carlos Baerga, Benito Santiago, and the Alomar brothers, Sandy Jr. and Roberto.

Age requirements set by the major leagues for signing amateur free agents underscore the different process of incorporation for foreign-born Latinos. Prior to 1984, foreign-born Latinos were deemed eligible to be signed as free agents upon turning sixteen years old. Responding to protests about abuses, the major leagues clarified their policy in 1984, raising the age to seventeen but allowing organizations to sign a player who is sixteen if he turns seventeen before the end of the relevant season or September 1, whichever is later.[8] A few organizations continued to sign younger players in violation of major-league rules, while others hid players by arranging with a player's family to have him attend a boarding school or a training academy until he was legally eligible to sign.

The legal and financial gap between inclusion in the amateur draft and incorporation as an undrafted free agent is palpable. Players chosen in the amateur draft are fully protected under the formalized guidelines of the major-league rules. These players can have legal representation and can seek legal relief to become a free agent if an organization fails to abide by the rules. The toll exacted for Latino foreignness versus being a drafted player is powerfully captured in the case of Dominican American superstar Alex Rodríguez. The Seattle Mariners selected eighteen-year-old Rodríguez with the first pick of the 1993 amateur draft. The $1.3 million signing bonus he received far exceeded what he would have been given as an undrafted free agent from the Dominican Republic. Rodríguez recognized the benefits of U.S. citizenship. "I'm really grateful I was born and raised in the U.S. . . . . I'm sure I would have been a top prospect [in the Dominican Republic,] but maybe I would have gotten $5,000 or $10,000. . . . The point is, it would have been a much tougher road." The stark difference in what foreign-born Latinos receive as signing bonuses is also poignantly captured in Sammy Sosa receiving the same amount ($3,500) as a signing bonus from the Texas Rangers in 1986 as the Brooklyn Dodgers paid to sign Jackie Robinson more than forty years earlier.[9]

Continued disparities in signing bonuses are a legacy of baseball's approach toward Latin America as a market to which it has long striven to secure unfettered access. Historically, the commissioner's office has not been overly committed to protecting Latino labor. Organized base-ball wanted Latin American prospects for their affordable entry-level labor and did not seek to incorporate them on equal terms. Its process for the acquisition of Dominican and Venezuelan prospects is structured to ensure such a labor surplus at the entry level that these players can be acquired for minuscule signing bonuses. The structure also takes advantage of long-held views about the entry of Latino labor in the U.S. labor market and in society as a whole. Opportunities extended to Latino laborers are emphasized as a positive feature, while the inequities of the process of incorporation are minimized.[10]

Dominican and Venezuelan league officials are at a disadvantage in altering the structure of incorporation into organized baseball. This stems partly from the working agreements negotiated by major-league commissioners and Latin American league officials. Originally a means to guarantee the participation of major leaguers in the winter leagues, the agreements set eligibility requirements in terms of big-league experience except for players undergoing rehabilitation. Major-league executives increasingly tightened the eligibility requirements to the detriment of the winter leagues, which are unable to fully capitalize on their country's best-known players since the tightened requirements drastically curtail the availability of even native-born major leaguers. As a result, attendance and fan interest in winter leagues have plummeted to well below the glory days of *beisbol romantico,* when Roberto Clemente, Willie Mays, and Hank Aaron could all be found roaming the outfield in Puerto Rico. The agreements worked to transform professional baseball teams in these countries into producers of talent mainly for export (participation in organized baseball).

Mexico proved an exception to the major leagues' approach to the acquisition of foreign-born Latino talent. An unexpected positive development arose for the Mexican League from the acrimonious relationship with the majors that resulted from the player raid engineered by Jorge Pasquel in the 1940s. Unencumbered by competition from the major leagues, which had blacklisted players from the Mexican circuit, Mexican League officials created a labor system that enabled them to protect their talent pool from external threats.

The low number of Mexican players who have performed in the major leagues in comparison with Caribbean Latino groups reflects the different processes involved in the procurement of foreign-born Latinos. Operated as a summer league, the Mexican League in the 1940s competed with North American leagues for talent. After the direct competition for players subsided in the early 1950s, the Mexican and major leagues formalized a process for purchasing talent from one another. The agreement prohibited major-league teams from directly signing a Mexican League player as an undrafted free agent. Instead to transfer a player's contract rights, major-league teams were required to negotiate a purchase price with the Mexican League team that held the contract.[11] As a result, major-league organizations had to pay significantly more to secure a Mexican League player than to acquire a Dominican or Venezuelan amateur free agent.

The higher cost made the transfer of Mexican League players to organized baseball a rarity. Organizations preferred to sign several dozen Dominican or Venezuelan prospects to develop through their farm system, which might yield one or two big leaguers. The Mexican players who were acquired were quite distinct from the undrafted free agents from Venezuela or the Dominican Republic. The Mexican Leaguer was an established professional with several years of experience, competing at the equivalent of AAA baseball—the highest minor-league classification.

The Dodgers' acquisition of Fernando Valenzuela in July 1979 from a Mexican League team for $120,000 illustrates the different system in place. The young Mexican pitcher quickly ascended through the Dodgers' farm system and enjoyed a fantastic start in 1981. Winning his first eight decisions and the hearts of Dodgers fans, a new cultural phenomenon, "Fernandomania," was born. Mexican and Mexican American fans poured into Dodgers Stadium whenever the stocky left-hander took the mound. Fernandomania spread through the entire circuit, as Latino fans came out to celebrate the Mexican pitching sensation who was helping vault the Dodgers to the top of the National League West.

Valenzuela's ascent made international headlines. In addition to his success on the ball field, his physical appearance strengthened his appeal. The prominence of his brownness and indigenousness made him a cultural hero to Mexicans and many Latinos. He was not racially ambiguous and was therefore quite distinct from those Latino (and Mexican) big leaguers in pre-integration days who had claimed Spanish blood, stressed European (often Castilian) ethnic roots, or kept tight-lipped about their Mexican ancestry.

SEARCHING FOR LATINO DIAMONDS IN THE ROUGH

Latin American scouting practices evolved out of precedents set mainly by the Washington Senators from the 1930s to the late 1950s and, to a lesser extent, the New York/San Francisco Giants organization after the start of integration. Once they instituted an amateur draft in 1965, the major leagues effectively denied Latinos born outside of North America the same economic benefits and legal protections afforded players defined as draft eligible. Instead, the minimum eligible age for foreign-born Latinos to sign as undrafted amateur free agents was set at sixteen. These standards served as an initial marker of Latino difference within organized baseball; Latinos entered in a more vulnerable position not just because of their cultural difference but also due to the system created by organized baseball.

The Washington Senators and Joe Cambria turned to Cuba as a strategy to limit player development costs by signing players who were anxious to seize the opportunity to enter organized baseball. In the position taken in the late 1990s by Andres Reiner, the Houston Astros' director of international scouting, one may hear the echoes of Joe Cambria's words about providing opportunity. Like Cambria, Reiner found it difficult to pay young Latino prospects significant signing bonuses and was annoyed by those who might escalate the purchase price. The Astros executive refused outright to negotiate with the agents hired by Venezuelan and Dominican prospects, "because they tend to inflate a player's value." When asked by the *Washington Post*'s Steve Fainaru about his approach to the Latin American market, Reiner responded, "I don't want to control the market. I just want to make the decision of how much a player is worth and how much I will pay him."[12]

Competition to sign a Latino prospect has traditionally produced an array of questionable practices that have become part of the "culture" of scouting and player acquisition in Latin America. Scouting practices in Latin American countries have not typically undergone the same level of scrutiny and enforcement as in the United States. Much to the contrary, it is a different terrain, where "free agency reigns, giving each major league team the incentive to be the first to sign promising prospects in Latin American countries."[13] For legal scholars Arturo Marcano and David Fidler, the lax enforcement of major-league rules governing the acquisition of Dominican and Venezuelan prospects raises questions about international labor relations and even the exploitation of Third World children. Major-league rules prohibit an organization from having a player in its camp until he is fourteen and from signing a prospect until he is sixteen. However, children in Venezuela and the Dominican Republic at times come to a scout's attention in their preteens. Just as troubling for many observers, the Dominican scouting innovation such as that represented by *buscónes* (independent talent evaluators) proved beyond the reach of major-league officials.

The infamous case of Laumin Bessa illuminates how scouting practices in Latin America depart from what the major leagues allow in the United States. Cleveland Indians scout Luis Aponte, a former big-league pitcher, signed Bessa, a fifteen-year-old Venezuelan prospect in 1998. Aponte then hid the teenager until he reached the age when he was legally eligible to sign according to major-league rules. After Bessa signed, Aponte and the Bessa family developed a disagreement around the signing bonus. Initially told by Aponte that Bessa's signing bonus was for $300,000, the Bessas received only $30,000 upon signing. The family soon learned that Aponte had independently decided to apportion the signing bonus and had made portions contingent on Bessa meeting certain criteria as to his development within the Cleveland organization; half of the initial signing bonus ($150,000) was payable when Bessa made Cleveland's major-league team.[14] Aponte's actions violated major-league rules on two counts: signing an underage player and dividing up his signing bonus. When the infractions were brought to the attention of the commissioner's office by *Washington Post* reporter Steve Fainaru, the Cleveland organization drew a fine and other sanctions.

Cleveland's organizational response to the Bessa affair attests to the risks and rewards involved in the pursuit of Latino prospects in the Dominican Republic and Venezuela. Cleveland did not fire Aponte, but rather defended its scout's violation of major-league rules, claiming he "was following normal business practices at the time."[15] Cleveland's stance typified the laissez-faire approach that has dominated the scouting of young Latino prospects in much of Latin America. To be sure, the Cleveland organization was not alone in signing underage prospects. The Florida Marlins, Los Angeles Dodgers, and Atlanta Braves have also been caught and penalized for violating the age eligibility rule. Sadly it is vulnerable Latino teenagers, who arguably need the most protection, who typically suffer from the underenforcement of major-league rules.

This lack of enforcement has facilitated the persistence of a "boatload mentality" toward signing Dominican and Venezuelan prospects. This attitude is seen in the signing bonuses the Cleveland Indians paid in 2001: approximately $700,000 spent to sign forty Latin American prospects, while Cleveland's top pick in the amateur draft received close to $1.7 million.[16] The result of a system operating under a boatload mentality, according to Angel Vargas, president of the Venezuelan Baseball Players Association, is the treatment of "Latino children and young men as commodities—a boatload of cheap Dominicans, as if these human beings were pieces of exported fruit."[17]

The difference made by the existence of a strong national league is also demonstrated in the acquisition of Japanese players. Unlike Dominican and Venezuelan prospects, Japanese players typically enter the U.S. baseball scene as established professionals. The structured process designed to protect the interests of the Japanese League ensures that players, such as Hideo Nomo and Hideki Irabu in the 1990s and Hideki Matsui and Ichiro Suzuki in the early twenty-first century, enter organized baseball at an entirely different point than foreign-born Latinos do. In the case of established Japanese League players, major-league organizations submit sealed bids for the exclusive right to negotiate with the player—bids that include financial compensation to the team losing the player and a preliminary contract proposal. Similar processes have been developed to govern the transfer of players from South Korea and Taiwan to organized baseball and to ensure that lesser-known prospects also receive economic benefits and legal protections.

The continued preference for younger Latino prospects has motivated late bloomers to engage in the "age game" in the hope of landing a contract with a major-league organization. Prospects manipulate their age by signing contracts under a sibling's name, falsifying a birth certificate, or entering into an agreement with an organization's scout. These tactics subtract anywhere from a few months to five or more years from a player's actual age. In an ironic twist, given their lack of enforcement of their own rules, major-league organizations have claimed that they have been victimized by the age game and that authentic documentation to validate a player's age is difficult to find.

The international political ramifications of baseball's lax enforcement of its rules came to the fore after the September 11 terrorist attacks. As part of tightened national security in the United States, the Immigration and Naturalization Service (INS) began to scrutinize all visa applications. Before the 2002 season opened, the INS required all major-league organizations applying for work visas to provide authentic documentation, of their applicants' ages. Compliance with INS requirements proved that authentic documents were in fact available, thus disproving the claim of major-league organizations about their lack of culpability in signing underage players. "This situation," Marcano and Fidler write, "suggests that major league teams have themselves been lax about requiring proper documents from players."[18]

Close attention to visa applications most immediately affected players from the Dominican Republic and Venezuela, the two largest groups of non–U.S. citizens in organized baseball. Those who had provided false information met swift repercussions. The Texas Rangers immediately released second baseman Marcus Agramonte when they discovered their "young" nineteen-year-old prospect was actually twenty-five years old. Miguel Richardson met a similar fate when the Seattle Mariners learned their supposedly twenty-two-year-old player was actually six years older. Investigation into the ages of foreign-born players continued in mid-May 2002, finding 126 players to have given false information about their age. However, contrary to claims by major-league organizations about being the unwitting victims of underage prospects who overstated their age, over 95 percent of those 126 players turned out to be older, not younger, than what they had originally claimed.[19]

The controversy over Dominican pitcher Adriano Rosario's signing with the Arizona Diamondbacks reveals how blurred the line between complicity and noninvolvement can become. The story broke in early May 2004 when an ESPN exposé revealed the subterfuge involved in Rosario's signing. On May 8 *Baseball America* reported that Ivan Noboa, a *buscón*, had attempted to extract 25 percent of Rosario's $400,000 signing bonus in violation of major-league rules, in addition to the $100,000 the Diamondbacks had already paid Noboa.[20] The fact that Noboa was the brother of Arizona's director of Latin American scouting, Junior Noboa, and had been listed as a Diamondbacks scout in the Dominican Republic the previous year raised further concerns. The Diamondbacks payment to Ivan Noboa also came under scrutiny, journalist Tom Farrey notes, since major-league rules "prohibit the payment of fees from a club to family members of club employees, as well as agents, for the recruitment of players."[21]

The Diamondbacks organization was further implicated in the Rosario affair when published reports announced that the Diamondbacks' Dominican scout Rafael Mena had encouraged the right-hander to alter his birth date and to sign under a different name. Thus the pitcher had signed using the name of his nephew Adriano Rosario, who was three years his junior; further investigation uncovered the player's real name, Ramon Antonio Peña Paulino. The ruse enabled all parties involved to extract a larger signing bonus for the prospect and commissions—a hard-throwing nineteen-year-old pitcher can command more than a twenty-two-year-old. Additional reports announced that the ballplayer's first agent, Rob Plummer, had advised against signing with Arizona under a false name. The young pitcher agreed nonetheless, prompting Plummer to quit—a claim disputed by Rosario's camp, which stated that Plummer had been fired when he agreed to work with Mena as a buscón. Although Mena later denied his role in the ruse, Rosario's new agent, Scott Boras, confirmed Plummer's version of the story. "Mena told him that if he used the (phony) name it would help him get more money from a team," Boras stated. "These are kids. They'll do anything the buscone [*sic*] tells them to do because they control these kids' lives."[22]

Rosario's case illuminates the impact that the system of *buscónes,* who operate outside the authority of Major League Baseball, has had in the Dominican Republic. Buscónes are independent talent evaluators who traverse the Dominican Republic searching for promising young ballplayers (typically between twelve and sixteen years old) whom they can train in preparation for a tryout before a big-league scout.[23] This valuable service to major-league organizations has saved them from making significant up-front investment to create infrastructure in the Dominican Republic, such as building their own baseball complex or hiring their own staff to operate a baseball academy. Once a buscón deems a prospect ready, he attempts to arrange a tryout. In the process, a buscón can form close relationships with specific organizations and their scouts, who reward him for providing their organizations with first notice on prospects. In some cases this relationship might evolve into formal employment for the buscón as an organizational scout.

The buscón system has drawn widespread attention from the North American sporting press as an operation rife with opportunities for exploitation. The cases of Rosario and Bessa are presented above as evidence of the system's flaws. Critics have complained that the player's interests are not fully protected, especially when the buscón is allowed to negotiate a prospect's signing bonus although he is not a legal representative, an agent. Others have pointed to the complicity of organized baseball officials, specifically their continuing to sign prospects developed by buscónes, thereby allowing them to maintain a significant role in the Dominican Republic. On the other hand, others note that the buscón system has emerged as a local response to the globalization of Major League Baseball, which has incorporated the Dominican Republic as a producer of affordable talent. The advent of the buscón allows Dominicans who are not affiliated with a major-league organization to have a role in the production of this talent and thereby earn income. In this sense, the buscón creates jobs that circulate additional capital in the local economy.

The manipulation of one's age and the innovation of the buscón system represent local strategies to counteract the economic ramifications of the major leagues' global turn. The quest to earn a shot at a tryout or to secure a larger signing bonus no doubt exerts pressure on impressionable teenagers and even slightly older prospects to engage in the age game or alter their names. The quest to earn a tryout and make it to the next level produces perverse results. The first time Major League Baseball conducted steroid testing at its Dominican Summer League in 2004, 11 percent of the players tested positive.

PAYING FOR AMERICA'S GAME

Critical attention to scouting activities and the actions of the young prospects in the Dominican Republic and Venezuela have produced new efforts to combat the system's failings. In 2002 Major League Baseball opened a league office in the Dominican Republic that created a local presence to better monitor the work of league members and buscónes. Updated facilities and closer monitoring of potential abuses increased the pressure on organizations to elevate their standards or risk operating at a competitive disadvantage in the markets that supply the largest number of foreign-born talent to organized baseball.[24] By 2005 all but two major-league organizations had baseball academies in the Dominican Republic to lessen their reliance on buscónes. Individual organizations have redoubled their efforts and committed resources to their Latin American operations. The increased scrutiny and greater attention to facilities has improved conditions in the Dominican Republic, and the average signing bonus for Dominican and Venezuelan prospects rose to $30,000 in 2005.

The major leagues turn to the Dominican Republic and Venezuela effectively maintained a separate system for the acquisition of amateur players from Latin America. The system contributed to the creation of Latino difference through selective exclusion. This is captured in the initial exclusion of Puerto Ricans from the amateur draft, thereby denying them the economic benefits and legal protections extended to all other U.S. citizens. Over twenty years passed before organized baseball addressed this policy, which ascribed second-class citizenship to Puerto Ricans. Nonetheless, discussions of a worldwide amateur draft have stalled in part because of the equal footing this system would give all amateur players, denying major-league organizations access to Latin America as an unfettered market and eliminating the exclusive status and economic advantage that U.S. and Canadian citizens receive when they enter organized baseball.

As if the difference between Latinos and Americans (U.S. born) is not wide enough, organized baseball's expanded scouting effort in Latin America was accompanied by a trend to select more college-level players in the amateur draft. Begun in the 1990s, the trend continued into the early twenty-first century. From the 2000 to the 2004 draft, the proportion of drafted players who signed with major-league clubs who have college or junior-college experience increased from 71.6 to 81.7 percent. This trend has changed the composite profile of players selected in the amateur draft. Current draftees, Arturo Marcano and David Fidler note, are "older, more mature, and better educated than draftees in the early years of the draft."[25] While major-league organizations increasingly prefer selecting more mature and developed college players, their preference in Latin America continues to be locating still-developing teenage boys in the hope of finding a major-league diamond in the rough.

Organized baseball's system in Latin America remains geared to the production of young surplus talent. In the Dominican Republic, baseball academies operate as a means of refining the raw talent cultivated by the buscónes. Limited to thirty-five attendees, around 25 percent of those who attend the baseball academies will "graduate" to play rookie ball in the United States; only about 5 percent will make it all the way to the majors.[26] Even those who do travel to the United States enter at the bottom of baseball's labor market. Their path to the big leagues reveals the reasons that inclusion does not necessarily translate into equality. Indeed, the very process of their inclusion reifies difference along lines of ethnicity, distinguishing between foreign-born Latinos, Asians, and North Americans.

12

Saying It Is So-sa!

I want people to be aware that some of the things I had to
hear when I was 20, all of sudden, I have to hear now when
I am 70.

Felipe Alou

We may be Latin, but we're not dumb. . . . We see everything.

Pedro Martínez

NEW CENTURY, FAMILIAR PROBLEMS

The participation of Latinos in U.S. professional baseball does more than
reflect popular racial perceptions and social conditions away from the
baseball diamond. The professional baseball scene operates as a public
forum where the meaning of difference between Latinos and other
racialized groups is played out before the American sporting public—
sometimes before such issues fully emerge in popular conversation. This
is acutely seen in discussions about the "browning of America." In the
aftermath of the adjusted 2000 census figures, debates about the significance of Latinos and their new status as the majority minority have become timely, particularly as pundits, scholars, and everyday people ponder the impact that Latinos will have on social relations, racial dynamics,
American (U.S.) culture, and the U.S. economy.

Media attention given to the exploits of such Latino stars as Alex Rodríguez, Sammy Sosa, Albert Pujols, and Pedro Martínez has made baseball fans acutely aware of the impact of Latinos on the game. The preva-
lence of Latinos among the game's all-stars and annual award winners
reflects the continuing demographic shift on the major-league diamond.
Latinos now represent baseball's majority minority. This new status be-

came official in 1997, when Latino participation first outpaced African Americans, and the gap has continued to widen. On opening day 2004, more than a quarter of all big leaguers were foreign-born Latinos (26 percent), based on calculations by sportswriter Travis Sawchik. And Latino participation has continued to spiral upward in spite of the United States' visa quota restrictions and tightened immigration procedures. Indeed, entering the 2005 season, U.S.- and foreign-born Latinos accounted for 44 percent of all players in organized baseball and filled nearly a quarter of all major-league roster spots.[1] These statistics indicate that the present and future prospects of major-league baseball hinge in large part on the participation of Latinos.

Greater on-field participation has been accompanied by increased attention to Latinos by the media and in the commercial marketplace. Whereas the structured process of incorporation into organized baseball has produced an economically defined notion of Latino, cultural productions of Latino in media coverage, marketing campaigns, and self-representations have combined to sustain the image of Latinos as persistent foreigners in baseball and U.S. society, arrivals in a "recent" wave. The public face constructed to represent Latinos distorts the Latino past within the game and powerfully elides the long history of Latino participation and the social forces that have shaped that participation.

Cultural productions that involve Latino figures in baseball merge the sporting world with the wider public. It is at two levels—racial understanding, and the continued association of Latino culture with deficiency—that I examine the marketing of Latinos and their self-representation to the U.S. public. The interrogation of the Latino marketing industry by anthropologist Arlene Davila's *Latinos, Inc.* provides a useful approach to examining cultural production. Specifically, Davila delineates the politics of self-representation and the packaging of Latino culture for the consumer market. "The reconstitution of individuals into consumers and populations into markets are central fields of cultural production that reverberate within public understandings of people's place, and hence of their rights and entitlements in a given society."[2]

Marketing strategies and self-representations shape popular perceptions of Latinos as a people, influence their behavior as consumers, and construct a place for them within U.S. society. Within marketing, the constant need to sustain a notion of Latinos as a unique market is based on framing recent arrivals as the *real* Latinos. In baseball, portrayals of Latino ballplayers as part of a recent wave divorce them from the history of Latino participation. This portrayal, moreover, facilitates the discounting of problems that affect Latinos as the grievances of the recently arrived rather than as parts of systemic issues with longer histories.

Even with the recent interest in Latino baseball, evident in the publication of books on the subject, understanding of the history of Latino participation remains limited, too often suffering from a myopic view of the Latino past in America's game. The marketing and even self-representations of Latino players consistently reinvent the Latino invasion, boom, explosion, or wave. This presentation of Latino history elides the connections between the current generation of Latino players and earlier generations.

From a longer historical view, Latino "invasions" of the big leagues have taken place approximately every generation. The invasion started in the 1910s with the entry of lighter-skinned Cubans such as Armando Marsans and Rafael Almeida. The late 1930s featured another wave of Latin Americans who replaced ballplayers who joined the war effort. In the 1950s Latinos such as Minnie Miñoso and Vic Power helped pioneer baseball's racial integration. And in the 1980s and 1990s, yet another wave crashed ashore as Jorge Bell, Tony Fernández, and Ramon Martínez, and other players emerged from training complexes in the Dominican Republic. During each wave the sporting press and those in baseball circles contemplated the impact the "introduction" of Latinos would have on the major-league game on the field (how the game is played) and off (fan reaction to the foreigners). In so doing, they constantly resurrected the figure of the Latino as recent arrival, thereby minimizing the social forces that shape the history of Latino participation in U.S. professional baseball—especially the transnational baseball circuit, which has largely determined which Latinos would perform professionally and where since the early twentieth century.

ACCOMMODATING LATINO DIFFERENCE

Major-league organizations have adopted new strategies to accommodate the increased participation of Latinos and the cultural adjustment they face. Pedro Martínez acknowledges the expanded efforts to address Latino concerns: "They are doing more. They're trying to actually educate us about how life is going to be in the United States because that's one of the most difficult adjustments we have to make." The centerpiece of Major League Baseball's effort is a Latin American language and cultural assimilation program, headed by former Venezuelan scout Sal Artiaga, that conducts clinics for foreign-born Latinos to assist in cultural adjustment.[3]

The current league-wide program builds on organizational efforts to provide a rudimentary preparation. Since the late 1980s, organizations have offered basic language instruction for their Latino prospects at their baseball academies and training complexes. Just as significant, teams began to hire minor-league coaches and managers who are bilingual, a practice critical at the lower levels where the highest percentage of foreign-born Latinos participate. Major-league teams also started to include at least one coach who was conversant in Spanish to facilitate communication with their Latino players.

The training complexes and baseball academies constructed in the Dominican Republic and to a lesser degree in Venezuela have performed multiple functions for major-league organizations. Led by the Toronto Blue Jays and Los Angeles Dodgers, the building of infrastructure (baseball parks, player housing) aided the evaluative functions involved in scouting and developing local players. These complexes also provide players with basic English-language instruction, improved diet (attendees are given three meals a day), and a regimen of physical training. Surrounded by fellow Dominicans and other Spanish-speaking Latinos, the language training the young players receive offers minimal preparation for their cultural adjustment.

Language instruction at the baseball academies, minor-league stops, and spring training camps does little to prepare the young players to deal with the English-language press. "Nobody actually teaches you how to deal with the media," Dominican pitching standout Pedro Martínez observes. Yet he was lucky: he benefited from his older brother Ramon having pitched in the majors and sharing his experiences dealing with the press in the United States.[4] Indeed, media relations rank high among the most daunting off-field tasks foreign-born Latinos encounter as professionals, and the financial stakes involved can be significant. The player who adroitly handles the media and his public image positions himself well for endorsement deals. Those who do not are often ridiculed by the sporting press for their inability to communicate and, over time, are often portrayed as unwilling to assimilate to the mainstream in the United States.

Press interactions present a different racial and cultural dynamic for Latinos than for North American players. Formulating a response to questions from the English-language media involves a complicated mental exercise, as Dominican native David Ortiz explains. "The thing is, you hear the question in English, you have to translate it in your mind to Spanish, think of an answer in Spanish, and then translate that to English."[5] The issue for Ortiz and other Latinos is that reporters often demand an immediate answer. Consequently, journalists turn to other players for postgame interviews, a practice that minimizes opportunities for Latinos to voice their reaction and become part of the storyline.

Fairness is at issue in the way journalists deal with the language and cultural divide in their treatment of Latinos, claims Cuban native Rafael Palmeiro, who arrived in the United States as a toddler in the late 1960s. "It's not fair for a reporter to quote a player that has maybe a little problem with English," Palmeiro observed in a 2003 interview. "They should try to clean it up a little bit and not make this player look bad."[6] Suggestions made by Latino players include requiring teams to have a media relations person and professional translators on hand to monitor interviews, more training for journalists to enable them to conduct interviews in Spanish, and more bilingual sportswriters covering the baseball beat.[7] The willingness of major-league organizations to retain an interpreter on their payroll to work with their Spanish-speaking players varies across the league, as seen in the case of Orlando "El Duque" Hernández and the New York Yankees during the 2002 season.

The battle between Hernández and the Yankees over keeping an interpreter on staff illustrated team officials' expectation that Spanish-speaking Latinos learn English or suffer the consequences. In 1998 Hernández's story of defection from Cuba and reports of his unusual pitching style and success with it, particularly during the postseason, captured the imagination of many baseball fans. In his fifth season in New York, team officials informed Hernández they would no longer carry his translator, Leo Astacio, on the payroll. When he offered to pay for the translator out of his own salary, the team refused. Instead, Yankees officials declared that the translator had become a "crutch" and that five years was ample time for the Cuban defector to have learned to communicate in English.[8]

Chicago White Sox manager Ozzie Guillén acknowledges that the current generation of Spanish-speaking players receives more instruction and mentoring than when he came up through the minors in the early 1980s. Yet the disparity between accommodations made for Asian players such as Ichiro Suzuki, Hideki Matsui, and Hideo Nomo and those afforded foreign-born Latinos remains a source of frustration. The gap in institutional resources dedicated to dealing with the language barrier for Japanese players versus Latinos perplexes Guillén. "It's not right," Guillén remarked while coaching for the Florida Marlins in 2002. "Why do they bring a guy from Japan to interpret for Japanese players, and they don't do it for Latin players? Why do Latin players have to suck it up and learn

English? Hideo Nomo isn't better than Pedro Martinez. Ichiro isn't better than Juan Gonzalez. It's not fair to the Latin players."[9] The numbers add credence to the outspoken Guillén's observation. Latinos, the vast majority of whom are foreign-born, represent over a quarter of all big leaguers, yet most teams remain reticent about permanently employing a translator to assist Latino players' media relations.

Interactions with the English-language press have proved just as challenging as learning a new language. Sports journalists tend not to fully comprehend the challenge involved in becoming conversationally fluent in a new language, Latino players insist. Others are bewildered by the effort some journalists expend to conjure up negative images of Latino players. "What makes me mad," one Latino player stated emphatically, "is they try to make us look like stupid guys or something because we don't know (English)."[10] For Pedro Martínez, the double standard inherent in the press's treatment is off-putting. Reflecting on the media response to Sosa's corked bat controversy, Martínez said in 2004, "I felt offended by having people laugh at the way Sammy speaks English. At least he's trying. It's not like [members of the media] are trying to become bilingual and talk to us and make it easier for us." The expectation is one-way: the Latino ballplayer is expected to adapt and learn the new language. That effort, Martínez declares, involves making matters easier for the press.[11]

The issue of who should bear the responsibility for adapting to the changing face of baseball encapsulates tensions over Latino difference. The composition of major-league players has changed dramatically since the start of integration, and even more so since baseball's global turn in the 1980s. No such change has transpired in the composition of the sportswriting corps covering baseball for the mainstream press. A member of the Spanish broadcast of Dodgers games since 1973 and recipient of the Ford Frick Award for broadcasting in 1998, Jaime Jarrín has observed the dramatic increase in Latino participation. As a thirty-year press veteran, the Ecuadorian native notes that little has changed in terms of the full-time baseball beat writers at English-language newspapers. According to Jarrín, fewer than ten baseball writers are fluent in Spanish, and perhaps fewer than five are conversant enough in Spanish that they can interview foreign-born Latinos in their native language.[12]

The slower pace of change in the press box than on the field has helped to maintain ideas about baseball's sociological function. In the face of baseball's growing diversity, a subtext of media coverage is the need for foreign-born Latinos to assimilate. The push for assimilation, especially

to learn English, stands in contrast to other professional team sports—
such as hockey and basketball—that have undergone their own internationalization yet celebrate their diversity in a different manner than
baseball. Pressure to adapt comes not only from external forces such as
the English-language press but also from other Latinos. After speaking
with Latino ballplayers at the start of the 2004 season, sportswriters Tom
Weir and Mike Dodd concluded that Spanish-speaking players "recognize the onus is on them to make the transition." Latino players stress
that it is their responsibility to at least try to become proficient in English. "I really had a hard time (trying) to communicate with people,"
said Sammy Sosa, who arrived in the United States as a sixteen-year-old
unable to speak English. "But I didn't have a choice. I had to learn it. . . .
Even sometimes I'd say something that I didn't understand what I was
saying, but at least I tried."[13]

Rather than a league-wide response to the problem of cultural adjustment, the major leagues have pursued responses at the organization
level. A number of organizations redoubled their efforts to assist their
players in learning English while coming up through the farm system.
The Boston Red Sox developed an intensive language instruction class
for minor leaguers from Spanish-speaking countries who were playing
for its Lowell Spinners affiliate. This course, implemented in 2004, com-
plemented similar classes held at Boston's baseball academies in the Dominican Republic and Venezuela. Director of player development Ben
Cherington explains the impetus for the structured program: "What we
found is the quicker the Latin players pick up the language, the quicker
they will become more confident in themselves in the United States and
the quicker they will be able to succeed." This focus on instruction in the
low minor leagues targets the levels where foreign-born Latinos are most
prevalent. In addition to boosting a player's chances to advance, language
instruction aids young players in gaining their independence. The ability to speak for himself in his interactions in public, especially with the
press, boosts a player's sense of masculinity.[14] This sense of voice and
masculinity is crucial to the agency Latino players can exercise in crafting a public image and manipulating perceptions through their linguistic abilities.

RE-CREATING LATINO DIFFERENCE: THE REVIVAL OF CHICO ESCUELA

Despite the relative decline in the number of Latino superstars performing in the major leagues in the 1970s, awareness of the Latino presence

actually increased during the decade. Cultural practices that differentiated Latinos from white and black participants in U.S. professional baseball worked to actively position Latinos as perpetual outsiders. Popular representations of Latinos gained prominence, whether it was Richard Pryor's character Charlie Snow masquerading as a Cuban in *Bingo Long Traveling All-Stars & Motor Kings* or Garrett Morris's character, Chico Escuela.

Released in 1976, *Bingo Long Traveling All-Stars & Motor Kings* hit movie theaters at a time when Negro leaguers were finally receiving recognition by the Hall of Fame and attention from historians seeking to recover the history of black baseball. A satirical portrayal of barnstorming in the Negro leagues, the movie, set in the late 1930s, depicts the life of African American players relegated to performing in professional baseball's backwaters. Richard Pryor's character, Snow, assumes a number of nonblack identities, including a thoroughly unconvincing performance as a Cuban who speaks "Spanish" hoping to land a shot at the majors. Pryor's performance lampooned the experience of players from the Spanish-speaking Americas, yet it also educated moviegoers about the different opportunities that existed for Latinos during baseball's segregated era. However, the performance glossed over how this only held true for a limited number of lighter-skinned Latinos, and that black Latinos were also profoundly affected by the color line.

African American comedian Garrett Morris's recurring character Chico Escuela on *Saturday Night Live* was another parody of a Latino ballplayer that shaped popular perceptions of Latinos. The Escuela character parodied a "Dominican" ballplayer turned sportscaster who spoke in a highly exaggerated Spanish accent and who responded to queries from reporters at mock press conferences during skits with the line "*Baysbol* has been *bery, bery* good to me." The character made comedic fodder of Latinos in the midst of a new wave of Latino players breaking into the major leagues. His catchphrase and portrayal took the image of the bumbling Latino player who cannot speak understandable English to an audience beyond baseball circles.

Performances of Latino identities, whether by players or other actors, exacerbated tensions, particularly when the performer attempted to destabilize popular perceptions of who is black, white, or Latino. After signing as a free agent with the New York Yankees in 1976, outfielder Reggie Jackson began performing on the sport's most recognized stage (Yankee Stadium) and in the most intense media market (New York City). One of new Yankees owner George Steinbrenner's first big free-agent signings, Jackson occasionally tired of the intense media scrutiny. At times, Jackson asserted the Latino part of his heritage in his interactions with the press. Although this heritage is clear in his full name, Reginald Martínez Jackson, most fans and many journalists were unaware that one of Jackson's grandparents was Puerto Rican. Jackson used this little-known fact to his advantage, frustrating the English-language press by responding to questions in Spanish or insisting that he would answer only questions that were asked in Spanish.[15] The performance antagonized journalists—why would Jackson, the well-known black player, start talking Spanish?

Initially celebrated for reviving fan interest and now clouded by the specter of performance enhancers, the 1998 home-run chase by Mark McGwire and Sammy Sosa after Roger Maris's single-season record also illuminated racial difference. The media's extensive coverage of McGwire's home-run assault on National League pitching into the late summer months seemingly caused the St. Louis Cardinals slugger to become increasingly surly. Conversely, although he received comparatively less attention, Sammy Sosa's affable interactions with the press and fans increasingly attracted supporters as he joined McGwire in the chase. Sosa's invocation of Chico Escuela's ever-lurking persona through his mimicking Escuela's familiar retort, "Beisbol has been very very good to me," at postgame press conferences added comic relief to intensified media coverage.

The resurrection of Chico Escuela in the midst of the home-run chase evokes the duality inherent in the clowning tradition in black baseball during the Jim Crow era. Clowning involved African American players performing various sleight-of-hand tricks—such as "shadow ball," in which players threw an imaginary ball around the infield—to attract larger crowds by providing additional entertainment for spectators. Not every Negro-league player or team engaged in clowning, however, due to its subtexts. Many players believed clowning lowered the appearance of professionalism involved in black baseball, since it sometimes meant sharing the field with players wearing costumes or acting out subservient roles reminiscent of antebellum days. The inferior economic position of black baseball compelled countless players to engage in clowning due to the potential financial benefits, most particularly, larger attendance revenues at barnstorming games.

The performance of Chico Escuela by Latino players involved a similar type of duality. On one level, Sammy Sosa reclaimed Escuela's "Latino" persona and gave it a Latino accent. According to Latino sportswriter and Sosa biographer Marcos Bretón, Sosa used Escuela's words "as a way of endearing himself to the media and sports fans. . . . As smart as he is talented, Sosa knew the words would make Americans laugh because, until recently, they were about all Americans knew about Latin players—that they talked funny."[16] Invoking Chico Escuela meant performing a familiar Latino figure—the gracious immigrant exuberant about receiving an opportunity to improve his life. Hidden in the subtleties of Sosa's performance was his use of racial knowledge to possibly extract financial gain by endearing himself to fans and marketers.

Sammy Sosa's affability in his interactions with the media during the intense 1998 season made him a more marketable figure. In subsequent years, marketers attempted to capitalize on Sosa's appeal in multiple markets—Latino, black, and mainstream North American. Sosa's success enabled marketers to herald him as a sports hero for mainstream America, a successful black man for the African American market, and a bilingual Dominican star to target the Latino audience. Success also gave him an audience for voicing his own concerns as a Latino. His new appeal and increased social capital came in handy late in 1998 when a devastating hurricane struck the Dominican Republic; Sosa called on his contacts to gather relief donations. Perhaps most telling of his elevated status, Sosa appeared as one of President Bill Clinton's guests at his last State of the Union Address, in 2000.

CORKED BATS, STEROIDS, AND LOADED LANGUAGE

The corked bat controversy involving Sammy Sosa three years later drew an international audience while pointing to the fragility of the public image created through media interactions. Mired in a season-long slump, Sosa, with one fateful swing during the June 3, 2003, game against the Tampa Devil Rays, saw his carefully crafted image shatter. The home plate umpire inspected the Dominican slugger's corked bat and ejected Sosa. The commissioner followed with a seven-game suspension for his violation of league rules. The repercussions for using a corked bat, however, went well beyond the suspension, touching on discourses on masculinity, race, and Latinos.

Few things are seen as more masculine today than the act of hitting a home run. Advertisers formulate marketing campaigns around this idea. The most provocative example occurred in 2001 when ESPN organized its advertising campaign for its baseball telecast around the expression "Chicks dig the long ball." The marketing campaign's play on the home run as a masculine display of virility and as symbolic of sexual potency exhibited the desire of league officials, team management, and advertising sponsors to capitalize on fan interest aroused by the power-hitting era. Indeed, increased home-run production drew larger game attendance and greater merchandise sales.

Media coverage of the 2003 corked bat incident revealed sharply divided lines. Sosa's status as a foreign-born Latino colored the positions of supporters and detractors. For supporters, his ingratiating attitude during the 1998 home run–record chase and his overall achievement had transformed him into the embodiment of the American immigrant success story. Detractors called into question his earlier power-hitting display and placed his individual failing within broader concerns about inflated displays of power resulting from the use of performance enhancers— whether steroids, Androstenedione, or illegally altered equipment. For these critics, Sosa's transgression captured the excesses of individuals who bend the rules to succeed, and a league bent on emphasizing masculine displays of power above all else.

The controversy evolved into the politics of cultural difference when the Associated Press (AP) released a June 3 wire story that quoted Sosa's response verbatim to a reporter's question about having been caught using a corked bat. "But when you make a mistake, you got to stood up and be there for it." Those in baseball circles debated whether the sportswriter or the AP editors had taken advantage of this moment of crisis to inflict additional harm. Latino players, fans, and Sosa supporters pondered the intent of those involved. They viewed as too convenient AP sports editor Terry Taylor's explanation that the quote was published as a result of "poor editing" or an oversight.[17] In this instance, the goal of getting good copy on the corked bat affair blinded both the journalist and his editor to the way their failure to "clean up" Sosa's quote portrayed him as less intelligent than his peers and unintelligible to readers.

The journalistic practice of cleaning up quotes reveals the politics of language and representation involved in the verbatim quote controversy. At issue is the power of the press to influence public perception. *Providence Journal* sportswriter Steven Krasner reflected on the deeper politics involved in the Sosa case. As often occurs with players who acquired English as a second language, Krasner notes, "some of his answers weren't worded correctly. He mixed a few tenses and misused a word or two." The established practice for print reporters, according to Krasner, was for them "to 'clean up' quotes if there are glaring grammatical mistakes, a common practice that doesn't alter the meaning of what was said."[18]

The rules for cleaning up quotes are governed by a common sensibility among journalists about avoiding embarrassing an interview subject when he misspeaks, according to Dan McGrath, associate managing editor for sports at the *Chicago Tribune*. Sosa presents an important case. "We don't have any hard and fast rules with regard to cleaning him up," McGrath explains. "We try to quote him as accurately as we can, as we would anybody, but if he misses on an idiom or a colloquialism, we try not to embarrass him."[19]

The subjective process involved in deciding to clean up a quote raises questions about power, privilege, and difference. Native English speakers such as politicians, corporate leaders, and even major-league officials regularly benefit from their quotes being cleaned up. Cases in which non-native English speakers such as a Latino ballplayer like Sosa do not benefit from the practice prompt concerns about the role of the media in the creation of public images. Latino journalists at the 2003 National Hispanic Journalists Conference decried the manner in which verbatim quotes of Latino players affect popular perceptions, leading many to see Latinos as unintelligent regardless of their individual speaking ability. Major-league baseball's executive vice president for baseball operations, Sandy Alderson, spoke at the conference, held within weeks of the controversial AP wire story, and faced questions about the story. The Ivy League–trained lawyer, who was born and raised in the United States, noted that he had often benefited from the sportswriters' practice of cleaning up quotes and, when pressed about the controversy replied, "In this case I don't know whether (Sosa) was viewed as a Spanish person who was speaking English or was it a question of the reporter feeling ethically bound to report the quote word for word rather than to rephrase."[20]

Latino players placed the media's mishandling of the Sosa corked bat and verbatim quote controversies within a longer history of slights. Pedro Martínez led a chorus of Latino players who demanded action from the Major League Players Association. He and other Latinos believed that the memorandum the Players Association issued advising Latino ballplayers who spoke English as a second language to do interviews with AP reporters in their native language did not go far enough.[21] The Latino ballplayer called on the union to demand that major-league baseball have translators on hand for all Latino player interviews. In the end, the pressure exerted worked to elicit a formal written apology to Sosa from the AP, but the demand for baseball to have translators at the ready was dropped.

The Associated Press's treatment of the Sosa corked bat incident seemingly confirmed the fears of Latino players that the English-language press only reinforced the public image of Latinos as moody, "hot-blooded" people who spoke unintelligible English. In an August 2003 interview, Pedro Martínez alluded to the anxiety Latino players experience in their dealings with the English-language press. "Sometimes, knowing as much as I know and understanding as much as I understand, I am afraid of the media."[22] For Martínez, the AP wire story was evidence of the press's manipulation when it came to its treatment of even Latino stars. "Sammy is a good example. They can make it look worse than it really is to sell papers." Unwilling to make fodder for journalists to sell papers, Latinos, from the inexperienced rookie to the well-traveled veteran, often avoid the press. Others, fearful that speaking out too vociferously about mistreatment might prompt retribution or portrayal as malcontents, remain silent, according to minor leaguer Rafael Riguero. "They'd rather quietly fit in," Riguero explains, "but for some, deep-down inside, they are bothered by it."[23]

(MIS)EDUCATION OF THE BASEBALL PUBLIC

The anxiety-ridden relationship between Latinos and the English-language press not only has influenced portrayals of Latinos within the contemporary print press but also reverberates within popular narratives of baseball history. The void created within the historical record—whether through Latinos' self-imposed silence or avoidance of the press or because of journalistic practices—minimizes Latino participation and contributes to the production of a limited Latino past within America's game. The selective silencing of the Latino past within popular narratives of baseball history affirms anthropologist Michel Rolph Trouillot's argument about power in the production of history. Trouillot sees no grand conspiracy at work in the production of silences in historical narratives. To the contrary, he stresses the agency of individual actors (both persons and social institutions) at the different stages in the production of these historical narratives. History is thus presented as more than a set of facts about the past but as a relationship between those in the present and the past.[24]

The miseducation of the baseball public arises out of cultural productions such as "Latino Legends" and "Black Aces" that present a slanted version of the past while projecting through the product a particular definition of Latino, black, and white. The production of a limited Latino past—and its corollary, a recent Latino history—arises from multiple factors, including decisions about whether to include or exclude Latinos in marketing campaigns. In August 2005 Major League Baseball (MLB) joined Chevrolet in launching the Latino Legends promotion. This campaign, baseball marketing officials acknowledged, was partially motivated to address the omission of Latinos, most specifically Roberto Clemente, from the Century 21 All-Century Team of twenty-five players. Clemente's omission upset Latino fans for several reasons, including a decision by MLB officials to bypass Clemente in favor of another player (Stan Musial) to fill the All-Century Team's final roster spot. The Latino Legends promotion produced its own controversy, however, through the promoters' selection of players to include on the ballot.

Protests immediately followed release of the Latino Legends ballot. A few complained about the exclusion of Ted Williams; others wondered why Reggie Jackson was left off. Both, supporters pointed out, had Latino heritage and Hall of Fame credentials. When pressed on the matter, major-league spokesman Carmine Tiso stated the promotion's organizers had "applied a litmus test" and "nominees had to have a direct connection to their Latino heritage." Keith Hernández, a former big leaguer who claims half-Spanish ancestry, differed with Tiso and the other promoters when it came to Jackson's case. "It wasn't well known about Ted," Hernández offers, "but Reggie Jackson's background was well documented to people involved in the game." Jackson was angered more by the litmus test used by the promotion's marketing officials than by his omission from the ballot. The Hall of Fame outfielder, whose grandmother was Puerto Rican and whose father, Martinez Jackson, had played in the Negro leagues, fired back: "They have no right to pass judgment on what I claim about my Latin heritage. . . . I just don't run my mouth about it."[25] Jackson's case reminds us that black Latinos often endure double invisibility in popular perceptions: too black to be perceived as Latino, too ethnic to be perceived as black in a U.S. context.

The overall lack of recognition of early Latino players produced additional complaints, particularly as it skewed the history of Latinos in the game. Although historian Samuel Regalado understood baseball's position in omitting Williams and Jackson, he observed, "Most of the recent players aren't pathfinders."[26] Indeed more than two-thirds of the players listed on the promotion's ballot had played only since the 1990s. Their inclusion instead of players from the 1950s and 1960s such as Vic Power, Tony Taylor, and Juan Pizarro who had starred as members of baseball's generation of integration pioneers reproduced a limited Latino past.

As a representation of Latino baseball history, the promotion also raised questions about the place of U.S.-born Latinos. The application of its litmus test failed to fully capture the role that migration for political and economic reasons had played in bringing generations of Latino settlers to the United States, producing talented U.S. Latino players such as Mike García, John Candelaria, and Nomar Garciaparra. The narrow litmus test minimized the historical connections between U.S.- and foreign-born Latinos, many of whom were subject to a similar racialization. Just as significant, as far back as the start of integration, when Mike García paired up with Mexican native Roberto "Beto" Avila, U.S.-born Latinos served as translators, roommates, and cultural intermediaries in introducing foreign-born Latinos to U.S. social customs. The promotion's litmus test effectively severed the current generation of Latinos from the transnational baseball network that Latinos had helped develop dating back to the early twentieth century and that first opened the opportunity to play professionally in the United States.

The narrow definition of Latino that limits acknowledgement of their place in baseball history was also manifested in the Black Aces. Founded by former major-league pitcher Jim "Mud Cat" Grant, the Black Aces club honors black pitchers who won twenty or more games in a single season. The club helps organize speaking engagements, Aces' appearances at sports memorabilia shows, and other promotions. The Black Aces club purposely excluded Latino pitchers of African descent. The exclusion of Cuban-born pitcher Luis Tiant by Grant and his co-authors, Tom Sabellico and Pat O'Brien, in their forthcoming book angered Tiant. "So why can't we be in that club?" asked Tiant, who was a four-time twenty-game winner. "I'm black. Maybe I'm not from here. But I'm black. . . . If I was born in Cuba or Africa, I'm still black." According to Tiant, Grant informed him that he was excluded because he was not African American— this evidently did not preclude the inclusion of Ferguson Jenkins, a black Canadian. Grant's explanation that a line had to be drawn somewhere proved arbitrary given that even Grant admitted that Tiant and Cuban pitcher Mike Cuellar, another four-time twenty-game winner, "had to live like we did. . . . They couldn't stay in hotels, couldn't drink from the [white] water fountains."[27] All the more unnerving for Tiant, Grant's forthcoming book mentions the achievements of Tiant's father in the Negro leagues, thereby severing the historical connection between the two generations of the Tiant family.

The exclusion of Afro-Latinos like Luis Tiant and Mike Cuellar from the Black Aces contributes to an ahistorical representation of Latinos, race, and the color line. Tiant's protests about his exclusion from the Black Aces reminded journalists and fans of the place of Afro-Latinos within this history. "I haven't been treated like a white person here. In the minor leagues, I wasn't white. I was black. We couldn't eat in the hotel. We couldn't eat in the restaurants. And now I'm not black?"[28] That it is an African American and one-time teammate of Tiant who is drawing the line that excludes Tiant and other darker-skinned Latinos makes the exclusion all the more ironic.

Tiant's poignant reflections reiterate the silencing of elements of the complex history of Latino participation in America's game. The Tiant family knows all too well the circumstances in which black Latinos participated within Jim Crow baseball and beyond. Tiant and other black Latinos like Minnie Miñoso lived the history of what it meant to be black and Latino in the U.S. playing field as change was occurring. Not to have their role recognized by their contemporaries, then as now, reveals that the lines have been redrawn within the popular understandings of race and that it remains incomprehensible to many that an individual can be black and brown.

The everyday contexts in which *Latino* is produced as foreign, less intelligent, and having a limited past resurfaced during a 2005 episode when a local broadcaster pilloried Latino players on the San Francisco Giants. Larry Krueger, a broadcaster on the Giants' flagship station (KNBR), described the team's Latino contingent as "brain-dead Caribbean hitters swinging nightly at slop" and lambasted manager Felipe Alou, "whose mind has turned to Cream of Wheat." The Giants players, Alou, and the front office protested the incendiary comments, which ultimately contributed to Krueger's dismissal.[29] The tirade affected Felipe Alou deeply, intimating that understandings of the plight of Latinos had not progressed since his days as a ballplayer as much as one might have supposed.

Krueger's comment fit a larger pattern within U.S. sporting culture that has portrayed Latino cultural practices (style of playing baseball) and behaviors (approach to the game) as deficiencies that handicap their individual success and hamper their team's ability to succeed. A witness to the media's treatment of Latinos, to changes in opportunities for Latinos, and to the major leagues' response to the changing face of America's game, Alou adamantly refused to accept the journalist's apology, insisting that "we should be beyond these stereotypes."[30] At a certain level, Krueger's rant must have reminded Alou and other Latinos about attitudes prevailing in the early to mid-1960s, when manager Alvin Dark banned Latinos from speaking Spanish and questioned their intelligence and desire to win. According to Moises Alou, the son of Felipe Alou and a veteran big leaguer, the ideas that sustained Dark's views on Latinos persist within organized baseball and the press. "In the minor leagues, people think all Dominicans, Mexicans, and Venezuelans are dumb. . . . [They] think if a guy doesn't speak English it's because he's stupid."[31]

Marketing, media coverage, and popular historical narratives combine to produce a cultural form of Latino identity that does not fully acknowledge the social forces that have shaped Latinos' experiences throughout baseball history. Presented primarily as recent arrivals, Latinos are divorced from their predecessors who influenced the involvement of the major and Negro leagues in the Spanish-speaking Americas. Reinventions of a "Latino wave" breaking into the U.S. playing field elide the longer history of Latino participation. This ahistorical perception promotes the denigration of Latinos as a group that is and remains culturally deficient, while it also discounts critiques made by Latino players and their supporters as expressions of people who refuse to assimilate or who are ungrateful for the opportunity they have been given to play America's game. Indeed, the notion of the Latino wave, as distinguished from the idea of generations of Latino players, persists in spite of the presence of individuals like Felipe Alou who are links to earlier eras.

The discourse about opportunities and the association of *Latino* with perpetual foreignness speaks to the location of Latinos in U.S society today. Latinos like Felipe Alou have waged a multigenerational campaign to have individual teams and organized baseball account, in their regular operations, for their cultural practices. The slow institutional response is partly the result of the incorporation of the majority of Latinos as a cheap labor source for future development. The parallels between their labor situation and Latino labor migrations at the institutional and state level are striking. Labor historian Carmen Whalen's claim that U.S. immigration policy and enforcement of labor laws has focused on Puerto Ricans as temporary workers is quite pertinent to understanding the institutional inertia. In the case of Puerto Rican labor migrations following the Second World War, Whalen observes: "As long as workers were viewed as temporary, few problems arose; however, the transition to permanent settlement sparked 'problems' and became 'a focal point of clashes between native and foreign populations.'"[32] Similar "problems" arise within organized baseball when Latinos call for changes that would leave a lasting imprint of the Latino presence on the culture of baseball—such as making translators standard employees of individual teams. These problems reveal the reticence regarding the changing face of baseball and possible revisions of the discourse about America's game as a tool to assimilate immigrants into Americans.

Conclusion
Still Playing America's Game

I never thought before what a queer thing the color line
is, anyway. Why it might be that the fellow who takes the
census could settle one's fate for life.

Bliss Perry, *The Plated City* (1895)

The discourse of baseball as the U.S. national pastime needing protection from those who would besmirch its purity continues to influence Americans, from well-heeled politicians to blue-collar fans. Congressional hearings about steroids in baseball, conversations on sports radio, and expanded electronic media coverage reiterate the symbolic significance attached to baseball as America's game. As a testament to the game's enduring symbolic power, the 2005 congressional hearings on steroids and baseball occurred against the backdrop of suspicions that baseball's home-run surge following the canceled 1994 season was the outcome of performance enhancers. The mid-March hearings put the vaunted ideas about America's game on display as some of the legends of the game were called to testify. Mark McGwire, the first player to break Roger Maris's single-season home-run record, steadfastly refused to answer questions about his possible steroid usage, declaring, "I'm not here to talk about the past." The entire scene, however, attested to how embedded the past remains for those who believe baseball is crucial to the American imagination.

As baseball continues to undertake its own form of globalization, Latinos are increasingly becoming the face of America's game. The rise of the Sosas, Martínezes, and Rodríguezes in baseball had already become regular fodder for fans, sports talk shows, and newspaper columns. When the subject of the increasing number of Latinos in the major leagues is raised the conversations often turn to issues other than their on-field performance: matters of race, place, and the state of America's game. To see Sammy Sosa, Rafael Palmeiro, and José Canseco testify before Congress not only indicated their involvement in the steroid scandal but also demonstrated how Latinos had become woven into the fabric of the game by the early twenty-first century. Their testimony at the hearings signaled to some the extent to which Latinos, even those raised in the United States, would go to secure a competitive edge.

The self-proclaimed father of steroids, José Canseco, embodied one aspect of the unbending desire to succeed by any means necessary, regardless of the potential physical toll. The son of Cuban parents who had fled Cuba in the 1970s, Canseco thus represented to many the perverse commitment to winning that afflicts some who entered the U.S. playing field, and, by symbolic parallel, U.S. society. Another son of Cuban immigrants who arrived in the 1970s, Rafael Palmeiro seemingly embodied a different strand. Accused by Canseco as a fellow steroid user, Palmeiro stared down the Congressional representatives, pointing his finger while emphatically declaring: "I have never used steroids. Period. I don't know how to say it any more clearly than that. Never." A month later, Palmeiro became the most established player to test positive under major leagues' new steroid testing program, although announcement of his positive result was postponed until July, after his grievance process was exhausted.[1]

Latinos were conspicuous in their presence within the steroid scandal. The first round of announced test results in early May included two dozen minor leaguers from Latin American countries who had tested positive—just over half of the forty-seven positive test results. The results on the minor-league and major-league levels provoked discussion about the place of Latinos in America's game. The struggle to get a shot at the major leagues, some claimed, had driven players to take the drugs in the hope of improving their performance and breaking into the majors. Others pointed to cultural misunderstandings as an explanation for the high percentage of Latino minor leaguers who had tested positive. A few looked to the buscón system and baseball academies in Latin America, wondering whether young prospects were unwitting victims of the effort to build up their bodies through (contaminated) nutritional supplements. The first round of testing conducted in the Dominican baseball academies during 2004 was extremely disturbing: 11 percent of more than eight hundred Dominicans tested positive for steroids or steroid precursors.[2] Whatever its cause, the steroid controversy had placed the prominence of Latinos in baseball on public display. Yet the history of the social forces and individual actors who had influenced the arrival and participation of Latinos remained largely hidden from view, buried by the notion of Latinos having a recent history and a limited past in America's game.

The entry of Latinos into U.S. professional baseball generally and organized baseball specifically was not the result of a series of disconnected events. Placed within the context of a transnational circuit that linked Havana and New York, San Juan and Chicago, Santo Domingo and San Francisco, both individuals and institutions shaped the movement of players, labor, capital, commodities, technical knowledge, and racial knowledge. This circulation created opportunities for Latinos to participate in professional baseball and thereby reshape its racial understandings. It is more than coincidence that Frank Bancroft led the first tour of Cuba in 1879, managed Vincent Nava (1884), and helped the Cincinnati Reds to sign Rafael Almeida and Armando Marsans in 1911. Bancroft was a transnational actor in the baseball world, one of organized baseball's most frequent visitors to Cuba. Similarly, the life of Alex Pompez attested to the possibilities of envisioning the Spanish-speaking Americas as inextricably linked to U.S. professional baseball. This vision was largely shaped by what he had witnessed as a youngster growing up in Tampa and Havana, where a national independence movement stretched beyond the borders of the island of Cuba and where an ideology inspired men and women from elsewhere within the Spanish-speaking Americas to join *la causa*. His genius lay in believing that he could mobilize a similar transnational network within the professional baseball world, first in the Negro leagues and then in the majors.

Focusing on the actors who moved within baseball's transnational circuit brings to view a site where racial understandings were negotiated and transformed to alter the terms of access at different locations. It is through this focus on Latinos and an examination of their limited incorporation into organized baseball that I explain the complex workings of baseball's color line as more than black and white; indeed, players from the Spanish-speaking Americas were the largest minority that participated in organized baseball during the Jim Crow era. In so doing I challenge the baseball historiography that simply categorizes the Cubans, Puerto Ricans, and Mexicans, among other Latinos, who entered organized baseball during the Jim Crow era as white. This argument consists

Baseball is a transnational process [handwritten margin note]

of more than mere semantics. It highlights the power of a social institution to define race and thereby determine the terms of inclusion as well as the racialization of Latinos as different from whites even after their inclusion in organized baseball. The argument also alters how we have traditionally viewed the interplay of labor, management, and markets in baseball's racial saga, vividly capturing the participation of management and labor in negotiating access to organized baseball and the meaning of racialized difference.

Precedent for the shifting terms under which individuals from the Spanish-speaking Americas entered organized baseball was established in the 1870s and early 1880s. Esteban Bellán and Vincent Nava gained access to a professional arena that had not yet fully or openly embraced racial segregation. At that point, concerns about racial eligibility were focused more on the players not being black than on their sharing whiteness with fellow players. This is most evident in the case of Nava, who, though allowed to perform in the National League from 1882 to 1884, was the subject of press coverage and strategic marketing that constantly reminded all of his foreignness.

Vincent Nava's place in baseball history has been submerged within a historical narrative that avoids grappling with the full complexity of the color line and instead fixates on its racial poles. As a result, baseball fans and historians are much more aware of Moses Fleet Walker's big-league trials and tribulations than Nava's entry and departure from the big leagues. This fixation continues to influence how baseball's racial history is understood and interrogated. In his fascinating analysis of New England author Bliss Perry's 1895 novel, *The Plated City*, literary scholar Robert Nowatzki argues that Fleet Walker was the inspiration for Perry's novel, which follows the professional travels of baseball player Tom Beaulieau. The ballplayer first performs in Connecticut, where he gains the favor of white fans although he is "colored." Beaulieau later acquires a sworn affidavit "testifying to his whiteness" and moves to California, where he assumes a Spanish identity and plays under the name *Mendoza*. But alas, a Connecticut-area fan spots Beaulieau performing in California and exposes his "colored" identity.

Interestingly, Nowatzki does not scrutinize the meaning of "Spanish" within the context of Perry's novel or within late-nineteenth-century racial understandings. Nowatzki fails to interrogate this despite Beaulieau's assumption of a Spanish surname and his taking on of a "Spanish" identity while playing in the California circuit. Rather, Nowatzki connects Perry's novel with Walker's dashed dreams of playing big-league ball. "Perhaps Perry had never heard of Walker," Nowatzki explains, "but there are some interesting parallels between the fictional third baseman and the flesh-and-blood catcher."[3]

The inverted parallels between Beaulieau's fictional travails and Vincent Nava's real life story make it quite plausible that Perry drew from the life of Nava. From 1882 through 1884, Nava performed throughout the New England area and was the subject of widespread press attention as the "Spanish" catcher of Providence's National League club. Like Perry's central character, Nava was allowed to play in professional baseball despite his "colored" identity through an arrangement with management. Moreover, Nava's inclusion in the big leagues was the result of the Spanish and Spaniards being racialized as nonwhite Others and as colored players. Indeed, the practice of applying the labels *Spanish* or *Spaniard* to African American players gained popularity only once Nava had appeared on the big-league scene, and was part of his legacy within baseball's racial past.

Established in the late 1880s as a means to exclude blacks, the ideologies that sustained organized baseball's color line were more than racial. Exclusion was rooted in discourses that validated the masculinity and respectability of those who continued to participate in organized baseball, while they also denigrated the excluded, thereby encoding white privilege into the culture of organized baseball. These discourses became part of the contested terrain where the excluded made claims for inclusion beyond demonstrated abilities on the athletic field of competition. Importantly, these discourses often prescribed the terms describing masculinity, respectability, and race-based ability that an individual or group used to contest his or its exclusion.

Local and national press coverage of the entry and participation of Latino players in organized baseball reveals that their admission did not signify acceptance as fellow whites but rather stressed their status as nonblack. This process of racial inclusion followed the precedent established by the entrance of Native Americans during the 1890s and 1900s. Indians, from Louis Sockalexis in the late 1890s to Charles Bender and John T. Meyers in the 1900s and 1910s, were continually reminded of their "red" status through acts of racialization by the press, fans, fellow players, and management. The complaint of future Hall of Famer Ed Delahanty that "the League has gone all to hell now that they're letting *them damn foreigners* in" vividly captured the place of Indian players along the color line. The entry of Cubans Rafael Almeida and Armando Marsans was framed in similar terms and prompted concerns about the impact that their inclusion in the big leagues would have on the color line. "Is Baseball to Lower Color Line?" asks a 1911 article about Cincinnati's signing of the two Cubans. The writer wonders whether their inclusion would "lower" the color line and signify a "step towards letting in the Negro."[4]

The discourse surrounding the entry of Native American and Latino players attests to red and bronze (brown) being located in between white and black poles on baseball's version of the color line. The incorporation of individuals from the Spanish-speaking Americas throughout the Jim Crow era captured a sophisticated system of racial understanding that was mapped onto the color line. Those involved in U.S. professional baseball mobilized a racial classification system that anticipated African American public intellectual Hubert Harrison's "new race consciousness," which categorized the world's people racially into five groups according to color versus nationality.[5] Rather than the creation of new categories when "colored" players sought entry into organized baseball, red, yellow, and brown categories and positions along the color line awaited their arrival.

The careful delineation between racialization, group self-identification, and a group's position along the color line in historian Tom Guglielmo's study *White on Arrival* is quite instructive here. Guglielmo demonstrates how neither the racialization of Italians nor their self-identification as an "Italian race" from the 1890s to the late 1930s precludes Italians from enjoying the benefits of whiteness in U.S. society. During this period, Guglielmo notes, Italian immigrants and their children were deeply racialized by a wide range of individuals and institutions that "criminalize[d] them mercilessly, restrict[ed] them from immigrating to the United States in large numbers, ostracize[d] them in various neighborhoods, and den[ied] them jobs on occasion." However, these individuals and institutions did not challenge Italian whiteness "in any sustained or systematic way."[6] The Italian case thus powerfully demonstrates that whiteness was no monolith and that one's ethnoracial background placed one in different locations along society's color line.

The story of Latinos and Jim Crow baseball reveals different locations for people of the "colored" races along the sport's color line. Latinos who did gain access to organized baseball prior to integration were not welcomed into that fraternity as fellow whites. To the contrary, baseball fans, officials, fellow players, and the press actively questioned claims of whiteness for Latinos. Thus, much like Native Americans, Latinos were given constant reminders that inclusion did not signify equality or racial sameness in America's game.

Notions of racial difference persisted after organized baseball's racial barrier was dismantled. This was what the pioneering generation of Latinos quickly discovered. Orestes Miñoso, Vic Power, Orlando Cepeda, Roberto Clemente, and Juan Marichal, among other darker-skinned Latinos, all continued to encounter the significance of their race and cultural difference inside and outside organized baseball. Miñoso and Power both hit the artificial impediments that prevented their earlier ascent into the big leagues and slowed the overall pace of integration, costing both several years in the major leagues. Cepeda, Clemente, and Marichal learned that their performance on the playing field would not always secure them acceptance off the field, and that many saw their cultural heritage as a deficit and not a potential benefit in an integrated setting. Indeed, one of the important lessons gleaned from the experience of Latinos in America's game is that racialized difference has continued to take on new forms, educating new generations of fans and observers as to the characteristics that mark Latinos as different.

The racialization of Latinos continues into the contemporary era in multiple forms. Organized baseball's structured process for the acquisition of amateur players ensures that foreign-born Latinos continue to enter at an economic disadvantage to North American players. This process reproduces a notion of *Latino* whereby their culture, ethnicity, and foreignness are inserted into financial considerations. The racialization of Latinos also persists through cultural productions that typically present Latinos as recent arrivals or outside the American mainstream. A 2005 nationally televised commercial for Pepsi featuring U.S.-born Latino Alex Rodríguez and Dominican native Vladimir Guerrero is a telling example. The commercial ends with the fluent English-speaking Rodríguez telling Guerrero with a heavily Spanish accent to "rrrun." Cultural productions such as this contribute to classifying Latinos, even the U.S.-born, as perpetual foreigners. The vast circulation of these cultural artifacts, moreover, enables the strategic disruption of Latinos' history of participation in baseball's transnational circuit and denies a basis through which Latinos can make their own claims about belonging in America's game.

The perception that Latinos possess only a recent past in America's game holds such power in U.S. popular perception that even an experienced Latino like Felipe Alou can be discredited when he speaks out against the racist depictions of Latinos. Those who claim that inclusion itself is what matters readily dismiss criticisms about structured inequalities. As a typical example of this simplistic notion of inclusion, *Reno*

Gazette-Journal writer Chuck Carlson claimed that Alou's refusal to accept Krueger's apology "only hurt [Alou's] case for racial sensitivity in this country." Krueger's diatribe (described in chapter 12) was part of the culture of sports radio, "done a thousand times a day in a thousand different places," according to Carlson, who cast Alou as "an overwrought bully who may need his own course in sensitivity training." Carlson thus evaded the substance of Alou's critique that Kruger's diatribe was representative of a social problem about perceptions of Latinos and not just an individual's misguided rant.

This book documents ways that racialization made a place for Latinos in America's game, and how that place changed over time. In so doing, it illuminates Latinos as actors, not just as people acted upon. Thus it reveals Latinos such as Alex Pompez, who as an entrepreneur and scout challenged traditional orthodoxies within baseball as a social and economic institution, and who as an individual challenged narrow definitions of who is black, Latino, and American. The study also illustrates ways that social institutions can affect racial understandings through their policies and practices, most evident in the approach organized baseball took in policing the color line, acquired Latino talent, and built and sustained its relationship with Latin American leagues. Finally, I have sought to counter the portrayal of Latinos as recent arrivals with a limited baseball past, a depiction so essential to the denigration of Latino cultural practices. The discourses that sustain the racialization of Latinos do not hold when placed in a longer historical framework. A closer examination of baseball history reveals a history of interconnections in which Latinos were critical participants in the drama of the Jim Crow color line, the evolution of racial understandings, and the continuation of baseball as America's game.

Appendix
Pioneering Latinos

Latino Barrier Breakers

Player	Black Baseball Team	Major-League Team
José Acosta	Long Branch (LB) Cubans, 1915	Washington Senators, 1920–22
Rafael Almeida	All Cubans, 1904–5	Cincinnati Reds, 1911–13
Angel "Pete" Aragon	LB Cubans, 1913	NY Yankees, 1914, 1916–17
Alfredo Cabrera	All Cubans, 1905	St. Louis Cardinals, 1913
Jack Calvo	LB Cubans, 1913–15	Senators, 1913, 1920
Tomas de la Cruz	Havana Cuban Stars, 1934	Reds, 1944
Pedro Dibut	Cuban Stars, 1923	Reds, 1924–25
Oscar Estrada	Cuban Stars, 1924–25	St. Louis Browns, 1929
Sal "Chico" Hernández	Indianapolis Clowns, 1945	Chicago Cubs, 1942–43
Ramon "Mike" Herrera	Cuban Stars, 1920–21	Boston Red Sox, 1925–26
Isidoro "Izzy" León	NY Cubans, 1948	Philadelphia Phillies, 1945
Adolfo Luque	Cuban Stars, 1912, LB Cubans, 1913	NY Giants, Boston Braves, Reds, Brooklyn Dodgers, 1914–15, 1918–35
Armando Marsans	All Cubans, 1905, Cuban Stars, 1923	Reds, Browns, Yankees, 1911–18

Latinos who participated in both the black baseball circuit and the major leagues. Drawn from Burgos, "Playing Ball in a Black and White Field of Dreams: Afro-Caribbean Ballplayers in the Negro Leagues, 1910–1950," *Journal of Negro History* 82:1 (Winter 1997): 67–104.

Latino Major Leaguers, Pre-1947

Debut Year	Player	Ethnicity/ Nationality	Team
1871	Esteban Bellán	Cuban	Troy Haymakers
1882	Vincent Nava	Mexican American	Providence Grays
1902	Louis Castro	Colombian	Philadelphia Athletics
1908	Frank Arellanes	Mexican American	Boston Red Sox
1911	Rafael Almeida	Cuban	Cincinnati Reds
1911	Armando Marsans	Cuban	Cincinnati Reds
1912	Miguel A. González	Cuban	Boston Braves
1913	Merito Acosta	Cuban	Washington Senators
1913	Alfredo Cabrera	Spanish Cuban	St. Louis Cardinals
1913	Jacinto "Jack" Calvo	Cuban	Washington Senators
1914	Angel Aragón	Cuban	New York Yankees
1914	Adolfo Luque	Cuban	Boston Braves
1915	Emilio Palmero	Cuban	New York Giants
1916	José Rodriguez	Cuban	New York Giants
1917	Manolo "Manuel" Cueto	Cuban	Cincinnati Reds
1918	Eusebio González	Cuban	Boston Red Sox
1918	Oscar Tuero	Cuban	St. Louis Cardinals
1920	José Acosta	Cuban	Washington Senators
1920	Ricardo Torres	Cuban	Washington Senators
1924	Pedro Dibut	Cuban	Cincinnati Reds
1925	Ramón "Mike" Herrera	Cuban	Boston Red Sox
1929	Oscar Estrada	Cuban	St. Louis Browns
1929	Al Lopez	Spanish American	Brooklyn Dodgers
1930	Vernon "Lefty" Gómez	Mexican American	New York Yankees
1933	Melo Almada	Mexican	Boston Red Sox
1935	José "Chili" Gómez	Mexican	Philadelphia Phillies
1935	Roberto Estalella	Cuban	Washington Senators
1937	Joe M. Gonzales	Mexican American	Boston Red Sox
1937	Fermín "Mike" Guerra	Cuban	Washington Senators
1938	Rene Monteaguado	Cuban	Washington Senators
1939	Alejandro Carrasquel	Venezuelan	Washington Senators
1940	Gilberto Torres	Cuban	Washington Senators
1941	Angel "Jack" Aragón	Cuban	New York Giants
1941	Roberto Ortiz	Cuban	Washington Senators

Debut Year	Player	Ethnicity/ Nationality	Team
1942	Hiram Bithorn	Puerto Rican	Chicago Cubs
1942	Froilan Fernandez	Spanish-American	Boston Braves
1942	Salvador "Chico" Hernández	Cuban	Chicago Cubs
1942	Jesse Flores	Mexican	Chicago Cubs
1943	Luis Rodríguez Olmo	Puerto Rican	Brooklyn Dodgers
1943	Antonio Ordeñana	Cuban	Pittsburgh Pirates
1943	Napoleón Reyes	Cuban	New York Giants
1944	Ralph "Putsy" Caballero	Spanish-American	Philadelphia Phillies
1944	Tomás de la Cruz	Cuban	Cincinnati Reds
1944	Pedro "Preston" Gómez	Cuban	Washington Senators
1944	Oliverio "Baby" Ortiz	Cuban	Washington Senators
1944	Jesús "Chucho" Ramos	Venezuelan	Cincinnati Reds
1944	Luis Suarez	Cuban	Washington Senators
1944	Carlos Santiago Ullrich	Cuban	Washington Senators
1944	Rogelio "Roy" Valdés	Cuban	Washington Senators
1945	Jorge Comellas	Cuban	Chicago Cubs
1945	Isidoro "Izzy" León	Cuban	Philadelphia Phillies
1945	Regino Otero	Cuban	Chicago Cubs
1945	Armando Roche	Cuban	Washington Senators
1945	Adrian Zabala	Cuban	New York Giants
1945	José Zardón	Cuban	Washington Senators

First Latino on Major-League Teams

Team	Year	Player	Nationality/Ethnicity
Philadelphia Athletics	1902	Luis Castro	Colombian
Boston Red Sox	1908	Frank Arellanes	Mexican American
Cincinnati Reds	1911	Rafael Almeida	Cuban
Boston Braves	1912	Miguel Angel González	Cuban
Washington Senators	1913	Merito Acosta	Cuban
New York Yankees	1914	Angel Aragon	Cuban
New York Giants	1915	Emilio Palmero	Cuban
St. Louis Cardinals	1918	Oscar Tuero	Cuban
Chicago White Sox	1922	José Acosta	Cuban
St. Louis Browns	1928	Oscar Estrada	Cuban
Brooklyn Dodgers	1930	Adolfo Luque	Cuban
Philadelphia Phillies	1935	José "Chili" Gómez	Mexican
Chicago Cubs	1942	Hiram Bithorn	Puerto Rican
Pittsburgh Pirates	1943	"Tony" Ordeñana	Cuban
Cleveland Indians	1948	Mike García	Mexican American
Detroit Tigers	1958	Ozzie Virgil	Dominican

Afro-Latino Pioneers, 1947–1959
(Name of first black player to integrate a team italicized)

Debut	Player	Team
April 19, 1949	Orestes Miñoso*	Cleveland Indians
April 18, 1951	Luis Marquez*	Boston Braves
April 18, 1951	Rafael "Ray" Noble*	New York Giants
May 1, 1951	*Orestes Miñoso*	Chicago White Sox
April 15, 1952	Hector Rodríguez*	Chicago White Sox
August 22, 1952	Edmundo "Sandy" Amoros*	Brooklyn Dodgers
April 17, 1953	Rubén Gómez	New York Giants
April 13, 1954	Vic Power	Philadelphia Athletics
April 17, 1954	*Nino Escalera*	Cincinnati Reds
September 6, 1954	*Carlos Paula*	Washington Senators
April 13, 1955	Wenceslao "Vince" González	Washington Senators
April 13, 1955	Roman Mejias	Pittsburgh Pirates
April 16, 1955	Juan Delis	Washington Senators
April 17, 1955	Roberto Clemente	Pittsburgh Pirates
April 17, 1955	Roberto Vargas*	Milwaukee Braves
April 20, 1955	Humberto Robinson	Milwaukee Braves
May 12, 1955	Hector López	Kansas City Athletics
June 18, 1955	Lino Dinoso*	Washington Senators
September 4, 1955	Vibert "Webbo" Clarke*	Washington Senators
September 13, 1955	Julio Becquer	Washington Senators
April 19, 1956	Pat Scantlebury*	Cincinnati Reds
June 21, 1956	Felix Mantilla	Milwaukee Braves
July 14, 1956	Humberto "Chico" Fernández	Brooklyn Dodgers
September 23, 1956	Ozzie Virgil Sr.	New York Giants
April 16, 1957	Valmy Thomas	New York Giants
April 21, 1957	Rene Valdez	Brooklyn Dodgers
May 4, 1957	Juan Pizarro	Milwaukee Braves
April 15, 1958	Orlando Cepeda	San Francisco Giants
April 15, 1958	Juan "Pancho" Herrera*	Philadelphia Phillies
April 15, 1958	Antonio "Tony" Taylor	Chicago Cubs
April 19, 1958	Osvaldo "Ozzie" Alvarez	Washington Senators
June 6, 1958	*Ozzie Virgil Sr.*	Detroit Tigers
June 8, 1958	Felipe Alou	San Francisco Giants
July 11, 1958	Daniel "Danny" Morejón	Washington Senators
April 18, 1959	Miguel "Mike" Cuellar	Cincinnati Reds
August 1, 1959	Zoilo Versalles	Washington Senators
August 4, 1959	José Págan	San Francisco Giants

*Performed in the Negro leagues

Notes

INTRODUCTION

1. Among the compelling studies of the relationship between white violence and neighborhood transition in the Midwest are Arnold Hirsch, *Making the Second Ghetto: Race and Housing in Chicago, 1940–1960* (Chicago: University of Chicago Press, 1998), and Tom Sugrue, *The Origins of the Urban Crisis: Race and Inequality in Postwar Detroit* (Princeton, NJ: Princeton University Press, 1998). For a case study about white resistance to busing that promoted the greater integration of public schools in the Northeast, see Ronald Formisano, *Boston against Busing: Race, Class, and Ethnicity in the 1960s and 1970s* (Chapel Hill: University of North Carolina Press, 2004).

2. I use "organized baseball" to refer to the leagues belonging to the National Agreement. I realize that some might infer that black baseball was therefore "disorganized"; however, my intention is to acknowledge the organization created in 1883 by major- and minor-league owners to wield influence over U.S. professional baseball.

3. These numbers are for the major leagues between 1870 and 1947 (inclusive of the National Association), and between 1905 and 1950 for the black baseball circuits. Totals are drawn from player entries listed in *The Baseball Encyclopedia: The Complete and Definitive Record of Major League Baseball*, 9th ed. (New York: MacMillan, 1993), and James A. Riley, *The Biographical Encyclopedia of Negro Baseball Leagues* (New York: Carroll & Graf, 1994).

4. Michel Rolph Trouillot, *Silencing the Past: Power and the Production of History* (Boston: Beacon Press, 1995).

5. Saxton quoted in Matthew Frye Jacobson, *Whiteness of a Different Color: European Immigration and the Alchemy of Race* (Cambridge, MA: Harvard University Press, 1998), 6.

6. Frank Guridy, "Racial Knowledge in Cuba: The Production of a Social Fact, 1912–1944," (Ph.D. diss., University of Michigan, 2001), 5. Examples of racial knowledge in action include the different immigrant groups, such as Japanese and Indians, that claimed "Caucasian" racial identity as the basis for their eligibility to acquire naturalized citizenship in the United States. See chapter 3, "Becoming Caucasian," and chapter 7, "Naturalization and the Courts," in Jacobson, *Whiteness of a Different Color,* 91–135, 223–45.

7. Omi and Winant, *Racial Formations in the United States: From the 1960s to the 1980s* (Philadelphia: Temple University Press, 1991), 55. For them, the Civil Rights Movement and the racial/identity politics that ensued demonstrated the processes whereby racial categories were formed, invested with significance by the state and society, and then made a source of contention when benefits were linked with distinct categories. Their examination thus ties the articulation of racial identity to claims made on state resources, particularly the impact that state policies had on racial identity in the latter half of the twentieth century.

8. Articulation of a Latino identity differs substantially from individual claims of Spanish descent. Spanish or even Hispanic identity, as deployed in the U.S. ethnoracial system, has often been understood as a nominally white European ethnic category that de-emphasizes the intermixture with indigenous and African (free and slave) groups that occurred in the peopling of the Spanish-speaking Americas. Furthermore, Spanish identity minimizes the role of the African diaspora in the formation of Latino, "Spanish," or "Hispanic" cultural practices in the United States and the Americas. This neglect has occurred despite notions of blackness and racial categories—such as *negro, afromestizo, mulatto, pardo*—that were articulated and socially constructed within each Spanish-speaking society.

9. Latino emerged as a pan-ethnic identity from a different set of historical circumstances than those that shaped regionally defined identities articulated by various groups of the Spanish-speaking Americas. From the seventeenth century through the mid-nineteenth century, individual settler groups articulated their identities based on several factors; most prominent among them were geographic location and family's national origin. As a result, a variety of regionally defined identities flourished throughout the Spanish-speaking Americas: Hispano in the Southwest, mainly New Mexico; Californio among people interspersed throughout California prior to its annexation by the United States; Tejano, Spanish-speaking residents of the Mexican province of Texas; and Spanish or Spaniards. U.S. territorial expansion on the North American continent during this period resulted in armed conflicts with Spanish then Mexican forces over land, self-rule, and national autonomy, producing countless skirmishes, the Mexican-American War (1848), and the War of 1898. These wars, which were influenced by U.S. imperial and colonial designs, reconfigured the nation-state boundaries of Mexico, Cuba, Puerto Rico, and the United States. Changes in nation-state configurations contributed to new articulations of identity by those residing in the newly acquired (or controlled) U.S. territories.

Studies of the formation of Latino ethnic identities that privileged national origins or regional articulations of Latino identity in the U.S. West and Southwest include George Sánchez, *Becoming Mexican American: Ethnicity, Culture, and Identity in Chicano Los Angeles, 1900–1945* (New York: Oxford University Press, 1993); Tomas Almáguer, *Racial Fault Lines: The Historical Origins of White Supremacy in California* (Berkeley and Los Angeles: University of California Press, 1995); David G. Gutierrez, *Walls and Mirrors: Mexican Americans, Mexican Immigrants, and the Politics of Ethnicity* (Berkeley: University of California Press, 1995); Lisbeth Haas, *Conquest and Historical Identities in California, 1769–1936* (Berkeley: University of California Press, 1995); Vicki Ruiz, *From Out of the Shadows: Mexican Women in Twentieth-Century America* (New York: Oxford University Press, 1998); and Joseph A. Rodríguez, "Becoming Latinos: Mexican Americans, Chicanos, and the Spanish Myth in the Urban Southwest," *Western Historical Quarterly* 29:2 (Summer 1998): 165–85. On the labor migration of Mexican nationals to the Midwest, see Zaragoza Vargas, *Proletarians of the North: A History of Mexican Industrial Workers in Detroit and the Midwest, 1917–1933* (Berkeley: University of California Press, 1999); and Dennis Noldes Valdes, *Al Norte: Agricultural Workers in the Great Lakes Region, 1917–1970* (Austin: University of Texas Press, 1990).

10. On class- and gender-based tensions over the development of leisure culture between industrialists, labor, and the middle class, see Roy Rosenzweig, *Eight Hours for What We Will: Workers and Leisure in an Industrial City, 1870–1920* (New York: Cambridge University Press, 1983); Kathy Peiss, *Cheap Amusements: Working-Class Women and Leisure in Turn-of-the-Century New York* (Philadelphia: Temple University Press, 1986); and Cindy S. Aron, *Working at Play: History of Vacations in the United States* (New York: Oxford University Press, 2001).

11. As a family, the Amaros raise important questions about Latino identity. How do we discuss the identity of these three generations of Amaro ballplayers? What aspect of their identity can be privileged while the integrity of their ethnic and racial experience is still maintained? Are they all Cuban? Do we consider one to be Cuban, another Mexican, and the youngest a Mexican-American? The movement of the Amaro family within professional baseball is outlined in Roberto González Echevarría's *Pride of Havana: The History of Cuban Baseball* (New York: Oxford University Press, 2000), 261.

12. The literature on transnationalism and Latinos has grown over the past ten years. The collaborative work of Nina Glick Schiller, Linda Basch, and Cristina Blanc-Szanton remains critical reading; see "From Immigrant to Transmigrant: Theorizing Transnational Migration," *Anthropological Quarterly* 68:1 (1996): 48–63. For recent discussions on transnationalism and Puerto Rican migrations, see Jorge Duany, *The Puerto Rican Nation on the Move: Identities on the Island and in the United States* (Chapel Hill: University of North Carolina Press, 2002); and Gina M. Pérez, *The Near Northwest Side Story: Migration, Displacement, & Puerto Rican Families* (Berkeley: University of California Press, 2004).

13. In this book, I use *Latino* as a panethnic identifier and refer to a Latino subgroup such as Mexican American, Cuban, or Dominican when discussing an issue that affected that specific group. Also, since the racialization of Latinos and

the categories used to describe them fused aspects of their national origins and cultural practices with characteristics perceived as racial (for example, physical features such as skin color), I refer to some of these categories as ethnoracial.

14. Recent works that focus on Latinos and baseball in the Caribbean include Marcos Bretón, *Away Games: The Life and Times of a Latin Ball Player* (New York: Simon & Schuster, 1999); Alan Klein, *Sugarball: The American Game, the Dominican Dream* (New Haven, CT: Yale University Press, 1991); Arturo J. Marcano Guevara and David P. Fidler, *Stealing Lives: The Globalization of Baseball and the Tragic Story of Alexis Quiroz* (Bloomington: University of Indiana Press, 2002); Samuel O. Regalado, *Viva Baseball!: Latin Major Leaguers and Their Special Hunger* (Urbana: University of Illinois Press, 1998); and Rob Ruck, *The Tropic of Baseball* (Westport, CT: Meckler, 1991).

15. We should keep in mind the particular ways our sense of national identity is shaped by the emergence of the modern nation-state, particularly in colonial and postcolonial settings. Could "Cuban" national identity exist before national independence was secured and any official state-coordinated program articulating *cubanidad* was enacted? Such questions illustrate how subject positions can predate nation-state formation.

16. Nineteenth-century Cuban nationalist leader José Martí coined the term *nuestra America* as a means of reconceptualizing hemispheric political, social, and economic relations at a time when the United States was becoming an increasingly dominant force. For a greater elaboration of *nuestra America*, see Jeffrey Belnap and Raúl Fernández, eds., *Jose Marti's "Our America": From National to Hemispheric Cultural Studies* (Durham, NC: Duke University Press, 1998); Sandhya Shulka and Heidi Tinsman, eds., "Our Americas: Political and Cultural Imaginings," special issue, *Radical History Review* 89 (Spring 2004).

The U.S. political role and the powerful sway of U.S. culture in the Americas have led to debates within American Studies regarding the discipline's boundaries as a field of inquiry and its incorporativeness of ethnic studies perspectives. See Patricia Nelson Limerick, "Insiders and Outsiders: The Borders of the USA and the Limits of the ASA: Presidential Address to the American Studies Association, 31 October 1996," *American Quarterly* 49:3 (September 1997): 449–69; Jane C. Desmond and Virginia Dominguez, "Resituating American Studies in a Critical Internationalism," *American Quarterly* 48:3 (September 1996): 475–90; Linda Kerber, "Diversity and the Transformation of American Studies," *American Quarterly* 41:3 (September 1989): 415–31; and Shelley Fisher Fishkin, "Interrogating 'Whiteness,' Complicating 'Blackness': Remapping American Culture," *American Quarterly* 47:3 (September 1995): 428–66. On debates on multiculturalism as an approach to American Studies, see Frances Aparício, "On Multiculturalism and Privilege: A Latina Perspective," *American Quarterly* 46:4 (December 1994): 575–88; John Higham, "Multiculturalism and Universalism: A History and Critique," *American Quarterly* 45:2 (June 1993): 195–219; and responses in same issue by Gerald Early, "American Education and the Postmodernist Impulse" (220–29); and by Nancy Hewitt, "A Response to John Higham" (237–42).

17. On multipositionality, see Earl Lewis, "Invoking Concepts, Problematizing Identities: The Life of Charles N. Hunter and the Implications for the Study of Gender and Labor," *Labor History* 34:2–3 (Spring–Summer 1993): 292–308.

18. Grant Farred, "Sport Isn't Everyday: Sport as the Ambivalent Language of Democracy," keynote address delivered at the Capitalizing on Sport conference, February 28, 2003, University of Illinois, Urbana-Champaign.

Historian Thomas Holt wonderfully explicates how the everyday can be used as the site for the replication of race. Holt asserts that in "everydayness," "race is reproduced via the marking of the racial Other and that racist ideas and practices are naturalized, made self-evident, and thus seemingly beyond audible change. It is at this level that race is reproduced long after its original historical stimulus—the slave trade and slavery—have faded. It is at this level that seemingly rational and ordinary folks commit irrational and extraordinary acts" (Holt, "Marking: Race, Race-Making, and the Writing of History," *American Historical Review* 100 [February 1995]: 7).

19. I prefer "War of 1898" to "Spanish-American War," the moniker formerly used by journalists, politicians, and scholars. This avoids the longer "Filipino-Cuban-Spanish-American War" and better captures the armed conflict that took place on two fronts—the Caribbean and the Pacific—and in three different countries. The United States intervened in local anti-colonial struggles against Spain in Cuba and the Philippines and invaded Puerto Rico, which had been granted a Charter of Autonomy by Spain in November 1897. After defeating Spanish forces, the United States signed the Treaty of Paris with Spain, whereby the United States took possession of the Philippines and Puerto Rico and established a transitional occupation government in Cuba.

1. A NATIONAL GAME EMERGES

Chadwick quoted in Warren Goldstein, *Playing for Keeps: A History of Early Baseball* (Ithaca, NY: Cornell University Press, 1989), 44.

1. *New York Clipper,* February 25, 1871.

2. For an early description of the war's impact on baseball's spread throughout the United States and the game's elevation to a national pastime, see chapter 7 in Albert G. Spalding, *America's National Game* (1911; repr., Lincoln: University of Nebraska Press, 1992).

3. In his memoir, Tampa native Evilio Grillo discusses his family's movement within the transnational circuit of labor before they settled in Tampa. Even so, economic downturns in Tampa would inspire Cuban residents to return to the island for seasonal work. See Evilio Grillo, *Black Cuban, Black American* (Houston: Arté Publico Press, 2002).

4. On Cuban immigration to the United States and the process of community formation, see Nancy Mirabal, "*De Aquí, De Allá:* Race, Empire, and Nation in the Making of Cuban Migrant Communities in New York and Tampa, 1823–1924," (Ph.D. diss., University of Michigan, 2001). On political alliances forged in New York between Cubans and Puerto Rican nationalists in the late nineteenth century, see Mirabal, "No Country But the One We Must Fight For," in *Mambo Montage: The Latinization of New York* (New York: Columbia University Press, 2001): 57–72.

5. González Echevarría, *Pride of Havana,* 82.

6. Ibid., 90. González Echevarría draws his information on Guilló and Zaldo

from interviews appearing in the *Diario de la Marina*, a leading Havana newspaper that began publishing in 1868. The interview with Teodoro Zaldo was published on January 20, 1924.

7. On baseball in nineteenth-century Cuba, see Louis A. Pérez, "Between Baseball and Bullfighting: The Quest for Nationality in Cuba, 1868–1898," *Journal of American History* (September 1994): 493–517; and Roberto González Echevarría, "The Game in Matanzas: On the Origins of Cuban Baseball," *Yale Review* 83 (July 1995): 62–94. On the Dominican Republic, see Ruck, *The Tropic of Baseball,* and Klein, *Sugarball.*

8. Historian Nancy Mirabal explores why New York City and Tampa developed into popular destinations for Cubans and details the political and economic factors that shaped their decision to leave the island from the 1840s through the mid-twentieth century. She challenges scholars to move beyond an exile model in analyzing Cubans' sojourn in the United States historically and better understanding the process of community making, identity formation, and the diverse factors that shaped the different waves of Cuban emigration and settlement in the United States. See Mirabal, "*De Aquí, De Allá.*"

9. Upon arrival in the United States, Bellán enrolled in the college's first grammar class and, according to documents located by a Fordham archivist, studied at Fordham until the 1867–68 academic year. The archivist explained that the college's three grammar classes were the equivalent of today's four-year high school, and completion of the following three grammar classes the equivalent of a bachelor's degree. Fordham University Library archivist Maurice Ahren to Lee Allen, December 9, 1969, Bellán Player File, National Baseball Library and Archive (hereafter NBLA).

10. In their respective works, Steven A. Reiss and Melvin Adelman examine the development of baseball in urban settings during the nineteenth century. One of the points both establish is baseball's initial place in the local sporting culture of the white-collar clerical class. This class of ballplayers consisted of men with some education and economic means. Due to his economic background as a Cuban attending a U.S.-based college, Bellán fit within this group. See Reiss, *City Games: The Evolution of American Urban Society and the Rise of Sports* (Urbana: University of Illinois Press, 1991); and section 2 in Adelman, *A Sporting Time: New York City and the Rise of Modern Athletics, 1820–1870* (Urbana: University of Illinois Press, 1990).

11. These percentages are drawn from my survey of enrollment cards for Fordham students who attended the college from the 1860s and 1880s and discussions with Patricia Kane, head of Archives and Special Collections (Student Enrollment Cards, Archives and Special Collections, Fordham University).

12. The Zaldo brothers played for Almendares as early as November 1, 1878, as indicated by a November 16, 1878, box score published in the *New York Clipper.* Almendares competed in Cuban professional baseball from 1879 to 1959. Ildefonso Ortega's article "Historia del Club Almendares," quoted in "Magazine 'Fotos' from Puerto Rico," Negro League Folder, Ashland Collection, NBLA. Fordham's baseball connection extended beyond the Caribbean and into other parts of Latin America. A member of the Fordham varsity baseball team

in the late 1880s, Nicaraguan David Arellano became a prominent figure in baseball's development in his native country and was a member of the first baseball team formed by the Managua Society of Recreation in 1890. Michael M. Oleksak and Mary Adams Oleksak, *Beisbol: Latin Americans and the Grand Old Game* (Indianapolis: Masters Press, 1996), 11.

13. The distinction between professional and semiprofessional arises from how players are paid. Semiprofessionals were paid primarily on a per-game cooperative basis. Professional players drew a salary based on a contract. For an overview of Bellán's career, see Robert L. Tiemann and Jose de Jesus Jiménez Jr., "Esteban Enrique Bellan (Steve)," in *Nineteenth Century Woodcuts*, 11; and Jimenez, "Esteban Bellan, the First Latin American Player to Play Organized Baseball in the United States," unpublished paper, Bellán Player File, NBLA.

14. Goldstein, *Playing for Keeps*, 98.

15. "Formation of the National Association of Base Ball Players (NABBP) in New York (1857)," in Dean A. Sullivan, ed., *Early Innings: A Documentary History of Baseball, 1825–1908* (Lincoln: University of Nebraska Press, 1995), p. 22, 54.

16. "The Exclusion of African Americans from the NABBP (1867)," in Sullivan, *Early Innings*, 68.

17. Goldstein, *Playing for Keeps*, 88.

18. *New York Clipper*, November 19, 1870.

19. This exclusion of African Americans from both professional and national baseball associations in the post–Civil War era coincides with the development of new visions of the American nation and the expansion of state power. On one hand, some Americans advocated a stronger central government that would actively assert, define, and protect the individual civil rights of all (male) citizens. On the other hand, Americans, regardless of region, invented new ways to subvert the social equality that passage of post–Civil War amendments and Reconstruction legislation sought to ensure. Thanks to Kate Masur for sharing this comment.

20. Spalding, *America's National Game*, 134.

21. Goldstein, *Playing for Keeps*, 34, 35.

22. Ibid., 46, 48.

23. Ibid., 23–24.

24. Ibid., 20, 38.

25. Spalding, *America's National Game*, 10–11.

26. Ibid., 190, 191.

27. Goldstein, *Playing for Keeps*, 31.

28. "A New Rule on Professional Players (1869)," in Sullivan, *Early Innings*, 72.

29. "Three Players Expelled for 'Selling' a Game (1865)," in Sullivan, *Early Innings*, 49–53; Spalding, *America's National Game*, 130.

30. Spalding, *America's National Game*, 134–35.

31. Ibid., 193.

32. Ibid.

33. "The NL Responds to the Manifesto (1889)," in *Early Innings*, 190.

34. Spalding, *America's National Game,* 194.

35. Goldstein, *Playing for Keeps,* 148; Spalding, *America's National Game,* 219.

36. According to baseball historian David Pietrusza, a "major" league's viability depended on four factors: money, leadership, player dissatisfaction, and necessity. See Pietrusza, *Major Leagues: The Formation, Sometimes Absorption, and Mostly Inevitable Demise of 18 Professional Baseball Organizations, 1871 to Present* (Jefferson, NC: McFarland, 1991), vii–viii.

37. Space does not permit a full account here of the maneuvers made to ensure the National League's supremacy in professional baseball. I will note that Hulbert's leadership style was quite similar to the monopolizing tactics employed by the era's industrial titans—Rockefeller, Morgan, and Carnegie—who built corporate empires by crushing smaller-scale competitors. Perhaps best capturing this monopolistic approach were Hulbert's mandates that forced leagues to join the National Agreement or risk National League teams raiding their rosters. On the labor history of professional baseball during this period, see Robert Burk, *Never Just a Game: Players, Owners, and American Baseball to 1920* (Chapel Hill: University of North Carolina Press, 1994), esp. chaps. 3–5. On Hulbert, see Robert Knight Barney and Frank Dallier, "'I'd Rather be a Lamp Post in Chicago, Than a Millionaire in Any Other City': William A. Hulbert, Civic Pride, and the Birth of the National League," *Nine* 2:1 (Fall 1993): 40–58.

38. Early in the twentieth century, the minor league system went from A-down to D-level leagues, which later evolved into the current minor-league classification system of AAA, AA, A, and Rookie League. For a commentary on the financial relationship between the major and minor leagues, see *Sporting News,* June 25, 1887.

39. Goldstein, *Playing for Keeps,* 151.

40. The Hop Bitters represented an ingenious form of marketing for a Rochester-based (New York) patent medicine company. The Bancroft-led team played against top-flight competition in the States and performed "so remarkably strong that it made a big hit throughout the country." Secondary sources provide conflicting dates for this first Cuban tour by a North American professional team, some as early as 1878, others as late as 1881. These sources agree that the Hop Bitters were the first U.S. professional team to tour the island. See "Giants Will Honor Frank Bancroft at Polo Grounds Wednesday," undated clipping [May 1917]; "The Pioneer Barnstormer," October 6, 1906; and "Starring in Sports," undated clipping, all in Frank Bancroft File, NBLA.

41. The war failed to resolve the central issue of Spanish rule or satisfy the nationalists' desire for autonomy. Indeed, not all members of the insurgent forces were pleased with the negotiated terms of the Pact of Zanjón, which ended the war. A displeased faction expressed its discontent by launching an offensive in the island's eastern provinces in late August 1879—a nine-month uprising known as *la guerra chiquita* (the Little War). See Ada Ferrer, *Insurgent Cuba* (Chapel Hill: University of North Carolina Press, 2000).

42. "Bancroft's First Cuban Invasion," *Sporting News,* January 14, 1909. Written upon Bancroft's return from his 1908 tour of Cuba with the Cincinnati Reds' barnstorming team, the article reflected on his first Cuban trip in 1879.

Although appearing in the *Sporting News,* the article was based on an interview of Bancroft by writer Charlie Zuber originally published in the *Cincinnati Times-Star.*

43. *Sporting Life,* January 2, 1897.

44. Felix Roberto Masud-Piloto, *From Welcomed Exiles to Illegal Immigrants: Cuban Immigration to the U.S., 1959–1995* (Lanham, MD: Rowman & Littlefield, 1996), 8–11.

45. *Sporting Life,* January 2, 1897; "Bancroft, Baseball Dean, Back on Job," undated clipping; Frank Bancroft File, NBLA.

46. *New York Clipper,* December 6, 1879, and Wenceslao Galvez y Delmonte, *El Base Ball en Cuba* (Habana: Imprenta Mercantil, de los Heredores de Santiago, 1889), 61; *New York Clipper,* September 6, 1879.

47. *Chicago Tribune,* December 7, 1879.

48. *Sporting Life,* January 14, 1885; *New York Clipper,* February 14, 1885; *El Figaro,* November 26, 1885 (based on an item reported in the *New York Herald*). Cullen served as Havana's manager, captain, and catcher for the 1884–85 campaign.

2. EARLY MANEUVERS

1. *Sporting Life,* May 20, 1899; A. G. Spink, *The National Game* (2nd ed., 1911; repr., Carbondale: Southern Illinois University Press, 2000), 110; *Washington Post,* September 29, 1907.

2. The gaps in primary materials contribute to unverifiable claims. One Internet website article proudly claims Nava as a native-born Cuban, concocting a story that he had been born in Cuba and was transported to San Francisco as an infant and speculating that his father "escaped from Cuba fleeing the obligatory military service and did not have the time to register his son's birth." Edwin "Kako" Vazquez, "Invasion Latina en las Grandes Ligas," accessed December 27, 2002, www.anotala.com/art001.asp (article translated by Adrian Burgos).

3. Maria Túa, personal communication with author regarding the traditional practice of using family names in Latin America, November 28, 2002.

4. U.S. Census Bureau, 1870 Census, Series M593, Roll 84, p. 626; Joel S. Franks, *Whose Baseball? The National Pastime and Cultural Diversity in California, 1859–1941* (Lanham, MD: Scarecrow Press, 2001), 46.

5. *New York Clipper,* September 26, 1868, and December 17, 1870. An intrasquad game played on Thanksgiving Day in 1870 between members of the American Baseball Club also featured players with Spanish surnames, Monteloy and Vallejo.

6. On racialization in California, particularly as it illuminates the creation of a racial hierarchy that elevated Spanish ancestry over indigenous and *afromestizo* roots, see Menchaca, *Recovering History Constructing Race: The Indian, Black, and White Roots of Mexican Americans* (Austin: University of Texas Press, 2001); and Haas, *Conquest and Historical Identities.* On the impact of the racialization of Mexicans through U.S. popular cultural forms on the motivations for U.S. action in the Mexican-American War and the lack of full enforcement of the Treaty of Guadalupe Hidalgo and citizenship rights thereafter,

see Shelley Streeby, *American Sensations: Class, Empire, and the Production of Popular Culture* (Berkeley and Los Angeles: University of California Press, 2002). For an overview of racial formation in Mexican American history, see Vicki Ruiz, "Morena/o, Blanca/o y Cafe con Leche: Racial Constructions in Chicana/o Historiography," *Estudios Mexicanos/Mexican Studies* 20:2 (Summer 2004): 343–59.

7. Josefa Simental Irwin, death record information, 1879D-1689, *San Francisco Call,* accessed November 28, 2002, http://feefhs.org/fdb2/6991/6991–204 .html. E-mail communication with Mario Longoria, October 3, 2001, and February 25, 2002. San Francisco City Directory, 1879, pp. 456, 470. Thanks to Bob Timmerman for sharing materials on Nava's life in San Francisco.

8. Ward played a fascinating role in race and labor relations in nineteenth-century baseball. A Columbia University law school graduate, he joined the struggle by the National Brotherhood of Base Ball Players (the Brotherhood) against management manipulation of the reserve rule. For coverage of the Brotherhood's campaign before formation of the Players League, see the *New York Clipper* between July 23, 1887, and November 26, 1887.

9. A *New York Clipper* article (December 7, 1878) listed the catcher as "V. Irwin"; at that moment he was the league's tenth leading hitter, with a .241 average. On California professional baseball during the late nineteenth century, see Joel S. Franks "Whose Baseball? Baseball in Nineteenth-Century Multicultural California," *Nine* 4:2 (Spring 1996): 246–62.

10. John Ward to Harry Wright, Boston, February 18, 1882; Harry Wright to John Ward, Boston, February 21, 1882, Harry Wright Scrapbook, Albert Spalding Baseball Collection, New York Public Library. Thanks to Mario Longoria, who is completing a full-length biography of Nava, for sharing copies of these communications.

11. Franks, *Whose Baseball?*, 102–8; *New York Clipper,* February 4, 1882, p. 753 (emphasis added); *New York Clipper,* March 25, 1882. The *New York Clipper* and *Providence Journal* covered the signing and arrival of Nava during the months preceding the 1882 campaign (*Providence Journal,* January 28, 1882; March 1, 1882; March 6, 1882).

12. *Providence Journal,* January 28, 1882 (annual meeting). Bloodgood was a partner in the patent medicine painkiller firm of Perry Davis & Son; see the 1882–86 Providence directories.

13. David Nemec, *The Beer and Whiskey League: The Illustrated History of the American Association—Baseball's Renegade Major League* (New York: Lyons & Burford, 1994).

14. *Providence Journal,* January 28, 1882, p. 8. Rick Stattler notes that the team management used Nava as a draw for games in Vermont and Connecticut towns. Stattler, "Vincent 'Sandy' Nava," unpublished manuscript, 8.

15. The concept of racial knowledge emerges from works on racialization and race-making that are grounded in the everyday world in which the multiple meanings are lived. Frank Guridy employs the concept in his study of race in early-twentieth-century Cuba, "Racial Knowledge in Cuba." See also Eduardo Bonilla-Silva, "Rethinking Racism: Towards a Structural Interpretation," *American Sociological Review* 62 (June 1997): 465–80; Barbara Jeanne Fields, "Slav-

ery, Race, and Ideology in the United States of America," *New Left Review* 181 (1990): 95–118; Holt, "Marking"; Evelyn Brooks Higginbotham, "African-American Women's History and the Metalanguage of Race," *Signs: Journal of Women in Culture and Society* 17 (Winter 1992): 251–74.

16. Gordon, *The Great Arizona Orphan Abduction* (Cambridge, MA: Harvard University Press, 1999). The case would eventually become the subject of a lawsuit by the New York Foundling Hospital, which arranged the original adoption. In a decision handed down by the U.S. Supreme Court, the adoptions were declared null and void because the adoptive parents, "Mexican Indians," were deemed unfit by "'mode of living, habits and education . . . to have the custody, care and education' of white children." Stephen Lassonde, "Family Values, 1904," *New York Times,* January 9, 2000.

17. David Voigt, *America through Baseball* (Chicago: Nelson-Hill, 1976), 111. Claims that Nava might be a Negro attest to the predominance of the black-white paradigm at the time historians began to revisit the history of America's game in the 1970s and 1980s. Collectively, scholars such as Voigt, Melvin Adelman, Steven Reiss, and Jules Tygiel moved the field beyond studies that focused on the making of heroes such as Babe Ruth, John McGraw, and Ty Cobb. By examining processes such as urbanization, modernization, and racial integration, they transformed the study of baseball, presenting the sport as a social institution in which Americans from various backgrounds negotiated their place in society. As important as this accomplishment was, their works did not interrogate racial difference beyond black and white.

18. *New York Clipper,* February 25 and April 22, 1882; *Chicago Tribune,* May 21, May 31, June 10, and June 22, 1883; *National Police Gazette,* October 4, 1884; *Providence Journal,* April 3, 1882, p. 8. To trace the initial transformation, see the *New York Clipper*'s coverage from January 21 to April 22, 1882.

19. Stattler, "Vincent 'Sandy' Nava," 8. Stattler refers to an article appearing in the *Providence Journal* on May 2, 1882, that discusses Nava's collecting tickets.

20. *New York Clipper,* April 22, 1882, p. 75; Stattler, "Vincent 'Sandy' Nava," p. 3.

21. Stattler, "Vincent 'Sandy' Nava," p. 11.

22. *Providence Journal,* April 1, 1882, p. 8. Substitutes entered a game only with the umpire's permission, and only if a starting player was injured or had taken ill during a game. Frederick Ivor-Campbell, "Extraordinary 1884: The Year of Baseball's First World Series," *National Pastime,* no. 13 (1993): 17.

23. *New York Clipper,* May 31, 1882, p. 7. Poem in *Providence Journal,* May 31, 1882, quoted in Stattler, "Vincent 'Sandy' Nava," 3.

24. *New York Clipper,* June 10, 1882, p. 16; *Providence Evening Telegram,* June 22, 1882, quoted in Stattler, "Vincent 'Sandy' Nava," 4.

25. Newspapers in Chicago, Detroit, and Providence printed these lyrics. See, for example, *Chicago Tribune,* June 25, 1882; *Detroit Free Press, Providence Evening Telegram,* June 27, 1882.

26. *New York Clipper,* March 27, 1883.

27. *Chicago Tribune,* July 28, 1882, and *New York Clipper,* August 5, 1882.

28. On the world series, see Frederick Ivor-Campbell, "Extraordinary 1884," 16–23; and Larry G. Bowman, "The First Worlds Championship of Professional Baseball: The New York Metropolitans and the Providence Grays, 1884," *Nine* 6:2 (Spring 1998): 2–14.

29. *New York Clipper,* October 11, 1884; *National Police Gazette,* November 8, 1884; *Sporting Life,* November 5, 1884.

30. On Nava's joining Baltimore, see *National Police Gazette,* June 27, 1885; *Sporting Life,* June 24, September 16, and December 16, 1885. On Nava's movement after the big leagues, see *National Police Gazette,* May 15, 1886; *New York Clipper,* January 29, 1887; and *Sporting News,* March 5, 1887.

31. E-mail communication with Mario Longoria, February 18, 2001. Longoria found the cemetery indicated on Nava's death certificate as his burial place. Although the cemetery was not listed in the National Register of Cemeteries, he and Norman Macht, a fellow member of the Society of American Baseball Researchers, found the church to which the cemetery belonged. They discovered that the cemetery was underneath a highway in Baltimore and that no other records were available.

32. Voigt, *America through Baseball,* 111. Although Voigt cited three primary sources for his description of Nava's identity, none of them refers to Nava as a Negro. In his 1910 publication, *The National Game,* Alfred Spink, editor of the *Sporting News,* refers to Nava as "a little Cuban" (p. 110). However, Voigt does not cite this work.

33. On the recovery of the impact of the African diaspora in Mexico—including the importation of slaves during Spanish colonial rule, the rise of *afromestizos,* and the role of blackness within the construction of national and racial identities—see Menchaca, *Recovering History, Constructing Race.*

34. *Chicago Tribune,* July 29, 1883. The *Tribune*'s description represents one of a handful of instances when Nava was specifically referred to as Cuban while he was an active player. This may again have stemmed from northeasterners' greater familiarity with the Cuban presence in baseball, due to Bellán and others having performed in local leagues and college teams.

35. Stefan Fatsis, "Mystery of Baseball: Was William White Game's First Black?" *Wall Street Journal,* January 30, 2004.

36. "Base Ball from a Colored Point of View," *Chicago Tribune,* August 24, 1870, quoted in John Freyer, "The 1870 Chicago Blue Stockings and Early Negro Baseball," paper presented at the Jerry Malloy Negro League Conference, June 18, 2005, Chicago.

37. *New York Freeman,* August 8, 1886. In New Jersey these hotels were located in such towns as Red Bank, Long Branch, Asbury Park, and Ocean Grove. At least six black baseball teams played in the hotel circuit in 1883: the West End Base Ball Club, Star Baseball Club of Keyport, Crescent B.B.C., Metropolitans, Long Branch, and Red Bank. Hotel industrialists like Henry Flagler in places such as St. Augustine, Florida, developed several of these hotels in the 1880s and 1890s. Florida-based hotels became extremely important to the development of black baseball in the 1900s when they hosted African American players and black teams such as the Cuban Giants. Information about teams and the hotels where they played are drawn from *New York Globe,* June 23, August 4 and 18, 1883.

38. *New York Globe,* May 24, 1884. From 1883 to 1889 Thompson worked at hotels in Boston, Babylon (Long Island), Philadelphia, and St. Augustine.

39. A native of St. Croix, S. K. Govern took the managerial helm of the Cuban Giants in 1886. The manager of the Manhattans of Washington (DC) team from 1881 to 1884, Govern made several trips to Cuba between 1881 and 1884, according to an 1886 *Trenton Times* article located by baseball historian Jerry Malloy. In his second year with the Cuban Giants, Govern made plans for a winter tour of Cuba following the 1886 campaign. Although it is unclear whether the Cuban leg of the team's trip came to fruition, the Cuban Giants did travel to Florida, making a stop in St. Augustine in 1886, where they would become regular wintertime visitors through the 1890s. Malloy, "Introduction" to *Sol White's History of Colored Base Ball, with Other Documents on the Early Black Game,* comp. Jerry Malloy (Lincoln: University of Nebraska Press, 1995), xl (hereafter *Sol White's History*); *New York Clipper,* July 31, 1886. For biographical information on Govern, see Rory Costello, "S.K. Govern: Black Baseball Renaissance Man," accessed October 10, 2003, http://home.nyc.rr.com/vibaseball/ govern.html.

40. Harlow, "Unrecognized Stars," *Esquire* (September 1938): 75.

41. In his introduction to *Sol White's History* (p. lx), Jerry Malloy states: "For several reasons, this rendition of events is far more plausible than White's. First, it was written twenty years before White's book and only two years after the fact. Furthermore, the article probably was based on an interview with [Frank] Thompson himself, who was employed by a Boston hotel at the time."

42. Team names are drawn from research conducted in nineteenth-century newspapers from the United States and Cuba including the *New York Clipper, Sporting Life, Sporting News, New York Age,* and *El Score* (Tampa) in the United States, and *El Score, El Pitcher,* and *El Figaro* in Cuba. On interactions between African American and Cuban teams, see Lisa Brock and Bijan Bayne, "Not Just Black: African-Americans, Cubans, and Baseball," in *Between Race and Empire: African-Americans and Cubans before the Cuban Revolution,* ed. Lisa Brock and Digna Castañeda Fuertes (Philadelphia: Temple University Press, 1998), 168–204.

43. *New York Globe,* August 11, 1883.

44. *National Police Gazette,* June 12, 1886.

45. This prose is an example of what African American scholar Evelyn Brooks Higginbotham labels a "metalanguage of race," whereby images, words, and styles gain racial significance beyond their regular meaning or definition. Indeed, through communication—verbal, visual, or textual—individuals engage in this metalanguage in daily conversations. As Higginbotham writes: "We must expose the role of race as a metalanguage by calling attention to its powerful, all-encompassing effect on the construction and representation of other social and power relations, namely, gender, class, and sexuality, . . . [and] recognize race as providing sites of dialogic exchange and contestation, since race has constituted a discursive toll for both oppression and liberation." Higginbotham, "African American Women's History and the Metalanguage of Race," 252.

46. "Cutting the Coons' Combs," *Binghamton Daily Leader,* June 10, 1887; *Sporting News,* June 28, 1886.

47. "Base Ball Notes," *Binghamton Daily Leader,* June 10, 1887.

48. Greg Bond lists the assortment of racial and national labels that were applied to African American players by sportswriters. See chapter 1, "'A Novelty . . . and an Intelligent Young Fellow,'" in "Whipped Curs and Real Men: Race, Manliness, and the Segregation of Organized Baseball in the Late Nineteenth Century" (master's thesis, University of Wisconsin, Madison, 1999).

49. *Sporting News,* April 23, 1887; *Toronto Daily Mail,* April 15, 1887. Thanks to Greg Bond for sharing the *Daily Mail* citation.

50. Among such historians, Mark Savoie argues that *Spaniard* was another code word for African American, based on his research findings, which included a July 1886 *Buffalo Express* reference to Frank Grant, an African American infielder, as a Spaniard. Savoie, "Drawing the Line: The Trials of African-American Baseball Players in the International League (1886–1889)," *Nine* 1:1 (Fall 1992): 44. On African American players being labeled Spanish in nineteenth-century professional baseball, see Jerry Jaye Wright, "From Giants to Monarchs: The 1890 Season of the Colored Monarchs of York, Pennsylvania," *Nine* 2:2 (Spring 1994): 248–49.

51. Anson and Nava appeared in more than ten games opposite each other. For box scores and recaps of some of the games in which Nava and Anson played against each other, see *Providence Evening Bulletin,* May 25, 26, and 28, and June 11 and 12, 1883, Spalding Scrapbook, NBLA; *Chicago Tribune,* June 10, 1882, and June 16, 1883; *New York Clipper,* July 8, 1882; October 21, 1882; June 2, 1883; May 17 and 24, 1884; and *Sporting Life,* May 21, 1884.

3. HOLDING THE LINE

Fowler quoted in Robert Peterson, *Only the Ball Was White: A History of Legendary Black Players and All-Black Professional Teams* (Englewood Cliffs, NJ: Prentice-Hall, 1970; repr., New York: Oxford University Press, 1992), 40.

1. Several works detail the formation of baseball's color line and its impact on North American professional baseball. See Jerry Malloy, "Out at Home: Baseball Draws the Color Line," *The National Pastime* (1983): 14–28; and Savoie, "Drawing the Line." On Walker's experience as Major League Baseball's first black player, see David Zang, *Fleet Walker's Divided Heart: The Life of Baseball's First Black Major Leaguer* (Lincoln: University of Nebraska Press, 1995), and "Oberlinian was First Negro Player in Major Leagues," *Oberlin Alumni Bulletin* (First Quarter 1946), in Moses Fleetwood Walker and Weldy Wilberforce Walker File, Ashland Collection, NBLA.

2. *Sol White's History,* 76.

3. *Toledo Daily Blade,* August 11, 1883, quoted in "PS," *The National Pastime* 2:2 (Fall 1983): 88; *National Police Gazette,* September 15, 1883. Moses Walker and his brother Weldy played in the American Association, a "major league," in 1884.

4. *Sol White's History,* 76.

5. Johnson, *Black Manhattan* (1930; repr., New York: Da Capo Press, 1991), 62–63.

6. Malloy, "The Pittsburgh Keystones and the 1887 Colored League: A Radical Concept in Team Ownership," in *Baseball in Pittsburgh* (Cleveland: SABR,

1995), 50. On the league's plans and ultimate demise, see *Binghamton Daily Leader,* April 7, 1887; *Sporting News,* May 21, 1887; and *New York Clipper,* March 19 and 26 and June 4, 1887.

7. Malloy, introduction to *Sol White's History,* xxii.

8. Clipping, "Story of an Old Timer—Bud Fowler's Long Siege on the Diamond," *Cincinnati Enquirer,* April 12, 1895, Fowler Player File, NBLA. Fowler's retirement in 1904 ended a career that spanned four decades. At various points in that career, he had played on all-black teams, managed traveling black teams, and stood alone as the sole black player on formerly all-white teams. *Sporting News,* July 19, 1890; and *Sporting Life,* February 4, 1899, April 8, 1899, and August 12, 1899.

9. *Binghamton Daily Leader,* July 5, 1887, quoted in *Labor-Community Reporter* 8:9 (September 1987), Bud Fowler Biographical File, NBLA. Richard White contends that Fowler's letter was part of a ruse by team management to cover up the actual reason he was being released: his race. See White, "Baseball's John Fowler: The 1887 Season in Binghamton, New York," *Afro-Americans in New York Life and History* 16:1 (January 1992): 7–17. Born John W. Jackson in 1858 to a free African American family in upstate New York, Fowler changed his name for reasons historians have not established. According to Bob Davids, he acquired his nickname "from his inclination to call most others by that name." Davids, *Memorial Observance for John (Bud) Fowler: Black Baseball Pioneer* (Manhattan, KS, 1987), 1, Fowler File, NBLA.

10. *Sporting News,* June 11, 1887.

11. *Binghamton Daily Leader* quoted in Davids, *Memorial Observance for John (Bud) Fowler,* 1.

12. *Binghamton Daily Leader,* June 19 and July 5, 1887; *Binghamton Daily Republican,* June 29, 1887.

13. *Binghamton Daily Leader,* July 16, 1887; *Sporting News,* July 23, 1887.

14. However, segregationist forces again voiced their displeasure and were scheming "to have colored players ousted from the International Association" in the middle of the 1888 campaign (*New York Clipper,* June 23, 1888). *Sporting News,* July 9 and July 30, November 19, and December 3, 1887.

15. "Ballplayers Do Not Burn," in *Sol White's History,* 140 (piece originally appeared in *Sporting Life,* October 24, 1891).

16. Quoted in Malloy, "Out at Home," p. 18. Fowler and fellow second baseman Frank Grant faced attempts to injure them by opponents with sharpened spikes so frequently that the two share credit for inventing shin guards.

17. *Binghamton Daily Leader,* June 6, 1887; *New York Clipper,* June 11, 1887; *Sporting News,* June 4 and 11, 1887. *Sol White's History,* 161; Savoie, "Drawing the Line," 50–52.

A team portrait controversy also erupted in the International League team in Buffalo. Several of Buffalo's white players initially refused to sit for the team portrait if it included their black teammate, Frank Grant. The team manager, however, convinced his players to end their protest without resorting to violence as had occurred in the Syracuse case. These protests illustrate the meaning that players attached to symbolic forms of social equality. See Malloy, "Out at Home," 23.

18. *National Police Gazette,* July 2, 1887. It should be noted that no International League team featured more than two African American players.

19. David Roediger, *The Wages of Whiteness: Race and the Making of the American Working Class* (New York: Verso, 1991), 148.

20. *National Police Gazette,* August 29, 1885 (emphasis added).

21. In current debates, masculinity is understood as a social and ideological construction that encapsulates society's thoughts, ideas, and expected behaviors concerning the male gender. In her important study of gender and race in the late nineteenth century, historian Gail Bederman established that in the 1890s a discursive shift occurred from "manly" to "masculinity." According to Bederman, manliness was "character or conduct worthy of a man" and "comprised all the worthy moral attributes which the Victorian middle class admired in a man." On the other hand, masculinity comprised "any characteristics, good or bad, that all men had . . . [and] more frequently than 'manly,' was applied across class or race boundaries; for, by definition, *all* men were masculine." *Manliness & Civilization: A Cultural History of Gender and Race in the United States, 1880–1917* (Chicago: University of Chicago Press, 1996), pp. 18–20.

On the role of gender in Redemption in North Carolina, see Glenda Gilmore, *Gender and Jim Crow* (Chapel Hill: University of North Carolina Press, 1998). On Reconstruction and the promises made (and broken), see Edward Ayers, *The Promise of the New South: Life after Reconstruction* (New York: Oxford University Press, 1992); Eric Foner, *Reconstruction: America's Unfinished Revolution* (New York: Harper & Row, 1988); and W. E. B. Du Bois, *Black Reconstruction in America, 1860–1880* (1935; repr., New York: Atheneum, 1992).

22. *Sporting News,* November 4, 1893.

23. *Sporting News,* August 25, 1888.

24. Bryan Di Salvatore, *A Clever Base-Ballist: The Life and Times of John Montgomery Ward* (New York: Pantheon, 1999): 219–22.

25. Peter Levine, *A. G. Spalding and the Rise of Baseball: The Promise of American Sport* (New York: Oxford University Press, 1985), 101–2. Duval was included on the tour in spite of protest by Anson. Malloy, "Out at Home," 24.

26. *New York Clipper,* June 16, 1888.

27. Newspaper clippings, Tommy Burns Personal Scrapbook, Giamatti Research Center, NBLA.

28. Levine, *A. G. Spalding and the Rise of Baseball,* 104. This incident and others in which Duval was the target of racial animus are documented in the scrapbook of Tommy Burns, one of the Chicago players who went on the world tour (Burns Personal Scrapbook, NBLA).

29. Greg Bond argues that the onset of segregation in organized baseball is linked to the evolution of "middle class attitudes towards African-Americans" in order to "conform to the mores of its core constituents," the fans. In this regard, in adopting segregation, organized baseball sought to validate the manliness and respectability of its participants in the public's mind. Bond, "Whipped Curs and Real Men," 4–5.

30. Thanks to Peter Laipson for his insightful comments on an early draft of this chapter.

31. It should be noted that maintaining baseball statistics first gained popu-

larity in the 1860s. Integral to this process was the creation of the box score, which recounted the team's and individual players' performances in two modes: an individual's game totals offensively and at times defensively; and an inning-by-inning recount of a team's production and team totals—a line score. Additionally, as historian Robert Burk notes, in the mid-1860s, baseball guides, similar in size and cost to dime novels, provided statistics that reflected a player's productivity and became quite popular among followers of the game. Burk, *Never Just a Game*, 45–46. For more on the development of box scores and statistics, see chapter 2, "The Mortar of Which Baseball Is Held Together," in Jules Tygiel, *Past Time: Baseball as History* (New York: Oxford University Press, 2000): 15–34.

32. Ava Baron, "An 'Other' Side of Gender Antagonism at Work: Men, Boys, and the Re-masculinization of Printers' Work, 1830–1920," in *Work Engendered: Toward a New History of American Labor* (Ithaca: Cornell University Press, 1991), 47–69. Also see David Montgomery, *The Fall of the House of Labor: The Workplace, the State, and American Labor Activism, 1865–1925* (New York: Cambridge University Press, 1993), esp. chs. 1–3. Thanks to Dolly Tua-Burgos for sharing these citations and for discussion about the gender dynamics unfolding in other professions during this time.

33. On the interactions between professional baseball magnates and urban politics, see chapter 2 and 3 in Steven Riess, *Touching Base: Professional Baseball and American Culture in the Progressive Era* (Westport, CT: Greenwood Press, 1980; repr., Urbana: University of Illinois Press, 1999), 54–98, 99–133.

34. The racial limitation of the Brotherhood's movement is seen in the formation of the Players League. Formed as a rival to the National League, the Players League also excluded African Americans. Their exclusion is noteworthy in that John Montgomery Ward had previously been rebuffed in his attempt to sign George Stovey for the New York Giants, a National League club, in 1887. Ward biographer Bryan Di Salvatore notes that the veteran ballplayer did consider signing a couple of darker-skinned players, described as "smoked Italians" and "Cubans," whose racial identity was ambiguous, for his Players League team in 1890. Di Salvatore, *A Clever Base-Ballist*, 427n237.

35. Ibid., 177.

36. "The 'Brotherhood Manifesto' (1889)," Sullivan, *Early Innings*, 188.

37. Di Salvatore, *A Clever Base-Ballist*, 159; "John Ward Attacks the Reserve Clause (1887)," in Sullivan, *Early Innings*, 161–70. For Ward's complete essay, see "Is the Base-Ball Player a Chattel?" *Lippincott's Magazine* 40 (August 1887): 310–19. For a recap of the Brotherhood's labor movement during the mid- to late 1880s, see "The Rebellion," newspaper clipping, April 5, 1890, John Montgomery Ward File, NBLA.

38. Thanks to Peter Laipson for reiterating this point in his comments.

39. Roediger, *The Wages of Whiteness*, 66.

40. Fowler's comment originally appeared in *Sporting Life*, 1895, quoted in Peterson, *Only the Ball was White*, 40. "Story of an Old Timer."

41. Exploration of Latino topics in sport history is a rather recent academic endeavor. The field has focused for the most part on the experience of European Americans and, to a lesser extent, on that of African Americans and Native Americans. Although calls for further incorporation of race theory have been made—

especially by Jeffrey Sammons in his 1994 *Journal of Sport History* article—the critical examination of whiteness, the intersection of race and gender, and racialization beyond black and white remains elusive. Sammons, "'Race' and Sport: A Critical, Historical Examination," *Journal of Sport History* 21:3 (Fall 1994): 203–78.

42. Matthew Pratt Guterl, "The New Race Consciousness: Race, Nation, and Empire in American Culture, 1910–1925," *Journal of World History* 10:2 (1999): 307–52.

4. BASEBALL SHOULD FOLLOW THE FLAG

1. Spalding, *America's National Game*, 377–78.

2. *Sporting News*, July 1, 1899.

3. *Sporting Life*, August 24, 1901.

4. Levine, *A. G. Spalding and the Rise of Baseball*, xiv.

5. North American occupiers placed everything, from marriage and sexual practices to personal hygiene and public health, under scrutiny. The occupation led to a flood of scientists, doctors, and other experts visiting the islands to examine the causes of the physical and cultural maladies of "our little neighbors." These imperial programs have served as fields ripe for scholarly examination of the American empire, particularly regarding gender roles, sexuality, and citizenship. On the impact of U.S. colonial rule on sexuality and marital practices in Puerto Rico, see Eileen Findlay Suarez, *Imposing Decency* (Durham, NC: Duke University Press, 1999). Also see Laura Briggs, *Reproducing Empire: Race, Sex, Science, and U.S. Imperialism in Puerto Rico* (Berkeley and Los Angeles: University of California Press, 2002); and Kelvin Santiago-Valles, "'Higher Womanhood' among the 'Lower Races': Julia McNair Henry in Puerto Rico and the 'Burdens' of 1898," *Radical History Review* 73 (Winter 1999): 47–73. For a nuanced study of the race and gender discourses that motivated U.S. expansionism in the late nineteenth and early twentieth century, see Bederman, *Manliness and Civilization*. For a study that analyzes the impact of U.S. imperialism at its various points of cultural contact, see Amy Kaplan and Donald Pease, eds., *Cultures of United States Imperialism* (Durham, NC: Duke University Press, 1993).

6. On the meanings that Cubans attached to baseball and the racial conflict that arose from the entry of Afro-Cubans into the professional game in the late nineteenth century, see Adrian Burgos Jr., "Entering Cuba's Other Playing Field: Cuban Baseball and the Choice between Race and Nation, 1887–1912," *Journal of Sport and Social Issues*, 29:1 (February 2005): 9–40. On baseball's arrival and development in Asia, see Joseph A. Reaves, *Taking in a Game: A History of Baseball in Asia* (Lincoln: University of Nebraska Press, 2002).

7. Robin Bachin, *Building the South Side: Urban Space and Civic Culture in Chicago, 1890–1919* (Chicago: University of Chicago Press, 2004), 210–12.

8. Jules Tygiel describes a cult of personality that followed these Irish American figures, and notes that they overcame prejudice and the tensions caused by their introduction to organized baseball of what was viewed as a working-class style. See chapter 3 in Tygiel, *Past Time*. For a typical rags-to-riches tale, see Horatio Alger, *Ragged Dick, and Mark, the Match Boy* (1868; repr., New York: Col-

lier Books, 1962). On the cultural indoctrination of immigrants, see James R. Barrett, "Americanization from the Bottom Up: Immigration and the Remaking of the Working Class in the United States, 1880–1930," *Journal of American History* 79 (December 1992): 996–1020.

9. John Bloom rightly notes that Native Americans also used sports as a forum to demonstrate their own desires for cultural and social autonomy that at times worked counter to the ideas that mainstream educational institutions and "Indian" schools attempted to impose. See *To Show What an Indian Can Do* (Minneapolis: University of Minnesota Press, 2000).

10. *New York Clipper,* February 25, 1882.

11. *El Sport* regularly updated Cuban fans about National League and American Association action, providing statistics and standings and reporting on post-season play, such as the 1886 "World Series" between St. Louis (American Association champs) and Chicago (the National League pennant winners). *El Sport,* November 11, 1886, and August 27, 1888.

12. *El Sport,* September 1, 1887.

13. *El Sport,* October 21, 1886; November 11, 1886; December 2, 1886; and January 8, 1887; *El Figaro,* October 23, 1886.

14. *Sporting News,* February 4, 1893.

15. Jorge Figueredo, *Beisbol Cubano: A un Paso de las Grandes Ligas, 1878–1961* (Jefferson, NC: McFarland Press, 2005), 16.

16. An important criterion for legal inclusion as white for much of U.S. history, according to Matthew Frye Jacobson and Mae Ngai, has been the idea of "racial eligibility for citizenship." This notion, they argue, arose from the 1790 Naturalization Law, which established the criteria for immigrating to the United States of whether one was a "free white person." The courts extended this notion to naturalization. Hence, naturalization was based on whiteness until immigration laws were revised in the early 1950s. On court cases in which the battle for legal recognition involved racially suspect Southern and Eastern Europeans, Asians, and Latin American nationals, see chapter 7, "Naturalization and the Courts," in Jacobson, *Whiteness of a Different Color,* pp. 223–45. On the creation of "national origins" and the use of "racial eligibility for citizenship," see Mae Ngai, "The Architecture of Race in American Immigration Law: A Reexamination of the Immigration Act of 1924," *Journal of American History* (June 1999): 67–92.

17. Jacobson, *Barbarian Virtues: The United States Encounters Foreign Peoples at Home and Abroad* (New York: Hill & Wang, 2000), 4, 8.

18. I separate the barnstorming trips of North American teams into two phases—1879 to 1912, and 1913 to 1947—to distinguish between the organizational basis of the barnstorming teams. Prior to the decrees made by American League president Ban Johnson in 1911 and by National Commission chairman Garry Herrmann, major-league teams could tour as intact teams—that is, players from a specific team could tour under the name of that club, e.g., the New York Giants. After the bans, North American players could tour only as members of all-star or "select" teams composed of players from different clubs, and they could not represent individual teams but rather toured under such names as the "All Americans." This second barnstorming phase could be subdivided

further if one considers that individual North Americans increasingly signed with specific Cuban teams.

19. Jorge Figueredo, *Cuban Baseball: A Statistical History, 1878–1961* (Jefferson, NC: McFarland Press, 2003), 9.

20. My use of *Indian* versus *Native American* in this chapter is done to remain consistent with the ways that contemporaries racialized members of Native communities in North America. Sockalexis has been the subject of two recent biographies: Brian McDonald, *Indian Summer: The Forgotten Story of Louis Sockalexis* (New York: Rodale, 2003); and David Fleitz, *Louis Sockalexis: The First Cleveland Indian* (Jefferson, NC: McFarland Press, 2001).

21. On federal efforts to assimilate Indians, see Frederick Hoxie, *A Final Promise: The Campaign to Assimilate the Indians, 1880–1920* (Lincoln: University of Nebraska Press, 1984). Among the more compelling examples of Americans seeing Indians and civilization on display was the Columbian Expedition held in Chicago during the 1893 World's Fair. For discussion of the fair as putting civilization on display, see Robert W. Rydell, *All the World's a Fair: Visions of Empire at American International Expositions, 1876–1916* (Chicago: University of Chicago Press, 1984); and Bederman, *Manliness and Civilization,* 31–40. On how the White City and the fair's layout mapped race and civilization onto the physical terrain, see the introduction to Bachin, *Building the South Side.*

22. Deloria, *Indians in Unexpected Places* (Lawrence: University of Kansas Press, 2004), 121.

23. McDonald, *Indian Summer,* 148.

24. Phil Deloria, *Playing Indian* (New Haven, CT: Yale University Press, 1998).

25. Quoted in Jeffrey Powers-Beck, *The American Indian Integration of Baseball* (Lincoln: University of Nebraska Press, 2004), 1.

26. This cartoon is reprinted in McDonald, *Indian Summer,* 45.

27. McDonald, *Indian Summer,* 131–32 (Baltimore), 142–43, (New York).

28. McDonald, *Indian Summer,* 149 (emphasis added).

29. "Sockalexis' Unpleasant Experience," *Sporting Life,* May 7, 1898. See also Louis Sockalexis Biographical File, NBLA.

30. For a critical discussion of the U.S. historiography concerning the War of 1898 and the role of Hearst and Pulitzer, see Louis Pérez, *The War of 1898: The United States in History and Historiography* (Chapel Hill: University of North Carolina Press, 1998). On the intersection between support for Cuba Libre and the impulse to "restore" American masculinity, see chapter 2, "Cuba and the Restoration of American Chivalry," in Kristin Hoganson, *Fighting for American Manhood: How Gender Politics Provoked the Spanish-American and Philippine-American Wars* (New Haven, CT: Yale University Press, 1998), 42–67.

31. *Sporting Life,* January 2, 1897.

32. *Sporting Life,* October 29, 1898.

33. *Sporting News,* October 1 and 29, 1898; *Sporting Life,* November 5, 1898.

34. *Sporting News,* July 1, 1899.

35. "Cuban Baseball Team Coming Here," *New York Times,* July 22, 1899; "The Cuban Baseball Team Arrives," *New York Times,* July 26, 1899; "A Cuban

Trip" and "Off for Cuba!" *Sporting Life,* September 5, 1900. Michael Lomax discusses the first wave of barnstorming trips by Cuban teams in fuller detail in his chapter "Rivalries, A New Frontier, and Reorganization" in *Black Baseball Entrepreneurs, 1860–1901: Operating by Any Means Necessary* (Syracuse, NY: Syracuse University Press, 2003).

36. *New York Sun,* July 26, 1899; August 24, 1899; September 3, 1899; and September 4, 1899. The All Cubans were initially scheduled to play games in Pennsylvania, Illinois, Indiana, Missouri, Connecticut, New York, and New Jersey. "Cuban Baseball Team Coming Here," *New York Times,* July 22, 1899. Thanks to Michael Lomax for sharing documents from the *New York Sun* on the All Cubans' initial tour.

37. This tour schedule is gleaned from coverage of Cuban barnstorming teams in multiple sources, including the *New York Age, Chicago Defender,* the *Sporting News, Sporting Life,* and *La Lucha* (Havana). An alternate tour route for Linares's team included arriving first in New Orleans in late March and then progressing northward to arrive in Chicago by late April or early May. The team would then barnstorm the Midwest before heading out to New York for the summer and departing for the Caribbean after their Labor Day games.

38. *Sporting Life,* February 28, 1891.

39. Peterson, *Only the Ball Was White,* 54. In January 1891 McGraw participated in a barnstorming tour of Cuba, playing with the Ocala team organized by fellow player Al Lawson. Ocala played all five teams that constituted the Cuban professional league during the 1891 season, exposing him to the island's professional talent.

40. Miles, *Ties That Bind: The Story of an Afro-Cherokee Family in Slavery and Freedom* (Berkeley and Los Angeles: University of California Press, 2005).

41. *New York Age,* July 23, 1949.

42. Peterson, *Only the Ball was White,* 55; *Sporting Life,* April 20, 1901.

43. Quoted in Jeffrey Powers-Beck, "'Chief': The American Indian Integration of Baseball, 1897–1945," *American Indian Quarterly* 25:4 (Fall 2001): 511.

44. *Havana Post,* July 27, 1913.

45. Powers-Beck, "'Chief,'" pp. 509–11.

46. *Louis,* instead of *Luis,* will be used in this chapter since this is the name that sportswriters used in talking about the Colombian native. *Sporting News,* March 11 and April 29, 1909.

47. After his college days, Castro signed with Utica of the New York State League before moving up to the Connecticut League; his time with the latter created a precedent whereby Latinos would play in this northeastern minor league before they appeared in the majors. *Sporting News,* November 27, 1941. This source is a letter to the editor written by Ernie Landgraf, who claimed to be an acquaintance of Castro's. Landgraf also claimed to have played a role in arranging the 1899 visit of the All Cubans and later sponsoring teams in San Juan and Ponce, Puerto Rico, in the winters of 1923–24 and 1924–25. Thanks to Dick Thompson, a member of the Society of American Baseball Researchers, for sharing this citation.

48. *Sporting Life,* May 31, 1902; June 14, 1902; and February 7, 1903. In 1908 Castro landed in the South Atlantic League (a Class C minor league), where

he managed the Augusta Tourists for several seasons. This initial managerial stint quite possibly made him the first Latino to manage a team in organized baseball. His last documented participation in organized baseball occurred in 1913, when he served as player-manager of the Portsmouth team (Virginia League). On Castro's stint in Baltimore, see *Sporting Life*, June 20 and July 25, 1903, and January 23, 1904. Activities as player-manager at Augusta and Portsmouth are covered in *Sporting News*, March 11 and April 29, 1909, and March 9, 1912.

49. The occupation of Castro's father probably resulted in the infielder acquiring the nickname "Jud." The Athletics met their teammate's father, Judge Louis M. Castro, at their end-of-season banquet. The team capped off its celebration with a "Spanish song" sung by Louis Castro. *Sporting Life*, October 11, 1902; *Sporting News*, January 3, 1903.

50. *Sporting News*, July 12, 1902.

51. *Sporting Life*, July 18, 1908; July 25, 1908. The columnist confused San Jose with San Francisco as the Pacific Coast League team from which Boston purchased Arellanes's contract.

52. *Sporting Life*, July 25 and December 12, 1908.

53. *Sporting Life*, December 12, 1908.

54. Back in his native California, Arellanes continued playing until the late 1910s before succumbing to pneumonia at age thirty-four on December 13, 1918. The birth date listed on the copy of Arellanes's death certificate included in his player file at the National Baseball Library and Archive, 1884, conflicts with the date provided in the *Baseball Encyclopedia*, January 28, 1882. Thus, he was either thirty-four or thirty-six years old when he died. Frank Arellanes Player File, NBLA.

5. "PUREST BARS OF CASTILIAN SOAP"

1. Figueredo, *Beisbol Cubano*, 41, 74.

2. Herrmann's response and the ban he decreed had two motivations. The Reds' team president also held the position of chairman of the National Commission, the governing body of the National League, the American League, and the rest of organized baseball. *Sporting Life*, December 26, 1908.

3. *Sporting News*, December 9, 1909.

4. *Sporting News*, January 5, 1911.

5. Sol White briefly discusses a tour made by the Cuban Stars of Santiago (organized by Manuel Camps), but perhaps more significant, his book includes photographs of some of these players. *Sol White's History*, 89–96.

6. *La Lucha*, March 14, 1910. With the gradual abolition of slavery on the island in 1880, Cuban sugar producers increasingly turned to Chinese "coolie" laborers to fill the growing labor shortage.

7. *Detroit News*, January 28, 1912. Research on the 1907 Scranton team conducted by baseball historian Peter Toot failed to yield any box scores in which either of the two Cubans appeared.

8. "Some Inside Facts on Cuban Players in America," undated newspaper clipping, Armando Marsans Player File, NBLA. Batters did not have the protection of batting helmets at this time. Thus, pitches thrown at a batter's head

had the capacity to inflict serious damage. Fisher later enjoyed a ten-year major-league career (1910–20), including eight years with the New York Yankees.

9. "Some Inside Facts."

10. *Sporting News,* April 16, 1908.

11. "Some Inside Facts," *Sporting News,* November 27, 1941 (emphasis added).

12. "Some Inside Facts." Padrón continued playing in the Negro leagues until 1926, appearing with Alejandro Pompez's Cuban Stars toward the end of his career. Among the elder statesmen of Cuban baseball players in 1921, Padrón still showed flashes of his former brilliance, leading the Cuban Stars over the "Tesreau Bears," which featured several former major leaguers—including former Cincinnati Reds player Manuel Cueto. *Chicago Defender,* May 14, 1921.

13. *Sporting News,* August 1911. Mansfield belonged to the Ohio-Pennsylvania League, a lower-tier minor league.

14. Figueredo, *Beisbol Cubano,* 80; *Atlanta Constitution,* April 2, 1916, A3. Interestingly, after listing the Long Branch players, the *Atlanta Constitution* stated, "All of the above are white players, of course." The paper's description did not account for Padrón's previous expulsion from New Britain and Mansfield or his rejection by the Chicago White Sox on racial grounds.

15. *Havana Post,* August 6, 1913.

16. Jake "Babe" Daubert, manager of the Brooklyn National League club that barnstormed Cuba in 1913, ranked Padrón high among the Cuban players he competed against during the tour. Of the fourteen Cubans he named, six later performed in the majors. *Havana Post,* November 14, 1913, and November 25, 1913.

17. *Sporting News,* January 5, 1911; November 10, 1910, and November 17, 1910. On the Athletics' trip, also see *Sporting News,* December 28, 1910, and *Cincinnati Enquirer,* December 4, 11, and 28–31, 1910.

18. Bancroft correspondence, "1080 1914" box, Garry Herrmann Papers, NBLA.

19. J. F. Sullivan to Garry Herrmann, January 2, 1911, "Unmarked Letters" file, Garry Herrmann Papers. On February 26 Almeida sent a letter to Herrmann with measurements for his uniform, indicating that preparations for his arrival with Cincinnati were already being made. Almeida to Herrmann, February 26, 1911, "1080 1914" box, Herrmann Papers. I am indebted to Tim Wiles, the Baseball Hall of Fame's public service librarian, for his assistance, and to fellow baseball historian Peter Toot for sharing documents from the Herrmann Papers.

20. In her study of American culture between the 1880s and 1920s, Gail Bederman notes the shift in the construction of gender from manliness to masculinity. Inherent to this shift was the confluence of ideas about civilization and race that lauded the cultural superiority of white Americans. This reshaped masculinity provides a cultural context in which to read coverage by North American sources of the integration of foreign-born Latin(o) players. See Bederman, "Remaking Manhood through Race and 'Civilization,'" in *Manliness and Civilization,* 1–42.

21. On August 3, the *Sporting News* noted the role that Cuban sportswriters Nuñez and Conte had played in planning the "Cuban invasion," the signing

of Almeida and Marsans. Bancroft had formed a working relationship with these sportswriters the previous winter when he led the Philadelphia Athletics on its barnstorming tour. *Sporting News,* August 3, 1911; *Cincinnati Enquirer,* December 27, 1910.

22. "Marsans was Cuba's First B.B. Graduate," newspaper clipping, September 1912, Marsans Player File, NBLA; *Sporting Life,* September 23, 1911.

23. Newspaper clipping, August 21, 1911, Marsans Player File, NBLA.

24. Undated newspaper clipping, Marsans Player File, NBLA.

25. "Marsans was Cuba's First B.B. Graduate."

26. Newspaper clipping, August 21, 1911.

27. *Sporting News,* July 13, 1911.

28. *Sporting News,* June 22, 1911 (emphasis added); *Cincinnati Enquirer,* June 23, 1911.

29. Newspaper clipping, May 1912, Marsans Player File, NBLA; *Sporting Life,* July 15, 1911.

30. Five days after the Cubans made their Cincinnati debut, the *Cincinnati Enquirer* also published photos of the Cuban duo, but they appeared in New Britain uniform. *Cincinnati Enquirer,* July 9, 1911.

31. Phelon, "Baseball in Cuba: The Great American Sport as an International Game," *Baseball Magazine,* May 1912, p. 35.

32. *Cincinnati Enquirer* passage quoted in Brock and Bayne, "Not Just Black," 185; *New York Times,* September 25, 1911.

33. *New York Times,* July 16, 1911.

34. *New York Age,* September 28, 1911.

35. Although conducted covertly, these attempts sparked rumors that circulated in baseball circles while the color line was in place. The stories still permeate the collective memory of surviving Negro leaguers. Negro leaguers allegedly approached included Larry Brown, a player with the Kansas City Monarchs, and Quincy Trouppe, who played many years in Puerto Rico and Mexico and whose career lasted long enough for him to appear in the majors after integration.

36. Peterson, *Only the Ball Was White,* 209.

37. Rogosin, *Invisible Men,* 159. Trouppe discussed his recruitment in his autobiography, *Twenty Years Too Soon: Prelude to Major-League Integrated Baseball* (Los Angeles: S & S Enterprises, c. 1977; repr., St. Louis: Missouri Historical Society Press, 1995).

38. Phelon, "Baseball in Cuba," 35.

39. *Sporting Life,* February 3, 1912. Consideration of this color line perhaps also reflected the island's tense racial climate. During this same year, rumors of an Afro-Cuban uprising in the eastern province of Oriente resulted in a brutal backlash as more than five thousand Afro-Cubans were massacred. For a lengthy discussion of these issues surrounding the Race War of 1912, see Aline Helg, *Our Rightful Share* (Chapel Hill: University of North Carolina Press, 1994).

40. As early as the late 1880s a conflict of vision emerged in Cuban baseball when Afro-Cubans sought to enter the profession of baseball on their own terms. Their efforts sparked a controversy regarding both the "proper place" of baseball in Cuban society and the role of Afro-Cubans in the island's national pastime as recast from a recreational activity to a professional career.

41. Control over the distribution of revenues generated by Cuban professional baseball was another critical issue in the movement to restructure the league. Noting that the men leading the exclusionary movement were "some of the best known sportsmen in Cuba" and "men of wealth and honor," a *Sporting Life* columnist highlighted the class element involved in this movement. *Sporting Life,* February 3, 1912.

42. Phelon, "Baseball in Cuba," 35; González Echevarría, *Pride of Havana,* 122.

43. *Sporting Life,* March 10, 1911.

44. *New York Age,* June 17, 1915.

45. Stetson Palmer, "Baseball the Game 'of All Nations,'" *Baseball Magazine,* October 1928, p. 488.

46. *New York Age,* April 27, 1935.

47. Quoted in Peter Toot, *Armando Marsans: The First Cuban Major League Baseball Player* (Jefferson, NC: McFarland, 2003), 40.

48. *Havana Post,* June 25, 1913, and July 7, 1913; Bretón, *Away Games,* 98. A Hall of Fame shortstop, Wagner played from 1897 to 1917, primarily with the National League's Pittsburgh Pirates.

49. Newspaper clipping, February 1914, Miguel Angel González Player File, NBLA; Ward, "Gonzalez, the Cuban Backstop," p. 34, in ibid.

50. *New York Times,* December 28, 1913. "Senor Emilio to get Chance with Giants to Show Just How Good He Is," March 1916; "Giants Sign Cuban Pitcher," October 1913; Harvey Conover, "Palmero, the Ageless Marvel," March 1914, newspaper clippings, Hicks Collection, December 1913, Palmero Player File, NBLA.

51. Sid Naroh, "They Say They'll Get Cuban," 1916 newspaper clipping, José Rodríguez Player File, NBLA.

52. Stephen Chicoine, "The Great Gallia: Texas's Melvin "Bert" Gallia and Ethnicity in Major League Baseball," *Southwestern Historical Quarterly* 105:4 (April 2004): 645.

53. Ibid., 639, 645.

54. Ibid., 639.

55. *New York Times,* July 16, 1911; February 27, 1914.

56. Newspaper clipping, October 1913, Palmero Player File, NBLA. On the occasion of Méndez's death in 1926, the *Amsterdam News* recalled McGraw's comments about the Cuban hurler: "If Méndez was even light enough to 'pass for white' he would have paid forty thousand grand for his release from the Cuban team." *Amsterdam News,* June 23, 1926.

57. "Cuban Tourists," *Sporting Life,* February 20, 1909 (emphasis added).

58. Ira Thomas, "How They Play Our National Game in Cuba," *Baseball Magazine,* March 1913, p. 62. A major-league catcher for ten years, Thomas played for the Athletics during their 1912 tour of Cuba, when the American League champs lost ten of their twelve games against Cuban teams.

59. *Sporting Life,* December 2, 1911. Lobert acted as the manager of the Phillies during their 1911 visit.

60. Phelon, "Baseball in Cuba," 30.

61. John Holway, *Blackball Stars: Negro League Pioneers* (New York: Car-

roll & Graf, 1992), 58. Brewer played for Méndez during the 1925 and 1926 seasons. There is still uncertainty concerning the cause of Méndez's death. In 1970 Peterson stated it was probably tuberculosis. James Riley, in his 1994 publication, gave bronchopneumonia as the cause of death; he did not indicate whether this assertion arose from new evidence. Riley, *Biographical Encyclopedia,* 546. For a history of the Monarchs, see Janet Bruce, *Kansas City Monarchs* (Lawrence: University Press of Kansas, 1985).

62. *Amsterdam News,* March 6, 1929. White's description comes from an article, "Old-Time Baseball Players," which was based on ongoing conversations within the black baseball community in New York. In a column written after major-league integration had begun, Wendell Smith included Méndez and Torriente among the Negro-league players from the 1920s and 1930s who would have strengthened any major-league club. *Pittsburgh Courier,* October 2, 1948.

63. "Primeros Pasos en el Professionalismo," p. 21, Jim Riley personal collection. Thanks to Jim Riley for sharing this document.

64. Torriente's most memorable day took place in his native Cuba in a November 1920 exhibition game. Cuban Stars owner and baseball official Abel Linares had scheduled a two-week visit by New York Yankees legend Babe Ruth. Tens of thousands came out to see Ruth perform, but Torriente stole the show. In the exhibition game Torriente outslugged Babe Ruth three homers to none, earning the nickname "The Black Babe Ruth." Jorge Figueredo, "November 4, 1920: The Day Torriente Outclassed Ruth," *Baseball Research Journal* (1982), Cristobal Torriente Player File, Ashland Collection, NBLA.

65. Holway, *Blackball Stars,* 126; "Christobel Torrienti" document, Cristobal Torriente Player File, Ashland Collection, NBLA.

66. *New York Age,* December 29, 1924, p. 6.

67. Mae M. Ngai argues that the Immigration Act's privileging of "national origins" in understanding race within a global context created a racial hierarchy among Americans. This hierarchy placed people of European descent into the category of white but distinguished among them according to desirability for the purpose of determining quotas. The act also mapped the rest of the world into nonwhite categories. In the case of those deemed nonwhite, the category "ineligible to citizenship" enabled government officials to assign certain countries lower quotas. See Ngai, "The Architecture of Race in American Immigration Law."

6. MAKING CUBAN STARS

1. Indicative of his wealth, Pompez contracted a local builder, J. H. Drew, to build a home for his family. The Pompez home was one of five residences that Drew built costing between $1,250 and $2,000. Arsenio M. Sanchez, "Incentives Helped to Build West Tampa," *Sunland Tribune* 11:1 (1985), Special Collections, University of South Florida.

José Gonzalo Pompez was part of the nineteenth-century wave of Cuban émigrés who settled in the United States and continued their push for Cuban independence. For a stunning literary history of Cuban exiles in the United States during the nineteenth century, see Rodrigo Lazo, *Writing to Cuba: Filibustering and Cuban Exiles in the United States* (Chapel Hill: University of North Carolina Press, 2004).

2. José Alvarez de la Vega, "Pompez affectionately remembers his trip to Puerto Rico. The *Hazaña* of Fabito in Shutting-Out his famous 'Cuban Stars.' From Triumph to Triumph, Good Opportunity for the New York Cubans," *Puerto Rican Deportivo* 4:7–8 (July–August 1947): 16 (hereafter, "Pompez affectionately remembers"; author's translation).

3. *Tampa Tribune,* October 26, 1888, Tony Pizzo Collection, Special Collections Library, University of South Florida, Tampa; Susan Greenbaum, *More Than Black: Afro-Cubans in Tampa* (Gainesville: University Press of Florida, 2002), 83; Alvarez de la Vega, "Pompez affectionately remembers," 16.

4. Greenbaum, *More Than Black,* 12; on schism within Tampa's Cuban community, see 103–10.

5. Ibid., 63.

6. Ibid., 60 (the Scrub), 12 ("ethnic boundaries"), 3 ("double-hyphenated lives").

7. Ibid., 347n4; Rufus Schatzberg, *Black Organized Crime in Harlem: 1920–1930* (New York: Garland, 1993), 115.

8. Alvarez de la Vega, "Pompez affectionately remembers," 15.

9. Luisin Rosario, "El Diamante Negro," newspaper clipping, Luis Alvelo Personal Collection (Scrapbook), Caguas, Puerto Rico (my translation).

10. Rosario, "El Diamante Negro."

11. League standings for the Eastern Colored and Negro National leagues can be found in Peterson, *Only the Ball Was White,* appendix A.

12. "Primeros Pasos en el Professionalismo," 21.

13. "Primeros Pasos en el Professionalismo," 23; Holway, "Martin Dihigo: El maestro," in *Blackball Stars,* 238.

14. *Chicago Defender,* July 5, 1919; May 14, 1921.

15. For discussion of West Indian and Caribbean migrations to Panama and then New York City, see Irma Watkins-Owens, *Blood Relations: Caribbean Immigrants and the Harlem Community, 1900–1930* (Bloomington: Indiana University Press, 1996).

16. For more on the squabbles over San (1926) and Montalvo (1927), see *New York Amsterdam News,* March 3, 1926; March 17, 1926; and *New York Age,* May 21, 1927; July 2, 1927.

17. *New York Age,* May 21, 1927.

18. *New York Age,* March 7 and 27, 1925.

19. *New York Age,* January 19, 1935; April 2, 1938.

20. *New York Age,* August 24, 1935.

21. *New York Age,* August 24, 1935; Alvarez de la Vega, "Pompez affectionately remembers," 16.

22. *New York Age,* October 5, 1935, p. 8; *Amsterdam News,* October 5, 1935, pp. 5, 12; "10,000 See Ruth Play," *New York Times,* September 30, 1935, p. 22. The *Times* article reported the score of the game as a 14–6 victory for the Cubans. The Cubans defeated the Babe Ruth All-Stars 6–1, as Lefty Tiant held Ruth to one hit in five turns at bat before a reported crowd of about five thousand. Ruth received $3,000 for his appearance.

23. *New York Age,* August 24, 1935; June 21, 1945; and April 17, 1948.

24. Watkins-Owens, *Blood Relations,* 4.

25. Watkins-Owens offers the concept of "intra-racial ethnic community" to explain black Harlem's heterogeneity; see ibid., chapter 10.

26. *Amsterdam News,* October 5, 1927. Claude McKay discusses the dynamics involved in the 1920s development of the "Puerto Rican section" in *Harlem: Negro Metropolis* (New York: E. P. Dutton, 1940), 89–90.

27. On the team's difficulties and inability to "jell," see Lewis Dial's column "The Sport Dial" in *New York Age,* June 8, 22, 1935. On Dial's proposed teams, see *New York Age,* July 27, 1935.

28. *Amsterdam News,* September 7, 28, 1935; *New York Age,* September 14, 28, 1935.

29. *New York Age,* January 28, 1928.

30. Alvarez de la Vega, "Pompez affectionately remembers," 15; *New York Age,* May 30, 1936.

31. For a discussion of numbers running in urban contexts, see Victoria Wolcott, "The Culture of the Informal Economy: Numbers Runners in Inter-War Black Detroit," *Radical History Review* 69 (1997): 46–75. On Pompez joining Schultz's outfit under duress and Schultz's hostile takeover of Harlem's scene, see chapter 9, "The Underground Entrepreneur," in Watkins-Owens, *Blood Relations,* 136–148. For more on Pompez's legal ordeal, see appendix A in James Overmyer, *Queen of the Negro Leagues: Effa Manley and the Newark Eagles* (Lanham, MD: Scarecrow Press, 1998), 272–79. On Gus Greenlee's place within Pittsburgh's sporting world, see Rob Ruck, *Sandlot Seasons: Sport in Black Pittsburgh* (Urbana: University of Illinois Press, 1993), esp. ch. 5.

32. McKay, *Harlem,* 107–9; *New York Times,* August 20, 1938.

33. *New York Times,* January 15, 1937; *New York Amsterdam News,* January 16, 1937.

34. On the effects of the struggle against segregation on the Civil Rights Movement in New York City, see Martha Biondi, *To Stand and Fight: The Struggle for Civil Rights in Postwar New York City* (Cambridge, MA: Harvard University Press, 2003).

35. McKay, *Harlem,* 109. According to Claude McKay, "each collector was remunerated with 10% of monies collected. . . . The controller's reward was 5% of the total sum turned over to the banker" (109).

36. Oscar Levis played in the black circuits from 1921 to 1934, mostly with Pompez's Cuban Stars (1921–29, 1931–32, 1934). Like Pompez, Levis testified at the Hines trial about his involvement in the policy racket. For Levis's testimony, see *New York Times,* August 20, 1938, p. 8. A native of Tampa, Mirabal performed in the black leagues from 1918 to 1934, primarily as a starting pitcher for the Cuban Stars (1921–34). After his playing career, Mirabal became Pompez's right-hand man, working as the New York Cubans' team president. Riley, *Biographical Encyclopedia,* 555–56.

37. Watkins-Owens offers a succinct description of the genesis of the numbers game and the role of Caribbean individuals in the development of Harlem's numbers in her chapter "The Underground Entrepreneur" in *Blood Relations,* 136–48.

38. Schatzberg, *Black Organized Crime in Harlem,* 115.

39. *New York Times,* August 20, 1938; Schatzberg, *Black Organized Crime in Harlem,* p. 115.

40. *New York Age,* May 21, 1937. Left without a club in 1937, several of the Cubans' Latino players opted to play in the Dominican Republic's fledging summer league, while others played in the Mexican league. *New York Age,* April 17, 1937.

41. On Pompez's indictment and flight, see *Pittsburgh Courier,* April 3, 1937; November 6, 1937; and *New York Times,* March 29, 1937. For his testimony at the Hines trial, see *New York Times,* March 30, 1937; August 18 and 20, 1938. Thanks to James Overmyer for sharing these important documents.

42. *New York Age,* April 2, 1938.

43. The Dyckman Projects, a basketball court, and a children's playground now occupy the grounds where Dyckman Oval once stood.

44. Neil Lanctot, *Negro League Baseball: The Rise and Fall of a Black Institution* (Philadelphia: University of Pennsylvania Press, 2004), 81.

45. Rodolfo and Matilda Fernández, interview with author, New York, February 1995 (hereafter, Fernández interview); Armando Vásquez, interview with author, New York, February 1995; Rafael "Ray" Noble, interview with author, New York, February 1995; Charlie Rivera, interview with author, Bronx, NY, February 1995. Each of these players mentioned that Pompez arranged for their housing. Vásquez, for one, mentioned living for a while with a Jamaican family that helped him learn English.

46. Fernández interview. Interestingly, prior to his twenty-year major-league career, Adolfo Luque played on two teams that participated in the black baseball circuits, the Cuban Stars (1912) and Long Branch Cubans (1913).

47. Piri Thomas, interview with author, New York, June 5, 1996 (hereafter, Thomas interview).

48. Everard Marius, interview with author, Harlem, NY, July 16, 1996 (hereafter, Marius interview).

49. Description of the different roles women performed is drawn from ethnographic interviews conducted with women and men who grew up or lived in Harlem from the 1940s through the 1960s. Miriam Jimenez Roman, interview with author, Harlem, NY, July 1996; Fernández interview; Thomas interview.

50. Albertus "Cleffie" Fennar, interview with author, Daytona Beach, FL, March 17, 1996.

51. Marius interview.

52. Vasquez interview.

53. James Weldon Johnson, *Along This Way: The Autobiography of James Weldon Johnson* (New York: Da Capo Press, 2000), 65. Thanks to Jerry Malloy for sharing this citation.

54. "1942 New York Cubans Player Roster," New York Cuban Stars File, Ashland Collection, NBLA. Orlando Cepeda with Charles Einstein, *My Ups and Downs in Baseball* (New York: G. P. Putnam's Son's, 1968), 26–27. The elder Cepeda died at age forty-nine. His nickname, *Perucho,* means "the Bull" in Spanish. Orlando Cepeda has been the subject of several books; for his most recent

effort see *Baby Bull: From Hardball to Hard Time and Back* (Dallas: Taylor Trade, 1998). For a previous effort, see Orlando Cepeda with Bob Markus, *High and Inside: Orlando Cepeda's Story* (South Bend, IN: Icarus, 1983).

55. Fernández interview.

56. *Amsterdam News,* June 10, 1939, quoted in Larry Lester, *Black Baseball's National Showcase: The East-West All-Star game, 1933–1953* (Lincoln: University of Nebraska Press, 2001), 122.

7. BECOMING CUBAN SENATORS

Gant and Smith quoted in Lester, *Black Baseball's National Showcase,* 185, 208.

1. Frio and Onigman, "'Good Field, No Hit': The Image of Latin American Baseball Players in the American Press, 1876–1946," *Revista/Review Interamericana* (1979): 203; *New York Age,* July 17, 1913. The latter, newspaper source discusses inquiries the New York Yankees made into Luque's availability while he was a pitcher with the Long Branch Cubans. The article appears to have been lifted from a *New York Evening Globe* article, "Cuban Pitcher is Likely to Be Signed for Trial with Yanks," July 1913, Adolfo Luque Player File, NBLA.

2. *New York Times,* August 8, 1923 (Stengel). Luque had gotten into a tussle three years earlier with home plate umpire Ed Klemm in a June 26, 1920, contest while pitching for the Cincinnati Reds versus the St. Louis Cardinals. According to Luque, he was verbally harangued by Klemm and retaliated. League officials suspended Luque for the attack. *New York Times,* June 27, 1920.

3. *New York Age,* February 25, 1939; newspaper clipping, May 4, 1933, Adolfo Luque Player File, NBLA.

4. *New York Age,* February 25, 1939.

5. *New York Age,* July 28, 1934.

6. "Caught First Pitch on Nose; Now He's Star as Dodger," undated newspaper clipping, Al López Player File, NBLA.

7. John J. Ward, "A Spanish-American Star," *Baseball Magazine,* March 1931, p. 447; and Ed Rumill, "A Topnotch Big Leaguer," *Baseball Magazine,* April 1944, p. 383.

8. "A Spanish-Speaking Battery," newspaper clipping, July 31, 1930, Adolfo Luque Player File, NBLA.

9. "All about Southpaw Gomez," newspaper clipping, February 26, 1930, Vernon "Lefty" Gomez Player File, NBLA. A 1931 *Sporting News* article on Gómez claimed that his father, Francisco Gómez, had been born in Madrid, Spain. Other sources state that the elder Gómez was a native Californian whose family had resided in the state for several generations. Published after Lefty Gómez's first full year in the majors, the claim made in the *Sporting News* article may have been a way to present the player as having "pure" Spanish roots versus a mixed Mexican past. "Gomez the Gorgeous, Yanks' Star Southpaw, Is Guarded like Precious Dresden China," *Sporting News,* November 12, 1931, newspaper clipping, Vernon "Lefty" Gomez Player File, NBLA.

10. "Spanish-Irish Gomez," undated newspaper clipping; untitled newspaper clipping, April 23, 1936, both in Vernon "Lefty" Gomez Player File, NBLA.

11. "All about Southpaw Gomez."

12. "Family Moved to California to Avoid War," newspaper clipping, September 9, 1933, Melo Almada Player File; Cunningham, "Grandstand Grandee," *Collier's,* August 24, 1935, Almada Player File; "A Mexican Revolution Gave Mel Almada to the Diamond," *Sporting News,* Almada Player File, NBLA.

13. On the participation of Mexican Americans and Mexican nationals in amateur and semiprofessional baseball in California, see José M. Alamillo, "*Peloteros* in Paradise: Mexican American Baseball and Oppositional Politics in Southern California, 1930–1950," *Western Historical Quarterly* 34:2 (Summer 2003): 191–211; and Alamillo, "Mexican American Baseball: Masculinity, Racial Struggle, and Labor Politics in Southern California, 1930–1950," in *Sports Matters: Race, Recreation, and Culture,* ed. John Bloom and Michael Willard (New York: New York University Press, 2002).

14. *Washington Post,* May 15, 1938, B4.

15. "Barnstormer to Big Leaguer," newspaper clipping, August 15, 1935, José "Chile" Gómez Player File, NBLA. Before comparing the paths that the two Mexican-born natives took, the article mistakenly claims that Bert Gallia, who pitched in the majors from 1912 to 1920, had "some Mexican blood in his veins, but he was a Texan from Laredo."

16. Ibid. According to this article, Gómez first toured the United States with a barnstorming team, the All-Mexican Stars. In games against some big-league players during the tour, he attracted their attention. Art Bramhall, a member of the Philadelphia Phillies in 1934, recommended Gómez to the club. A good showing at a tryout with the club led to his signing; prior to joining the Phillies, Gómez had also played more than five years in the Mexican League.

17. Robert Dominguez, "Teddy Beisbol Joins Roster of Latino Greats," *New York Daily News,* March 31, 2004, www.nydailynews.com/entertainment/culture/story/179269p-155821c. html (last accessed May 31, 2004).

18. Ted Williams with John Underwood, *My Turn at Bat: The Story of My Life* (New York: Simon & Schuster, 1969, 1988), 28–29. Thanks to Neal Traven for sharing this citation, and to Eric Enders for providing additional materials on Ted Williams's family history.

19. On the impact of Mexican repatriation on Mexican American communities, see Sánchez, *Becoming Mexican American,* and Ruiz, *From Out of the Shadows.*

20. Peter Bjarkman, *Baseball with a Latin Beat* (Jefferson, NC: McFarland, 1994), 119.

21. González Echevarría, *Pride of Havana,* 269. Another critique of Cambria is provided in Heuer, "The Cuban Slide: Who Really Broke Baseball's Color Barrier?" *Chicago Reader,* September 26, 1997, p. 12.

22. *Washington Post,* August 17, 1932.

23. *Washington Post,* August 19 and December 13, 1932. Berg would later serve as a spy for the United States during the Second World War; see Nicholas Dawidoff, *The Catcher Was a Spy: The Mysterious Life of Moe Berg* (New York: Vintage, 1995).

24. *New York World Telegram,* April 4, 1939.

25. *Daily Worker,* September 3, 1942.

26. *Washington Post,* February 17, 1939.

27. Sam Murphy, "Barefoot Boy Learned to Hit on Cuban Farm," undated newspaper clipping, Estalella Player File, NBLA.

28. Newspaper clipping, *Sporting News,* October 9, 1935, Estalella Player File, NBLA.

29. Shirley Povich, "Bob Estalella, Cuban, Is Back Again," newspaper clipping, March 14, 1938, Estalella Player File, NBLA; Bretón, *Away Games,* 100. Despite the resentment occasionally expressed in public, Estalella went on to play a total of nine seasons in the majors spanning 1935 to 1949; he spent several intermediate years in the minors and played in the Mexican League from 1946 to 1948.

30. Heuer, "Cuban Slide," 12. Thanks to black baseball researcher Michael Marsh for sharing this article, which discusses major-league baseball's two Bobby Estalellas, the grandfather, who played with the Senators, and the grandson Bobby, who played in the majors from 1996 to 2004 and retired before the start of the 2006 season.

31. Brad Snyder, *Beyond the Shadow of the Senators: The Untold Story of the Homestead Grays and the Integration of Baseball* (New York: Contemporary Books, 2003), 70, 71.

32. Ibid., 70, 72.

33. *Daily Worker,* July 13, 1942.

34. Newspaper clipping, *Washington Post,* June 1, 1939, Alejandro Carrasquel Player File, NBLA.

35. *Washington Post,* February 23, 1939. Other newspaper reports referred to Carrasquel as Alex Alexandra.

36. Newspaper clipping, August 20, 1941, Alejandro Carrasquel Player File, NBLA; *Washington Post,* March 22, 1943.

37. *New York Times,* May 30, 1939.

38. Oleksak and Oleksak, *Beisbol,* 33; *Washington Post,* March 16, 1948, and July 25, 1950.

39. Oleksak and Oleksak, *Beisbol,* 33.

40. *Washington Post,* March 14, 1938.

41. *Daily Worker,* May 31, 1942.

42. González Echevarría, *Pride of Havana,* 270.

43. Newspaper clipping, September 22, 1944, Roberto Ortiz Player File, NBLA; *Sporting News,* September 28, 1944, and "Browns Defeat Senators, Trail by Half a Game," newspaper clipping, September 22, 1944, Ortiz Player File, NBLA.

44. "Rumbas over Obstacles," newspaper clipping, April 10, 1936, Estalella Player File, *The Sporting News* Archive, St. Louis (hereafter TSNA).

45. Snyder, *Beyond the Shadow of the Senators,* 70, 73.

46. "Carrasquel, Vibrant Venezuelan, Improves English—Puts Lots of It on Ball for Harris, Who Fired Him in '41," undated newspaper clipping, Alex Carrasquel Player File, TSNA.

47. "Cuban Turns Washington Spring Camp into Circus, but Scout Cambria's 'Finds' Are No Clowns on Field," newspaper clipping, Cambria Player File, TSNA; Shirley Povich, *The Washington Senators* (New York, G. P. Putnam's Sons, 1954), 209; "Cuban Turns Washington Spring Camp."

48. Newspaper clipping, May 9, 1951, Fermín "Mike" Guerra Player File, NBLA; Povich, *Washington Senators*, 233.

49. *Washington Post,* March 30, 1942.

50. Establishing the exact number of Latinos who participated in minor-league baseball is a tedious process that involves scouring the statistics of more than fifty years' worth of baseball annuals, such as *Spalding Baseball Guide, Reach Baseball Guide,* and *The Sporting News Annual Register,* searching for Spanish surnames, an inexact science at best.

8. PLAYING IN THE WORLD JIM CROW MADE

Williams quoted in Jules Tygiel, *Baseball's Great Experiment: Jackie Robinson and His Legacy* (New York: Oxford University Press, 1983), 25.

1. Wells quoted in Lester, *Black Baseball's National Showcase*, 222–23. These different social and work conditions, as well as the greater organizational strength of the Mexican League compared with other professional leagues in the Spanish-speaking Americas, partly explain the lower numbers of Mexican players in the major leagues historically.

2. In each of these cases African Americans saw their plight as connected to other people of African descent not just in the United States but internationally. Although pursuing different agendas and distinct political ideologies, these actions reveal how African Americans and other Americans of the African diaspora acted on a diasporic political consciousness in the early to mid-twentieth century. For critical assessments of these moments and their impact on how African Americans envisioned their world, see Robin Kelly, *Race Rebels: Culture, Politics, and the Black Working Class* (New York: Free Press, 1994), and Penny Von Eschen, *Race against Empire: Black Americans and Anticolonialism, 1937–1957* (Ithaca, NY: Cornell University Press, 1997). On the relationship between African Americans and Cubans, see Brock and Castañeda Fuertes, eds., *Between Race and Empire.*

3. Although white Americans went south for Caribbean winter ball, I label this scene an "African American player's market" because of the substantial difference in salaries between the major leagues and Negro leagues. Not only were African Americans a hot commodity, but they could also earn substantially higher salaries than what they drew monthly during the Negro-league season.

4. Wilmer Fields, *My Life in the Negro Leagues: An Autobiography by Wilmer Fields* (Westport, CT: Meckler, 1992), 24.

5. Fernández interview. From 1949 to 1960 the winter-league season culminated in the Caribbean World Series. In its first manifestation, the round-robin tournament featured the champions of the Cuban, Puerto Rican, Panamanian, and Venezuelan leagues. Black went on to impress the team's manager, Brooklyn Dodgers second baseman Billy Herman, who contacted the Dodgers' front office, leading to their signing of Black.

6. Bienvenido Rodríguez, interview with author, Ponce, Puerto Rico, June 22, 1995. Major-league teams recognized Trouppe's skill as a talent evaluator after his playing career ended in the early 1950s. He worked as a scout for the St. Louis Cardinals for ten years. Riley, *The Biographical Encyclopedia,* 792.

7. Quoted in "Here in Mexico, I am a Man!" *Miami Herald,* Mexico Edition, February 22, 2004, available online at http://geocities.com/jonclark500/blackslmb.html (accessed August 13, 2005).

8. *New York Age,* April 12, 1941.

9. "Here in Mexico, I am a Man!"

10. Untitled newspaper clipping, April 1, 1946, *New York World-Telegram,* "Mike" Fermin Guerra Player File, NBLA. Olmo's salary numbers are drawn from "Mexican Government Seen behind League," *New York World-Telegram,* newspaper clipping, February 23, 1946, Luis Rodríguez Olmo Player File, NBLA.

11. "American Players in Mexico Put OK on New Surroundings," *New York World Telegram,* newspaper clipping, April 6, 1946, Roberto Ortiz Player File, NBLA. There were mitigating circumstances in Torres's case: he had lost a five-year-old son the previous year, and his wife suffered complications during a pregnancy. Torres returned to Cuba just before the Senators opened the 1946 campaign. The opportunity to play in Mexico proved more amenable to the grieving parents after the birth of their child. In January 1947 the *Sporting News* reported: "Torres may jump to Mexico. He toyed with the idea last spring, and had the support of Mrs. Torres. The bond of language, the greeting of friends swayed the lovely Senora Torres." *Sporting News,* January 8, 1947, and *Washington Post,* April 2, 1946, newspaper clippings, Gilberto Torres Player File, NBLA.

12. "Giants Fear More Players May Be Lured to Mexico," *New York World-Telegram,* newspaper clipping, April 1, 1946, Napoleon Reyes Player File, NBLA.

13. George Compton and Adolfo Solórzano, "Latins on the Diamond," *Américas* 3 (1951); Philip M. Hoose, *Necessities: Racial Barriers in American Sports* (New York: Random House, 1987), 101.

14. Larry Lester lists the names of thirty-three Negro leaguers who served during the Second World War. Lester, *Black Baseball's National Showcase,* 207–8.

15. *New York Times,* April 16, 1944; "Selective Service Rules Cubans Resident Aliens," undated newspaper clipping, "Mike" Fermin Guerra Player File, NBLA.

16. "Griffs Lose 3 Mainstays as Latins Go," newspaper clipping, July 1, 1944, "Mike" Fermin Guerra Player File, NBLA; Dan Daniel, "Daniel's Dope" column, *New York World Telegram,* newspaper clipping, August 3, 1944, Roberto Ortiz Player File, NBLA.

17. *Daily Worker,* May 14, 1943; newspaper clipping, May 6, 1943, Sal Hernández, TSNA. Some confusion initially arose about Hernández's last name due to the popular cultural tradition of using both parent's surnames: his full name was Salvador José Hernández Ramos. As a result, the Cuban catcher played several years in the minor leagues as Ramos before appearing in the majors as Hernández. The Cuban native was also misidentified early in his career as Ramon Hernández. *Sporting News,* March 3, 1986.

18. "Espionage on Diamond," newspaper clipping, July 30, 1942, Bithorn Clipping File, TSNA; *Daily Worker,* May 16, 1943; *Chicago Tribune,* June 2, 1943.

19. *Daily Worker,* December 13, 1943.

20. Determining Bithorn's status had posed a problem for baseball officials in his native Puerto Rico. In another demonstration of the contextual nature of racial perceptions, Puerto Rican league officials initially classified Bithorn as a *blanquito* (white). More than a reference to his skin color, the classification, according to Puerto Rican baseball historian Luis Alvelo, questioned Bithorn's Puerto Rican identity. Due to this perception, officials designated Bithorn a *refuerzo* when he joined the Puerto Rican Professional Winter League in its inaugural campaign in 1938. After a brief investigation, officials reversed their initial ruling, allowing Bithorn to play as a *nativo*.

21. *New York Age*, July 25, 1942.

22. *Daily Worker*, March 13, 1943.

23. *Daily Worker*, August 13, 1943.

24. *New York Daily News*, April 28, 2003; Howard Bryant, *Shut Out: A Story of Race and Baseball in Boston* (New York: Routledge, 2002), 36–40. The two Negro leaguers showed up at the Dodgers' spring training camp with sportswriters Joe Bostic (Harlem's *People's Voice*), Wendell Smith (*Pittsburgh Courier*), and Nat Low (*Daily Worker*). Details of the impromptu tryout were reported in the *New York Daily News* and other local New York papers and Black weeklies (www.dailynews.com/city_life/big_town/v-pfriendly/story/79194p-72847c.html, accessed January 12, 2004).

25. González Echevarría, *Pride of Havana*, 45.

26. Albertus "Cleffie" Fennar interview; newspaper clipping, November 7, 1940, Tommy de la Cruz Player File, NBLA.

27. *Washington Post*, March 17, 1936 (Senators camp); *New York Times*, February 20, 1937 (Giants camp); *New York Times*, April 16, 1944 (Reds camp).

28. *New York Times*, August 16, 1944.

29. *New York Age*, February 21, 1942.

30. Bretón, *Away Games*, 100.

31. *New York Age*, July 25, 1942. This article mistakenly identifies Venezuelan native Alejandro "Chico" Carrasquel as Cuban.

32. Heuer, "The Cuban Slide," 12.

33. Bretón, *Away Games*, 100.

34. *Washington Post*, April 13, 1946.

35. *New York Times*, December 13, 1946.

9. LATINOS AND BASEBALL INTEGRATION

Power quoted in Danny Peary, "Vic Power Remembers His Playing Days," *Sports Collector's Digest* (March 9, 1990): 201. The second epigraph is taken from Orlando Cepeda, "Foreword," in Minnie Miñoso with Herb Fagen, *Just Call Me Minnie: My Six Decades in Baseball* (Champaign, IL: Sagamore, 1994), xi.

1. *New York Age*, April 27, 1935, October 16, 1937. The black newspaper's campaign to have black players on all the New York City teams continued into the early 1950s. Writers from the *New York Age* and the *Amsterdam News* raised the subject during every baseball campaign until the last of the city's teams, the Yankees, finally had a black player. For representative columns of this campaign, see *New York Age*, October 16, 1937; August 15, 1942; April 14, 1945; No-

vember 24, 1945; October 16, 1948; November 6, 1948; and April 23, 1949. It was by no means an effort driven solely by New York City sportswriters; the most notable advocate of integration was Wendell Smith, *Pittsburgh Courier* columnist. For an examination of Smith's prominent role, see David Wiggins, "Wendell Smith, the *Pittsburgh Courier-Journal* and the Campaign to Include Blacks in Organized Baseball, 1933–1945," *Journal of Sport History*, 10:2 (Summer 1983): 5–29.

2. Snyder, *Beyond the Shadow of the Senators*, pp. 131, 207–8; Lester, *Black Baseball's National Showcase*, 208; Lanctot, *Negro League Baseball*, 249.

3. *New York Times*, October 25, 1945; *Washington Post*, October 26, 1945.

4. *Washington Post*, October 26, 1945; Rogosin, *Invisible Men*, 159–60. Red Smith's "a Senegambian somewhere in the Cuban batpile" comment originally appeared in the *Pittsburgh Courier*, November 3, 1945.

5. *Daily Worker*, September 3, 1942.

6. Heuer, "Cuban Slide," 12.

7. Newspaper clipping, October 3, 1935, Estalella Player File, NBLA.

8. *New York Times*, March 5 and 8, 1942. The Cuban All-Stars team was an amalgamation of top Cuban players from the recently finished Cuban winter-league season.

9. Bjarkman, *Baseball with a Latin Beat*, 148–49; Bruce Brown, "Cuban Baseball," *Atlantic Monthly* (June 1984): 112. Brown draws on the published works of Edel Casas, a Cuban sportswriter from the 1940s and 1950s, for the details of the García and Rickey interview.

10. Lester, *Black Baseball's National Showcase*, 224.

11. *Pittsburgh Courier*, June 23, 1945, Wendell Smith Papers, NBLA.

12. *New York Times*, September 20, 1947.

13. *New York Times*, September 24, 1947.

14. *New York Times*, September 25, 1947.

15. *New York Times*, September 29, 1947.

16. Tygiel, *Baseball's Great Experiment*, 213.

17. Ibid. An economic alliance between the organizations had begun in 1936 when the Eagles started renting Ruppert Stadium in Newark, the home park of the Yankees' highest minor-league team, named after former Yankees owner Colonel Jacob Ruppert.

18. Ibid., 214.

19. Lester, *Black Baseball's National Showcase*, 318.

20. Quoted in ibid., 316.

21. Quoted in ibid., 316–18.

22. *New York Age*, September 24, 1948.

23. Lanctot, *Negro League Baseball*, 348.

24. Anthropologist Peter Wade elucidates the problem of reifying the bipolar racial classification system that has existed in the United States. Wade notes that scholars occasionally slip into naturalizing the two categories of black and white, and calls for examining local articulations of race. *Blackness and Race Mixture: The Dynamics of Racial Identity in Colombia* (Baltimore: Johns Hopkins University Press, 1993): 343–46.

25. In his recent contribution to the historiography of baseball integration, Bruce Adelson places Latinos such as Felipe Alou and Orlando Cepeda alongside African Americans as part of the first wave of players who integrated clubs throughout the United States. See Adelson, *Brushing Back Jim Crow: The Integration of Minor-League Baseball in the American South* (Charlottesville: University Press of Virginia, 1999); and Larry Moffi and James Kronstadt, *Crossing the Line: Black Major Leaguers, 1947–1959* (Jefferson, NC: McFarland, 1994).

26. Breton, "Giants Lost Latin Stars," *Sacramento Bee,* August 29–30, 1993, p. 8.

27. Brock and Bayne, "Not Just Black," 168.

28. Miñoso with Fagen, *Just Call Me Minnie,* xi.

29. The seminal work on baseball integration continues to be Jules Tygiel, *Baseball's Great Experiment.* For other studies that focus on Robinson and the Dodgers, see Arnold Rampersad, *Jackie Robinson: A Biography* (New York: Ballantine Books, 1997); Tygiel, ed., *The Jackie Robinson Reader: Perspectives on an American Hero* (New York: Plume Books, 1998); and Carl E. Prince, *Brooklyn's Dodgers: The Bums, the Borough, and the Best of Baseball, 1947–1957* (New York: Oxford University Press, 1996).

10. TROUBLING THE WATERS

1. *Sporting News,* July 16, 1947.

2. Armando Vásquez, interview with author, July 1, 2005, New York; Monte Irvin, interview with author, July 25, 2005, Cooperstown, NY; Lester, *Black Baseball's National Showcase,* 363–65. Vásquez was a first baseman for the Clowns' 1952 team, on which Aaron was an aspiring shortstop.

The number of transactions between the Giants' and Cubans' franchises between 1948 and 1950 contradicts historian Neil Lanctot's claim that the arrangement between the Giants and Pompez was "largely informal." Lanctot does acknowledge that this relationship "did parallel the 'working agreements' in effect throughout Organized Baseball allowing major or high minor league teams first option on a lower level club's players in exchange for financial support." Lanctot, *Negro League Baseball,* 348.

3. Letter to *Wall Street Journal,* John S. (Jack) Schwarz, April 11, 1984.

4. Felipe Alou, interview conducted by Larry Hogan, March 2004, Scottsdale, AZ.

5. Bretón, *Away Games,* 49 (emphasis added).

6. These scouts included Jesse Thomas, brother of former New York Cubans first baseman Dave "Showboat" Thomas. Jesse spotted a sixteen-year-old Willie McCovey playing baseball in the Mobile playgrounds. *New York Times,* August 6, 1959.

7. Robert Boyle, "The Private World of the Negro Ballplayer," *Sports Illustrated,* March 21, 1960, p. 74.

8. Ibid., 18.

9. Ibid., 18. While Pompez was arrested at least four times for involvement

in Harlem's numbers scene, there are no records of any arrests after his plea arrangement in 1939, when he turned state's evidence in exchange for probation.

10. Ibid., 19.

11. Tom Weir and Blane Bachelor, "Spanish-Speaking Players Get Lessons in American Life," *USA Today,* April 13, 2004, www.usatoday.com. Each spring training roster had forty men.

12. *Washington Post,* August 2, 1957.

13. Boyle, "Private World," 19.

14. Quoted in Regalado, *Viva Baseball!* 72.

15. Tygiel, *Baseball's Great Experiment,* 281.

16. *Washington Post,* October 14, 1953.

17. Bjarkman, *Baseball with a Latin Beat,* 91; Vic Power, interview with author, June 1995, Bayamon, Puerto Rico; "Power Proves His Case," *Sport,* August 1956, pp. 44–45; and newspaper clipping, *Philadelphia Daily News,* September 11, 1964, Vic Power Player File, NBLA.

18. Instituted in 1958, the Gold Glove award is given to the top fielder at each position as decided by vote among all major-league team managers. Tygiel, *Baseball's Greatest Experiment,* 296.

19. Peary, "Vic Power Remembers His Playing Days," 201. The Yankees traded Power to the Philadelphia Athletics early in 1954; Power made his major-league debut with the Athletics during the 1954 season. Elston Howard would earn the distinction as the first black player to appear for the Yankees in the following campaign, 1955.

20. Ibid., 201.

21. Julio and Ana Navarro, interview with author, Bayamon, Puerto Rico, June 9, 1995.

22. Regalado, *Viva Baseball!* 52.

23. *Sporting News,* July 5, 1950.

24. Bill Roeder, "Bums Need a Spanish Dictionary," newspaper clipping, August 22, 1952, Sandy Amoros Player File, NBLA.

25. Larry R. Gerlach, "Crime and Punishment: The Marichal-Roseboro Incident," *Nine* 12:2 (Spring 2004): 3.

26. Ibid. Gerlach also notes that other matters weighed on both players' minds. A resident of Watts, Roseboro played in the series aware that, less than two weeks earlier, race riots had erupted in his Los Angeles neighborhood. Marichal entered the series concerned with the deteriorating political conditions in the Dominican Republic, which had been occupied by twenty thousand U.S. Marines since April.

27. *New York Times,* August 24, 1965, Juan Marichal Player File, NBLA.

28. *New York World Telegram,* August 30, 1965, Juan Marichal Player File, NBLA.

29. Dick Young, "Young Ideas," *New York Daily News,* August 26, 1965, Marichal Player File, NBLA.

30. Bjarkman, *Baseball with a Latin Beat,* 138n2, 229. Dark's comment originally appeared in a 1964 interview with *New York Newsday* sportswriter Stan Isaacs.

31. Regalado, *Viva Baseball!* 85 (Cepeda), 98 (Alou).

32. Ibid., 86.

33. Dan Daniel, "Gonzalez Making Fortune in Cuba, but He Isn't Happy," *New York World Telegram*, July 25, 1947, Miguel Angel González Player File, NBLA.

34. *Sporting News*, July 24, 1957, Miguel Angel González Player File, NBLA.

35. Daniel, "Gonzalez Making Fortune in Cuba."

36. Weir and Bachelor, "Spanish-Speaking Players Get Lessons in American Life."

37. *New York Times*, November 11, 1960.

38. For the development of Cuban amateur baseball in the Castro era, see Milton Jamail, *Full Count: Inside Cuban Baseball* (Carbondale: Southern Illinois University Press, 2002).

39. *New York Times*, November 11, 1960.

40. "Pascual, Ramos, Minoso, among Those Affected," newspaper clipping, January 4, 1961, Pedro Ramos Player File, NBLA; *New York Times*, January 7, 1961.

41. *Sporting News*, September 4, 1965.

42. Regalado, *Viva Baseball!* 144.

43. Ibid., 143.

44. Frick negotiated an agreement in early 1963 with the leagues in Puerto Rico, the Dominican Republic, and Venezuela. The agreement stated that "major leaguers are allowed to play winter ball, but only in their own home countries." The winter league teams also agreed not to sign U.S. players who had not secured permission from their major-league club and the commissioner. "Latins Rhumba to Frick Tune—Fined $2,500," *Sporting News*, February 16, 1963, p. 4; Regalado, *Viva Baseball!* 143.

45. Regalado, *Viva Baseball!* 143.

46. Bob Stevens, "Latins Have Rep in Frick's Office," newspaper clipping, March 16, 1963, Felipe Alou Player File, NBLA.

47. Nicholas Dawidoff, "The Struggles of Sandy A," 79–81, undated magazine clipping, Sandy Amoros Player File, NBLA; *New York Times*, June 28, 1992, p. 32.

48. Dawidoff, "The Struggles of Sandy A," 80. On the changing context of Cuban emigration to the United States, see Masud-Piloto, *From Welcomed Exiles to Illegal Immigrants*.

49. Vásquez interview; Milton Gross, "Tragic Downfall of a World Series Hero," *Sports Scene*, November 1971, p. 76, Amoros Player File, NBLA.

50. *New York Times*, June 6, 1992, Amoros Player File, NBLA.

51. Dawidoff, "The Struggles of Sandy A," 81.

52. *Syracuse Post-Standard*, July 17, 1973, p. 12, Zoilo Versalles Player File, NBLA; Bretón, *Away Games*, 140–43; *New York Times*, June 11, 1995.

53. Fernández interview.

54. A public television channel in Milwaukee, WMVS, filmed part of its documentary *Jonron: A Look at Baseball's Immortal Latinos* (1983) during one of these reunion games. This documentary is part of the Film and Recorded Sound Collection, NBLA. Vásquez showed me a picture of Celia Cruz's visit to one of the reunion games (Vásquez interview).

55. Fernández interview.

56. *Amsterdam News,* March 2, 1932.

57. Bill Liston, "The Man: Tiant," *1975 Boston Scorebook,* 8–9, Luis Tiant Player File, NBLA. The Cuban government granted Tiant's mother a temporary visa in 1968 to visit her son and his family in Mexico.

58. Apparently inspired by his parent's visit, Tiant won two games in the World Series against Cincinnati that Boston lost in a heartbreaking seven-game series. Maury Allen, "Of Destiny Man," newspaper clipping, October 14, 1975, Luis Tiant Jr. Player File, NBLA. For a discussion of the Tiant father-son combination, see John Holway, "Will the Real Luis Tiant Please Stand Up," *Baseball Digest* (February 1976): 74–78.

59. Bjarkman, *Baseball with a Latin Beat,* 91; Perry, "Vic Powers Remembers His Playing Days," 203.

60. On the impact of accents in job discrimination and on notions of American identity, see Mari J. Matsuda, "Voices of America: Accent, Antidiscrimination Law, and a Jurisprudence for the Last Reconstruction," *Yale Law Journal* 100:5 (March 1991): 1329–1407.

61. Hoose, *Necessities,* 93.

62. A man's and his family's honor was rooted in his ability to protect and defend the virginity of the female members of his family. The underside of this honor system, therefore, was the violence that often sustained the dominant ideology of race and gender. Although legal recourse was available to a family to punish a man who "deflowered" one of its women, disenfranchised men often resorted to physical violence, either against the "fallen" woman or the violating man, in order to maintain the family's honor. This system, of course, did not survive in its old form. Historian Eileen Findlay Suarez provides a comprehensive examination of the way this system of honor shaped understandings of gender and race in *Imposing Decency: The Politics of Sexuality and Race in Puerto Rico, 1870–1920* (Durham, NC: Duke University Press, 1999).

63. *New York Times,* March 27, 1955, A2; *Washington Post,* March 27, 1955, C4.

64. Steve Wulf, "Arriba Roberto," *Sports Illustrated* (December 28, 1992–January 4, 1993), 117.

65. Hoose, *Necessities,* 102.

66. Regalado, *Viva Baseball!* 122.

67. Ibid., 123.

68. Ibid.

69. Luis Mayoral, "*El Hombre*—The Man: Roberto Clemente," undated magazine article, Roberto Clemente Player File, NBLA.

11. LATINOS AND BASEBALL'S GLOBAL TURN

Fainaru and Sanchez quoted in Andrew Kalloch, "From the Barrio to the Big Leagues: Latin Americans & the National Pastime," *The Undergraduate Quarterly* 1:2 (January–March 2005): 93. Klein quoted in ibid., 98.

1. Ted Williams Induction Speech, National Baseball Hall of Fame, July 1966. Thanks to Dick Clark for sharing this excerpt from Williams's speech.

2. Historian Sam Regalado charts the composition of each decade of Latin American-born players in *Viva Baseball!* (see 7, 40, 117, 140, and 171). Also see Bjarkman, *Baseball with a Latin Beat,* 385–86.

3. *Washington Post,* March 5, 1958.

4. "No Bonuses for Cambria," newspaper clipping, October 1962, Joe Cambria File, TSNA.

5. Ibid.

6. Robert Boyle, "The Latins Storm Las Grandes Ligas," *Sports Illustrated,* August 9, 1965, 26.

7. Regalado, "'Latin Players on the Cheap': Professional Baseball Recruitment in Latin America and the Neocolonialist Tradition," *Indiana Journal of Global Legal Studies* 8:1 (Fall 2000): p. 5 of 8, http://ijgls.indiana.edu/archive/08/01/regalado.shtml (last accessed June 3, 2002).

8. Oleksak and Oleksak, *Beisbol,* 142; Marcano Guevara and Fidler, *Stealing Lives,* 32.

9. Elliot Almond and Lupe Gervas, "A Cultural Curveball," *San Jose Mercury News* and *Nuevo Mundo,* July 23, 2003, www.belleville.com/mld/belleville/sports/baseball/mlb/635790.html (last accessed April 7, 2004); Bretón, *Away Games,* 39.

10. This point is made by a number of Latino historians who have studied the incorporation of Latino labor in the United States. See, for example, Carmen Whalen, *From Puerto Rico to Philadelphia: Puerto Rican Workers and Postwar Economies* (Philadelphia: Temple University Press, 2001); Camille Guerin-Gonzalez, *Mexican Workers and American Dreams: Immigration, Repatriation, and California Farm Labor, 1900–1939* (New Brunswick, NJ: Rutgers University Press, 1994).

11. Marcano and Fidler, *Stealing Lives,* 23–24, 28.

12. Steve Fainaru, "Baseball's Minor Infractions," *Washington Post,* October 26, 2001, D1.

13. Marcano and Fidler, *Stealing Lives,* 30.

14. Fainaru, "Baseball's Minor Infractions." Marcano and Fidler also discuss the Bessa case at length; see chapter 3 of *Stealing Lives.*

15. Fainaru, "Baseball's Minor Infractions."

16. Ibid.

17. Marcano and Fidler, *Stealing Lives,* p. 29.

18. Ibid., 36.

19. "Dawn of a New Age," *Baseball America,* May 13, 2002, www.baseballamerica.com/today/features/agechart.html (last accessed May 13, 2002).

20. Ed Price, "Rosario Signing Raises Red Flag," *Baseball America,* May 8, 2004, www.baseballamerica.com/today/news/040508rosario (last accessed June 5, 2004); Tom Farrey, "Boras Confirms Player Used False Identity," May 18, 2004, http://sports.espn.go.com/mlb/news/story?id=1803614 (last accessed June 5, 2004). Later reports stated that Ivan Noboa had agreed to have the pitcher sign with the Diamondbacks, although the Los Angeles Dodgers had offered the prospect a $750,000 signing bonus; however, the Dodgers refused to pay Noboa directly, telling the *buscón* to negotiate his fee with the prospect.

21. Farrey, "Boras Confirms Player Used False Identity."

22. "In exchange for keeping quiet about Rosario's identity, Mena wanted between $20,000 and $40,000 of his signing bonus," according to Rosario's former agent Rob Plummer. Farrey, "Boras Confirms Player Used False Identity." The Rosario story was the subject of several featured segments during April and May 2004 on ESPN and ESPN.com. It was also the subject of a story on ESPN2's *Cold Pizza,* May 20, 2004, which featured interviews of ESPN *Deportes* reporter Ernesto Jerez and player agent Rob Plummer.

23. Marcano and Fidler, *Stealing Lives,* 37.

24. Jonathan Mahler, "Building the Beisbol Brand," *New York Times,* July 31, 2005, www.nytimes.com/2005/07/31/magazine/31METS.html (last accessed September 25, 2005).

25. Jorge Ortiz, "Culture Gap Draws Attention to High Proportion of Latinos Caught in the Web of Drugs, Steroids," *San Francisco Chronicle,* May 6, 2005, p. D1, http://sfgate/cgi-bin/article.cgi?file=/c/a/2005/05/06/MINORS.TMP (last accessed October 13, 2005); Marcano and Fidler, *Stealing Lives,* 27.

26. Mahler, "Building the Beisbol Brand."

12. SAYING IT IS SO-SA!

Alou quoted in "Alou: Let Host Stay," *San Francisco Chronicle,* August 9, 2005, C-5. Alou made his comments during his appearance on ESPN's *Outside the Lines* program that aired August 8, 2005. Pedro Martínez quoted in Almond and Gervas, "A Cultural Curveball."

1. Ozzie González, "Latinos in the Major Leagues: The 1999 Breakdown," posted April 1999, www.latinosportslegends.com/LatinsinMLB.htm (last accessed May 22, 2004). "More Foreigners in Majors for Sixth Straight Year," posted April 2, 2003, www.ESPN.com/MLB—Baseball's flood of foreign players continues to rise.htm (last accessed April 2, 2003). Sawchik, "Fair Baseball Globalization," *HispanicBusiness.com,* April 19, 2004, www.hispanicbusiness.com/news.htm (last accessed May 22, 2004). The methodology that Sawchik uses in arriving at his figures is unclear, the most significant issue being whether he included U.S.-born Latinos in his calculations. In their April 13, 2004, article, *USA Today* sportswriters Tom Weir and Blane Bachelor provided a figure of 23.5 percent for Latinos on major-league opening-day rosters. Weir and Bachelor, "Spanish-Speaking Players Get Lessons in American Life." Dan Klores, "Viva Baseball," aired September 23, 2005, Spike TV. Major League Baseball Press Release, "29.2 percent of Major League Baseball Players born outside the U.S.," posted April 7, 2005, http://mlb.mlb/NASApp/mlb/content/printerfriendly/mlb/y2005/m04/d07/c100306/ (last accessed August 24, 2005). On tightened immigration restrictions on quotas, see Kevin Baxter, "Teams Scramble to Secure Work Visas," *Miami Herald,* October 9, 2004.

2. Arlene Davila, *Latinos, Inc.: The Marketing and Making of a People* (Berkeley: University of California Press, 2001), 2.

3. Rodriguez, "Adjusting to Majors Has a New Meaning," *New York Times,* July 23, 2003.

4. Krasner, "Words Often Come Back to Haunt Them."

5. Ibid.

6. Weir and Dodd, "Talking to Each Other," *USA Today,* April 13, 2004, www.usatoday.com/sports/baseball/2004–04–13-language-barriers_x.htm (last accessed May 22, 2004); Alan Ginsberg, "Ramirez a Proud American," May 11, 2004, http://boston.redsox.mlb.com/NASApp/mlb/bos/news/bos_news.jsp?ymd =20040511&contentid=741017&vkey=news_bos&fext=.jsp (last accessed May 30, 2004).

7. Weir and Dodd, "Talking to Each Other."

8. Howard Bryant, personal communication with author, April 5, 2003; Bryant, "In Plain English, Language Barrier a Huge Obstacle," *Boston Herald,* September 28, 2004; Bob Klapisch, "Fight Could Hurt Duque's Playoff Status," *ESPN.com,* September 18, 2002, http://espn.go.com/mlb/columns/klapisch_bob/ 1433520.html (last accessed September 26, 2005). Anthony McCarron, "George Remains Zoo Keeper," *New York Daily News,* February 4, 2003, www.nydaily news.com/sports/story/59661p-55879c.html (last accessed May 31, 2004). A baseball beat writer who has covered the Yankees and Boston Red Sox during his career, Bryant broke the Hernández story during the 2002 season.

Interestingly, on occasions when his translator was unavailable, Hernández turned to fellow Latinos on the Yankees. Jorge Posada, a Latino of Cuban descent raised in Puerto Rico, typically stepped in as the translator. However, Posada's translation for Hernández's eloquent comments during postgame interviews did not always capture the nuances and emotions of what Hernández was saying—much was lost in the layman's translation. The Yankees eventually relented and allowed Astacio to return as Hernández's interpreter during the 2002 playoffs. Astacio continued to work for the Yankees translating for another Cuban defector signed by the team, José Contreras.

9. Weir and Dodd, "Talking to Each Other"; David Andriesen, "Full Count: SI's Reilly Inspires More Queries for Top Jocks," *Seattle Post-Intelligencer,* July 5, 2002, http://seattlepi.nwsource.com/baseball/77362_daveo5.shtml (last accessed May 31, 2004).

10. Weir and Dodd, "Talking to Each Other."

11. Ibid.

12. Ibid.

13. Ibid.

14. Andy Nesbitt, "English Class a Hit with Latino Ballplayers," *Boston Globe,* July 22, 2004.

15. Juan Vene, personal interview with author, Bronx, New York, June 1996. When Major League Baseball (MLB) organized the "Latino Legends" promotion sponsored by Chevrolet, allowing fans to select players for the all-time Latino team, Jackson was not included, in part because he did not pass the MLB marketing department's litmus test of having a close identification with his heritage. Richard Sandomir, "Who's a Latino Baseball Legend?" *New York Times,* August 26, 2005.

16. Bretón, *Away Games,* 35.

17. Gloria Rodriguez, "Adjusting to Majors Has a New Meaning," *New York Times,* July 23, 2003.

18. Krasner, "Words Often Come Back to Haunt Them."

19. Weir and Dodd, "Talking to Each Other."

20. Krasner, "Words Often Come Back to Haunt Them."

21. Almond and Gervas, "A Cultural Curveball"; José de Jesús Ortiz, "An Issue of Interpretation: Hispanic Players Advised to Address AP Reporters in Native Tongues," *Houston Chronicle*, June 14, 2003, www.chron.com/cs/CDA/ssistory .mpl/sports/1952269 (last accessed May 30, 2004).

22. Almond and Gervas, "A Cultural Curveball."

23. Steven Krasner, "Words Often Come Back to Haunt Them," *Providence Journal*, August 27, 2003; Almond and Gervas, "A Cultural Curveball."

24. Trouillot, *Silencing the Past*, 26–29.

25. Richard Sandomir, "Who's a Latino Baseball Legend?" *New York Times*, August 26, 2005.

26. Sandomir, "Who's a Latino Baseball Legend?"

27. Mike Bernardino, "Ace Issue Not Black and White," *Ft. Lauderdale Sun-Sentinel*, September 21, 2005, 1C.

28. Ibid.

29. John Ryan, "Latinos' Rough Road to Majors," *San Jose Mercury News*, September 22, 2005, www.mercurynews.com/mld/mercurynews/sports/baseball/mlb/san_francisco_giants/12709250.htm (last accessed September 24, 2005); "Station Won't Fire Host after Apology," *ESPN.com*, August 6, 2005, http:// sports.espn.go.com/espn/print?id+2126396&type=story (last accessed September 25, 2005).

30. Ryan, "Latinos' Rough Road to Majors."

31. Henry Schulman, "Host's One-Week Suspension Not Enough for Alou," *San Francisco Chronicle*, August 7, 2005, D-5.

32. Whalen, *From Puerto Rico to Philadelphia*, 6.

CONCLUSION

Perry quoted in Robert Nowatzki, "Foul Lines and the Color Line: Baseball and Race at the Turn of the Twentieth Century," *Nine* 11:1 (Fall 2002): 87.

1. Jose Canseco, *Juiced: Wild Times, Rampant 'Roids, Smash Hits, and How Baseball Got Big* (New York: Regan Books, 2005); on Palmeiro's testimony and subsequent suspension for his positive test results, see coverage in *Baltimore Sun*, especially "Palmeiro's Congressional Testimony," August 2; "Palmeiro Learned of Failed Test in May," August 3; "Palmeiro Saga Enters Theater of the Absurd," September 23; and "Palmeiro Needs to Inject Some Answer Now," September 25, 2005.

2. Ortiz, "Culture Gap Draws Attention."

3. Nowatzki, "Foul Lines and the Color Line," 83.

4. McDonald, *Indian Summer*, 149; 1911 article quoted in Nick C. Wilson, *Early Latino Ballplayers in the United States: Major, Minor, and Negro Leagues, 1901–1949* (Jefferson, NC: McFarland, 2005), 29.

5. Guterl, "The New Race Consciousness," 309. Historian Matthew Pratt Guterl situates the emergence of this new race consciousness in the post–World

War I era, a time of African American migrations to the urban north, the rise of African American radicalism, the initial outburst of anti-colonialism, and the United States' new role in the world economic system.

6. Guglielmo, *White on Arrival: Italians, Race, Color, and Power in Chicago, 1890–1945* (New York: Oxford University Press, 2003): 175–76.

Selected Bibliography

ARCHIVAL COLLECTIONS

Archivo Nacional, Havana
Biblioteca Nacional José Marti, Havana
Centro de Estudios Puertorriqueños, Hunter College, New York, NY
    Jesus Colón Papers
    Justo Martí Photographic Collection
    Sports (newspaper clippings) Vertical Folder
Cienfuegos Provincial Archive (Cuba)
Fordham University Archives and Special Collections Library, Bronx, NY
    Student Enrollment Cards
    The Fordham Monthly (student newspaper), 1887
Luis Alvelo Personal Collection, Caguas, Puerto Rico
National Baseball Library and Archive, Cooperstown, NY
    Ashland Collection
    Effa Manley Scrapbook
    Garry Herrmann Papers
    Negro Leagues Collection
    Negro League Newspaper Clippings, 1930–1960 File
    Negro League Newspaper Clippings, 1990–Present File
    Player Files
    Spanish Articles on the Negro Leagues File
    Subject Files

321

Rhode Island Historical Society, Providence
The Sporting News Archive, St. Louis, MO
    Player Biographical Clippings Files
University of South Florida Special Collections, Tampa, FL
    Tony Pizzo Papers
    La Union Marti-Maceo Papers

INTERVIEWS

Conducted by Adrian Burgos Jr. unless otherwise noted.

Alou, Felipe. Interview by Larry Hogan, March 3, 2004.
Alvelo, Luis. June 6, 1995.
Cabrera, Lorenzo "Chiquitin." April 3, 1999.
Fennar, Albertus "Cleffie." March 17, 1996.
Fernández, Rodolfo and Matilda. February 23, 1995.
Guilbe, Felix. June 24, 1995.
Irvin, Monte. July 25, 2005.
Jimenez, Miriam. July 25, 1996
Marius, Everard. July 16, 1996.
Navarro, Emilio "Millito." June 21, 1995.
Navarro, Julio and Ana. June 18, 1995.
Noble, Rafael "Ray." February 25, 1995.
Osborne, Claritha "Peaches." July 30, 1996.
Pereira, José "Pepin." August 25, 1999.
Power, Vic. June 17, 1995.
Rivera, Charlie. August 14, 1995.
Rodríguez, Bienvenido. June 22, 1995.
Sierra, Pedro. August 8, 1998.
Thomas, Piri. June 5, 1996.
Tua, Maria and Pedro. June 12, 1996.
Vargas, Roberto. June 19, 1995.
Vásquez, Armando. February 24, 1995; July 1, 2005.

NEWSPAPERS AND SERIALS
CUBA (HAVANA, UNLESS OTHERWISE NOTED)

El Comercio, (Cienfuegos, Cuba)
Diario de la Marina
El Figaro
El Habanista
Havana Post
La Lucha
El Pitcher
El Score
El Sport

UNITED STATES

Amsterdam News (NY)
Baltimore Afro-American
Baseball Magazine
Binghamton Daily Leader
Binghamton Daily Republican
Chicago Defender
Chicago Tribune
Cincinnati Post-Gazette
National Police Gazette
New York Age
New York Clipper
New York Times
Pittsburgh Courier
Providence Evening Dispatch
Providence Journal
Providence Sun Bulletin
El Score (Tampa)
Sporting Life
The Sporting News
Washington Post

PUBLISHED PRIMARY SOURCES

Aaron, Hank, with Lonnie Wheeler. *I Had a Hammer: The Hank Aaron Story.* New York: Harper Collins, 1991.

Almond, Elliot, and Lupe Gervas. "A Cultural Curveball." *San Jose Mercury News,* July 23, 2003. www.belleville.com/mld/belleville/sports/baseball/mlb/635790.html.

Alvarez de la Vega, José. "Pompez Affectionately Remembers His Trip to Puerto Rico. The *Hazaña* of Fabito in Shutting-Out his Famous 'Cuban Stars.' From Triumph to Triumph, Good Opportunity for the New York Cubans." *Puerto Rican Deportivo* 4:7–8 (July–August 1947): 14–17.

Andriesen, David. "Full Count: SI's Reilly Inspires More Queries for Top Jocks." *Seattle Post-Intelligencer* July 5, 2002, http://seattlepi.nwsource.com/baseball/77362_dave05.shtml.

Baseball Extra: A Newspaper History of the Glorious Game from Its Beginnings to the Present. Compiled by Eric C. Caren. Edison, NJ: Castle Books, 2000.

Cepeda, Orlando, with Charles Einstein. *My Ups and Downs in Baseball.* New York: G. P. Putnam's Sons, 1968.

Colon, Jesus. *The Way It Was and Other Writings.* Houston: Arte Publico Press, 1993.

———. *A Puerto Rican in New York and Other Sketches.* Foreword by Juan Flores. New York: International, 1982.

Dominguez, Robert. "Teddy Beisbol Joins Roster of Latino Greats." *New York Daily News,* March 31, 2004. www.nydailynews.com/entertainment/culture/story/179269p-155821c.html.

Fainaru, Steve. "Baseball's Minor Infractions." *Washington Post,* October 26, 2001, D1.

Farrey, Tom. "Boras Confirms Player Used False Identity." *ESPN.com.* May 18, 2004. http://sports.espn.go.com/mlb/news/story?id = 1803614.

Fields, Wilmer. *My Life in the Negro Leagues.* Westport, CT: Meckler Books, 1992.

Galvez y Delmonte, Wenceslao. *El Base Ball en Cuba.* Habana: Imprenta Mercantil, de los Heredores de Santiago, 1889.

Ginsberg, Alan. "Ramirez a Proud American." mlb.com. May 11, 2004. http://boston.redsox.mlb.com/NASApp/mlb/bos/news/bos_news.jsp?ymd=20040511&content_id=741017&vkey=news_bos&fext=.jsp.

Grillo, Evelio. *Black Cuban, Black American: A Memoir.* Houston: Arté Publico Press, 2002.

Gross, Milton. "Tragic Downfall of a World Series Hero." *Sports Scene,* November 1971, pp. 75–80.

Harlow, Alvin. "Unrecognized Stars." *Esquire,* September 1938.

Iglesias, Cesar Andreau, ed. *Memoirs of Bernardo Vega: A Contribution to the History of the Puerto Rican Community in New York.* New York: Monthly Review Press, 1984.

Irvin, Monte, with James A. Riley. *Nice Guys Finish First: The Autobiography of Monte Irvin.* New York: Carroll & Graf, 1996.

Jesús Ortiz, José de. "An Issue of Interpretation: Hispanic Players Advised to Address AP Reporters in Native Tongues." *Houston Chronicle,* June 14, 2003. www.chron.com/cs/CDA/ssistory.mpl/sports/1952269.

Leonard, Buck, with James A. Riley. *The Black Lou Gehrig: An Autobiography.* New York: Carroll & Graf, 1995.

McCarron, Anthony. "George Remains Zoo Keeper." *New York Daily News,* February 4, 2003. www.nydailynews.com/sports/story/59661p-55879c.html.

Miñoso, Minnie, with Herb Fagen. *Just Call Me Minnie: My Six Decades in Baseball.* Champaign, IL: Sagamore, 1994.

"More Foreigners in Majors for Sixth Straight Year." *ESPN.com,* April 2, 2003. www.ESPN.com/MLB—Baseball's flood of foreign players continues to rise.htm.

Paige, Satchel. *Maybe I'll Pitch Forever.* Lincoln: University of Nebraska Press, 1993.

Peary, Danny. "Vic Power Remembers His Playing Days." *Sports Collector's Digest,* March 9, 1990, p. 201.

Phelon, Bill. "Baseball in Cuba: The Great American Sport as an International Game." *Baseball Magazine,* May 1912, p. 35.

Price, Ed. "Rosario Signing Raises Red Flag." *Baseball America,* May 8, 2004. www.baseballamerica.com/today/news/040508rosario.

Rosa, Wilfredo. "Francisco Coimbre, gloria del béisbol de Puerto Rico." *El Boricua: Organo Oficial de la Federacion de Pueblos de Puerto Rico,* no. 2 (December 1993): 24.

Sawchik, Travis. "Fair Baseball Globalization." *Hispanic Business.com,* April 19, 2004. www.hispanicbusiness.com/news.htm.

Shecter, Leonard. "Vic Power's New, Wonderful World." *Sport,* May 1963, p. 69.

Spalding, Albert Goodwill. *America's National Game.* New York: American Sports Publishing Co., 1911. Reprint, Lincoln: University of Nebraska Press, 1992.

Spink, Alfred. *The National Game.* Carbondale: Southern Illinois University Press, 2000.

Sullivan, Dean. *Early Innings: A Documentary History of Baseball, 1825–1908.* Lincoln: University of Nebraska Press, 1995.

Thomas, Piri. *Down These Mean Streets.* New York: Knopf, 1967.

Troupe, Quincy. *Twenty Years Too Soon: Prelude to Major-League Integrated Baseball.* Los Angeles: S&S Enterprises, c. 1977. Reprint, Kansas City: Missouri Historical Society Press, 1995.

"Unsplendid Splinter: Cubs Rally Past Rays after Sosa's Ignominious Ejection" (unsigned AP wire story). *Sports Illustrated S.I.com,* June 3, 2003. http://sports illustrated.cnn.com/baseball/news/2003/06/03/sosa_ejected_ap.

Ward, John Montgomery. "Is the Base-Ball Player a Chattel?" *Lippincott's Magazine* 40 (August 1887): 310–19.

Weir, Tom, and Blane Bachelor, "Spanish-Speaking Players Get Lessons in American Life." *USA Today,* April 13, 2004. www.usatoday.com/sports/baseball/2004–04–13-cover-latinos_x.htm.

White, Sol. *Sol White's History of Colored Base Ball, With Other Documents on the Early Black Game.* Introduction by Jerry Malloy. Lincoln: University of Nebraska Press, 1995.

BOOKS AND ARTICLES

Acosta-Belén, Edna, and Carlos E. Santiago, "Merging Borders: The Remapping of America." *Latino Review of Books* 1:1 (Spring 1995): 2–12.

Adelman, Melvin. *A Sporting Time: New York City and the Rise of Modern Athletics.* Urbana: University of Illinois Press, 1986.

Adelson, Bruce. *Brushing Back Jim Crow: The Integration of Minor-League Baseball in the American South.* Charlottesville: University Press of Virginia, 1999.

Alamillo, José M. "*Peloteros* in Paradise: Mexican American Baseball and Oppositional Politics in Southern California, 1930–1950." *Western Historical Quarterly* 34:2 (Summer 2003): 191–211.

———. "Mexican American Baseball: Masculinity, Racial Struggle, and Labor Politics in Southern California, 1930–1950." In *Sports Matters: Race, Recreation, and Culture,* edited by John Bloom and Michael Willard. New York: New York University Press, 2002.

Allen, Lee. *100 Years of Baseball.* New York: Bartholomew House, 1950.

———. *The Cincinnati Reds.* New York: G. P. Putnam's Sons, 1948.

Almaguer, Tomas. *Racial Fault Lines: The Historical Origins of White Supremacy in California.* Berkeley and Los Angeles: University of California Press, 1994.

Anderson, Benedict. *Imagined Communities: Reflections on the Origins and Spread of Nationalism.* New York: Verso Books, 1991.

Aparicio, Frances. "Performing the Caribbean in American Studies." *American Quarterly* 50:3 (September 1998): 636–44.

———. "On Sub-versive Signifiers: U.S. Latina/o Writers Tropicalize English." *American Literature* 66:4 (December 1994): 797.

———. "Language on Language: Metalinguistic Discourse in the Poetry of U.S. Latinos." *Latino Studies Journal* 2:1 (January 1991): 58–74.

Aparicio, Frances, and Susan Chavéz-Silverman, eds. *Tropicalizations: Transcultural Representations of Latinidad*. Hanover, NH: New England University Press, 1995.

Arbena, Joseph. "Sports Language, Cultural Imperialism, and the Anti-Imperialist Critique in Latin America." *Studies in Latin American Popular Culture* 14 (1995): 129–41.

———. "Sport and the Promotion of Nationalism in Latin America: A Preliminary Interpretation." *Studies in Latin American Popular Culture* 11 (1992): 143–55.

———, ed. *Sport and Society in Latin America: Diffusion, Dependency, and the Rise of Mass Culture*. New York: Greenwood Press, 1988.

Arnesen, Eric. "Up from Exclusion: Black and White Workers, Race, and the State of Labor History." *Reviews in American Labor History* 26:1 (1998): 146–74.

Ayers, Edward. *The Promise of the New South: Life after Reconstruction*. New York: Oxford University Press, 1992.

Bachin, Robin F. *Building the South Side: Urban Space and Civic Culture in Chicago, 1890–1919*. Chicago: University of Chicago Press, 2004.

Bak, Richard. *Turkey Stearnes and the Detroit Stars: The Negro Leagues in Detroit, 1919–1933*. Detroit: Wayne State University Press, 1994.

Bankes, James. *The Pittsburgh Crawfords: The Lives & Times of Black Baseball's Most Exciting Team*. Dubuque, IA: Wm. C. Brown, 1991.

Barkley Brown, Elsa. "Negotiating and Transforming the Public Sphere: African American Political Life in the Transition from Slavery to Freedom." *Public Culture* 7 (Fall 1994): 107–46.

Barney, Robert Knight, and Frank Dallier. "'I'd Rather Be a Lamp Post in Chicago Than a Millionaire in Any Other City': William A. Hurlbert, Civic Pride, and the Birth of the National League." *Nine* 2:1 (Fall 1993): 40–58.

Baron, Ava, ed. *Work Engendered: Toward a New History of American Labor*. Ithaca, NY: Cornell University Press, 1991.

Barrett, James R. "Whiteness Studies: Anything Here for Historians of the Working Class?" *International Labor and Working-Class History* 60 (Fall 2001): 33–42.

———. "Americanization from the Bottom Up: Immigration and the Remaking of the Working Class in the United States, 1880–1930." *Journal of American History* 79 (Dec. 1992): 996–1020.

Barrett, James, and David Roediger, "In Between Peoples: Race, Nationality and the 'New Immigrant' Working Class." *Journal of American Ethnic History* 16 (1997): 3–44.

The Baseball Encyclopedia: The Complete and Definitive Record of Major League Baseball. 9th ed. New York: MacMillan, 1993.

Baud, Michiel. *Peasants and Tobacco in the Dominican Republic, 1870–1930.* Knoxville: University of Tennessee Press, 1995.

———. "The Struggle for Autonomy: Peasant Resistance to Capitalism in the Dominican Republic, 1870–1924." In *Labour in the Caribbean,* edited by Malcolm Cross and Gad Heuman, 120–40. London: MacMillan, 1988.

Bay, Mia. *The White Image in the Black Mind: African American Ideas about White People, 1830–1925.* New York: Oxford University Press, 2000.

Bederman, Gail. *Manliness and Civilization: A Cultural History of Gender and Race in the United States, 1880–1917.* Chicago: University of Chicago Press, 1995.

Benmayor, Rina, Ana Juarbe, Celia Alvaréz, and Blanca Vásquez. *Stories to Live By: Continuity and Change in Three Generations of Puerto Rican Women.* New York: Centro de Estudios Puertorriqueños, 1987.

Bergad, Laird. *Cuban Rural Society in the Nineteenth Century.* Princeton, NJ: Princeton University Press, 1990.

Berlin, Ira. "Time, Space, and the Evolution of Afro-American Society on British Mainland North America." *American Historical Review* 85 (1980): 44–78.

Betances, Emilio. "Social Classes and the Origin of the Modern State: The Dominican Republic, 1844–1930." *Latin American Perspectives* 22:3 (Summer 1995): 20–40.

Bjarkmann, Peter. *Baseball with a Latin Beat.* Jefferson, NC: McFarland, 1994.

Blanco, Tomas. *El prejudicio racial en Puerto Rico: Con estudio preliminar de Arcadio Díaz Quiñones.* Rio Piedras, Puerto Rico: Ediciones Huracán, 1985.

Bloom, John, and Michael Willard, eds. *Sports Matters: Race, Recreation, and Culture.* New York: New York University Press, 2002.

Bolton, Todd. "Beisbol behind the Veil: Latin Americans in the Negro Leagues." *Ragtyme Sports* (December 1994): 23–25.

———. "Pompez' Greatest Aggregation: The 1935 New York Cubans." Unpublished paper.

Bond, Greg. "Whipped Curs and Real Men: Race, Manliness, and the Segregation of Organized Baseball in the Late Nineteenth Century." Master's thesis, University of Wisconsin–Madison, 1999.

Bonilla, Frank, ed. *Borderless Borders: U.S. Latinos, Latin Americans, and the Paradox of Interdependence.* Philadelphia: Temple University Press, 1998.

Bonilla-Silva, Eduardo. "Rethinking Racism: Towards a Structural Interpretation." *American Sociological Review* 62 (June 1997): 465–80.

Bowman, Larry G. "The First Worlds Championship of Professional Baseball: The New York Metropolitans and the Providence Grays, 1884." *Nine* 6:2 (Spring 1998): 2–14.

Bretón, Marcos. *Away Games: The Life and Times of a Latin Ball Player.* New York: Simon & Schuster, 1999.

———. "Hope Lives on Field of Lost Dreams." *Sacramento Bee,* August 29–30, 1993, pp. 1–8.

Brock, Lisa, and Digna Castañeda Fuertes, eds. *Between Race and Empire: African-Americans and Cubans before the Cuban Revolution.* Philadelphia: Temple University Press, 1998.

Brown, Bruce. "Cuban Baseball." *Atlantic Monthly,* June 1984, p. 111.

Briggs, Laura. *Reproducing Empire: Race, Sex, Science, and U.S. Imperialism in Puerto Rico.* Berkeley and Los Angeles: University of California Press, 2002.

Briley, Ron. "Roman Mejias: Houston's First Major League Latin Star and the Troubled Legacy of Race Relations in the Lone Star State." *Nine* 10:1 (Fall 2001): 73–88.

Bruce, Janet. *Kansas City Monarchs.* Lawrence: University Press of Kansas, 1987.

Bryant, Howard. *Shut Out: A Story of Race and Baseball in Boston.* New York: Routledge, 2002.

Burgos, Adrian Jr. "'The Latins from Manhattan': Confronting Race and Building Community in Jim Crow Baseball, 1906–1950." In *Mambo Montage: The Latinization of New York,* edited by Arlene Davila and Agustin Lao-Montes, 73–95. New York: Columbia University Press, 2001.

———. "Playing Ball in a Black and White Field of Dreams: Afro-Caribbean Ballplayers in the Negro Leagues, 1910–1950." *Journal of Negro History* 82:1 (Winter 1997): 67–104.

Burk, Robert F. *Never Just a Game: Players, Owners, and American Baseball to 1920.* Chapel Hill: University of North Carolina Press, 1994.

Cabán, Pedro. "Moving from the Margins to Where? Three Decades of Latino/a Studies." *Latino Studies* 1:1 (March 2003): 5–36.

———. "The New Synthesis of Latin American and Latino Studies." In *Borderless Borders: U.S. Latinos, Latin Americans, and the Paradoxes of Interdependence,* edited by Frank Bonilla, 195–215. Philadelphia: Temple University Press, 1998.

Cahn, Susan K. "Sport Talk: Oral History and Its Uses, Problems, and Possibilities for Sport History." *Journal of American History* (September 1994): 594–609.

Calder, Bruce. *The Impact of Intervention: The Dominican Republic during the U.S. Occupation of 1916–1924.* Austin: University of Texas Press, 1984.

Captain, Gwendolyn. "Enter Ladies and Gentlemen of Color: Gender, Sport, and the Ideal of African American Manhood and Womanhood during the Late Nineteenth and Early Twentieth Centuries." *Journal of Sport History* 18:1 (Spring 1991): 81–102.

Chicoine, Stephen. "The Great Gallia: Texas's Melvin "Bert" Gallia and Ethnicity in Major League Baseball." *Southwestern Historical Quarterly* 105:4 (April 2004): 635–62.

Clark, Dick, and Larry Lester. *The Negro Leagues Book.* Cleveland: Society of American Baseball Researchers, 1994.

Cockcroft, James D. *Latinos in Beisbol.* New York: Franklin Watts, 1996.

Cohen, Lizabeth. *Making a New Deal: Industrial Workers in Chicago, 1919–1939.* New York: Cambridge University Press, 1990.

———. "Encountering Mass Culture at the Grassroots: The Experience of Chicago Workers in the 1920s." *American Quarterly* 41 (March 1989): 6–33.

Conzen, Kathleen Neils, et al., "The Invention of Ethnicity: A Perspective from the U.S.A." *Journal of American Ethnic History* (Fall 1992): 3–41.

Costas, Rafael. *Enciclopedia Beisbol Ponce Leones, 1938–1987.* Santo Domingo: n.p., n.d.

Costello, Rory. "S. K. Govern: Black Baseball Renaissance Man." *Baseball in the Virgin Islands*. http://home.nyc.rr.com/vibaseball/govern.html.

Davila, Arlene. *Latinos, Inc: The Marketing and Making of a People*. Berkeley and Los Angeles: University of California Press, 2001.

Davila, Arlene, and Agustin Lao-Montes, eds. *Mambo Montage: The Latinization of New York*. New York: Columbia University Press, 2001.

Davis, Mike. *Magical Urbanism: Latinos Reinvent the U.S. City*. New York: Verso, 2001.

Dawidoff, Nicholas. *The Catcher Was a Spy: The Mysterious Life of Moe Berg*. New York: Vintage, 1995.

Debono, Paul. *The Indianapolis ABCs: History of a Premier Team in the Negro Leagues*. Jefferson, NC: McFarland, 1997.

De Genova, Nicholas. "Race, Space, and the Reinvention of Latin America in Chicago." *Latin American Perspectives* 25:5 (September 1998): 87–116.

de la Fuente, Alejandro. "Race, National Discourse, and Politics in Cuba." *Latin American Perspectives* 25:3 (May 1998): 43–69.

Deloria, Phil. *Indians in Unexpected Places*. Lawrence: University of Kansas Press, 2004.

———. *Playing Indian*. New Haven: Yale University Press, 1998.

Derby, Lauren. "Gringo Chicken with Worms: Food and Nationalism in the Dominican Republic." In *Close Encounters of Empire: Writing the Cultural History of U.S.-Latin American Relations*, edited by Gilbert M. Joseph et al., 451–93. Durham, NC: Duke University Press, 1998.

Desmond, Jane C., and Virginia Dominguez. "Resituating American Studies in a Critical Internationalism." *American Quarterly* 48:3 (September 1996): 475–90.

Di Salvatore, Bryan. *A Clever Base-Ballist: The Life and Times of John Montgomery Ward*. New York: Pantheon, 1999.

Dixon, Phil, with Patrick J. Hanigan. *The Negro Baseball Leagues: A Photographic History*. Mattituck, NY: Amereon Ltd., 1992.

Dorinson, Joe, and Joram Warmund. *Jackie Robinson: Race, Sports, and the American Dream*. New York: M. E. Sharpe, 1998.

Duany, Jorge. "Nation, Migration, Identity: The Case of Puerto Ricans." *Latino Studies* (2003): 424–44.

———. "Reconstructing Racial Identity: Ethnicity, Color, and Class among Dominicans in the United States and Puerto Rico." *Latin American Perspectives* 25:3 (May 1998): 147–72.

———. "Common Threads or Disparate Agendas? Recent Research on Migration from and to Puerto Rico." *Centro de Estudios Puertorriqueños* 7:1 (Winter 1994–95/Spring 1995): 60–77.

———. "Ethnicity in the Spanish Caribbean: Notes on the Consolidation of Creole Identity in Cuba and Puerto Rico." *Ethnic Groups* 6:2 (1985): 99–123.

Du Bois, W. E. B. *Black Reconstruction in America, 1860–1880*. Reprint, New York: Atheneum, 1992.

———. *The Souls of Black Folk*. Reprint, Greenwich, CT: 1961.

Fainaru, Steve, and Ray Sánchez. *The Duke of Havana: Baseball, Cuba, and the Search for the American Dream*. New York: Villard, 2001.

Ferrer, Ada. *Insurgent Cuba: Race, Nation, and Revolution, 1868–1898*. Chapel Hill: University of North Carolina Press, 1999.

———. "To Make a Free Nation: Race and the Struggle for Independence in Cuba, 1868–1898." Ph.D. dissertation, University of Michigan, 1995.

Ferrer Aguilar, Narciso E. "La Historia del Beisbol en Cienfuegos entre los años 1888–1920." Trabajo de Diploma de Instituto Superior Técnico de Cienfuegos, Facultdad de Cultura Fisica: 1991–1992 [Work for Diploma Cienfuegos Superior Technical Institute, Physical Culture Faculty].

Fields, Barbara J. "Slavery, Race, and Ideology in the United States of America." *New Left Review* no. 181 (May–June 1990): 95–118.

Figueredo, Jorge. *Beisbol Cubano: A un Paso de las Grandes Ligas, 1878–1961*. Jefferson, NC: McFarland, 2005.

———. *Cuban Baseball: A Statistical History, 1878–1961*. Jefferson, NC: McFarland, 2003.

Findlay Suarez, Eileen. *Imposing Decency: The Politics of Sexuality and Race in Puerto Rico, 1870–1920*. Durham, NC: Duke University Press, 1999.

———. "Love in the Tropics: Marriage, Divorce, and the Construction of Benevolent Colonialism in Puerto Rico, 1898–1910." In *Close Encounters of Empire: Writing the Cultural History of U.S.-Latin American Relations*, edited by Gilbert M. Joseph, 139–172. Durham, NC: Duke University Press, 1998.

Fishkin, Shelley Fisher. "'Interrogating 'Whiteness,' Complicating 'Blackness': Remapping American Culture." *American Quarterly* 47:3 (September 1995): 428–66.

Fleitz, David. *Louis Sockalexis: The First Cleveland Indian*. Jefferson, NC: McFarland, 2001.

Flores, Juan. *From Bomba to Hip-Hop: Puerto Rican Culture and Latino Identity*. New York: Columbia University Press, 2000.

———. "Latino Studies: New Contexts, New Concepts." *Harvard Educational Review* 67:2 (Summer 1997): 208–21.

———. "Pan-Latino/Trans-Latino: Puerto Ricans in 'New Nueva York.'" *Centro de Estudios Puertorriqueños* 8:1/2 (Spring 1996): 170–86.

———. "Broken English Memories." *Modern Language Quarterly* 57:2 (June 1996): 381–95.

———. *Divided Borders: Essays on Puerto Rican Identity*. Houston: Arte Público Press, 1993.

———. "'Que Assimilated, Brother, Yo Soy Asimilao': The Structuring of Puerto Rican Identity in the U.S." *Journal of Ethnic Studies* 13:3 (1985): 1–16.

Foley, Neil. *The White Scourge: Anglos, Blacks, and Mexicans in Central Texas, 1880–1930*. Berkeley and Los Angeles: University of California Press, 1997.

Foner, Eric. *The Story of American Freedom*. New York: W. W. Norton, 1998.

———. *Reconstruction: America's Unfinished Revolution*. New York: Harper & Row, 1988.

Formisano, Ronald. *Boston against Busing: Race, Class, and Ethnicity in the 1960s and 1970s*. Chapel Hill: University of North Carolina Press, 2004.

Franks, Joel S. *Whose Baseball? The National Pastime and Cultural Diversity in California, 1859–1941*. New York: Rowman & Littlefield, 2001.

———. "Whose Baseball? Baseball in Nineteenth-Century Multicultural California." *Nine* 4:2 (Spring 1996): 246–62.

———. "Sweeney of San Francisco: A Local Boy Makes Good, Then Not So Good." *Baseball History* (Winter 1987–88): 52–62.

———. "Of Heroes and Boors: Early Bay-Area Baseball." *Baseball Research Journal*, no. 16 (1987): 45–47.

Fraser, Steve, and Gary Gerstle, eds. *The Rise and Fall of the New Deal Order, 1930–1980*. Princeton, NJ: Princeton University Press, 1989.

Frio, Daniel, and Marc Onigman. "'Good Field, No Hit': The Image of Latin American Baseball Players in the American Press, 1876–1946." *Revista/Review Interamericana* (1979): 199–208.

———. "Baseball Triumphs of Latin Players Obscured by Ethnic Slurs, Jokes." *Washington Post*, March 5, 1978.

Gaines, Kevin. *Uplifting the Race: Black Leadership, Politics, and Culture in the Twentieth Century.* Chapel Hill: University of North Carolina Press, 1996.

Gerlach, Larry. "Crime and Punishment: The Marichal-Roseboro Incident." *Nine* 12:2 (2004): 1–28.

Gerstle, Gary. "Race and the Myth of the Liberal Consensus." *Journal of American History* 82 (September 1995): 579–86.

———. *Working Class Americanism: The Politics of Labor in a Textile City, 1914–1960*. New York: Cambridge University Press, 1989.

Gilman, Sander L. "Black Bodies, White Bodies: Toward an Iconography of Female Sexuality in Late-Nineteenth-Century Art, Medicine, and Literature." In *Race, Writing, and Difference*, edited by Henry Louis Gates, Jr., 223–261. Chicago: University of Chicago Press, 1986.

Gilroy, Paul. *The Black Atlantic: Modernity and Double Consciousness.* Cambridge, MA: Harvard University Press, 1993.

Glasser, Ruth. "*En Casa en Connecticut:* Towards a Historiography of Puerto Ricans Outside of New York." *Centro de Estudios Puertorriqueños* 7:1 (Winter 1994–95/Spring1995): 50–59.

———. *My Music Is My Flag: Puerto Rican Musicians and Their New York Communities, 1917–1940*. Berkeley and Los Angeles: University of California Press, 1995.

Goldstein, Warren. *Playing for Keeps: A History of Early Baseball.* Ithaca, NY: Cornell University Press, 1989.

González Echevarría, Roberto. *The Pride of Havana: A History of Cuban Baseball.* New York: Oxford University Press, 1999.

———. "The Game in Matanzas: On the Origins of Cuban Baseball." *Yale Review* 83 (July 1995): 62–94.

González, José Luis. *Puerto Rico: The Four-Storeyed Country.* Translated by Gerald Guiness. Princeton, NJ: Weiner Markus, 1993.

González, Juan. *Harvest of Empire.* New York: Penguin Press, 2000.

González, Ozzie. "Latinos in the Major Leagues: The 1999 Breakdown." April 1999. www.latinosportslegends.com/LatinsinMLB.htm.

Gordon, Linda. *The Great Arizona Abduction.* Cambridge, MA: Harvard University Press, 1999.

Gorn, Elliot. *The Manly Art: Bare-Knuckled Prize Fighting.* Ithaca, NY: Cornell University Press, 1984.

Greenbaum, Susan D. *More Than Black: Afro-Cubans in Tampa.* Gainesville: University Press of Florida, 2002.

———. "Afro-Cubans in Exile: Tampa, Florida, 1886–1984." *Cuban Studies/Estudios Cubanos* 15:1 (Winter 1985): 59–72.

Greenberg, Cheryl. *"Or Does It Explode?": Black Harlem in the Great Depression.* New York: Oxford University Press, 1991.

Grossman, James R. *Land of Hope: Chicago Black Southerners and the Great Migration.* Chicago: University of Chicago Press, 1989.

Guerin-Gonzalez, Camille. *Mexican Workers and American Dreams: Immigration, Repatriation, and California Farm Labor, 1900–1939.* New Brunswick, NJ: Rutgers University Press, 1994.

Guglielmo, Tom. *White on Arrival: Italians, Race, Color, and Power in Chicago, 1890–1945.* New York: Oxford University Press, 2003.

Guridy, Frank A. "From Solidarity to Cross-Fertilization: Afro-Cuban/African American Interaction during the 1930s and 1940s." *Radical History Review* 87 (2003): 19–48.

———. "Racial Knowledge in Cuba: The Production of a Social Fact, 1912–1944." Ph.D. dissertation, University of Michigan, 2001.

Guterl, Matthew Pratt. *The Color of Race in America, 1900–1940.* Cambridge, MA: Harvard University Press, 2001.

———. "The New Race Consciousness: Race, Nation, and Empire in American Culture, 1910–1925." *Journal of World History* 10:2 (1999): 307–52.

Gutierrez, David G. "Migration, Emergent Ethnicity, and the 'Third Space': The Shifting Politics of Nationalism in Greater Mexico." *Journal of American History* 86:2 (September 1999): 481–517.

———. *Walls and Mirrors: Mexican Americans, Mexican Immigrants, and the Politics of Ethnicity.* Berkeley and Los Angeles: University of California Press, 1995.

———. "Significant to Whom? Mexican Americans and the History of the American West." *Western Historical Quarterly* 24 (November 1993): 519–39.

Haas, Lisbeth. *Conquest and Historical Identities in California, 1769–1936.* Berkeley and Los Angeles: University of California Press, 1995.

Hall, Stuart. "Negotiating Caribbean Identities." *New Left Review,* no. 209 (1995): 1–14.

———. "Cultural Identity and Diaspora." In *Identity: Community, Culture, Difference,* edited by Jonathan Rutherford, 222–37. London: Lawrence & Wishart, 1990.

Hamilton, Nora, and Chinchilla Norma Stolz. "Central American Migrations: A Framework for Analysis." In *Structuring Latina and Latino Lives in the United States,* edited by Mary Romero, 81–100. New York: Routledge, 1997.

Harrison, C. Keith. "Scholar or Baller in American Higher Education? A Visual Elicitation and Qualitative Assessment of the Student-athlete's Mindset." *NASAP Journal* 5:1 (Spring 2002): 66–81.

Heaphy, Leslie. *The Negro Leagues, 1869–1960.* Jefferson, NC: McFarland, 2003.

Helg, Aline. *Our Rightful Share: The Afro-Cuban Struggle for Equality, 1886–1912*. Chapel Hill: University of North Carolina Press, 1995.

Heuer, Robert. "The Cuban Slide: Who Really Broke Baseball's Color Barrier?" *Chicago Reader*, September 26, 1997, p. 12.

Hewitt, Nancy. "A Response to John Higham." *American Quarterly* 45:2 (June 1993): 237–42.

———. "The Voice of Virile Labor: Labor Militancy, Community, Solidarity, and Gender Identity among Tampa's Latin Workers." In *Work Engendered: Toward a New History of American Labor*, edited by Ava Baron. Ithaca, NY: Cornell University Press, 1991.

Higginbotham, Evelyn Brooks. "African-American Women's History and the Metalanguage of Race." *Signs: Journal of Women in Culture and Society* 17 (Winter 1992): 251–74.

Higham, John. *Stranger in the Land: Patterns of American Nativism, 1860–1925*. 2nd ed. New Brunswick, NJ: Rutgers University Press, 1988.

———. *Send These to Me: Immigrants in Urban America*. Baltimore: Johns Hopkins University Press, 1984.

Hirsch, Arnold R. *Making the Second Ghetto: Race and Housing in Chicago, 1940–1960*. Chicago: University of Chicago Press, 1999.

———. "Massive Resistance in the Urban North: Trumbull Park, Chicago, 1953–1966." *Journal of American History* 82 (September 1995): 522–50.

History Task Force. *Labor Migration under Capitalism: The Puerto Rican Experience*. New York: Monthly Review Press, 1979.

Hoffnung-Garskopf, Jesse. "The Migrations of Arturo Schomburg: On Being Antillano, Negro, and Puerto Rican in New York, 1891–1938." *Journal of American Ethnic History* 21 (Fall 2002): 3–49.

Hoganson, Kristin L. *Fighting for American Manhood: How Gender Politics Provoked the Spanish-American and Philippine-American Wars*. New Haven, CT: Yale University Press, 1998.

Holt, Thomas. "Marking: Race, Race-making, and the Writing of History." *American Historical Review* 100:1 (February 1995): 1–20.

———. "'An Empire over the Mind': Emancipation, Race, and Ideology in the British West Indies and the American South." In *Race, Region, and Reconstruction*, edited by J. Morgan Kousser, 283–313. New York: Oxford University Press, 1982.

Holway, John. *Voices from the Great Black Baseball Leagues*. New York: Da Capo Press, 1992.

———. *Black Diamonds*. Westport, CT: Meckler Publishing, 1989.

———. *Blackball Stars: Negro League Pioneers*. Westport, CT: Meckler Books, 1988. Reprint, New York: Carroll & Graf, 1992.

Honey, Michael K. *Southern Labor and Black Civil Rights: Organizing Memphis Workers*. Urbana: University of Illinois Press, 1993.

Hoose, Philip M. *Necessities: Racial Barriers in American Sports*. New York: Random House, 1987.

Hoxie, Frederick. *A Final Promise: The Campaign to Assimilate the Indians, 1880–1920*. Lincoln: University of Nebraska Press, 1984.

Ivor-Campbell, Frederick. "Extraordinary 1884: The Year of Baseball's First World Series." *National Pastime*, no. 13 (1993): 16–23.

Jacobson, Matthew Frye. *Barbarian Virtues: The United States Encounters Foreign Peoples at Home and Abroad*. New York: Hill & Wang, 2000.

———. *Whiteness of a Different Color: European Immigrants and the Alchemy of Race*. Cambridge, MA: Harvard University Press, 1998.

James, C. L. R. *Beyond a Boundary*. Durham, NC: Duke University Press, 1983.

James, Winston. *Holding Aloft the Banner of Ethiopia: Caribbean Radicalism in Early Twentieth-Century America*. New York: Verso, 1998.

———. "Afro-Puerto Rican Radicalism in the United States: Reflections on the Political Trajectories of Arturo Schomburgh and Jesus Colon." *Centro de Estudios Puertorriqueños* 8:1–2 (Spring 1996): 92–127.

Jimenez Roman, Mirian. "*Un hombre (negro) del pueblo*: Jose Celso Barbosa and the Puerto Rican 'Race' Towards Whiteness." *Centro de Estudios Puertorriqueños* 8:1/2 (Spring 1996): 8–29.

Johnson, James W. *Black Manhattan*. Reprint, New York: Da Capo Press, 1991.

Johnson, Susan L. "'A Memory So Sweet to Soldiers': The Significance of Gender in the History of the American West." *Western Historical Quarterly* 24 (November 1993): 495–517.

Joseph, Gilbert. "Forging the Regional Pastime: Baseball and Class in Yucatán." In *Sport and Society in Latin America: Diffusion, Dependency, and the Rise of Mass Culture*, edited by Joseph Arbena, 29–61. New York: Greenwood Press, 1988.

Joseph, Gilbert, et al., eds. *Close Encounters of Empire: Writing the Cultural History of U.S.–Latin American Relations*. Durham, NC: Duke University Press, 1998.

Juffer, Jane. "Who's the Man? Sammy Sosa, Latinos, and Televisual Redefinitions of the American National Pastime." *Journal of Sport and Social Issues* 26:4 (November 2002): 337–59.

Kaplan, Amy, and Donald Pease, eds. *Cultures of United States Imperialism*. Durham, NC: Duke University Press, 1993.

Kasinitz, Philip. *Caribbean New York: Black Immigrants and the Politics of Race*. Ithaca, NY: Cornell University Press, 1992.

Kazal, Russell A. "Revisiting Assimilation: The Rise, Fall, and Reappraisal of a Concept in American Ethnic History." *American Historical Review* 100:2 (April 1995): 437–71.

Kelley, Brent. *The Negro Leagues Revisited: Conversations with 66 More Baseball Heroes*. Jefferson, NC: McFarland, 2000.

Kelley, Robin D. G. "'But a Local Phase of a World Problem': Black History's Global Vision." *Journal of American History* 86:3 (December 1999): 1045–77.

———. *Race Rebels: Culture, Politics, and the Black Working Class*. New York: Free Press, 1994.

———. "Notes on Deconstructing 'the Folk.'" *American Historical Review* (December 1992): 1400–8.

Kerber, Linda. "Diversity and the Transformation of American Studies." *American Quarterly* 41:3 (September 1989): 415–31.

Kirsch, Gary B. "Baseball Spectators, 1855–1870." *Baseball History* (Fall 1987): 4–20.

Klein, Alan M. *Baseball on the Border: A Tale of Two Laredos*. Princeton, NJ: Princeton University Press, 1997.

———. "Culture, Politics, and Baseball in the Dominican Republic." *Latin American Perspectives* 22:3 (Summer 1995): 111–30.

———. *Sugarball: The American Game, the Dominican Dream*. New Haven, CT: Yale University Press, 1991.

———. "Sport and Colonialism in Latin America and the Caribbean." *Studies in Latin American Popular Culture* 10 (1991): 257–71.

Knight, Franklin. *The Caribbean: The Genesis of a Fragmented Nationalism*. New York: Oxford University Press, 1990.

———. *Slave Society in Cuba during the Nineteenth Century*. Madison: University of Wisconsin Press, 1970.

Knight, Franklin, and Colin Palmer, eds. *The Modern Caribbean*. Chapel Hill: University of North Carolina Press, 1989.

Kolchin, Peter. "Whiteness Studies: The New History of Race in America." *Journal of American History* 89:1 (2002): 154–73.

Koshy, Susan. "Morphing Race into Ethnicity: Asian Americans and Critical Transformations of Whiteness." *boundary* 2 28:1 (2001): 153–94.

Kropp, Phoebe. "Citizens of the Past? Olvera Street and the Construction of Race and Memory in 1930s Los Angeles." *Radical History Review* 81 (2001): 35–60.

LaFeber, Walter. *The Cambridge History of American Foreign Relations: The American Search for Opportunity, 1865–1913*. New York: Cambridge University Press, 1993.

Lamb, Chris. "'I Never Want to Take Another Trip like This One': Jackie Robinson's Journey to Integrate Baseball." *Journal of Sport History* 24:2 (Summer 1997): 177–91.

Lamb, Chris, and Glen Bleske. "The Road to October 23, 1945: The Press and the Integration of Baseball." *Nine* 6:1 (Fall 1997): 48–68.

Lanctot, Neil. *Negro League Baseball: The Rise and Fall of a Black Institution*. Philadelphia: University of Pennsylvania Press, 2004.

———. *Fair Dealing and Clean Playing: The Hildale Club and the Development of Black Professional Baseball, 1910–1932*. Jefferson, NC: McFarland, 1994.

Lao, Agustin. "Resources of Hope: Imagining the Young Lords and the Politics of Identity." *Centro de Estudios Puertorriqueños* 7:1 (Winter 1994–95/Spring 1995): 34–49.

Lee, Erika. "The Chinese Exclusion Example: Race, Immigration, and American Gatekeeping, 1882–1924." *Journal of American Ethnic History* (Spring 2002): 36–62.

Legrand, Catherine. "Informal Resistance on a Dominican Sugar Plantation during the Nineteenth Century to the Trujillo Dictatorship." *Hispanic American Historical Review* 75:4 (November 1994): 555–96.

Leonard, Karen. *Making Ethnic Choices: California's Punjabi Mexican Americans*. Philadelphia: Temple University Press, 1992.

Lester, Larry. *Black Baseball's National Showcase: The East-West All-Star Game, 1933–1953*. Lincoln: University of Nebraska Press, 2001.

Levine, Lawrence. "The Folklore of Industrial Society: Popular Culture and Its Audiences." *American Historical Review* 97:5 (December 1992): 1369–99.

———. *Highbrow/Lowbrow: The Emergence of Cultural Hierarchy in America.* Cambridge, MA: Harvard University Press, 1988.

———. *Black Culture and Black Consciousness: Afro-American Folk Thought from Slavery to Freedom.* New York: Oxford University Press, 1977.

Levine, Peter. *Ellis Island to Ebbets Field: Sport and the American Jewish Experience.* New York: Oxford University Press, 1992.

———. *A. G. Spalding and the Rise of Baseball: The Promise of American Sport.* New York: Oxford University Press, 1985.

Lewis, David Levering. *W. E. B. Du Bois: The Biography of a Race, 1868–1919.* New York: Henry Holt, 1993.

———. *When Harlem Was in Vogue.* New York: Vintage, 1981.

Lewis, Earl. "Connecting Memory, Self, and the Power of Place in African American Urban History." *Journal of Urban History* 21:3 (March 1995): 347–71.

———. "Race." In *Encyclopedia of the United States in the Twentieth Century,* edited by Stanley Kutler, 129–160. New York: Scribners, 1995.

———. "'To Turn as on a Pivot': Writing African American into a History of Overlapping Diasporas." *American Historical Review* 100:3 (June 1995): 765–87.

———. "Invoking Concepts, Problematizing Identities: The Life of Charles N. Hunter and the Implications for the Study of Gender and Labor." *Labor History* 34:2–3 (Spring–Summer 1993): 292–308.

Limerick, Patricia Nelson. *The Legacy of Conquest: The Unbroken Past of the American West.* New York: W. W. Norton, 1987.

———. "Insiders and Outsiders: The Borders of the USA and the Limits of the ASA: Presidential Address to the American Studies Association, 31 October 1996." *American Quarterly* 49:3 (September 1997): 449–69.

Lipsitz, George. *Possessive Investment in Whiteness.* Philadelphia: Temple University Press, 1998.

———. "The Possessive Investment in Whiteness: Racialized Social Democracy and the 'White' Problem in American Studies." *American Quarterly* 47:3 (September 1995): 369–87.

———. *Rainbow at Midnight: Labor and Culture in the 1940s.* Urbana: University of Illinois Press, 1994.

———. *Time Passages: Collective Memory and American Popular Music.* Minneapolis: University of Minnesota Press, 1990.

Lomax, Michael. *Black Baseball Entrepreneurs, 1860–1901: Operating by Any Means Necessary.* Syracuse, NY: Syracuse University Press, 2003.

———. "Black Entrepreneurship in the National Pastime: The Rise of Semiprofessional Baseball in Black Chicago, 1890–1915." *Journal of Sport History* 25:1 (Spring 1998): 43–64.

Lott, Eric. *Love and Theft: Blackface Minstrelsy and the American Working Class.* New York: Oxford University Press, 1995.

Lowe, Lisa. "Heterogeneity, Hybridity, Multiplicity: Marking Asian American Difference." *Diaspora* (Spring 1991): 24–44.

Maldonado, Edwin. "Contract Labor and the Origins of Puerto Rican Communities in the United States." *International Migration Review* 13 (Spring 1979): 103–21.

Malloy, Jerry. "The Strange Career of Sol White, Black Baseball's First Historian." *Nine* 4:2 (Spring 1996): 217–36.

———. "The Pittsburgh Keystones and the 1887 Colored League: A Radical Concept in Team Ownership." *Baseball in Pittsburgh*. Cleveland: Society of American Baseball Researchers, 1995.

———. "The Birth of the Cuban Giants: The Origins of Black Professional Baseball." *Nine* 2:2 (Spring 1994): 233–46.

———. "Out at Home: Baseball Draws the Color Line." *The National Pastime* (1983): 14–28.

Mankekar, Purnima. "Reflections on Diasporic Identities: A Prolegomenon to an Analysis of Political Bifocality." *Diaspora* 3:3 (1994): 349–71.

Marcano, Arturo, and David Fidler. *Stealing Lives: The Globalization of Baseball and the Tragic Story of Alexis Quiroz*. Bloomington: Indiana University Press, 2003.

Martinez-Alier, Verena. *Marriage, Class, and Colour in Nineteenth-Century Cuba: A Study of Racial Attitudes and Sexual Values in a Slave Society*. Ann Arbor: University of Michigan Press, 1989.

Martinez-Fernandez, Luis. "Puerto Rico in the Whirlwind of 1898: Conflict, Continuity, and Change." *OAH Magazine of History* (Spring 1998): 24–29.

Masud Piloto, Félix. *From Welcomed Exile to Illegal Immigrant: Cuban Immigration to the U.S., 1959–1995*. Lanham, MD: Rowman & Littlefield, 1996.

———. *With Open Arms: Cuban Migration to the United States*. Lanham, MD: Rowman & Littlefield, 1988.

Mayoral, Luis Rodriguez. *Más Allá de un Sueño*. Hato Rey, Puerto Rico: Romallo Bros. Printing Inc., 1981.

McDonald, Brian. *Indian Summer: The Forgotten Story of Louis Sockalexis*. New York: Rodale, 2003.

McGovern, Eileen. "José Martí and the Politics of Journalism." *Cuban Studies* 25 (1995): 123–46.

McLeod, Marc C. "Undesirable Aliens: Race, Ethnicity, and Nationalism in the Comparison of Haitian and British West Indian Immigrant Workers in Cuba, 1912–1939." *Journal of Social History* 31:3 (Spring 1998): 599–623.

Menchaca, Martha. *Recovering History, Constructing Race: The Indian, Black, and White Roots of Mexican Americans*. Austin: University of Texas Press, 2001.

Mintz, Sidney. *Caribbean Transformations*. New York: Columbia University Press, 1989.

———. *Worker in the Cane: A Puerto Rican Life History*. New York: W. W. Norton, 1974.

Mirabal, Nancy. "*De Aquí, De Allá*: Race, Empire, and Nation in the Making of Cuban Migrant Communities in New York and Tampa, 1823–1924." Ph.D. dissertation, University of Michigan, 2001.

———. "No Country but the One We Must Fight For." In *Mambo Montage: The Latinization of New York*, edited by Arlene Davila and Agustin Lao-Montes, 57–72. New York: Columbia University Press, 2001.

———. "Telling Silences and Making Community." In *Between Race and Em-*

pire: African-Americans and Cubans before the Cuban Revolution, edited by Lisa Brock and Digna Fuentes Castañeda, 49–69. Philadelphia: Temple University Press, 1998.

Moffi, Larry, and James Kronstadt. *Crossing the Line: Black Major Leaguers, 1947–1959.* Jefferson, NC: McFarland, 1994.

Montgomery, Charles. "Becoming 'Spanish-American': Race and Rhetoric in New Mexico Politics, 1880–1928." *Journal of American Ethnic History* 20 (Summer 2001): 59–84.

Montgomery, David. *The Fall of the House of Labor: The Workplace, the State, and American Labor Activism, 1865–1925.* New York: Cambridge University Press, 1987.

Moore, Glenn. "Ideology on the Sportspage: Newspapers, Baseball, and Ideological Conflict in the Gilded Age." *Journal of Sport History* 23:3 (Fall 1996): 228–55.

Mormino, Gary R., and George Pozzetta. *The Immigrant World of Ybor City: Italians and Their Latino Neighbors in Tampa, 1885–1985.* Urbana: University of Illinois Press, 1987.

Morrison, Toni. *Playing in the Dark: Whiteness and the Literary Imagination.* Cambridge, MA: Harvard University Press, 1992.

Mumford, Kevin. *Interzones: Black/White Sex Districts in Chicago and New York in the Early Twentieth Century.* New York: Columbia University Press, 1997.

Nemec, David. *The Beer & Whiskey League: The Illustrated History of the American Association, Baseball's Renegade Major League.* New York: Lyons & Burford, 1994.

Ngai, Mae. "The Architecture of Race in American Immigration Law: A Reexamination of the Immigration Act of 1924." *Journal of American History* 87 (June 1999): 67–92.

Nowatzki, Robert. "Foul Lines and the Color Line." *Nine* 11:1 (Fall 2002): 82–88.

Oboler, Susan. *Ethnic Labels/Latino Lives: The Politics of (Re)Presentation.* Minneapolis: University of Minnesota Press, 1995.

———. "The Politics of Labeling: Latino/a Cultural Identities of Self and Others." *Latin American Perspectives* 19:4 (Fall 1992): 18–36.

Oleksak, Michael M., and Mary Adams Oleksak. *Latin Americans and the Grand Old Game.* Grand Rapids: Masters Press, 1991.

O'Malley, Michael. "Specie and Species: Race and the Money Question in Nineteenth-Century America." *American Historical Review* 99:2 (April 1994): 369–95.

Omi, Michael, and Howard Winant. *Racial Formations in the United States: From the 1960s to the 1980s.* New York: Routledge, 1994.

Orsi, Robert Anthony. *The Madonna of 115th Street: Faith and Community in Italian Harlem, 1880–1950.* New Haven, CT: Yale University Press, 1985.

Otto, Frank. "Playing Baseball in America: Puerto Rican Memories." *Nine* 4:2 (Spring 1996): 362–75.

Overmyer, James. *Queen of the Negro Leagues: Effa Manley and the Negro Leagues.* Lanham, MD: Scarecrow Press, 1998.

Padilla, Felix M. *Puerto Rican Chicago.* Notre Dame, IN: University of Notre Dame Press, 1987.

———. *Latino Ethnic Consciousness: The Case of Mexican Americans and Puerto Ricans in Chicago.* Notre Dame, IN: University of Notre Dame Press, 1985.

Painter, Nell Irvin. "Thinking about the Languages of Money and Race: A Response to Michael O'Malley, 'Specie and Species.'" *American Historical Review* 99: 2 (April 1994): 396–404.

Patterson, Thomas G. "U.S. Intervention in Cuba, 1898: Interpreting the Spanish-American-Cuban-Filipine War." *OAH Magazine of History* (Spring 1998): 5–10.

Patterson, Tiffany, and Robin Kelley. "Unfinished Migrations: Reflections in the African Diaspora and the Making of the Modern World." *African Studies Review* 43:1 (April 2000): 47–68.

Pérez, Gina M., *The Near Northwest Side Story: Migration, Displacement, and Puerto Rican Families.* Berkeley and Los Angeles: University of California Press, 2004.

———. "An Upbeat Wide Side Story: Puerto Ricans and Postwar Racial Politics in Chicago." *Centro* 13:2 (Fall 2001): 46–71.

Pérez, Louis A. *Becoming Cuban.* Chapel Hill: University of North Carolina Press, 1999.

———. "1898: A War of the World." *OAH Magazine of History* (Spring 1998): 3–4.

———. *The War of 1898: The United States in History and Historiography.* Chapel Hill: University of North Carolina Press, 1998.

———. *Cuba between Reform and Revolution.* New York: Oxford University Press, 1995.

———. "Between Baseball and Bullfighting: The Quest for Nationality in Cuba, 1868–1898." *Journal of American History* (September 1994): 493–517.

———. *Cuba and the United States: Ties of Singular Intimacy.* Athens: University of Georgia Press, 1990.

———. "Politics, Peasants, and People of Color: The 1912 'Race War' in Cuba Reconsidered." *Hispanic American Historical Review* 66:3 (August 1986): 509–39.

———. *Cuba between Empires, 1878–1902.* Pittsburgh: University of Pittsburgh Press, 1982.

Pérez Firmat, Gustavo. *Life on the Hyphen: The Cuban-American Way.* Austin: University of Texas Press, 1994.

Peterson, Robert. *Only the Ball Was White: A History of Legendary Black Players and All-Black Professional Teams.* New York: Oxford University Press, 1992.

Pietrusza, David. *Major Leagues: The Formation, Sometimes Absorption, and Mostly Inevitable Demise of 18 Professional Baseball Organizations, 1871 to Present.* Jefferson, NC: McFarland, 1991.

Pope, Steven. "Negotiating the 'Folk Highway' of the Nation: Sport, Public Culture, and American Identity, 1870–1940." *Journal of Social History* 27 (Winter 1993): 327–40.

Powers-Beck, Jeffrey. *The American Indian Integration of Baseball.* Lincoln: University of Nebraska Press, 2004.

———. "'Chief': The American Indian Integration of Baseball, 1897–1945." *American Indian Quarterly* 25:4 (Fall 2001): 508–38.

Poyo, Gerald E. *"With All and for the Good of All": The Emergence of Popular Nationalism in the Cuban Communities of the United States, 1846–1898.* Durham, NC: Duke University Press, 1989.

Prince, Carl. *Brooklyn's Dodgers: The Bums, the Borough, and the Best of Baseball, 1947–1957.* New York: Oxford University Press, 1996.

Ramos-Zayas, Ana Y. *National Performances: The Politics of Class, Race, and Space in Puerto Rican Chicago.* Chicago: University of Chicago Press, 2003.

Rampersad, Arnold. *Jackie Robinson: A Biography.* New York: Knopf, 1997.

Reaves, Joseph A. *Taking in a Game: A History of Baseball in Asia.* Lincoln: University of Nebraska Press, 2002.

Regalado, Samuel. "Hey Chico! The Latin Identity in Major League Baseball." *Nine* 11:1 (2003): 16–24.

———. *Viva Baseball! Latin Major Leaguers and Their Special Hunger.* Urbana: University of Illinois Press, 1998.

———. "'Image is Everything': Latin Baseball Players and the United States Press." *Studies in Latin American Popular Culture* 13 (1994): 101–14.

———. "The Minor League Experience of Latin American Baseball Players in Western Communities, 1950–1970." *Journal of the West* (January 1987): 65–70.

———. "Baseball in the Barrios: The Scene in East Los Angeles since World War II." *Baseball History* 1: 2 (Summer 1986): 47–59.

Reisler, James. *Black Writers/Black Baseball.* Jefferson, NC: McFarland, 1994.

Riess, Steven A. "I Am Not a Baseball Historian." *Rethinking History* 5:1 (March 2001): 27–41.

———. *Touching Base: Professional Baseball and American Culture in the Progressive Era.* Reprint, Urbana: University of Illinois Press, 1999.

———. *City Games: The Evolution of American Urban Society and the Rise of Sports.* Urbana: University of Illinois Press, 1989.

Riley, James A. *The Biographical Encyclopedia of Negro Baseball Leagues.* New York: Carroll & Graf, 1994.

———. *Dandy, Day, and the Devil.* Cocoa, FL: TK Publishers, 1987.

Rodríguez, Clara E., Aida Castro, Oscar Garcia, and Analisa Torres. "Latino Racial Identity: In the Eye of the Beholder." *Latino Studies Journal* 2:3 (September 1991): 33–47.

Rodríguez, Clara. "Puerto Rican Studies." *American Quarterly* 42:3 (September 1990): 437–55.

———. *Puerto Ricans: Born in the U.S.A.* Westminister, MA: Unwin & Hyman, 1989.

———. "Puerto Ricans: Between Black and White." *New York Affairs* 1:4 (1973): 97–101.

Rodríguez, Joseph A. "Becoming Latinos: Mexican Americans, Chicanos, and the Spanish Myth in the Urban Southwest." *Western Historical Quarterly* 29:2 (Summer 1998): 165–85.

———. "Ethnicity in the Horizontal City: Mexican Americans and the Chicano Movement in San Jose, California." *Journal of Urban History* 21 (July 1995): 597–621.

Rodríguez, Richard. *Brown: The Last Discovery of America.* New York: Penguin Books, 2003.

Rodríguez-Morazzani, Roberto. "Beyond the Rainbow: Mapping the Discourse on Puerto Ricans and 'Race.'" *Centro de Estudios Puertorriqueños* 8:1/2 (Spring 1996): 128–49.

———. "Puerto Rican Political Generations in New York: Pioneros, Young Turks and Radicals." *Centro de Estudios Puertorriqueños* 4:1 (Winter 1991–92): 96–116.

Roediger, David R. *Colored White: Transcending the Racial Past.* Berkeley and Los Angeles: University of California Press, 2002.

———. *The Wages of Whiteness: Race and the Making of the American Working Class.* New York: Verso, 1991.

Rogin, Michael. "Making America Home: Racial Masquerade and Ethnic Assimilation in the Transition to Talking Photos." *Journal of American History* 79 (December 1992): 1050–77.

Rogosinn, Donn. *Invisible Men: Life in Baseball's Negro Leagues.* Reprint, New York: Kodansha, 1995.

Rosenzweig, Roy. *Eight Hours for What We Will: Work, Workers, and Leisure in an Industrial City, 1870–1920.* New York: Cambridge University Press, 1983.

Rouse, Roger. "Mexican Migration and the Social Space of Post Modernism." *Diaspora* 1:1 (Spring 1991): 8–23.

Ruck, Rob. "Baseball and Community: From Pittsburgh's Hill to San Pedro's Canefields." *Nine* 7:1 (Fall 1998): 2–15.

———. *The Sandlot Season: Sport in Black Pittsburgh.* Urbana: University of Illinois Press, 1993.

———. *The Tropic of Baseball.* Westport, CT: Meckler Publishing, 1991.

Ruiz, Vicki. *From Out of the Shadows: Mexican Women in Twentieth-Century America.* New York: Oxford University Press, 1998.

Rumbaut, Ruben G. "The Americas: Latin American and Caribbean People in the United States." In *Americas: New Interpretive Essays,* edited by Alfred Stepan, 275–307. New York: Oxford University Press, 1992.

Rydell, Robert W. *All the World's a Fair: Visions of Empire at American International Expositions, 1876–1916.* Chicago: University of Chicago Press, 1984.

Sammons, Jeffrey. "'Race' and Sport: A Critical, Historical Examination." *Journal of Sport History* 21:3 (Fall 1994): 203–78.

Sanabria, Carlos. "Patriotism and Class Conflict in the Puerto Rican Community in New York during the 1920s." *Latino Studies Journal* 2:2 (May 1991): 3–16.

Sánchez, George J. "'Y Tú, Qúe?' (Y2K): Latino History in the New Millennium." In *Latinos: Remaking the Americas,* edited by Marcelo Suárez-Orozco and Mariela Páez, 45–58. Berkeley and Los Angeles: University of California Press, 2002.

———. "Race, Nation, and Culture in Recent Immigration Studies." *Journal of American Ethnic History* 18 (Summer 1999): 66–84.

———. *Becoming Mexican American: Ethnicity, Culture, and Identity in Chicano Los Angeles, 1900–1945.* New York: Oxford University Press, 1993.

Sánchez-Korrol, Virginia. *From Colonia to Community: The History of Puerto Ricans in New York City.* Berkeley and Los Angeles: University of California Press, 1994.

Santiago-Valles, Kelvin. "'Higher Womanhood' among the 'Lower Races': Julia McNair Henry in Puerto Rico and the 'Burdens' of 1898." *Radical History Review* 73 (Winter 1999): 47–73.

———. *"Subject People" and Colonial Discourses: Economic Transformation and Social Disorder in Puerto Rico, 1898–1947.* Albany: State University of New York Press, 1994.

———. "The Unruly City and the Mental Landscape of Colonized Identities: Intellectually Contested Nationality in Puerto Rico, 1945–1985." *Social Text* 38 (Spring 1994): 149–63.

Savoie, Mark. "Drawing the Line: The Trials of African-American Baseball Players in the International League (1886–1889)." *Nine* 1:1 (Fall 1992): 42–60.

Saxton, Alexander. *The Rise and Fall of the White Republic: Class Politics and Mass Culture in Nineteenth-Century America.* New York: Verso, 1990.

Scarano, Francisco. "The *Jíbaro* Masquerade and the Subaltern Politics of Creole Identity Formation in Puerto Rico, 1745–1823." *American Historical Review* 101 (December 1996): 1398–1431.

———. *Sugar and Slavery in Puerto Rico: The Plantation Economy of Ponce, 1800–1850.* Madison: University of Wisconsin Press, 1984.

Schmidt-Nowara, Chris. "'Spanish' Cuba: Race and Class in Spanish and Cuban Antislavery Ideology, 1861–1868." *Cuban Studies* 25 (1995): 101–22.

Schneider, Dorothee. "Naturalization and United States Citizenship in Two Periods of Mass Migrations: 1894–1930, 1965–2000." *Journal of American Ethnic History* (Fall 2001): 50–82.

Scott, James. *Domination and the Art of Resistance: Hidden Transcripts.* New Haven, CT: Yale University Press, 1990.

Scott, Rebecca J. "'The Lower Class of Whites' and the 'Negro Element': Race, Social Identity and Politics in Central Cuba, 1899–1909." In *La Nacion Soñada: Cuba, Puerto Rico y Filipinas ante el 98,* edited by Consuelo Naranjo, Miguel A. Puig-Samper, and Luis M. García Mora, 179–91. Madrid: Doce Calles, 1996.

———. "Defining the Boundaries of Freedom in the World of Cane: Cuba, Brazil, and Louisiana after Emancipation." *American Historical Review* 99 (February 1994): 70–102.

———. "Exploring the Meaning of Freedom: Postemancipation Societies in Comparative Perspective." *Hispanic American Historical Review* 68 (August 1988): 407–28.

———. *Slave Emancipation in Cuba: The Transition to Free Labor, 1860–1899.* Princeton, NJ: Princeton University Press, 1985.

Singletary, Wes. *Al Lopez: The Life of Baseball's El Senor.* Jefferson, NC: McFarland, 1999.

Slotkin, Richard. *Gunfighter Nation: The Myth of the Frontier in Twentieth-Century America.* New York: Harper, 1992.

———. *Regeneration through Violence: The Mythology of the American Frontier, 1600–1860.* Middletown, CT: Wesleyan University Press, 1973.

Snyder, Brad. *Beyond the Shadows of the Senators: The Untold Story of the*

Homestead Grays and the Integration of Baseball. New York: Contemporary Books, 2003.

Springwood, Charles Fruehling. *Cooperstown to Dyersville: A Geography of Baseball Nostalgia*. Boulder, CO: Westview Press, 1996.

———. "Where Have You Gone, Joe DiMaggio? Discourses of Nation, Family, and Masculinity in Dyersville, IA." *Cultural Studies* 1 (1996): 183–208.

Stattler, Rick. "Vincent 'Sandy' Nava." Unpublished manuscript.

Stephens, Michelle. "Black Transnationalism and the Politics of National Identity: West Indian Intellectuals in Harlem in the Age of War and Revolution." *American Quarterly* 50:3 (September 1998): 592–608.

Sugrue, Thomas J. *Origins of the Urban Crisis: Race and Inequality in Postwar Detroit*. Princeton, NJ: Princeton University Press, 2005.

———. "Crabgrass-Roots Politics: Race, Rights, and the Reaction against Liberalism in the Urban North, 1940–1964." *Journal of American History* 82 (September 1995): 551–78.

Thorn, John, and Mark Rucker, eds. "Special Pictorial Issue: The Nineteenth Century." *The National Pastime* 3:1 (1984).

Tölölyan, Khachig. "Rethinking Diaspora(s) Stateless Power in the Transnational Movement." *Diaspora* 5:1 (1996): 3–36.

Toot, Peter. *Armando Marsans: The First Cuban Major League Baseball Player*. Jefferson, NC: McFarland, 2003.

Torres, Angel. *La historia del beisbol Cubano, 1878–1976*. Los Angeles: self-published, 1976.

Torres-Saillant, Silvio, and Ramona Hernández. *The Dominican Americans*. Westport, CT: Greenwood Press, 1998.

Trotter, Joe William, Jr., ed. *The Great Migration in Historical Perspective*. Bloomington: Indiana University Press, 1991.

Trouillot, Michel-Rolph. *Silencing the Past: Power and the Production of History*. Boston: Beacon Press, 1995.

Tygiel, Jules. *Past Time: Baseball as History*. New York: Oxford Univ. Press, 2000.

———. *The Jackie Robinson Reader: Perspectives of an American Hero*. New York: Plume Books, 1997.

———. *Baseball's Greatest Experiment: Jackie Robinson & His Legacy*. New York: Oxford University Press, 1983.

Van Hyning, Thomas. *Puerto Rico's Winter League: A History of Major League Baseball's Launching Pad*. Jefferson, NC: McFarland, 1995.

Vargas, Zaragoza. *Proletarians of the North: A History of Mexican Industrial Workers in Detroit and the Midwest, 1917–1933*. Berkeley and Los Angeles: University of California Press, 1999.

Vázquez, Edwin "Kako." "Invasion Latina en el Beisbol de las Grandes Ligas." *Galerias Net*, undated. www.galeriasnet.com.mx/Revista/deportes/invasion latina.html.

Voigt, David. *America through Baseball*. Chicago: Nelson-Hill, 1976.

Von Eschen, Penny. *Race against Empire: Black Americans and Anticolonialism, 1937–1957*. Ithaca, NY: Cornell University Press, 1997.

Wade, Peter. *Blackness and Race Mixture: The Dynamics of Racial Identity in Colombia*. Baltimore: Johns Hopkins University Press, 1993.

Watkins-Owens, Irma. *Blood Relations: Caribbean Immigrants and the Harlem Community, 1900–1930.* Bloomington: Indiana University Press, 1996.

Whalen, Carmen. *From Puerto Rico to Philadelphia: Puerto Rican Workers and Postwar Economies.* Philadelphia: Temple University Press, 2001.

White, Richard. "Baseball's John Fowler: The 1887 Season in Binghamton, New York." *Afro-Americans in New York Life and History* 16:1 (January 1992): 7–17.

Wiggins, David K. "Wendell Smith, the *Pittsburgh Courier-Journal,* and the Campaign to Include Blacks in Organized Baseball, 1933–1945." *Journal of Sport History* 10:2 (Summer 1983): 5–29.

Wright, Jerry Jaye. "From Giants to Monarchs: The 1890 Season of the Colored Monarchs of York, Pennsylvania." *Nine* 2:2 (Spring 1994): 248–59.

Zang, David W. *Fleet Walker's Divided Heart: The Life of Baseball's First Black Major Leaguer.* Lincoln: University of Nebraska Press, 1995.

Index

Text:	10/13 Sabon
Display:	Sabon
Compositor:	Integrated Composition Systems, Inc.
Indexer:	Sharon Sweeney
Printer and binder:	Thomson-Shore, Inc.